Sociology

Sociology

Jack Nobbs BSc (Econ.) Dip.Soc.

Robert Hine BA M Phil

Margaret E. Flemming BA (Hons), MA, Ph D

Revised Second Edition

Macmillan Education
London and Basingstoke

First published 1975
Reprinted 1976 (twice), 1977, 1978
Second edition 1979
Reprinted 1980
Revised Second Edition 1980
Reprinted 1981
Reprinted with further revisions 1982
Reprinted 1983

Published by
MACMILLAN EDUCATION LTD
Houndmills, Basingstoke, Hampshire RG21 2XS
and London
Associated companies in Delhi, Dublin,
Hong Kong, Johannesburg, Lagos, Melbourne,
New York, Singapore, and Tokyo

Filmset by BAS Printers Limited, Over Wallop, Hampshire
Printed in Hong Kong

Preface

When I wrote the first preface to this book four years ago, I referred to the debate about whether the ideas, concepts and approaches of sociology were appropriate for students at GCE Ordinary Level. Not all the issues in that debate have yet been resolved but the continuing increase in the number of examination candidates indicates—to some extent—that teachers and students now accept sociology as an integral part of the curriculum.

In 1974, I welcomed *Sociology*, saying that I found it 'interesting, stimulating and valuable' for both students and teachers. My views have been shared by the many students and teachers who have used *Sociology* since then, confirming its value as a textbook.

Revision of the book so soon after its original publication is a praiseworthy move by the authors. Not only does it ensure that the book remains in step with social changes, but it also acknowledges the need for students of sociology to be aware of the constantly changing nature of the material involved in the subject.

It is gratifying, therefore, to see this new edition and I feel sure that students and teachers will find (as previous readers have found) that both in range and presentation *Sociology* is a very worthwhile contribution to the study of the subject.

T. Schofield
Chief Examiner
GCE 'O' Level Sociology
Associated Examining Board

1 February 1978

Editor's note

A great advantage of this book is that it combines the expertise of three experienced teachers. There has been a continuous cross-fertilisation of ideas about the approach, methods and content. The aim has been to bring together the experience of two men and a woman who have taught sociology in both schools and colleges.

This revised edition has followed four reprints within three years of the first publication. At the outset the authors recognised that the nature of the subject would require periodic revision of the book; however, our decision to make substantial alterations has been based primarily on the changing demands of syllabuses and the ever increasing volume of published material. It also provides the opportunity to update statistical data wherever possible.

Amongst the various changes we have decided to make are the inclusion of a reading list at the end of each chapter, the addition of a glossary and the expansion of the index.

Before undertaking the revision a number of sociologists and teachers were asked for their advice and criticism. Whilst it would never be possible to accommodate all the proposals, we hope we have met most of the suggestions made to us. I should like to place on record the special contribution by Bob Hine in editorial changes which have helped to produce the improved updated second edition. Also our thanks are due to Wanda Verity, formerly Head of Social Studies at Claremont High School, Brent, for her thorough appraisal of the material and to Helen Davies of Ashridge Management College, who undertook so much of the secretarial and administrative work.

Our aim since the beginning has been to establish as truly comprehensive a book as possible; given the limitations of price and length, we hope we have moved a step nearer this goal. For teachers and students seeking further exercises and stimulus material of various kinds, a *Workbook* has been prepared to accompany *Sociology*.

Jack Nobbs
General Editor

Acknowledgements

The authors and publisher wish to thank the following who have kindly given permission for the use of copyright material:
The Associated Examining Board for use of A.E.B. Questions set in G.C.E. Papers; B. T. Batsford Limited for table from *The Wealth of Britain* by S. Pollard and D. W. Crossley; Bedford Square Press for table from *Socially Deprived Families in Britain* by Dr. Holman; Central Office of Information for two maps from *Density of Population 1961* and *Percentage Change in Population 1951–61* and two diagrams from *Britain 1972*, An Official Handbook; The Controller of Her Majesty's Stationery Office for extracts and tables from H.M.S.O. publications; Granada Publications Limited for tables from *The Home and the School* by J. W. B. Douglas (MacGibbon & Kee), and a figure from *The Effects of Television* by J. D. Halloran; Harvard University Press for a table from *Marriage and Divorce: A Social and Economic Study* by Hugh Carter and Paul C. Glick; Independent Broadcasting Authority for an illustration from *I.T.V. 1973*; JICNARS for table from *National Leadership Survey*, July 1974– December 1974; Lloyds Bank Limited for chart from *Lloyds Bank Review*, July 1969; New Science Publications for extracts and tables from *New Society*, London (the weekly review of the social sciences); Oxford Delegacy of Local Examinations for use of Oxford G.C.E. Questions; Penguin Books Limited for tables from *Voters, Parties and Leaders*, by Jean Blondel, *Sense and Nonsense in Psychology* by H. J. Eysenck and *Must Labour Lose?* by Abrams and Rose; Routledge & Kegan Paul Limited for extracts and tables from published work; Times Newspapers Limited for tables 'Occupations of MPs Elected October 1974' from *The Times*, March 1974 and 'Educational Background of MPs Elected October 1974' from *The Times*, October 1974; United Nations for tables and chart from copyright publications; University of Cambridge for a table from *University Reporter*.

The author and publishers wish to acknowledge the following photograph sources:
Barnabys Picture Library p. 273; Bib. Nationale p. 10 bottom left; Brighton Polytechnic—Faculty of Applied Sciences p. 137; British Railways Board p. 47; Camera Press pp. 41, 314, 345; Central Office of Information, Crown Copyright p. 198; Brian Chaplin p. 19; Community Service Volunteers p. 241; Daily

Mirror p. 333; Dept. of Health & Social Security, Crown Copyright p. 239; Electricity Council p. 275; Flamborough C.E. School p. 122 bottom; Fontarel Ltd. p. 189; Friends Service Council p. 247; Granada Television pp. 64 (World in Action) 188 (The Messengers); Henry Grant pp. 109, 132; Greater London Council p. 228; Francis Hodges p. 359; Lanchester Polytechnic p. 136; London Express News & Features Service pp. 87, 116, 205, 305, 315, 346; Keystone Press Agency pp. 207, 208, 211; Margaret Murray p. 57; North London News Ltd. p. 293; Norwich City Corporation p. 245; Oxfam p. 170; Pace Group p. 263; Paul Popper Ltd. p. 204; Post Office p. 283; Press Assoc. Ltd. p. 326; R.T.H.P.L. pp. 10 top, 226, 229; Rowntree Mackintosh Ltd. p. 279; Salvation Army Information Services p. 310; Shelter (Nick Hedges) p. 249; The *Sun* p. 332; Thames Television p. 122 top; Topix p. 343 top; Ullstein Bilderdienst p. 10 bottom right; UNESCO p. 343 bottom; Janine Wiedel p. 166

The publishers would also like to thank the following for permission to re-draw artwork:
Fig. 3.5 J. Klein—Samples from English Culture Vol 1. Routledge & Kegan Paul Ltd.
Fig. 3.7 Population Trends No. 2 1975. Permission of the Controller of Her Majesty's Stationery Office.
Fig. 3.8 Social Trends No. 7 1976. Permission of the Controller of Her Majesty's Stationery Office.
Fig. 5.9 Social Trends. Permission of the Controller of Her Majesty's Stationery Office.
Fig. 9.2 Social Trends. Permission of the Controller of Her Majesty's Stationery Office.
Fig. 10.2 This diagram appeared in New Society, London, the weekly review of the social sciences.
Fig. 11.1 Social Trends. Permission of the Controller of Her Majesty's Stationery Office.
Fig. 11.2 This diagram appeared in New Society, London, the weekly review of the social sciences.
Fig. 11.3 This diagram appeared in New Society, London, the weekly review of the social sciences.

The publishers have made every effort to trace copyright holders, but if they have inadvertently overlooked any they will be pleased to make the necessary arrangement at the first opportunity.

Contents

1 **Approaches to the Study of Society**
Unit 1 What is sociology?
Topic 1.1   What is meant by society and social system?   2
Topic 1.2   Sociology and social science   4

Unit 2 Sociology as a science
Topic 2.1   How scientific is social science?   7
Topic 2.2   Some theories of social science   8

Unit 3 The tools of the sociologist
Topic 3.1   Sampling   12
Topic 3.2   Social surveys   17
Topic 3.3   Questionnaires   18
Topic 3.4   Methods of observation   22
Further reading   24
GCE questions   24

2 **Social Differences**
Unit 4 What is stratification?
Topic 4.1   Estate   26
Topic 4.2   Social class   28
Topic 4.3   Caste   30

Unit 5 Social mobility
Topic 5.1   Factors affecting social mobility   32
Topic 5.2   Self-assigned class   34

Unit 6 Social structure and social change
Topic 6.1   The social structure of Britain   39
Topic 6.2   How class affects our lives   40

Unit 7 Status and power
Topic 7.1   Status   42
Topic 7.2   Power   43
Further reading   45
GCE questions   45

3 The Family

Unit 8   The family in society

Topic 8.1   Types of families   48
Topic 8.2   What are the social functions of the family?   51
Topic 8.3   Can we do without the family?   55
Topic 8.4   Marriage   56

Unit 9   The family in Britain today

Topic 9.1   The family in industrialised societies   58
Topic 9.2   The traditional working–class extended family   60
Topic 9.3   The privatised working–class family   63
Topic 9.4   The middle-class family   65

Unit 10   The family and social change

Topic 10.1   Family life in nineteenth-century Britain   67
Topic 10.2   Changes in family size   70
Topic 10.3   Parents and children   73
Topic 10.4   The woman's role   75
Topic 10.5   Marriage and divorce   90
Further reading   102
GCE questions   103

4   Education

Unit 11   The development of education

Topic 11.1   The functions of education   105
Topic 11.2   The growth of education   107
Topic 11.3   The tripartite system   109
Topic 11.4   The comprehensive system   112

Unit 12   Education and social class

Topic 12.1   Socio-linguistics and early learning   117
Topic 12.2   Education and attainment   123
Topic 12.3   Arguments in education   130

Unit 13   Further education

Topic 13.1   Further education   134
Topic 13.2   Youth culture   139
Further reading   142
GCE questions   142

5   Population

Unit 14   Demography

Topic 14.1   The study of population   145
Topic 14.2   The census in Britain   146

Unit 15 The size of a population
Topic 15.1   The population of Britain   147
Topic 15.2   The birth rate   151
Topic 15.3   The death rate   152
Topic 15.4   Infant mortality   155
Topic 15.5   Emigration and immigration   156

Unit 16 Population distribution
Topic 16.1   Sex distribution   159
Topic 16.2   Age distribution   162
Topic 16.3   Geographical distribution   164
Topic 16.4   Internal migration   165

Unit 17   The future population
Topic 17.1   A population policy for Britain?   167
Topic 17.2   World population trends   169
Further reading   172
GCE questions   172

6 Communications and the Mass Media
Unit 18   Communications
Topic 18.1   The importance of communicating   176
Topic 18.2   What do we communicate?   177

Unit 19   The press
Topic 19.1   What is the press?   178
Topic 19.2   Who reads what?   180

Unit 20   Radio and television
Topic 20.1   Radio   182
Topic 20.2   Television   183

Unit 21   Influence of the mass media
Topic 21.1   Advertising   189
Topic 21.2   The power of the press   190
Further reading   193
GCE questions   193

7   Government and Politics
Unit 22   Government
Topic 22.1   The meaning of government   195
Topic 22.2   Government in the United Kingdom   196
Topic 22.3   The passage of legislation   198
Topic 22.4   The separation of powers   199
Topic 22.5   Local government   199

Unit 23   The electorate

Topic 23.1   Abstentionism   202
Topic 23.2   The voters   206

Unit 24   The political parties

Topic 24.1   The Conservative Party   210
Topic 24.2   The Labour Party   211
Topic 24.3   The Liberal Party   212
Topic 24.4   Membership of political parties   213
Topic 24.5   Political motivation   214

Unit 25   Politics outside the parties

Topic 25.1   Interest groups   216
Topic 25.2   The Establishment   219
Topic 25.3   Politics in Britain   221
Further reading   222
GCE questions   223

8   The Welfare Society

Unit 26   The background to welfare

Topic 26.1   Poverty through the ages   225
Topic 26.2   The origins and development of the welfare society   232

Unit 27   The modern Welfare State

Topic 27.1   Social services   235
Topic 27.2   The National Health Service   236
Topic 27.3   Housing   242
Topic 27.4   Voluntary organisations   246
Topic 27.5   The Welfare State and the family   250
Further reading   252
GCE questions   252

9   The Economy and Employment

Unit 28   Work and the economy

Topic 28.1   Why do we work?   254
Topic 28.2   Employment and unemployment   257
Topic 28.3   The distribution of income and wealth   265

Unit 29   The organisation of work

Topic 29.1   The division of labour   270
Topic 29.2   Alienation   272
Topic 29.3   Technology and automation   274
Topic 29.4   Relationship between employer and employee   277

Unit 30   Work and leisure
Topic 30.1   Occupations   282
Topic 30.2   Leisure   285
Further reading   288
GCE questions   289

10   Social Control
Unit 31   Social order and social control
Topic 31.1   Social order   292
Topic 31.2   Formal social control   294
Topic 31.3   Informal social control   295

Unit 32   Religion: another type of social control
Topic 32.1   Beliefs and belief systems   298
Topic 32.2   What part does religion play in society?   301
Topic 32.3   Secularisation   302
Topic 32.4   Religion in Britain   302

Unit 33   The law
Topic 33.1   Law and morality   312
Topic 33.2   The police   314
Topic 33.3   The judicial system   317
Topic 33.4   The penal system   323
Further reading   329
GCE questions   329

11   Social Problems
Unit 34   Deviancy and crime
Topic 34.1   Deviancy   331
Topic 34.2   Crime and juvenile delinquency   334

Unit 35   Drug-taking
Topic 35.1   What are drugs?   338
Topic 35.2   Drug-taking in Britain   340
Topic 35.3   Alcoholism   346

Unit 36   Some other social problems
Topic 36.1   Illegitimacy   349
Topic 36.2   Abortion   351
Topic 36.3   Suicide   353

Unit 37   Minority groups and social integration
Topic 37.1   Minority groups   357
Topic 37.2   Race relations   363

Further reading   369
GCE questions   370

12   The Individual and Society
Unit 38   What makes the individual?
Topic 38.1   Intelligence and personality   371
Topic 38.2   Class, education and the individual   372
Topic 38.3   Work, welfare and the individual   373
Unit 39   Society today
Topic 39.1   How society is shaped   375
Topic 39.2   The future of society   377
GCE questions   380

Glossary   384

Index of authors and published works   411

General Index   417

1 Approaches to the Study of Society
Unit 1 What is Sociology?

Over the past thirty years sociology has grown in popularity and developed considerably, so we would expect people to know more about the subject than they generally do. Many have a notion that sociology is about people: but some think that sociology is all about helping the unfortunate and doing welfare work, while others think that sociology is the same as socialism and is a means of bringing revolution to our schools and colleges. Certainly sociology is about people. But understanding some of the problems of people is only a part of sociology. It is true that sociology does lead the student to look very closely at the society in which he lives. But for many years sociology was banned in the Soviet Union as a bourgeois ideology, so the leading European Communist country did not think of sociology as being particularly revolutionary.

Looking in the *Oxford English Dictionary* we read that sociology is 'the study of the history and nature of human society'. But we all have different ideas about what is meant by human society. So perhaps the best way to discover the meaning of the word 'sociology' is to find out what the study of sociology involves.

The word 'sociology' was first used by the French philosopher Auguste Comte in the late 1830s, and was more firmly established as a discipline by theorists such as Émile Durkheim and Karl Marx. Since then other writers have placed their own interpretation upon its meaning and have arrived at a definition which is generally acceptable:

Sociology is the scientific and systematic study of people in groups. It usually means looking for patterns of behaviour among people living in organised social groups.

Later on we shall see exactly what is meant by 'scientific' and 'systematic', but for the moment let us assume that these words refer to the thorough and organised way in which we, as sociologists, study how people live.

Throughout the world people live in groups: the smallest grouping is usually the family, and the largest group is a nation or possibly a federation of nations; in between are a host of different groups such as a school, workplace, neighbourhood, village or town, and we refer to these as social groups. It is easy for us to think of the family as a group, but it is harder to work out precisely who belongs to a particular community. As sociologists we must always define the limits of any community which is to be studied. For example, if we are making a study of a school we must say from the outset whether or not we will be considering the caretaker as part of our study.

All groups have some kind of organisation and purpose to them, and the way in which people of the group behave towards one another tells us something about the nature of the group. Sociologists look for these patterns of behaviour, and try to understand the causes which shape them.

Is sociology just common sense?

What makes sociology an exciting subject is that it tells us more about ourselves and the way in which we live. There are those who regard the findings of sociologists as just common sense which any good observer of society would have realised. What such people fail to appreciate is that although the sociologist often starts his studies with a sensible idea, for example, that people who receive less education do not get as good jobs as those who have had more education, he then sets about finding out, with a degree of academically acceptable precision, whether this is really the case, and what proportion of poorly educated people in fact have been able to get good jobs. Even more important, sociologists often are able to disprove widely-held wrong ideas about the society in which we live. For example, sociologists such as Peter Townsend draw attention to the continued existence of wide-scale poverty in the United Kingdom.

1.1   What is meant by society and social system?

Society may be regarded as a living organism whose structure is being constantly renewed. (Radcliffe-Brown)

The word 'society' is one of the least precise sociological terms: it can be used to describe a modern industrial state or a dozen bushmen wandering in the Kalahari desert. These days 'society' is usually employed to mean a country or a nation. Once again we have the problem of setting the limits of our definition. Societies are usually found in one place; their people have common patterns of behaviour; they have rules which are usually observed by the majority of their members, but which may be changing constantly, although they are always identifiable. Four factors usually characterise a society:

1   geographical location (where groups live)
2   common habits and customs ⎫
3   the maintenance of order   ⎬ (how people behave)
                                           ⎭
4   self-perpetuation (children being born).

These days if a sociologist is dealing with a specific society he looks at the formation of its *social system*. The social system is formed by the way in which individuals in a society behave and interact. Studying this interaction between two or more individuals gives us an understanding of *social relationships*. Every member of society has some form of social relationship with everyone whom he may come into contact with or deal with in some way. The family as a group has certain patterns of behaviour within that group: children may treat their parents with respect; a man may expect his wife to do the cooking while she may expect him to do the decorating. These social relationships within the family constitute part of its *social structure*. On a larger scale, for example, in a school or factory, the patterns of behaviour found between various members of the group are also social relationships, and this whole network of different relationships creates another kind of structure. Taken altogether, the various structures (family, school, factory, neighbourhood, town, etc.) form the social system.

All groups involve social relationships, but the existence of a social relationship does not necessarily mean the existence of a group. An example of a social relationship that does not entail a group would be that of two Englishmen staying at the same hotel in a foreign country, having never been properly introduced, yet acknowledging each other's presence by saying 'good morning' at breakfast; this simple greeting creates a social relationship of a temporary kind and no more.

Groups, as opposed to mere social relationships, usually involve some kind of co-operation to achieve a particular end. The common goal of a school is to educate its pupils, therefore there is co-operation between pupils and teachers to achieve this aim. Every member of the school has certain rights, obligations, and duties to perform: the pupil has the right to attend lessons; the teacher is obliged to teach; and the head has a duty to run the school. These rights and obligations are essentially rules of behaviour. Quite obviously not all members of the group have the same rights and obligations. There are many common characteristics that a group may have but the two most basic ones are:

1   co-operation
2   a sense of belonging.

Societies are made up of people: people are born, age and eventually die. For this simple reason societies are constantly changing with time. Social relationships change and so too do social structures and the social system they form. It is one of the tasks of the sociologist to look at the changes that are occurring in society. Later we shall examine more closely the factors which make for social change, but we should also realise that there are factors which renew the structure of society as well as changing it. Many of the institutions of society such as the educational system, the economic system, the religious system, and the legal system, may provide the basis for some social change but in other ways they are responsible for passing on traditions and practices that will help maintain the fabric of society.

1.2   Sociology and social science

The term *social science* is a general one meaning the study of human relationships in society; for this reason some people equate social science with sociology; however, this will not help us in a definition of either. Instead let us say that sociology may be regarded as a branch or *discipline* of social science. Elements or parts of the other disciplines of social science such as economics, politics, anthropology, psychology, demography, history and even philosophy, are contained within sociology; but elements of sociology are likewise found in the other social science disciplines. All the social science disciplines examine human relationships from a particular viewpoint, but sociology may perhaps claim a broader perspective of society (see Figure 1.1). For when a sociological study focuses upon a particular group within society it will inevitably consider the forces which may affect that group and which are dealt with by other disciplines, such as economics or psychology, before reaching conclusions from a sociological viewpoint.

How is sociology related to the other disciplines of social science?

Sociology may be regarded as being to social science what mathematics is to the natural sciences of, say, physics or chemistry: a vital component which cements the discipline together. A student of politics or economics cannot afford to neglect sociology in his studies, just as it would be impossible to study physics without some knowledge of mathematics.

The social sciences

History is the study of events which were created by people (geology is history without people). Historians this century have been increasingly aware of the need to understand events in the light of social factors such as increases in population, the psychology of individuals, or the importance of social classes. There are specialised branches of history—economic history, social history, political history—but all involve human activity and human relationships in the study of the past.

Economics is concerned with getting and spending: the study of the spending and financial habits of people. The economist is concerned with the use that people make of money and capital resources. Sociologists try to establish the economic patterns of different groupings and the extent to which economic forces affect people's lives.

Politics is the study of governments and power. The sociologist studies

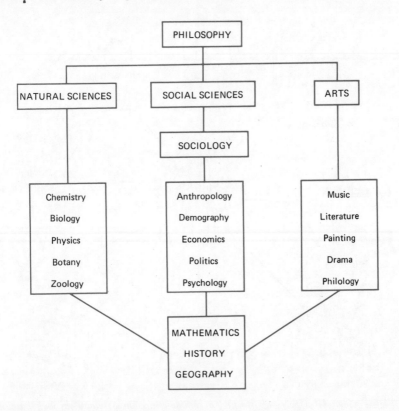

Figure 1.1 *The relationship between sociology and other studies*

the nature and composition of groups who seek or who have attained power. Voting behaviour interests political sociologists and psephologists.

Demography is the scientific study of population. Perhaps it may be regarded as sociology on a large scale. Demographers look at changes in the population and sociologists relate these changes to society.

Psychology is a discipline of social science concerned with the experience and behaviour of people, how they react to certain conditions. Sociologists are usually more concerned with psychology applied to groups. (Psychology is often confused with psychiatry which is a discipline of medical science.)

Anthropology (the science of man) is one of the disciplines closest to sociology. The anthropologist used to be concerned primarily with the biological changes in human development, but social anthropology today

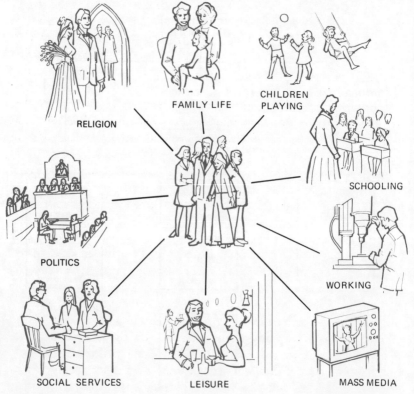

Figure 1.2   *All aspects of life find a common link in sociology through human relationships*

may in many instances be regarded as sociology for our purposes.

All the disciplines of social science are concerned with human behaviour patterns. Each has developed its own specialisations, but has found a common link in sociology through human relationships. (See Figure 1.2.)

Unit 2 Sociology as a Science

2.1 How scientific is social science?

It is accepted that the natural sciences such as chemistry, physics and biology, are 'scientific', yet some people doubt whether the social sciences can be regarded as being scientific in the same way. Of course, it really depends upon what is meant by 'science': the original Latin word, *scientia*, means knowledge, but the modern word 'science' has come to have a more specialised meaning. The careful, systematic way in which the natural scientist conducts his experiments and possibly makes predictions from the results of his work, causes his work to be regarded as 'scientific'.

One of the arguments against the social sciences being scientific is that they concern people in their human relationships, and as people vary as individuals there is no consistency of behaviour. An experiment connected with the natural sciences can be repeated anywhere in the world by another natural scientist and the same results will be obtained: this is because the natural scientist conducts his experiments on *matter*. But even if it were possible to set up experimental conditions with human beings, without putting them at physiological or psychological risk, it is argued that the variations between individuals (let alone societies) would be so great as to make any results meaningless. People who argue in this way add that even members of the same family vary, so that it would be of little use to compare findings made in a study of a British community to those of, say, an Arab community. But this argument reveals a lack of understanding of both the sociologist's aims and *sociological evidence*. An individual's behaviour may be of interest to a psychiatrist or social psychologist, but usually sociologists are looking for *common patterns of behaviour* found in groups, and comparisons with other groups can be sociologically significant. The surprising thing is that although we may have individual personalities and different genetic constructions, we do tend to have fairly regular behaviour patterns, and the sociologist is able to obtain a considerable amount of information about societies and communities by observing and comparing these patterns.

The sociologist sets about gathering information in a systematic and thorough way which is quite scientific. The techniques of gathering evidence (known as *data*) for a sociological investigation may include the use of statistics, and statistics as a branch of mathematics is scientifically acceptable.

One of the tests applied to a scientific subject is whether predictions can be made about it, given that certain conditions prevail. For example, when a chemist pours the right proportions of hydrochloric acid and sodium hydroxide together he can predict that the result will be salt and water, but as sociologists we cannot really predict with the same degree of accuracy how people will behave. In fact the social scientist is not concerned with a one hundred per cent degree of accuracy about people, and totally accurate predictions about human behaviour are not necessary in social science. The natural sciences do not always stand up to the same tests of one hundred per cent accuracy. Meteorology is a branch of natural science, but is the weather forecaster always right? All disciplines of natural science and social science have their particular techniques of investigation; each is as accurate as its limitations of investigation will allow. If projections are made in the social sciences they are used only as guides towards the ways in which people *might* behave in the future, not as pointers to how they *will* behave.

2.2   Some theories of social science

Do sociologists always agree with each other about their subject?

Just as doctors conduct a diagnosis of their patients, so too sociologists make a diagnosis of society. Not all doctors agree on their findings or the ways of approaching particular illnesses, and neither do all sociologists agree on their findings. There are many theories of social science and ideas about the nature of society. Anyone may claim to know what is wrong with society and what ought to be done to remedy its problems. Anyone may have distinct views about such matters as politics, economics and race relations. The difference between a qualified sociologist and the ordinary man in the street is that the sociologist will accumulate data in a systematic way about some of the problems of society, instead of pronouncing what should be done purely from his own personal observations. Sociology and most other social science disciplines have the following four characteristics, which are similar to those of many natural science disciplines.

1 Sociology is *empirical*. This means that it is based upon things observed and intelligent reasoning about them, and not upon supernatural phenomena.

2 Sociology is *theoretical*. The observations made are summarised in a logical way as part of a theory about the nature of society.

3 Sociology is *non-ethical*. Sociologists do not question whether their observations of society are necessarily good or bad for society (although very often this rule is bent somewhat in writing up observations). The observations are conducted without bias one way or another.

4 Sociology is *cumulative*. Different sociological theories are constructed out of other theories which have been modified or corrected in the light of fresh evidence.

Although there are many different theories of sociology, most sociologists construct their own theories out of the many, choosing those parts of the different theories that seem best and most accurate. For example, two important groups of theories have been *historical* and *functionalist* yet few sociologists would rely completely on either as a means of analysis or explanation of social theory.

Historical theories have fallen into two groups: one which sought to look at society as a whole and saw society undergoing an evolutionary process; the other which does not seek to explain everything about society in terms of history but rather looks for changes that are occurring. The first group was originally characterised by Auguste Comte (1798–1857) and Karl Marx (1818–1883). Marx's influence upon social theory has been considerable. He developed his theory after he had amassed a great deal of historical and economic data, and this theory sought to explain mainly in terms of economics everything about what had happened in history, what was happening, and what would happen to society. The all-embracing theory of Marx was first seriously challenged by Max Weber (1864–1920). Weber held that Marx's theories were too economically biased, and because no social scientist is able to look at the whole of society in depth a complete explanation of society was not possible.

Functionalist theories were largely developed by social anthropologists during this century. A number of leading academics still subscribe to functionalist views, but most modern sociologists reject the main conclusions of these theories. The functionalist view is that everyone has a set position and task in society (function) and that we are all interdependent upon one another in the successful running of society. Because functionalism is unable to explain adequately the changes that

Four founding fathers of sociology

Auguste Comte (1798–1857)

Karl Marx (1818–1883)

Émile Durkheim (1858–1917)

Max Weber (1864–1920)

take place in society the term *dysfunction* was invented to explain how revolutions and dissatisfaction occurred to produce social change.

Of course, we cannot elaborate upon all the theories of sociology as they are too numerous to mention. Nevertheless it would be useful if students of sociology, particularly those who may wish to pursue it to a higher level, looked up something about the contributors to the development of the subject and other theories of society. A useful book for this is Brian Fay's *Social Theory and Political Practice* (Allen & Unwin, 1975).

Unit 3 The Tools of the Sociologist

A study of the way in which sociologists make their observations and gather data will give us a clearer idea about the nature of the subject. Once we have found out *how* sociologists work we are able to see the kinds of problems and questions that are dealt with in this subject.

Today what is known as the *quantitative approach* is used by most sociologists. It involves four principles of investigation based upon the empirical method:

1   the observation of some aspect of society
2   the accumulation of data about this aspect
3   the putting together (correlation) of this data
4   the reporting of these findings.

Before a sociologist investigates an aspect of society he usually has some idea of theory, known as an *hypothesis*, about what he may find when his investigation is concluded. The sociologist must take care not to let his hypothesis affect his conclusions by only looking for evidence which will support his original idea and disregarding any evidence which may disprove his hypothesis. A sociologist must be completely unbiased when conducting investigations and writing up his conclusions. Indeed, he must expose his findings to the most rigorous testing to see whether his hypothesis is valid. If a sociologist allows his personal feelings and possible prejudices to shape his investigation and conclusion, then his findings will not have a scientific validity. Let us consider an extreme example. A sociologist holds the view that poor children who come from broken homes will become juvenile delinquents. In order to prove his hypothesis he investigates the cases of several hundred juvenile delinquents who came from poor homes and whose parents were divorced or separated. Because all the cases meet his requirements of a poor background and a broken home, his response rate is one hundred per cent correct, owing to his selection of just those juvenile delinquents. What the sociologist failed to do was to consider the many more (the majority perhaps) of children who were poor and who came from broken homes, but who did not become delinquents; nor did the sociologist look for other causes of delinquency which may have caused children from wealthy and stable homes to become juvenile delinquents. Employing the correct principles of investigation, this so-called sociologist was wrong because:

1   His observation was prejudiced.
2   The data, ie information, that he accumulated on juvenile delinquency, was chosen to prove his hypothesis.
3   His correlation of data did not consider the possibility of other causes of delinquency.
4   No doubt such a bad sociologist reported his findings in a biased manner.
5   His sample was unrepresentative of the total population.

Fortunately there are few of these so-called 'sociologists'. When mistakes are made in sociological investigation it is usually due to the investigator's failure to see or consider one or two vital factors. This happened in a most spectacular way before the United States Presidential election of 1936. A popular magazine took the names of ten million voters from telephone directories and sent them postcard ballots to express their preference for either the Republican or the Democratic candidate. Two million replies were received, perhaps the largest poll ever conducted in history, giving Landon the Republican candidate 60 per cent and Roosevelt the Democrat 40 per cent of the vote. On election day itself the actual result reversed these figures and Roosevelt won handsomely. In those days less than a third of Americans had telephones, usually the financially better off who tended to be Republicans, and not likely to vote for Roosevelt anyway. This mistake is not likely to be repeated in future by organisers of opinion polls.

3.1   Sampling

The lesson of the Presidential election of 1936 is that sociologists must take the greatest of care when deciding which people will be part of the sample investigated. Ideally a sociological investigation should include everyone under investigation, known as the population, but just as it would have been impossible to find out the opinions of every single

American voter in 1936 over a short period of time, so too it is often impossible for a sociologist to consider everybody in his investigation. For this reason samples are taken of the population: population in this sense means everyone under consideration when data is being gathered, not the whole number of people in a country. Sometimes a whole nation may become the 'population', eg when a census is being conducted (see Topic 14.2).

What is a representative sample?

In general, the larger the sample taken the more representative of the population it will be — provided that bias and sampling errors are avoided as far as possible. For a survey, no matter how large, would be biased if only motorists were asked whether the tax on petrol should be lowered, or only families with two children were investigated as to the adequacy of the family allowance. Bias could occur in many ways if the sample is not carefully thought out, therefore sociologists try to make their sample as representative of the population as possible.

Two factors usually limit a sample, just as they limit any investigation:

1 time
2 money.

The more time and money a sociologist has at his disposal, the more thorough his investigation can be; more time and money could mean a larger sample, and perhaps a more accurate conclusion. If we wished to investigate the problem of homelessness in Britain and had several years and plenty of money we could employ many investigators. Because resources of both time and money are usually limited, we should use them to the best advantage. A wise way of using our resources would be to concentrate them in those towns and cities where most homelessness is found, rather than to seek out cases in places where it is not so great a problem.

The ideal sample size is when no appreciable gain can be obtained by increasing the size of the sample.

Methods of sampling

Random sampling (Figure 1.3) is a general term meaning each individual in the population has an equal chance of being picked out for investigation, and samples are chosen on a more or less haphazard basis.

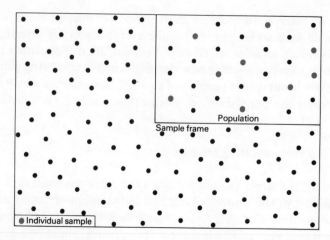

Figure 1.3 *Random sampling*

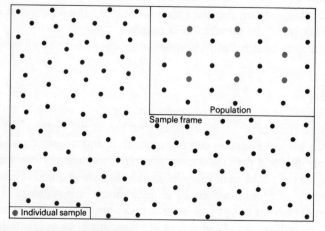

Figure 1.4 *Systematic sampling*

For example, an investigator stops the first person he meets in a street, interviews him, and then stops the next person he meets, irrespective of how many people may have passed him during the interview.

Systematic sampling (Figure 1.4) is another method when, say, every hundredth person is chosen from the electoral register. The electoral register is known as the *sample frame*. Peter Townsend in his study *The Family Life of Old People* (Penguin 1963) chose at random one doctor in three from the locality under investigation, and then selected every tenth elderly patient on the doctors' files.

Sometimes there are difficulties involved, such as finding that people drawn from a list may live some distance from each other and locating them may prove time-consuming and expensive. In this case the area under investigation, such as a town, might be divided into a section on a map and the random/systematic samples are then taken from the more confined area; this is known as *cluster sampling*.

Possibly the best method of avoiding error in most investigations is to divide the population into blocks or strata (layers) on a specified basis such as by income, age, sex, or education in proportions previously learnt from other investigations where data is already available. We may know that 8 per cent of the national population are unskilled manual workers, therefore 8 per cent of the sample is chosen from unskilled manual workers. The distribution of these subdivided groups means in effect that each stratum becomes a population on its own, and this method is termed *stratified sampling* (Figure 1.5).

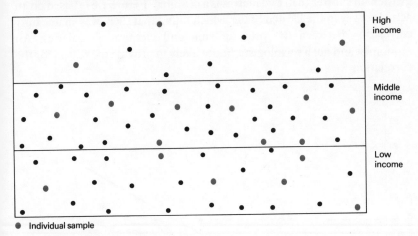

● Individual sample

Figure 1.5   *Stratified sampling*

Quota sampling is when a group of investigators are given the task of finding a set number of people in a given proportion of social characteristics, eg half male and half female, one-sixth old age pensioners, and so forth. Commercial surveying organisations use this method of *judgement sampling* where known proportions of the population exist.

All methods of sampling involve the use of *statistics* as an essential mathematical technique. Disraeli once condemned their use in his famous observation that there were 'Lies, damned lies, and statistics';

someone else spoke of statistics as being the means of lying with precision. No competent sociologist, however, can afford to neglect statistics. Because the use of statistics *is* so important in all fields of social science it is usually taught as part of most sociology courses in universities and other institutions of higher education. The correct use of statistics can provide the basis for good judgement in sociology as they enable us to allow for error in sampling and thereby make for precision in our findings. The use of statistics can indicate whether the outcome of our investigation is likely to be of significance, or whether the result could have been obtained by random chance. Whilst statistics are an invaluable tool of the sociologist they also require careful and accurate interpretation. Alone, statistical findings cannot indicate the real relationships between different sets of data. It might be found, for example, that 95 per cent of all convicted criminals are male, right-handed, and under two metres tall, but clearly not every right-handed gentleman shorter than two metres is a criminal. Figure 1.6 is based on an actual survey in the United States which found that there was an uncanny correlation between the price of rum and clergymen's salaries. An economist and not a sociologist is more likely to provide the reason for the correlation.

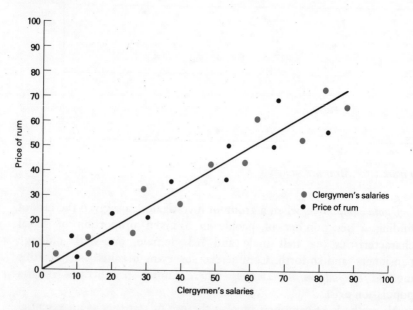

Figure 1.6 *An apparent correlation, but sociologically meaningless, between the price of rum and clergymen's salaries over the same period of time*

3.2   Social surveys

Sociologists usually gather data and other information by carrying out a *social survey*. A social survey involves systematically gathering facts about people. C. A. Moser, describing social surveys in his book *Survey Methods in Social Investigation* (Heinemann Educational Books, 1971) states, 'When it comes to the subject matter the only common factor is that they are concerned with demographic characteristics, the social environment, the activities or opinions or attitudes of some group of people.' There have been some famous exceptions, mainly in the last century, but almost all modern social surveys try to keep to the rules of being unbiased and systematic. Equally, although there are many ways of conducting social surveys, the two limitations which apply to sampling, time and money, restrict the depths to which any survey may go. There are, nevertheless, three steps which should be followed before undertaking a social survey:

1   gather as much existing information as possible about the subject of the survey
2   decide how far the survey will go
3   whenever possible carry out a *pre-test* or *pilot survey* before commencing the main survey.

Existing information can take many different forms: usually it is published material such as books, newspapers, or government reports. It may involve asking advice from experts in the subject that is to be surveyed. The reason existing information ought to be considered is that it would be pointless to repeat a survey which had already adequately covered the subject. Even more important, consideration of other works will provide pointers to what is likely to be found in the survey, together with some of the problems that may be encountered. If the problems of a previous survey can be planned for, or, better still, avoided, time and effort can be concentrated elsewhere. The original hypothesis of the investigators may well be amended after information has been gained from this preliminary study. Existing information often provides interesting material for comparison once the survey has been conducted. It might, for example, be interesting to compare the spending habits of young people in a survey conducted today with the results of a similar study conducted ten years ago, and see what changes, if any, have taken place.

The aim of a survey should be defined at the outset, taking into consideration the limits imposed by time and money and the amount of information already available. A poorly organised survey could result in the gathering of a mass of pointless and irrelevant information, and the omission of much important material. Once the resources for conducting the social survey have been established the searching out of information can be organised systematically within the bounds of those resources.

Pre-testing or pilot surveys are often valuable because they may show up faults in the design of the survey. For example, questions may be included which people do not understand, or which might lead them to give wrong answers. A pilot survey of, say, 5 per cent of the population that is to be surveyed may give an indication of the likely *response rate*: it will show how many people would be prepared to answer questions. If a pilot survey showed that only half of the people surveyed (known as *respondents*) were prepared to answer questions and the population of the survey was to be 500, then 1000 respondents would need to be found to achieve the target of 500. Pre-testing and pilot surveys may reveal how long it takes on average to answer the questions. If it were found that a survey planned to take five minutes for each respondent took ten minutes in pre-testing, then it would be necessary to double the time allowed in order to get adequate replies, and time might not be inexhaustible.

3.3 Questionnaires

In the last century, social surveys were often carried out by one investigator who recorded his observations after living among and talking to people who interested him. One of the most famous nineteenth-century works of sociological interest is Henry Mayhew's *London Labour and the London Poor*, which was first published in 1851. With two collaborators Mayhew interviewed thousands of Londoners and wrote a fascinating account of their ways of life and the many trades that flourished in the capital more than a century ago. Another survey was B. Seebohm Rowntree's *Poverty: A Study of Town Life*, which was carried out in York in 1899.

These days more than ninety per cent of social surveys involve the use of a *questionnaire* of some kind. This can take a number of forms. Either the respondent is asked a series of questions, the answers to which are filled in on a form by an interviewer, or else the respondents complete the forms themselves. Depending on the kind of information sought, both methods have their advantages and disadvantages.

The questions that are asked in questionnaires can be of the type where the respondent is asked a set question and marks off an appropriate or

Completing a questionnaire

limited reply. For example, to the question 'How much money do you earn before all deductions?' the respondent may be asked to reply by ticking one of a number of boxes, labelled perhaps:

under £60 per week ☐	£60–£70 per week ☐
£70–£80 per week ☐	£80–£90 per week ☐
£90–£100 per week ☐	£100–£110 per week ☐
over £110 per week ☐	

This type of question is known as the *pre-coded* variety, another example, the 1971 census form, is found on pp. 148–9 (Figure 5.1).

When the respondent is asked to answer a general question, such as 'What do you think of the Government's economic policy?' in his own words, either writing down his reply or dictating it to the interviewer, this is known as an *open-ended* question. For obvious reasons pre-coded questions are easier to analyse and computers may be used to do this in large surveys, but often they cannot easily be used to gauge accurately such things as the strength of a respondent's feelings on certain matters.

The usual method of using questionnaires is to have a trained interviewer. When the interviewer, who may be a comparative, and often a complete, stranger to the respondent conducts a face-to-face interview, we call this a *formal interview*. Formal interviewing requires special skills on the part of the interviewer. In the first instance the interviewer often has to find the respondents and encourage them to answer the questions. The only compulsory questionnaire is the census form which is discussed in Chapter 5, so to get replies from reluctant respondents to other questions may be quite difficult. During a formal interview the interviewer must try to give an impression of 'neutrality', firstly so that the respondent does not give replies which he thinks the interviewer would like to hear, and secondly so that the respondent is not embarrassed to answer any of the questions on the questionnaire. Middle-aged women have been found to be the best kind of interviewers as they seem to get on well with people of all ages and social backgrounds. *Informal interviewing* is more difficult than formal interviewing: this is when the interviewer tries to get a more relaxed atmosphere in order to draw out the respondent's feelings, opinions and confidences, and yet subsequently reports his findings in an objective, ie non-biased, way. Very often informal interviewing is a *follow-up* to formal interviews after a respondent has shown some interesting characteristics which the investigators wish to look at in greater depth. Considerable skill on the part of the interviewers is required for this kind of work, as they must build up a relationship with the respondent, be objective, and yet not destroy the respondent's trust or divulge publicly what they have been told in confidence.

The commonest form of investigation without an interviewer is the use of *mail questionnaires*, when a respondent is sent the questionnaire through the post accompanied by a pre-paid envelope for the reply. The two main advantages of the mail questionnaire are that it is cheap and results can be obtained rapidly. If costs are limited, then the difference between paying a day's wage to a trained interviewer who may be able to see a dozen respondents, and posting out several hundred questionnaires for the same price, may be a deciding factor. It has been the experience of investigators using the mail questionnaire that they receive between two-thirds and three-quarters of the replies within the first week (this does *not* mean a response rate of 66–75 per cent); after three weeks there are hardly any replies at all. Sometimes questionnaires ask a question which would be best answered by a family discussing the reply: for example, a question on family expenditure. Sociologists call this *intra-household consultation*. If people can reply to the questionnaire at their leisure, or at least when they are all together and not just when the interviewer calls, then a more precise reply may be obtained, especially if they have to look up documents to give a reply. Questions of an intimate personal nature often receive a better response with the anonymity of a mail questionnaire than if they are asked by a strange interviewer. Some people say that if the interviewer is not properly trained, such things as his speech, dress and manner may put off the respondent, and that this does not happen with a mail questionnaire. Quite often interviewers have difficulty in making contact with selected respondents from a carefully chosen representative sample, and time may be lost before the meeting is arranged. This too will not happen with mail questionnaires.

The main disadvantage of mail questionnaires, and therefore an advantage of having trained interviewers, is that there is always a chance of the wording being confusing and the questions being misunderstood: for this reason the choice of words in all types of questionnaire is of the greatest importance. The answers given to a mail questionnaire must be taken as final, and no allowance is made for the possibility of people misunderstanding questions and being inaccurate in their replies. Sometimes questions require a spontaneous response, before the respondent has the chance to think up a reply and obviously this is not possible with a mail questionnaire. Other questions may be of a 'follow-up' type depending upon the answer to one particular question, eg 'Do you take part in an active sport? If "Yes" which one, and for how long each week?' If the respondent has had the chance to read through all the questions before answering, he may frame his replies to match all the questions. On occasions the truthful answer can only be obtained when a husband or wife is not present: a husband may not like to fill out the real answer to a question on how much he spends on beer each week in an intra-household consultation.

Sometimes interviewers add extra information about respondents after an interview, perhaps giving an assessment of the character, environment and even honesty of the respondent. This cannot be done with a mail questionnaire. Such factors as the type of question to be asked, the time and money available, and perhaps the need for extra information about the respondent, must all be taken into account before deciding the appropriate type of questionnaire and interviewing techniques to be used.

3.4   Methods of observation

As has been said, most surveys involve a questionnaire of some kind, but important sociological research has been conducted using other kinds of social survey. Instead of seeking a mass of information that question-naires might provide, some investigators prefer to gain an impression of many aspects of their subjects' behaviour which could not be contained in a series of questions no matter how well devised. The general name for this kind of investigation is the *observational approach*. Television documentaries, often about social problems, use this technique by filming the conditions under which people live, the way in which they speak and what their attitudes to things are—a *qualitative* rather than a *quantitative* approach is used.

There are some kinds of social activity and situations where it is best for the investigator to live among the subjects of his research. This is known as *participant observation*. Usually this method is employed when dealing with small communities, such as villages, or primitive tribes. The insight gained by living and working among small communities can be far greater than it would have been if the observer were an outsider and not accepted by the community. Provided the participant observer is constantly aware of the need to be objective in his study (and this could prove difficult as he is bound to develop friendships, or his very presence might cause his subjects to act unnaturally) a deep understanding of the community is possible.

In contrast to observation there are techniques of surveying which use only existing data and archive material such as government documents or similar published information. These techniques are usually employed in large-scale research projects where demographic material is the source of the sociologists' work. Quite often different sets of data are compared over a period of time, and changes or differences are recorded. Case studies of individuals are used by social psychologists, but by their nature they can only be on a small scale.

A *longitudinal study* is an investigation where the same population is observed periodically over a time-span of several years. An example of a longitudinal study is the *birth cohort* of 17 000 children born in one week in 1958 (see Topic 12.2) who were observed and tested on a regular basis. The main disadvantage of this type of investigation is the possibility of

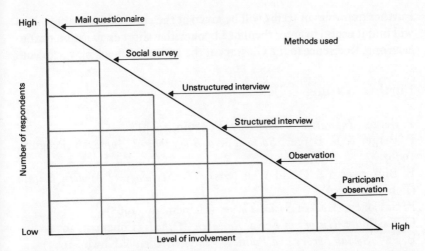

Figure 1.7   *Theoretical diagram showing the level of involvement of the sociologist in the different methods of social investigation*

losing contact with the members of the population. The 1958 study was fairly successful in this regard as only 582 could not be traced by 1973.

How do sociologists decide which approach to use?

The nature of the subject to be studied largely determines the method of approach. The resources available determine the depth to which investigations can be carried out. The rest of this book examines various aspects of society, or the different groups into which people form themselves. If we investigate the way in which people behave towards one another, and the structure of different institutions, we shall gradually build up a picture of the society in which we live. Before we could begin to study society we have had to learn the ways in which sociological investigation is conducted and some of the theories on which sociology is based.

Terms used in this chapter

quantitive	observational	dysfunction
longitudinal study	anthropology	pilot survey
social relationship	behaviour patterns	pre-coded questionnaire
social system	empirical	social groups
social structure	hypothesis	non-ethical

Further examples of terms will be given at the end of each chapter. You will find it useful to enter them in a book with a short explanation next to each one. Reference to the Glossary at the end of this book may help you.

Further reading

P. Berger, *Invitation to Sociology* (Penguin, 1963)
P. Berger & B. Berger, *Sociology: a Biographical Approach* (Penguin, 1976)
E. Butterworth & David Weir (eds), *The Sociology of Modern Britain* (Fontana, 1970)
P. S. Cohen, *Modern Social Theory* (Heinemann, 1968)
G. Easthope, *History of Social Research Methods* (Longman, 1974)
B. Fay, *Social Theory and Political Practice* (Allen & Unwin, 1975)
M. J. Moroney, *Facts from Figures* (Penguin, 1962)
C. A. Moser, *Survey Methods in Social Investigation* (Heinemann, 1971)
M. D. Shipman, *Limitations of Social Research* (Longman, 1972)
M. Stacey, *Methods of Social Research* (Pergamon, 1969)
P. Worsley, *Introducing Sociology* (Penguin, 1970)
P. Worsley (ed.), *Modern Sociology Introductory Readings* (Penguin, 1972)

Questions from GCE 'O' Level Sociology Examination Papers

1   Sociology is not a collection of facts but a different way of seeing the world. Illustrate. (AEB, November 1972)
2   It has been suggested that a scientific method includes the following six processes:
i   identifying a specific problem
ii   selecting appropriate methods to study the problem
iii   collecting relevant data
iv   analysing the data
v   interpreting the data
vi   reporting findings and conclusions.
Take any sociological study that you are familiar with and show how it fits in (or does not fit in) with the six stages quoted above. Make sure that you refer clearly to *one* particular piece of research. (AEB, June 1973)
3   Describe and explain some of the methods used by sociologists in their studies. Give examples from *one* piece of relevant research. (AEB, November 1972)

4   What do you understand by scientific method? To what extent are sociologists scientific? (AEB, November 1974)

5   (a) What is meant by a sampling frame?
(b)   Why is stratifying important when designing a sample?
(c)   What are the advantages and disadvantages of longitudinal studies? (AEB, June 1976)

6   What would be the main points to consider if you were designing a survey within your school or college? Use the following notes as a guide: aims/hypothesis; sample and sampling frame; collection of information; analysis of information.
(A detailed questionnaire is not required.) (AEB, November 1975)

7   Explain clearly but briefly what you understand by *three* of the following terms:

experiment	group
questionnaire	hypothesis.

(AEB, November 1970)

8   Explain what is meant by *one* of the following kinds of sociological research methods and describe its use in *one* sociological study with which you are familiar: random sampling, participant observation, or a longitudinal study. (AEB, November 1974)

9   Describe two different methods which sociologists have used to obtain information. (AEB, November 1976)

10   Describe the important considerations to be borne in mind when designing a postal questionnaire. (Use examples but a full questionnaire is not required.) (AEB, June 1978)

11   *Either*: Compare postal questionnaires with open-ended interviews as methods of gaining information for sociological research.
Or: Explain with examples what is meant by a stratified random sample. Discuss the advantages and limitations of this form of sampling. (AEB, June 1979)

12   Select the most suitable method of collecting information for sociological research into each of the following. Give reasons for your choice of the method to be used in each case and examine some of its weaknesses.
(a)   The response of family doctors towards a suggested new system of patient consultations throughout England and Wales.
(b)   The lifestyle of a group of gypsies.
(c)   The attitudes of local residents to a new hostel for unmarried mothers in the neighbourhood.
(You are not required to give detailed examples in any case or to discuss sampling procedures.) (AEB, June 1981)

2 Social Differences
Unit 4 What is Stratification?

A characteristic common to almost all societies is the way in which they may divide up into different layers or *strata*. In industrial societies such as Britain today we may think of a simple division into two *classes*, a working class and a middle class (leaving for the moment the tricky definition of class). Earlier this century there was also a recognisable upper class, but this group is now identified by most sociologists as having merged with the middle class. Some other terms of stratification employed are *estate*, *status*, and in Indian society, *caste*. All these terms imply some kind of ranking or hierarchy. Throughout history strata have been recognisable: in ancient times there were slaves and freemen, in medieval society there were lords and villeins. As time passes different divisions have emerged, reflecting the changes that have taken place in society, yet hierarchies have continued to exist, and sociologists have sought to understand the reasons for these divisions; some have advanced theories as to how the differences between them could be eliminated. Even in countries where revolutions have occurred and ideals such as those of the French Revolution—Liberty, Equality and Fraternity— have provided the inspiration for change, eventually some new hierarchy has asserted itself.

Stratification provides sociologists with a convenient means of distinguishing between different groups, and even of distinguishing divisions within groups themselves; yet too often the terms of stratification appear rather loose and care must be taken in their definition.

4.1 Estate

Estate systems existed in Europe from late Roman times even into the last century in some countries. The hierarchy in medieval England was structured as in Figure 2.1. Essentially the system was based upon the ownership of land, and in the higher ranks, upon the numbers of fighting men that could be provided in times of war. Since power rests ultimately

Royalty
Nobility $\rightarrow$ Free tenants $\rightarrow$ Cottars
Lesser gentry   Villeins   Serfs

Figure 2.1   The feudal hierarchy

upon military force, those who possessed arms and controlled numbers of fighting men were unwilling to allow their authority to be weakened by any change in the system. The Church reinforced this rigid hierarchy: the medieval Church too had its upper and lower ranks, which ranged from powerful archbishops to poor village priests, and it regarded with suspicion any ideas which might appear to threaten its own position in the social order. Anyone who challenged the feudal order or the teachings of the Church might be regarded as a heretic and liable to the most extreme penalties. Thus we have two estates, the nobility and the Church. Later a third estate developed: the townspeople increased their power from about the twelfth century onwards until they were able to dominate society in the late eighteenth and nineteenth century with the coming of industrialisation. The summoning of the 'Estates General' in Paris in May 1789 was the prelude to the French Revolution, since it was the Third Estate or *bourgeoisie* who demonstrated their newfound power in the famous 'Tennis Court Oath', by demanding a National Assembly in France.

The rise of the Third Estate has been attributed to a number of factors, ranging from the Black Death to the establishment of the Protestant religion. One theory is that the Black Death, the plague that swept Europe between 1347 and 1350, killing a third or more of the population, caused the depleted agricultural population to demand higher farm wages and this in turn encouraged the land owners to turn to wool production on a larger scale in England. Land owners were no longer dependent upon subsistence farming, and merchants and townspeople grew prosperous on the new trade. Trading is linked to the growth of towns and industrialisation; Max Weber, and R. H. Tawney (in his book *Religion and the Rise of Capitalism*), maintained that industrialisation occurred in Europe because of the Protestants' freedom to lend money and indulge in commerce. The Catholic Church had forbidden the lending of money at high interest rates as the sin of usury, thereby stifling commerce, while to Protestants such as the Calvinists success in business was held to be a sign of God's favour. Whatever theory is advanced for the development of commerce, and we have given just two examples from many, it is a fact that the growth of towns and cities meant that power passed from the landowning aristocracy to the merchant classes in the eighteenth and nineteenth centuries.

4.2   Social class

Of all the different terms of stratification the word 'class' is perhaps the most confusing and even sociologists interpret the term differently. If we talk about the working class or middle class, certain images come to mind, yet we may all have different conceptions of class. Karl Marx was one of the first writers to analyse class differences, in the middle of the last century. He saw class as being a phenomenon of any society where ownership of wealth and the means of production, factories or land, gave an economic basis for stratification.

In *The Communist Manifesto* (1847), written in collaboration with Friedrich Engels, Marx outlined different stages in history in which the ownership of property gave one group control over others. From ancient society based on slavery to feudal society resting upon the labour of villeins and serfs, the group which controlled and owned the means of producing food and goods was the dominant class. Marx argued that there was a constant struggle, a class struggle, and this conflict between the different classes brought about changes in society. He believed that in the nineteenth century the bourgeoisie, who owned and controlled the means of production in the capitalist system, dominated the wage-earners or *proletariat*. Everything, Marx said, depended upon the ownership of capital (wealth)—it shaped religion, government, and even the family. In other words, economic relationships determined all other relationships. The class struggle between the proletariat and bourgeoisie would eventually end in a victory for the working class if they were to unite and overthrow the owners of capital. Of course, many of Marx's observations were based upon the appalling conditions that were the results of industrialisation in the nineteenth century where little was done to alleviate the distress of the poor. Nevertheless, he made the essential point that class was primarily based upon economic circumstances.

Separated from Marx by half a century, Max Weber (1864–1920) had seen a further development of capitalist society. Instead of the small middle class (shopkeepers and small farmers) being drawn down into the working class as Marx had predicted, the middle classes had grown in importance and number. The main reasons for this were the development of education and literacy, and the increase in working-class participation in government and politics through an extension of the franchise (see Chapter 7). This new middle class, consisting of such people as clerks and skilled workers, had no wish to overthrow the existing social system. For their part, the working classes were organising themselves into trade unions and gaining increased benefits from raised standards of living.

Both Marx and Weber saw class as being related to the economic conditions of an industrialised society. If we were asked what it was that constituted class, we would usually reply that it was income, or education, or the kind of job that someone has. Usually sociologists base definitions of class upon occupation, because the kind of occupation that someone has is to some extent dependent upon their education and it will give us an idea of the income that they have. Obviously class cannot be based upon income alone. Would an unskilled labourer who won thousands of pounds on the football pools automatically join the middle classes? Is a newly qualified teacher, who earns less than a docker, a member of the working class? The type of occupation that someone has would seem to be the best guide to the classification of classes. This use of occupation to give a rough guide to class is found in newspaper reports, and in courts, where together with an accused person's full name, age and address, their occupation is also requested.

The Registrar General, who is in charge of the government's statistical department, divides the population into five classes based upon occupation, with a division of Class 3 into manual and non-manual workers after the 1971 census. (See Table 2.1.)

		1971
Class 1	capitalists, managers, scientists, professionals, *eg* architects, doctors, lawyers, university teachers, etc.	3.6%
Class 2	lower professionals, intermediate, *eg* small shopkeepers, farmers, teachers, airline pilots, etc.	17.8%
Class 3	skilled workers, clerical workers, *eg* miners, butchers, electricians, bricklayers, draughtsmen, secretaries, shop assistants, etc.	21.1% (non-manual) 28.4% (manual)
Class 4	semi-skilled workers, *eg* bus conductors, fishermen, postmen, telephone operators, farm workers, packers, etc.	20.9%
Class 5	unskilled workers, *eg* labourers, messengers, cleaners, porters, kitchen hands, etc.	8.2%

Table 2.1   The Registrar General's five-point occupational scale

The Registrar General's five-point scale was originally drawn up in 1911, since when many changes have taken place in the kinds of occupations that people have (*occupational structure*) with the result that the scale has become somewhat vague and rather limited in its scope. In 1950 John Hall and D. Caradog Jones developed a seven-point scale also based upon occupations (Table 2.2). Many sociologists recognise that the Hall–Jones scale has its limitations, for example some believe that it is too biased in favour of *white-collar* (non-manual) workers, yet compared with the Registrar General's scale it is more sophisticated. Usually sociologists use adaptations of the Hall–Jones scale in their work.

Class 1   professional and high administrative
Class 2   managerial and executive
Class 3   inspectional, supervisory and other non-manual, higher grade
Class 4   inspectional, supervisory and other non-manual, lower grade
Class 5   skilled manual and routine grades of non-manual
Class 6   semi-skilled manual
Class 7   unskilled manual

Table 2.2   The Hall–Jones scale

So far we have talked of the working class and the middle class, and said that the upper class has merged with the middle class during this century. Many people still presume that there is an upper class, but although they were recognisable as landed gentry in the eighteenth and nineteenth centuries, they are not recognised as such today by most sociologists (unless we mean the three or four thousand members of the aristocracy who constitute less than a ten-thousandth part of the population, which is far too few to constitute a distinct social class). On the continent a fourth class is made up of the peasantry, who are small farmers of their own land, which usually does not exceed forty acres. Because of the enclosure of the land in Britain which began in Elizabethan times and reached a peak during the industrial revolution, a peasant class is not found in Britain today—with possible exceptions in the highland areas of Scotland and Wales. In Britain only three per cent of the population is engaged in farming, but in France about a sixth of the population is connected in some way with agriculture; the peasant class is thus of importance to Continental sociologists.

4.3   Caste

The Indian caste system has interested sociologists for many years. Some 3500 years ago invaders from the north, known as *Aryans*, imposed the caste system; there is no conclusive evidence that they originated the idea of caste in India, but it seems to be the most likely explanation. The Hindu religion divides the population into five basic groups. The four highest groups are known as *Varnas* (colours) and beneath them come a group without caste, the *Untouchables*. The four Varnas consist of:

1   *Brahmans*   a priest caste
2   *Kshatriyas*   a military caste
3   *Vaishyas*   a merchant or agricultural caste
4   *Sudras*   a labouring caste.

Within these groups there are thousands of subdivisions; among the *Brahmans* there are more than 500 subdivisions and there are over 200 divisions of people without caste. Caste affects the whole way of Indian life despite laws against discrimination such as the Indian Constitution's law of 1950 which officially abolished 'untouchability'. To a large extent skin colour differentiated caste (the lighter the colouring the higher the caste) but the occupational structure of India does not truly reflect caste—for example not all *Kshatriyas* are soldiers, and many *Sudras* have made money in business. Even so, caste is still important in Indian society and attitudes have changed little since India's independence in 1947.

It is clear that any understanding of caste must be accompanied by a knowledge of Hinduism. The doctrine of *karma* maintains that anyone who behaves well on earth will enter a higher caste after rebirth, in other words Hindus believe in reincarnation, and it is this that keeps people within their allotted caste without too much resentment. In recent times, nevertheless, many untouchables have turned to Buddhism (which does not recognise caste differences and is a separate religion) as a means of obtaining self-respect. There are strict laws on what food may be eaten by Hindus; one authority (J. H. Hutton, *Caste in India: Its Nature, Function and Origins*, Oxford University Press, 1963) considers that these rules on food maintain the system more than anything else. Marriage is not permitted between different castes, so membership of one caste is hereditary and permanent. The religious restrictions (known as *taboos*) ensure that very little contact occurs on a social level between castes. The caste system is, as a consequence, very rigid and unlikely to change. As we have seen with the estate system in Europe, change occurs with commercialisation and industrialisation. India is still largely a rural society, and this has helped to maintain the caste system. The vast geographical distances of India have also meant that there are considerable regional differences in the position of various castes—some have prospered despite a low caste, usually through the purchase of land after success in commerce, while others have remained poor in isolated villages. Professor F. G. Bailey (*Tribe, Caste and Nation*, Manchester University Press, 1960) believes that the caste system has profoundly altered since India's independence, but the roots of the system based upon tradition and ritual are still strong.

Unit 5 Social Mobility

As we have seen, estate and caste systems are rather rigid, making it difficult for anyone to get out of the position in society into which he is born. In the early development of industrialisation during the nineteenth century, people were no longer tied to the land and were free to seek jobs in the towns, but the harsh conditions of employment with low wages and slum conditions (Marx referred to the industrial proletariat as 'wage slaves') did not really entail much more freedom for most of the population. By the end of the century, however, conditions were improving and new kinds of jobs were created. Increasing educational opportunities and some political power did allow certain groups to better themselves: to give just one example, the founding of the Amalgamated Society of Engineers in 1851 marked the beginning of a new craftsman's union whose members' services were clearly needed by the manufacturing employers, and so engineers were able to improve their economic and social position. The growth of the new middle classes at the end of the century came only from the newly-educated working class. Improved economic status meant an improved social status; the possibility of changing position in the hierarchy is termed *social mobility*. When someone improves his or her position in society, this is known as *upward mobility*. A much rarer occurrence is when someone falls to a lower position in the social hierarchy and this is termed *downward mobility*. Sociologists usually measure social mobility by comparing occupations over a generation: if the son of an unskilled labourer becomes the director of a merchant bank then upward mobility has taken place (such a rise would indeed be rare).

5.1 Factors affecting social mobility

The case of the engineers in the nineteenth century is an example of one of the causes of mobility: the development of a new kind of skill or type of job, especially when the numbers of people who have that particular skill are limited, means that upward mobility can take place because of a change in occupational structure. Another, more recent, change in the occupational structure has been the development of electronics and technology. Computer programmers are an example of a new occupation which has grown out of a change in the occupational structure. Generally the advance of technology and economic growth mean the creation of more jobs higher up the social scale: instead of the muscle power of six unskilled labourers digging a trench, one skilled machine operator driving an excavator can do the job, and do it more efficiently. Economic growth has meant that there are more people in middle–class occupations year by year. (GCE question 4 on page 289 illustrates occupational changes over fifty-five years.)

Education too is an important factor in upward mobility, because the better an education one has, and the higher the qualifications that are gained, the more likely it will be that an occupation higher up the social scale can be obtained. A labourer's son who gets a university place is not likely to become a labourer himself. Education is a fairly clear means to upward mobility.

In Britain there are regional differences in the kinds of jobs open to school-leavers. In a remote valley where coal is mined, employment available to the school-leaver who is not prepared, or is even unable, to move, may be restricted to mining. In a small town where there are a few little factories the choice is also very restricted.

Motivation is an important factor affecting mobility. There may be restrictions of an economic kind on the type of job open to someone, but if there is a motivation or determination strong enough either to move somewhere where the opportunities for advancement are greater, or to go on to further study and gain higher qualifications, then upward mobility may be achieved.

The number of children in a family will also play its part in social mobility. Over a generation the larger families of manual workers may mean that some of the children of the manual workers will enter occupations of a non-manual kind through the changes that occur in the occupational structure.

Factors which affect social mobility are:

1 occupational structure
2 education
3 distribution of opportunity
4 motivation
5 family size
6 marriage (see cover photograph).

One of the difficulties of calculating social mobility, when measured over a generation, is to establish a constant point on the social scale: what was regarded as low social status thirty years ago may be more highly regarded today, or the reverse may have happened. During the years between the wars a secure clerical job held high status at a time of high unemployment. Are such jobs so well regarded today? At what point on the scale do we place, or how much prestige are we to attach to, new types of job that have been created over a generation? The variables, such as income, education, or life styles, that constitute class make it difficult to establish the relevant point on the ever-moving social scale or *index of occupation*. The social mobility between father and son, termed *intergenerational mobility*, is dependent upon the numbers of occupations of one kind within the population. If the number of bricklayers, in proportion to the total population, were to remain constant over a generation, and a bricklayer's son became a solicitor, then (given that the number of solicitors in relation to the total population had also remained constant) we would have an example of *perfect mobility*. Such conditions of constant occupational structure are few. If we take a point on a scale today and contrast the different positions of, say, father and son we can only make general comparisons from it, yet these can be interesting, as Table 2.3 reveals. International comparison of social mobility would provide an even more complex task.

Ralph Turner ('Sponsored and Contest Mobility and the School System', *American Sociological Review*, Vol. XXV, 1960) considered the question of social mobility. He defined two 'ideal' forms of mobility which he termed *contest* and *sponsored* mobility. Contest mobility is the form of mobility where the top positions in society are dependent principally upon the ability and effort of the individual, and where institutions such as the famous public schools have little control over mobility. Sponsored mobility is the form of mobility where recruits to the leading positions in society are chosen, not so much on individual merit, but by selection from their own class by the upper strata. In Britain both forms of mobility exist, but as we shall see in subsequent chapters, and as Turner argues, the sponsored form is more dominant.

5.2 Self-assigned class

Marx considered that when the working class fully understood their position in society, that is to say the way in which they were exploited by the factory owners or landowners, they would rise in a revolution; this awareness he called *class-consciousness*. More than a century ago there

Father's occupation	Professional and high administrative	Managerial and executive	Higher inspectional and supervisory	Lower inspectional and supervisory	Skilled	Semi-skilled	Unskilled
	1 %	2 %	3 %	4 %	5 %	6 %	7 %
Prof and high admin	38.8	14.6	20.2	6.2	14.0	4.7	1.5
Managerial and executive	10.7	26.7	22.7	12.0	20.6	5.3	2.0
Higher insp and supervisory	3.5	10.1	18.8	19.1	35.7	6.7	6.1
Lower insp and supervisory	2.1	3.9	11.2	21.2	43.0	12.4	6.2
Skilled manual	0.9	2.4	7.5	12.3	47.3	17.1	12.5
Semi-skilled manual	0.0	1.3	4.1	8.8	39.1	31.2	15.5
Unskilled manual	0.0	0.8	3.6	8.3	36.3	23.5	27.4

Table 2.3 Sons' occupations in relation to fathers' occupations (men aged 21 and over, England and Wales—sons' present occupation)
(Source: *Social Mobility in Britain*, ed. D. V. Glass, Routledge & Kegan Paul, 1954)

were clear divisions in society between the worker and wealthy capitalist, but today the divisions of class may not be so readily apparent. We may have many different views about what is meant by class and the extent to which divisions exist. Some people maintain that we are moving towards a *classless society*, whilst others feel that there are still marked class differences. Some of the criteria that sociologists use to define class are: occupation, education, income, power, prestige, life style, speech patterns, and possibly appearance; yet attitudes towards class are also of importance. Some of the differences between working–class and middle–class groups are revealed in their overall view of society known as *social perspectives*.

What are the different social perspectives?

The middle class tend to regard society as a kind of ladder where it is possible to move up the hierarchy rung by rung (see Figure 2.2). Through such things as ability, initiative or hard work it is possible to 'get

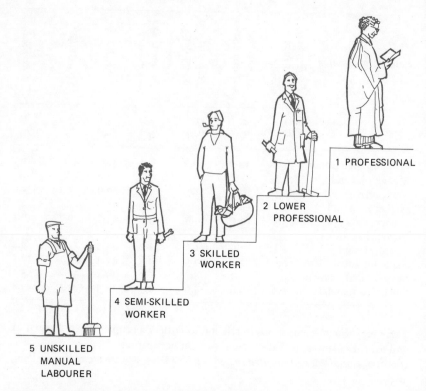

Figure 2.2   Registrar General's five-point scale of occupational structure

on', even though this may mean sacrifices at some stage of an individual's life. This perspective is one of *individualism*. A working-class perspective is to divide society up into *us* and *them* (the latter may refer to governments, landlords, bosses or virtually any official who has some kind of authority). The division is more or less permanent, unless one is lucky, so for the most part you must put up with your lot and try to make the best of things as they are now rather than worrying too much about the future. This perspective is termed *collectivist* as it is a view of society as being the two groups *us* and *them*.

Sociologists are interested in the way in which people regard their own position in society, and the position of others. When asked about class most people would say that there are three classes in society, an upper class, a middle class, and a working class. We have already said that there is no such thing as an upper class in sociological terms because class involves so many factors and it is impossible to differentiate between the upper and middle classes (using whichever scale we choose) in many of the factors other than occupation that constitute class. We shall, however, see that there are many differences between the broad classifications of working class and middle class. No social survey these days will include the category upper class. If asked which class they belonged to themselves, a large number of people would place themselves in a category higher than that assigned to them by the Registrar General, or indeed any other sociologist's scale. A survey by F. M. Martin in Greenwich and Hertford in the 1950s found that a quarter of the manual (working-class) respondents thought of themselves as being middle-class (*Social Mobility in Britain*, ed. D. V. Glass, Routledge & Kegan Paul, 1954). In a later survey (1961) Mark Abrams and R. Rose found that the percentage of working-class people who thought of themselves as being middle-class was even higher. Although their book *Must Labour Lose?* was mainly concerned with political attitudes, these figures confirm the tendency to think of oneself as being in a higher social class than one really is.

It is clear from this kind of survey that most people recognise that there are class differences. In order to make themselves seem more important, perhaps for reasons of snobbery, a fair percentage will place themselves on a scale higher than their true position.

The value that is placed upon the different jobs held by people is related to an overall view of society. It is surprising perhaps that there is often a considerable agreement when people are asked to rank types of employment in order of importance. In 1956 Michael Young and Peter Willmott gave a list of thirty occupations (graded by the Hall–Jones scale) to a number of East End of London manual workers (remembering that the Hall–Jones scale is biased in favour of middle-class occupations). The East Enders were asked to grade the occupations according to their ideas of importance; what emerged was a high degree of similarity between Hall–Jones's ranking and the East Enders' ranking at the top and to some extent the bottom ends of the list. In the middle and towards the lower end of the list the East Enders gave more importance to skilled manual occupations and less importance to the less skilled non-manuals jobs. The criteria upon which the East Enders based their choices included ability, education, income, social standing, and how much the occupation contributed towards the good of society. A small group of the sample were found to have very different views from their fellow respondents; these tended to place more emphasis on the social contribution of the occupation, ie the benefit to society of the occupation. Doctors of medicine always head the list when the criterion of benefit to society is applied, though this is not really surprising as similar surveys conducted in other countries have also found that doctors invariably headed the list. In 1973 a Law Society study of attitudes towards various professions put estate agents at the bottom of the list of popularity and usefulness.

	Labour voters %	Other voters %
Upper middle class	0	3
Middle class	14	31
Lower middle class	16	16
Total who thought themselves to be middle-class	30	50
Skilled working class	27	28
Labouring working class	40	18
Total who thought themselves to be working-class	67	46
Don't know	3	4
	100	100

Table 2.4   Self-assigned class of manual workers
(Source: Abrams and Rose, *Must Labour Lose?*)

Unit 6   Social Structure and Social Change

In Chapter 1 it was noted briefly that there is interaction between individuals and between groups in the form of social relationships. The network or patterns of these social relationships create a social structure; as the relationships change, the structures of society change. Here is one example which may help in understanding this idea: 150 years ago a workman was economically weak, others were ready to do his job for the same low wages, conditions of employment were poor, and the workman was humble before his employer and would address him in a subservient manner; workmen are in a stronger economic position today, particularly when labour is scarce, and this being the case the employer will address the workman with some respect; a change in the social relationship between employer and employee has taken place.

Patterns of social behaviour (usually in groups) = social structure

Most of this book is an examination of different aspects of behaviour: behaviour in the family, behaviour in the educational system, behaviour of people who act differently from most others, and so forth. Taken as a whole this builds up a picture of the social structure of contemporary Britain. We cannot freeze society at a given moment in time in our examination of society today, but we can examine the general trends, as well as the changes that have already taken place, against a background of life in contemporary Britain.

6.1   The social structure of Britain

It /ould be wrong to assume that sociology consists of a series of separate studies of aspects of society such as the family, the educational system or the economic system. The way in which we are brought up in the family, the way in which we learn at school, the way in which people behave towards us at work are all part of a process of experience that affects our attitudes and makes us what we are as individuals. However, we are not examining individuals, but society as a whole. If we study how the family is related to the educational system, how the educational system is related to the economic system, etc., we shall see the structure of our social system. Attitudes are important because different attitudes produce different forms of behaviour; and the most basic difference of attitude found in society as a whole is that which exists between different classes. There are a host of other differences, differences by age, sex, religion, race, and many more, but for simplicity most sociologists use class differences as a starting point since they underlie many of the major differences in society.

How do class differences affect the social structure?

The constant changing or *dynamism* of society means that sociologists need frequently to change their theories in the light of fresh evidence of social change. One theory is that class differences are disappearing in Britain as the better-off members of the working class are beginning to adopt middle-class life styles and values. This is known as the process of *embourgeoisement*, and is the view of F. Zweig founded upon his study of highly paid workers in four industries (*The Worker in an Affluent Society*, Heinemann Educational Books, 1961). Some of the middle-class patterns adopted took the form of a change in family relationships and the purchase of material possessions formerly enjoyed only by the middle classes. An opposite view is taken by J. H. Goldthorpe and others in their book *The Affluent Worker in the Class Structure* (Cambridge University Press, 1969). Deliberately looking for evidence of embourgeoisement, they did find a resemblance in life styles to those of the middle class among some of the better-off working class, but in the important question of attitudes and values fundamental differences still existed between the classes. The former working-class *us* and *them* perspective had been replaced by the view that social status (standing) depended upon income and spending habits.

Class, although not entirely resting upon economic circumstances, is, as we have seen, tied largely to the economic factor of occupation. Certainly the number of manual occupations decreases in Britain year by year and changes in the occupational structure contribute towards upward mobility. Economic change certainly causes social change, but the important element of *behaviour* is largely shaped by the attitudes and values found in the family, amongst friends, and the experience of school and work. It is here that the working class and middle class divide in their experience of life, and these divisions remain through life.

6.2   How class affects our lives

Quite naturally we associate a person's life style with his class. A manual labourer from the East End of London will have a different way of life from a stockbroker living in a Sussex village. We would expect different patterns of behaviour from a vicar's wife and a trawlerman's wife. Although we are conscious of some of the differences of class, it may be difficult to pinpoint exactly what makes those subtle differences. Before we hear someone speak we may try to sum people up by their age and the clothes they are wearing; hearing them speak may provide a pointer towards their social class because of accent and choice of words. If they tell us their occupation we have an even clearer picture of their social class. Why should these things be meaningful, and of how much importance is class in our lives?

We shall see later how the upbringing of a child and the kind of education received, together with the experience of work, more or less condition us in advance to our place in society. If the embourgeoisement process is carried to its logical conclusion class differences will become so minimal that eventually we shall be living in a classless society. Unfortunately conditions such as family environment, schooling and occupation that create and reinforce social class differences are still

Visual social differences

strong, and although there are many changes in class behaviour, there are
equally powerful forces which maintain a division between the working
class and the middle class. In his book *Social Class Differences in Britain*
(Open Books, 1977) Ivan Reid examined the differences between social
classes. He used a large number of surveys, censuses, opinion polls, and
other statistical data. His overall conclusion is that the higher up the
social scale one is, the better the quality and, even the happier the life that
will be led. To give just a few examples from his findings: middle-class
and professional people tend to live longer, are healthier from birth, have
happier marriages, live in better homes, visit the doctor less, retain more
teeth, suffer less from almost every disease, play more sport, join more
clubs, commit suicide less, and smoke less. As most British sociologists
use social class and status as an essential means of analysis, these and
many other differences will appear throughout this book.

It is true that most members of the working class enjoy a greater
material prosperity than ever before, but the middle classes have enjoyed
increased benefits too. The Welfare State was instituted during and
immediately after World War II to create equality of opportunity in
education for all, and to provide security for the aged, sick and
unemployed (see Chapter 8). Professor R. M. Titmuss in his *Essays on
'The Welfare State'* (Allen & Unwin, 1963) argues that in reality the middle
classes have gained far more from the provisions of the Welfare State than
have the working class. Several examples may provide some illustration:

1 The cost of education beyond the school-leaving age is high, but this is a privilege enjoyed proportionately far more by the middle class than the working class.

2 House purchase provides income tax relief greater than any subsidies received by rent-paying tenants of council or private accommodation. A house will rise in value and, with inflation, the mortgage repayments become less in real terms. A far greater percentage of the middle class than the working class purchase their own house, and find it easier to obtain mortgages. Recently, however, high costs of building and stricter standards of quality, which apply to council houses, have meant that on average a new council house costs more to build than a private one.

3 Because the middle class are more familiar with their rights and speak with greater authority to such people as doctors or officials they are likely to receive more considerate treatment.

4 Credit and more favourable repayment terms are more likely to be made available to people in middle-class occupations which are considered secure and carry pensions.

Problems of homelessness and poverty are still found in Britain and, with rare exceptions, these are working-class problems. If we lived in a classless society with full equality of opportunity for all in education, adequate sickness and unemployment benefits and pensions not geared to previous earnings, we might be nearer the ideals of the creators of the Welfare State. Unfortunately the machinery that provides the benefits cannot help being biased towards the middle class, while the working class are often unaware of some of the benefits that they might enjoy through such things as further education and investment for the future. As we shall see in Chapter 8, it is officially estimated that some seven million Britons, one-eighth of the total population, live on or below the minimum level of income thought necessary by the government to provide a basic living standard.

Unit 7 Status and Power

7.1 Status

We have already come across the word 'status' when considering the ranking given to various occupations. Status may be defined as the social honour or prestige that is given to certain positions in society. It is the position occupied by a person or group relative to others in the same social system. To begin with, this position is determined by the family circumstances into which a child is born, the kind of education received and the occupation that is followed. The hierarchy that seems inevitably to be found in almost all societies means that there will be different status groups. Through life it is possible to change one's status by achievement comparable to others—in the case of occupational status either through upward or downward mobility. The status held by an individual or group will determine their rights, duties and behaviour towards others.

What is the difference between class and status?

Max Weber, in his book *Class, Status and Power*, distinguished between class and status in advanced industrial societies. Weber was interested in the way in which the new middle classes had gained so much political power; he felt that this was not only due to their class position. The prestige and success of the middle classes he considered due to their status in society. Social classes were stratified by Marx according to their relationship with the means of production (as wage-earning employees or as a professional class) and their wealth. Status groups were stratified by Weber according to such things as education, occupation and what he termed 'styles of life', making finer distinctions between groups than Marx's economic definition. Changes in status are more rapid than changes in class over any given period of time, for example the status accorded to a First Division professional footballer or to a pop star is greater now than it was twenty years ago, but there has been little fundamental change in class over the same period. Not so long ago air hostesses were accorded considerable status, but today the job does not seem as glamorous as it did, being regarded by some people as simply that of a flying waitress.

Because status provides more subtle gradings than class differences sociologists these days have tended to look more towards status differences in their analysis of society. This means that less importance is given to economic interests and emphasis is given to the status or prestige which various groups enjoy within the community. Such studies often occur at times when there is least class conflict, but when strikes and economic crises occur (to give but two examples) attention may be directed towards power.

7.2 Power

In the last century the problems of social class could be clearly associated with political power, but when the threat of revolution subsided as the working class gained the vote (if not political power) attention was turned towards the problems of democracy. In recent times the action of some trade unionists such as the miners' strike in 1973-4, is seen by some as a challenge to our democratic system, and the question is raised whether the Government should govern or give way to the demands of powerful trade unionists who hold key jobs in the economic system. At the same time, as John Raynor (*The Middle Class*, Longman, 1969) says, 'Power in our society is a feature of many social groups and manifests itself in the middle class in the associations and groups connected with it; business groups, professional associations, civic societies etc., are all holders of power in varying degrees at both community and national level.'

In Britain our political parties obtain their unity essentially through their representation of class interests. In other countries religious groupings may provide the basis of political parties. Identification with a status group, rather than identification with a class interest, may cause some to support a particular party.

In the last resort all power rests on force or, as the late Chairman Mao put it, 'power comes from the barrel of a gun', but because more than ninety-nine per cent of the people of Britain recognise the right of the Government to govern by passing laws, the Government does not require force of arms to gain acceptance of its authority. This situation exists largely owing to the fact that people feel that they are being represented in Parliament, or that they are able to change the Government in a peaceful way at election times. There are some theories of power, such as those of Vilfredo Pareto (1848-1923) or Gaetano Mosca (1848-1941) who maintain that the small group at the top of the social hierarchy, the élite, are always in real control of society, no matter which political party may run the Government. Other theorists, such as C. Wright Mills in his book *The Power Elite* (Oxford University Press, 1956), consider that power circulates between different status groups, one being at the top for a while and eventually being replaced by another. A third theory, as advanced by James Burnham in *The Managerial Revolution* (Greenwood, 1972), is that society is moving towards a situation where political control is moving out of the hands of the traditional top status groups and passing to a new class of managers and experts who may not own the enterprises in which they work but are vital to the direction of big business and the economy and therefore in reality have overall political control (see Topic 29.3).

Most of the chapters which follow this one are at least in part an examination of the ways in which class and status affect society.

Terms used in this chapter

strata	dynamism	styles of life
hierarchy	social perspective	contest mobility
manual worker	classification	sponsored mobility
collectivist	ranking	class consciousness
social mobility	embourgeoisement	

Further reading

A. Béteille, *Social Inequality* (Penguin, 1969)

T. B. Bottomore, *Classes in Modern Society* (Allen & Unwin, 1965)

F. Field, *Unequal Britain* (Arrow, 1974)

A. Giddens, *Capitalism and Modern Social Theory* (Cambridge University Press, 1977)

J. H. Goldthorpe, *The Affluent Worker in the Class Structure* (Cambridge University Press, 1969)

P. Laurie, *Meet Your Friendly Social System* (Hutchinson, 1974)

F. Parkin (ed.), *The Social Analysis of Class Structure* (Harper & Row, 1974)

J. Raynor, *The Middle Class* (Longman, 1969)

G. Rose, *The Working Class* (Longman, 1968)

I. Reid, *Social Class Differences in Britain* (Open Books, 1977)

Questions from GCE 'O' Level Sociology Examination Papers

1 Distinguish between middle and working class, and discuss the major differences between the two. (Oxford Local Examinations, Summer 1970)

2 What do you understand by 'the working class'? How is it changing? (Oxford Local Examinations, Summer 1971)

3 'When people's behaviour takes account of the existence of others, and is affected by expectations about others, we call it social.' Give three examples of different kinds of social behaviour and describe the roles and norms associated with each of your examples. (AEB, November 1972)

4 In what ways has the economic and social situation of the middle class changed since 1945? (Oxford Local Examinations, 1974)

5 What do sociologists mean by 'social mobility'? What are the problems involved in measuring social mobility? (Oxford Local Examinations, 1974)

6 Discuss the suggestion that Britain has become a 'classless' society. (Oxford Local Examinations, 1975)

7   What are the arguments surrounding the suggestion that we are all becoming 'middle class'? (AEB, November 1974)

8   The coalminer and the assembly-line worker might both be described as 'working class'. Explain the differences in life style, general values and behaviour which exist between them despite the fact that they are members of the same 'social class'. (AEB, November 1974)

9   The manual worker has become more affluent in recent years. Does this mean that he is now middle-class? (AEB, June 1976)

10   'Marxists believe that modern industrial societies are divided into two major classes according to the ownership or non-ownership of capital or property . . .'
'In Britain official statistics published by the Registrar General describe *social class* and *socio-economic group* in terms of occupation.' (S. R. Parker et al, *Sociology of Industry*, 1967)
How useful are the above ways of looking at stratification in modern Britain?
(AEB, June 1979)

11   (a) Briefly describe any *one* kind of social stratification other than social class.
(b)   Describe *two* different ways in which social class may be defined. (AEB, June 1980)

3 The Family
Unit 8 The Family in Society

There are four people in the photograph: a woman, a man and two children. We usually describe people grouped together in this way as a *family*. Most of us have had some experience of being a member of a family group in the course of our lives. For example, we may have grown up in a group which included people we called *father*, *mother*, *brother* and *sister*. These are all terms which are primarily confined to people who are part of a family group. Also, books, magazines, films and television programmes have shown us the lives of other family groups, real or imaginary, so that we have all formed ideas about the family. However, we must remember that sociologists are interested in the general

A modern family

characteristics of human behaviour rather than in the lives of individual human beings. Personal experience is a good place to start from, but it cannot give us the whole picture. In looking at the family, it is useful to draw on personal experiences when, for example, these can shed light on the more widespread patterns of human behaviour, but on the whole we shall be concentrating on the most general characteristics of the family in society.

In its widest sense 'family' refers to a group of people who think of themselves as belonging to a separate group in society and who are related to one another by ties of either blood or marriage. This group is also recognised by other members of society who see these individuals as tied to one another by certain relationships. According to L. Broom and P. Selznick (*Sociology*, Harper & Row, 1969) the family mediates between the individual and society, helping him to take his place in the wider world.

8.1   Types of families

The terms, father, mother, brother, sister, refer to certain positions in the family group. These positions are made obvious by the way the people who occupy them behave. For example, a mother looks after her baby, and a husband and wife show affection towards one another. These positions are called *social statuses* and 'social roles' are the patterns of behaviour which we expect from a person occupying a particular social status. The sexual and social roles of husband and wife are often described as *conjugal roles*. The family takes many forms in society, the most fundamental of which is the *nuclear family* (sometimes also called the *conjugal family*).

The family

The nuclear family   For a group to be called a nuclear family there must at some time be a father, mother and at least one child. The family in the photograph at the beginning of the chapter is an example of a nuclear family. This type of family structure is found in almost all societies, although the length of time in which the family remains in this form varies even within the same society. The physical fact of a man and a woman producing (or adopting) a child lies at the heart of this pattern of family structure. When the nuclear family is viewed from the point of view of the children's position in the group, then it is called the *family of origin.* By contrast, when the children grow up and have children of their own they will be looking at the family group from the social status of parents. Looked at from this point of view, the nuclear family is called the *family of procreation.*

Statuses and roles together make up the organisation of the family, and this called its *structure.* There is a way of showing the structure of a family group by using symbols. In Figure 3.1 the symbol △ is used to denote a male, the symbol O to denote a female and = to denote their sexual union. How would you describe the social structure of this family group?

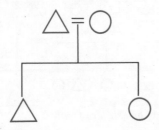

Figure 3.1   An example of a nuclear family

This family group has one father, one mother, and two children. Each child has either a brother or a sister. Brothers and sisters are called *siblings* so we can say that each child has one sibling. We can describe the pattern of the social structure of the family by using diagrams and by referring to the statuses and roles within it, but it is important to remember that the family is not really a concrete object in society that is always the same; it is part of society and is influenced by changes in that society. At any time a single family will be changing if only because the people who occupy the positions of father, mother, and children will be growing older and the children will soon start to fill positions of father and mother in a new family which they have made for themselves. Families therefore have *life-cycles.*

The extended family   The *extended family* (sometimes also called the *consanguine family*) is a common family structure and includes within it the nuclear family pattern. It has been suggested by C. Rosser and C. Harris in *The Family and Social Change* (Routledge & Kegan Paul, 1965) that the extended family is 'any persistent kinship-grouping of persons related by descent, marriage or adoption, which is wider than the (nuclear) family, in that it characteristically spans three generations from grandparents to grandchildren'. All the members of the group do not need to live under one roof for a family group to be an extended family. The structure of one such extended family is shown in Figure 3.2. Where are the nuclear families in the diagram?

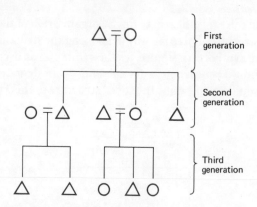

Figure 3.2   An example of an extended family

The extended family may be 'patrilineal', 'matrilineal' or 'bilineal'. A 'patrilineal' extended family reckons descent through the male line.

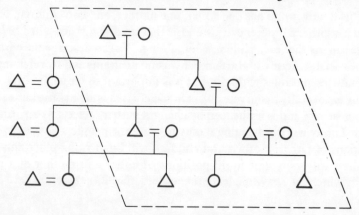

Figure 3.3   A patrilineal extended family: broken lines indicate the boundaries of this patrilineal extended family

Where the father is the formal head of the family and has complete authority, then this is called a 'patriarchal' family. The patrilineal, patriarchal type of family existed throughout China before the first decades of the twentieth century. An extended family reckoning descent through the female line is termed 'matrilineal'. Where this arises it affects the pattern of rights and duties of the women of the family. If women have the main authority in the family, it is called a 'matriarchal' family. For example, in the society of the Zũni American Indians women control the house, its furnishings, the fields and the produce of the fields. The birth of the first child enhances the role of the husband who may only then acquire a little authority in the family unit. An extended family is 'bilineal' where descent or the inheritance of goods is regarded as determined equally by the male and the female line. It is argued that bilateral descent is typical of modern western extended families, and that for example, the British family has this characteristic. Figure 3.3 illustrates the social structure of an example of a patrilineal extended family.

8.2 What are the social functions of the family?

Nurturance

A child born into society must be fed and looked after. In many societies, the parents of the child are responsible for his welfare and, in this way, perform a function for society in general by looking after the next generation and ensuring that it will survive.

Socialisation

As the child grows up, surrounded by brothers and sisters, his 'peer group', his parents and, sometimes, by members of the extended family group, he will gradually learn things about the society in which he lives. For example, he will learn its language, its ideas about right and wrong, its ideas about what is funny and what is serious and so forth. In other words, the child will learn the *culture* of his society through his contact with, at first, the members of his family. The sociologist calls the way in which an individual acquires the culture of his society *socialisation*.

An important part of the process of socialisation concerns the way in which, from infancy, the individual develops into a social being, having his own unique 'self', but able to function effectively in interaction with others in society. Sigmund Freud, G. H. Mead, E. H. Erikson, Jean Piaget and L. Kohlberg are among the many people who have studied aspects of socialisation and all have their different theories. However, here, we will confine ourselves to looking at the most general points that can be made about the process of socialisation. The earliest years of socialisation are called *primary socialisation*. It is thought that, while infants are born with some innate capacities, derived from their heredity, their environmental experience is important in shaping their development. For example, through interaction with other people the child learns what patterns of behaviour are expected of him. Much of this process of role learning occurs as a result of imitative behaviour, which is then respectively reinforced or discouraged by parents' praise or criticism. Initially, the infant learns to pattern his behaviour after those that he sees around him. In fact, they become his 'models'. However, the process is not indiscriminate. Research suggests that imitative behaviour initially occurs where the models are persons important to the infant as providers of food, shelter, comfort and affection. The threat of withdrawal of these important gratifications makes the parents especially important to the child and for this reason he begins to model his personal behaviour after theirs. This has been called 'personal modelling'. By contrast, 'positional modelling' occurs when a child is impressed by the amount of control and power an individual has over everyday circumstances by virtue of the position he holds. For example, to a child, a teacher has a good deal of authority by virtue of his position. This leads to imitative role modelling, but the role performance is associated with the position rather than the personal characteristics of the occupant of the social status involved.

Research indicates that there are social class differences in the way in which parents bring up their children. For example, middle-class parents are more likely than working-class parents to control their children's behaviour by subtle verbal and psychological means, such as the withdrawal of love. A working-class parent is more likely to punish his child with a slap. Differences in working-class and middle-class cultures have effects also on the language development of children. For example, Basil Bernstein has pointed out how middle-class children tend to use an elaborated speech code, whereas working-class children use a restricted speech code. (This is considered in more detail in Topic 12.1.)

Socialisation is not confined to interaction between parents and their children, nor does it finish in childhood but goes on through life. At the present time, research by social scientists indicates that the early years of socialisation are important in the development of the individual because they have enduring effects on his ideas and attitudes.

The behaviour that is considered naturally masculine or feminine is, in large part, the product of the culture of the society. Through socialisation, the individual learns the appropriate *sex roles* of society. For example, in our society, we consider anything involving hard manual work to be man's work. However, it is not unusual in African societies, such as the Arusha, for women to toil in the fields and carry the heavy loads. Children explore the roles they will play as father or mother in adult life in their games, and, in our society, when parents give children toys, girls are usually given dolls and boys motor-cars, and this *anticipatory socialisation* has the effect of preserving the traditional differences in the sex roles. At the present time, many people are concerned about the way in which our culture limits the choice of behaviour open to the sexes. It has been argued that socialisation into culturally-defined sex roles is partly to do with the expectations of people in complementary role positions. For example, daughters' femininity is associated with fathers' expectations that their daughters should hold 'feminine' attitudes and behave in 'feminine' ways. This suggests that changes in the role performance of men and women can be brought about by changes in the expectations which members of the opposite sex have of one another.

Economic and supportive functions of the family

In some societies, where there are no modern industrial methods of factory production, the extended family is the most important unit in society. As a member of the extended family, an individual is able to eat and have somewhere to sleep, and also is able to count on someone looking after him if he is ill. In such traditional societies, the extended family is the unit around which all other activities are built. For example, the Masai are a people who live in the areas that we know as the countries of Kenya and Tanzania. Their main activity is looking after their herds of cattle, sheep and goats which supply them with a staple diet of meat, milk and blood. Each extended family has its own herd; and men, women and children all have separate parts to play in looking after and tending these animals. The children of the Masai are socialised into the Masai language which has words for every tiny aspect of the condition of the cattle. Children growing up in our culture are socialised into a language which does not have the same vocabulary in defining the condition of cattle, because cattle do not have the same importance for us.

In contrast to the Masai, the Sisala of northern Ghana are farmers and live in settled villages. Also, some of their activities are affected by western culture, for example, through formal schooling. Each extended family lives in a compound, with the head of the family, the 'house-owner', controlling the use and distribution of cattle and food produced on the family farm. Usually the large patrilineal family comprises the families of procreation of at least two brothers, and the younger generation from these families. Sometimes individual family members own small plots of land and a few fowl and goats. In the family, the birth of a child symbolises the wife's womanhood and cements the marriage bond between husband and wife. The father of many offspring is respected because the work his children will do will bring him wealth and authority. In play, girls imitate their mothers' work by pretending to prepare millet by grinding sand between two stones, making porridge and gathering firewood and water. Boys learn to work in the fields, first by imitating their fathers and brothers in their play and then, when they want to join in, by being given jobs to do such as feeding the poultry, frightening away the cows from the crops and preparing the midday meal.

Assigning a position for the individual in society

In such a traditional society a person's work and responsibilities are decided not by passing examinations, as in our own society, but by factors such as his age and whether or not he is married. The traditional society is therefore based on *ascribed* rather than *achieved* status. For example, in Sisala society participation in real work begins at about four for a girl and six for a boy. The girl is taught by her elder sisters, her mother and father's other wives. After about the age of seven, she will have a little more contact with the men in the family and will be concerned with the activities allocated to women in this society. A boy reaches manhood at about fifteen years old and, in addition to learning farming, he learns one occupational specialisation, usually from a relative. For example, a man can become a specialist in weaving, sewing, leather-working, weapon making, hunting, blacksmithing or divining. He marries at about eighteen but must continue to defer to the decisions of his elders and is still subject to his father and father's brothers for basic daily needs until about the age of thirty. This leads to friction as a husband's authority over his wife and children is not complete under these circumstances.

In Masai society, a man who is becoming old will go through a ceremony which establishes him as an old man in society. After the ceremony, his role has changed and he will not join in cattle-raiding expeditions with the younger men. In Sisala society age is revered. At about fifty a man becomes too old to work in the fields and so he comes to occupy the status of an 'elder man', with greater authority in village affairs. When a woman is past childbearing she is called an 'elder woman' and, where she is the senior wife, will become the confidante of her husband. She is given this status of a masculine identity as a mark of her past duty and loyalty to her husband's family.

Irrespective of whether a society is based on achieved or ascribed status, universally the family provides a position for the individual, giving him a setting from which to relate to the wider society.

At this point we can summarise the functions which the family performs in the following list:

1 *Biological and supportive functions*

   a) It provides a legitimate situation in which the gratification of sexual needs can be met on a regular basis.

   b) It supports human reproduction in the social setting.

   c) It provides for the nurturance of the dependent child.

   d) It provides for the satisfaction of individual emotional needs.

2 *Social and economic functions*

   a) It transmits culture, and socialises the young into society.

   b) It acts as an agent of social control, regulating the behaviour of its members.

   c) It provides economic support for its members.

   d) It provides a position for the individual in society, giving him a place from which to relate to the wider society.

8.3   Can we do without the family?

Although the family performs numerous functions in society, this does not necessarily mean that there is no possibility of anything else taking its place. There have been many planned experiments which have tried to find other ways by which, for example, children can be brought up in society. Examples of experiments in communal living, where children are the concern of the society as a whole, are groups such as the Israeli kibbutzim and the communes of the People's Republic of China. However, it would be misleading to think of these experiments as providing complete alternatives to the family in society. For example, the allocation of social functions, such as child-rearing, to other groups does not mean that the family has no significance in society, rather that it is freed from that particular activity in the context of the different demands of a communal society.

The Israeli kibbutz has been watched with interest by many sociologists, as it provides a way of testing the idea that whatever social arrangements are designed, the family will never altogether disappear. In the early kibbutzim, infants were taken to Children's Houses after only a short time with their parents. The physical separation from their family continued into adult life, the children growing up together and being looked after by specially trained nurses (called *metaplets*) and teachers, only being at their parents' home or seeing their parents for a few hours each day. Women therefore were free to take on any work on the same terms as men. Today, these patterns are changing and the separation between parents and children is less complete; in many kibbutzim, children return to spend the night at their parents' flat, and women are involved in the traditionally feminine types of work such as working in the communal kitchen or laundry.

In the communes of the People's Republic of China, the family is supported in its social role by the presence of communal services, such as free crèches, nurseries and canteens. The provision of these services in the commune releases members of the family for participation in the work of the commune.

8.4 Marriage

A wedding is a ceremony at which marriage is recognised by society. What, then, is marriage? Again, we are looking at patterns of relationships between people. The wedding service is an official way in which new relationships between a man and a woman, as husband and wife, are recognised by the couple themselves and established in the eyes of the society to which they belong.

Marriage does not necessarily always take place between one man and one woman (see Figure 3.4). For example, the Masai practise a form of polygamy, called polygyny; that is, Masai men take more than one woman as their wife. This has many social and economic advantages for the group. For example, when a man has more than one wife they may combine their herds and place them under the care of one or two of their children. Polygyny also creates a hierarchy of social statuses and roles within the family. For example, in the Masai family, the first wife always has more authority and the right to wield this over the wives who follow. Her son has all the rights of an heir, inheriting the herds and ultimately becoming the male head of the family. Tensions and conflicts do arise between the different wives, but there are strong loyalties towards female relatives in Masai families and this often helps to resolve conflicts. For example, by custom, a man is expected to please his mother, therefore the eldest son will take note first of his mother's wishes. If this gives rise to complaint among the other wives, their fathers and brothers will be willing to take up the complaints with the head of the family. The Sisala also practise polygyny and prefer this to be the marriage of a man to two

Masai women and children, Kenya

Type	Description		Examples
MONOGAMY	One man + One woman	Husband + Wife	Great Britain; Europe; USA, most western societies
POLYGYNY	One man + Several wives (simultaneously)	Husband + Wives	The Masai of East Africa; the Sisala of Northern Ghana; Moslem societies e.g. Egypt allows a man four wives
POLYANDRY	One woman + Several husbands This is less usual than POLYGYNY	Wife + Husbands	Marquesan Islands, Tibet
POLYGAMY	This is a category which embraces POLYGYNY and POLYANDRY. It is sometimes used as a general term to replace these.		As in second and third categories above

Figure 3.4 *Forms of marriage*

sisters. This is because it is said that sisters do not quarrel as much as women who are strangers to one another. At marriage a *bride price*, usually a cow, is paid by the groom's family to the wife's kin. A woman is expected to adjust from her role as daughter and sister to wife and mother in her husband's people. The stress of this situation often leads to early divorce. Then, because she is not allowed to re-marry, a woman will remain in her father's house as a daughter.

In our society, romantic ideas about marriage abound. It is generally thought that people fall in love and that this is the basis for their decision to marry. All this would sound very strange to many people, for instance in the Sisala society, or Afghanistan and other Moslem societies, where marriage is customarily arranged by the respective parents of the couple. The social recognition given to marriage makes it more likely that the parents of children born into society will continue to remain together while they care for their offspring. In many societies, children are an economic asset. For example, in the Masai, fathers want many children, particularly boys, as they can help in looking after the herd and later go on raids to bring back more cattle to the group. In our society, children are not so economically important to the family and many married couples decide to have only one or two children. In this way marriage has become separated from the idea of having children and the happiness of husband and wife is often looked on as being just as important as raising children.

Unit 9 The Family in Britain Today

In advertising family holidays by the sea, British Rail sometimes makes use of posters showing a mother, a father and two or three children playing in the sunshine at the seaside. Pictures like this show us how we have come to think of the family in our society as typically being the nuclear family.

9.1 The family in industrialised societies

Today families made up of two generations, parents and children, are usually found living together under one roof. The widespread presence of the nuclear family has led some sociologists to suggest that there is a 'fit' between the demands of living in industrialised society and the nuclear family. For example, in an industrialised society men are required to fill jobs as industry expands. This demand for working men, and men skilled in certain occupations means that there must be a labour force which is prepared to move to places where the jobs arise. It is argued that a person who is a member of the nuclear family is more free to do this than a person bound by many close ties with his relatives.

In industrial societies a decline has taken place in the range of activities which are performed by the family. For example, in terms of economic functions, the members of the extended family in an industrial society, such as Britain, are not so closely dependent on one another for support as in traditional societies. In our society there are organisations outside the family group, such as the factory or the office, where we can be employed and earn money by which to support ourselves. Also, the workplace is separated from our home and it may be some distance away from where we live; we may have to travel to work each day for a regular forty-hour week. We can see that, in these ways, economic functions are the concern of other specialised groups in society. For example, a man goes to his work at the local branch of Barclays Bank, in return for which he receives a salary. He will spend this on the things he needs, such as food sold in multiple food stores such as Safeway's, clothes sold by such stores as Marks and Spencer's, and light and heating supplied by the Electricity Board. The family today, therefore, is a unit which uses up goods in society rather than being a unit which spends its time producing goods, for the benefit of family members.

There are other ways in which the functions performed by the family in traditional societies have come to be the concern of specialised groups in modern industrialised society. For example, in Britain today, the knowledge and skills which are needed by people living in society change very quickly. No one family can ever hope to pass on to its children a wide enough variety of new knowledge and skills. There are instead schools and colleges which, to some extent, supplement the social function of the family in socialising children into the culture of society.

Most schools and colleges in Britain today are provided by the State. Government departments and local authorities are responsible also for the provision of other services such as the National Health Service, social security benefits, child allowances, pensions, low-rental housing, homes for the care of old people. The services of the Welfare State then, contribute to the economic security and well-being of the members of the society. In this way, the Welfare State modifies and supports many of the social functions which, in non-industrialised societies, are largely the concern of the extended family unit.

According to MacIver and Page in their book *Society* (Macmillan, 1950) although the 'non-essential social functions' of the family have been taken over by other agencies in the modern industrialised society, the *essential social functions* remain as concerns of the nuclear family. These essential social functions are: having children, looking after them and socialising them into the culture of the society. The reproductive function of the family is limited to sexual relations between certain adults. For example in our society it is usually held that sexual relations ought to be confined to husband and wife. In this way the children born in society are the responsibility of and cared for by particular adults.

9.2   The traditional working-class extended family

In some localities the extended family remains a vigorous part of the individual's experience of growing up in a family. These are traditional working-class areas which have a history of employment in difficult and strenuous manual occupations such as coal-mining, working on the docks, shipbuilding and deep-sea fishing. In these traditional working-class areas, families have lived and worked for generations, members of the extended family living close to one another, often next door or on the same street. This makes it possible for relatives to see a lot of one another, and to be at hand whenever help is needed. This pattern is called a *mutual support system* and, whether by habit or from choice, this pattern of relationships is characteristic of traditional working-class communities. The sociologist calls such areas *close-knit communities*.

'Mum' and her married daughter

In a traditional working-class community, a woman usually expects to keep up a close relationship with her mother after marriage. This is not difficult as 'Mum' usually lives close by. Family life often centres on the close relationship which exists between 'Mum' and her married daughters. Michael Young and Peter Willmott in *Family and Kinship in East London* (Routledge & Kegan Paul, 1956) found that in Bethnal Green there was a considerable degree of contact between married daughters and their mothers (see Table 3.1).

Willmott and Young found that 'Mum' helped her married daughter in many ways: for example she might 'speak for' a house for her daughter by explaining the daughter's position to the rent collector and asking him to reserve a house when one became available. In traditional working-class communities 'Mum' is also at hand to help her daughter by looking after the children while their mother goes out to a job during the day.

(General sample—133 married women with mothers alive
and not in the same dwelling)

Residence of mother	Number of married women	Women who saw their mother in previous 24 hours
Same street or block of flats	23	23
Elsewhere in Bethnal Green	49	33
Adjacent borough	25	4
Elsewhere	36	3

Table 3.1   Contacts of women according to distance of mothers
(Source: Michael Young and Peter Willmott, *Family and Kinship in East London*, Routledge & Kegan Paul, 1956)

Husband and wife

In looking at the relationship between husband and wife in traditional working-class families we must remember that this relationship usually takes in the relationship between the wife and her mother. The lives of husband and wife are closely bound up with what is going on round at 'Mum's place'.

   The wife's role is usually throught of as being properly concerned with

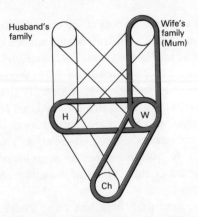

Figure 3.5   Relationships in the traditional working-class family. (Note: the red lines indicate stronger relationships.)
(Source: J. Klein, *Samples from English Culture*, Vol. 1, Routledge & Kegan Paul, 1965)

looking after the children and the home. The husband is the breadwinner but domestic chores or helping with the children are not seen as being appropriate to the masculine role. Leisure-time activities are also often carried on separately, husbands spending time with their workmates and women with their female relatives and friends. The separation between husband and wife often extends to the point where the wife does not know, or think it any of her business to know, how much money her husband earns. This type of conjugal role relationship is termed *segregated conjugal role*.

The way of life of younger married couples appears to be changing so that now husbands do not think it unmanly to give their wife a little help with some domestic chores. The different patterns of family life which are shown in the course of plays, advertisements or shows on television may be one of the reasons underlying these changes.

Parents and children

Relationships between parents and children are also changing. For example Michael Young and Peter Willmott in *Family and Kinship in East London* noticed how young fathers were spending time at the weekend playing with their children, taking them for a row on the lake in a nearby park.

Old people

The close contact between members of the extended family in traditional working-class communities is an important source of support for old people. A recent study, *Old People in Three Industrial Societies* by the sociologists G. Shanas, P. Townsend and J. D. Wedderburn (Atherton Press, New York, 1968), investigated the social circumstances of old people in three industrial societies, Britain, the USA and Denmark. This sheds light on the hypothesis that there is little support between extended family members in modern industrialised societies. The researchers drew on the replies given to questionnaires by samples of 2500 persons of pensionable age in each country. The informants were living in private households.

The researchers found that there was some variety in the degree of integration which older family members had with the nuclear family group. The majority of old people in all three countries, however, have children and live in the vicinity of at least one of these children. There is mutual help between these old people and their families. The role of the older relative is as a contributing member of the family rather than as a dependant. 'Help' took the form of old people assisting their children in emergencies, helping with housekeeping and home repairs, giving gifts on holidays and birthdays, looking after grandchildren, and having children and grandchildren to stay as weekend guests. Children gave their parents assistance in emergencies, and gifts on birthdays and holidays, help with the housekeeping, home repairs, outings, etc.

9.3 The privatised working-class family

Many recent changes in the wider social structures have affected the old, traditional working-class communities. For example, rehousing schemes have drawn families away from close-knit communities and this has affected relationships between members of the extended family. The effects of this change on the organisation of the family is noted by Willmott and Young in their study of Bethnal Green families living on a new housing estate on the outskirts of London. The separation of the nuclear family from the extended family group encourages the family to spend more time with each other and to spend money on their home, their children and *home-centred activities*. In a recent study, Michael Young and Peter Willmott (*The Symmetrical Family*, Penguin, 1975) suggest that modern technology, in removing creative forms of work, causes husbands to turn to the home as place of self-expression and fulfilment. The life of the nuclear family is more private and self-contained, carried on free of close contact with everyone else in the neighbourhood. This *privatisation* is described by Willmott and Young as a change from face-to-face relationships to window-to-window relationships. The presence of the privatised family pattern amongst the working class was also noted by John Goldthorpe and David Lockwood in their study, *The Affluent Worker*. In this they studied the family, working life and political views of the relatively well-paid car workers in Luton. Despite the seeming parallels between the privatised family and the middle-class family, Goldthorpe and Lockwood concluded that the growth of the privatised family in the more affluent working class does not constitute a movement of the working class into the middle class. The privatised family pattern therefore remains characteristic of the new working classes.

Husband and wife

Conjugal role relationships have also changed, husband and wife

A husband parted from his wife has five children to bring up

increasingly acting as partners and sharing activities to do with the home
and the children. In other words, segregated conjugal roles are changing
to become *joint conjugal roles*. For example, in her study of housebound
mothers, Hannah Gavron (*The Captive Wife*, Routledge & Kegan Paul,
1966) notes a young working-class wife who recalls: 'My father was never
at home, not so's you'd notice, while my husband, well he's at home all
the time and that makes for sharing.' In this study, Hannah Gavron
describes how many of the working-class mothers, at home with young
children and living away from the friends and family that they had known
when they were growing up in a traditional working-class area, were very

miserable and looked to their husbands as the only relief which they had from isolation and loneliness. Hannah Gavron suggests that, in these circumstances, joint conjugal roles are an expression of a desire for emotional closeness on the part of working-class couples.

Parents and children

We have seen that with privatisation, parents turn their attention to their own immediate family of procreation, spending time and money on the home and on their children.

The family structure and life styles of the more prosperous working class today might lead us to think that this group has really now become part of the middle class. However, Peter Willmott and Michael Young, in a study in which they considered the social organisation of the East London suburb of Woodford (*Family and Class in a London Suburb*, Routledge & Kegan Paul, 1960), found that despite outward appearances: 'Inside people's minds . . . the boundaries of class are still closely drawn'. In suburban Woodford, families of middle- and working-class background remained socially separate groups in the community.

9.4   The middle-class family

The social structure of the middle-class family today is typically the nuclear family pattern. The middle-class family is generally interested in 'getting on'. This desire for upward social mobility is reflected in a willingness to move to new areas if this means a better job or promotion. This results in the nuclear family often living many kilometres from members of the extended family group. Middle-class residential districts are areas where there is shifting population, few people being either related to one another or knowing one another closely. This type of community is called a *loose-knit community*.

Husband and wife

In middle-class families the geographical separation of men and women from their parents frequently begins when the individual takes some form of training or extended education at a college or a university. This separation from kinfolk and the experience of leading independent lives affects the way in which husbands and wives get along together. In middle-class families it is often thought appropriate that husband and wife share the responsibilities of looking after the home and the children.

Also the couple are likely to have mutual friends of both sexes, and leisure time is frequently spent by husband and wife together. In *The Captive Wife*, Hannah Gavron suggests that middle-class joint conjugal roles, in contrast to privatised working-class conjugal roles, are a way in which husband and wife show that they expect the individual to be able to carry on and enjoy a high level of independence within marriage. In some middle-class families wives may continue in their career after marriage and see this as equally important as their role as wife and mother. Under these circumstances, home-centredness is displaced by a primary concern with activities outside the home, both husbands and wives fulfilling themselves in those activities which are not home-centred.

Parents and children

In middle-class families, parents tend to raise their children according to current ideas of experts about how children should be brought up. Usually, this means parents attach importance to such things as taking the children on visits to plays, concerts, exhibitions, museums and historic places, giving them books to read, arranging music lessons, and encouraging children to express their ideas and opinions. Parents also encourage their children to spend time on school work, rather than, for example, sitting watching television. Middle-class parents, by encouraging their children to sacrifice present pleasures, often hope that their children will secure future goals and rewards such as having interesting and rewarding jobs.

The middle-class extended family

In middle-class families the distance which separates parents and married children reduces the amount of personal contact possible between members of the extended family. However, most middle-class families have telephones and are able to keep in touch by frequent telephone calls. In addition to telephone calls, letters and visits by car help to keep members of the middle-class family in contact with one another. Raymond Firth, Jane Hubert and Anthony Forge, in their study *Families and Their Relatives* (Routledge & Kegan Paul, 1970) found that members of the immediate family of origin keep in contact with one another, regardless of distance, but beyond this group, geographical distance had more of an effect on the level of contact. For example (in middle-class families): 'Attitudes to kin have something (of the quality) of a bond with selected people thought to persist irrespective of geography, and maintained by periodic activity, perhaps mainly by correspondence'. In *Middle-Class Families* Colin Bell noted how parents of married children often discreetly provide financial support for the young couple particularly at times such as the birth of their first grandchild. In the interests of a career, many middle-class people postpone taking a paid job in order to take courses at colleges and universities. Young married couples therefore have a low income at the outset of their married life and financial help from parents and in-laws helps them over this period in the economic life-cycle of the family.

Conclusion

Although the nuclear family is the group which is usually found living together under one roof in Britain today, the extended family still plays an important part in the way people of all social classes live. The Welfare State replaced some of the functions of the family and has relieved it from many of its immediate anxieties in caring for members. In these circumstances, the nuclear family is more free to develop closer emotional ties. This development is important if we consider how much anonymity an individual may experience in society today. For example, at work many people are involved in dull repetitive activities and they can easily be replaced by someone else. At home, with his family, the individual involved in such occupations may be able to compensate a little for the frustrations and anonymity which he experiences at work.

Unit 10 The Family and Social Change

10.1 Family life in nineteenth-century Britain

Industrialisation and urbanisation

Before industrialisation work was carried on by the extended family in the home:

My mother taught me (while too young to weave) to earn my bread by carding and spinning cotton, winding linen or cotton weft for my father and elder brothers at the loom until I became of sufficient age and strength for my father to put me on to a loom.

(W. Radcliffe, *Origin of the New System of Manufacture* (1828), quoted in Asa Briggs, *1700–1815: How They Lived*, Blackwell, 1969)

The family is part of society and therefore it influences, and is itself influenced by, changes in the wider social structure. Among the most significant of such changes have been the processes of industrialisation and urbanisation which began in this country in the eighteenth century.

Industrialisation brought the factory system. This meant a decline in the hand-production of goods, an activity which was centred on production by the extended family carried on in the home, and the growth of machine-production of goods, carried on in factories in towns. Workers worked for wages, their labour and goods that they produced being effectively owned by the factory owner. Some of the traditions of the family-centred method of production carried over into the factory system. For example, the factory system inherited the custom of child labour and the belief that this was socially acceptable. Such attitudes only began to disappear after the passing of various Factory Acts in the 1830s and 1840s, limiting child labour. The growth of factories brought with it the growth of towns.

This urbanisation was a result of the influx of workers from the countryside, leaving behind the older generation of the extended family, and seeking better wages in the factories. Although the evils of town life and the degradation of factory workers have been amply recorded, there were some good things that resulted from this change in the family's way of life. For example, home-centred production had meant all family members working long, irregular hours in order to complete production on time and ensure their livelihood. When work was transferred to the factory, family members worked long hours, but they were more likely to be regular hours. Also, they were more likely to receive regular wages independently—a fact which, it has been suggested, may have given the wife a little freedom, for the first time in her life. Despite this, the disadvantages were severe. Urban conditions were very bad indeed, and malnutrition was rampant in the working classes and the urban poor. Under these hopeless circumstances, there was no incentive for workers to save, even if wages allowed this, and family life was constantly threatened by violence and drunkenness.

Today the family in Britain is part of a fully industrialised and urbanised society. In contrast to the nineteenth century, mass-produced goods, such as foodstuffs, cars, televisions, electric irons and vacuum cleaners are commonplace, everyday things. Almost all paid work is carried on at a place of work outside the home, and typically it is members of the nuclear family rather than the extended family who live together under one roof. Industrialisation and urbanisation have been powerful forces in changing the structure and function of the family in Britain over the last two centuries. This has occurred directly through the changes which have followed from work being taken outside the home, but also directly through legislative and other changes which have arisen in order to make modern, industrialised society a better place to live in. For example, the work of trade unions and the services of the Welfare State have helped to guarantee the family some income even in times of unemployment or ill health. Children are able to receive free education at State schools until they are sixteen. More people can read and write, and ideas are passed on more rapidly because of the circulation of newspapers and magazines and the effect of radio and television. Many married women go out to work and legislation exists to safeguard equality between the sexes in many areas, both at work and in family life.

In order to understand the changes which have occurred in the structure and function of the family over about the last hundred years, it is necessary to examine more closely what the family was like in the nineteenth century, and to see how changes in its organisation since then have had an effect on the pattern of life in society today.

Family life

In Victorian times it was a popular idea that family life was the backbone of the life of the country and therefore the family was looked upon as a very important part of society. The Queen's own family life was taken as a model and, as the highest praise of Prince Albert at his death, the editor of *The Times* wrote:

The Prince was always seen to most advantage in that particular character which of all others most commends itself to the English heart—the head of a well regulated English family.
(The London Times, 1861)

By the middle of the nineteenth century, the manufacturing industries were expanding and the factory owners and businessmen who had prospered from the rise of industry had emerged as a new social class, the middle class. In fact, the word itself only came into the English language about this time. The middle class, with their newly-acquired wealth, lacked the social recognition that was given the aristocracy and the old-established upper-class families. In an attempt to gain this recognition, wealthier middle-class families often imitated the way of life of upper-class families. The importance and solidarity of family life in the middle classes became an influential model for the rest of society.

In middle-class families it was important for a man to postpone marriage until he could afford to support a wife in the same circumstances as she had enjoyed in her parents' home. It was not considered appropriate for the daughter to work in order to hasten her own wedding day. Instead a considerable amount of time typically elapsed before a man had accumulated enough money and security to contemplate marriage. This resulted in a pattern of late marriage, a man often not marrying until well into his thirties. It has been suggested that this late marriage pattern and the double standard about chastity before marriage which existed in Victorian times, could be considered as going some way towards explaining the widespread prostitution found in nineteenth-century Britain.

In addition to late marriage, marriage was by no means universal. National marriage rates declined sharply between 1821 and 1851. In the middle classes the unmarried were provided for by the family and often lived with their relatives. The pattern of late and non-universal marriage which has been described, has been called the 'European marriage pattern' by Hajnal. This is because, at the time, this marriage pattern was found throughout western Europe.

In working-class families, the ideas of respectability and solid family life were usually held in high regard, but the reality of hard, manual work for long hours, under poor conditions and with low wages, often made such a way of life impossible. In *The Symmetrical Family*, Young and Willmott suggest that therefore, at the outset, the effect of new technology of industrialisation was to disrupt family solidarity in these social classes, thus disturbing the customary social and economic relationships between man and wife, parents and children. There are many descriptions by nineteenth-century writers of the very poorest urban population whose conditions of life were so wretched that family life, as understood by the prosperous middle classes, was virtually impossible. The insecurity of daily life may have been one of the reasons accounting for the widespread custom for men and women to live together as common-law husbands and wives, rather than as legally married partners. Many individuals lived as vagrants with no permanent experience of being a member of a family group.

We will concentrate on some of the more conspicuous changes which have taken place in the course of the last hundred years.

10.2 Changes in family size

The nineteenth-century family was larger than the family today. Among the middle class, the average family size was five or six children for couples who were married in the 1870s, while among the working class, families were usually even larger.

No. of live births	Proportion of women (per 1000) with specified no. of births who were first married in:		
	1870–79	*1900–09*	*1925*
0	83	113	161
1 or 2	125	335	506
3 or 4	181	277	221
5 to 9	434	246	106
10 or more	177	29	6
ALL	1000	1000	1000

Table 3.2 Distribution of women marrying in 1870–79, 1900–09 and 1925, with varying numbers of live births
(Source: *Papers of the Royal Commission on Population*, Vol. 6, Table 2)

The number of children living, however, did not always reflect the number of pregnancies that had taken place. This was because, owing to factors such as poor health, bad housing, deficient nutrition, costs of medical services and poorer knowledge and education about caring for mothers and their babies, more children died in infancy than today.

The average family size today is a little over two children for couples completing their family in recent years. However, in examining statistics on family size it is important to notice that family size figures for recently married couples do not necessarily represent their completed family size. Cross-section figures can be misleading. The table below shows how correct family size figures may be estimated using marriage cohort data.

The reason for the long-term decline in family size lies with the decision of couples to plan the number of children that they want, and the availability of reliable forms of contraception. The decline in family size began in the middle classes in the second half of the nineteenth century. It has been suggested by J. A. Banks (*Prosperity and Parenthood*, Routledge & Kegan Paul, 1954) that the decline that occurred around the 1870s was a reflection of the middle classes adopting family planning when they were experiencing a threat to their newly-acquired wealth and social status by the rise of competition from foreign industry and a

Average number of live births at marriage duration:	Year of marriage								
	1935 –39	1940 –44	1945 –49	1950 –54	1955 –59	1960 –64	1965 –69	1971	1972
2 years	0.55	0.50	0.65	0.60	0.63	0.69	0.64	0.52	0.48
5 years	1.05	1.10	1.26	1.37	1.48	1.37			
10 years	1.67	1.73	1.83	1.92	2.07	2.10			
15 years	1.96	1.98	2.11	2.20	2.30				
Completed family size	2.07	2.09	2.22	2.30	2.38				

Table 3.3 Average family size in Great Britain at specified durations of marriage
(Source: Social Trends, No. 7, 1976, p. 69, Table 1.15, CSO)

decline in business profits. Faced with the problem of maintaining the traditionally large family on a declining income, the middle classes made the decision to limit family size. The move to adopt family planning in the middle classes was followed later by a similar move among working-class families. In The Symmetrical Family, Young and Willmott see the lag in the adoption of family planning between the two social classes as an indication of a general principle underlying social change in the family since the second half of the nineteenth century. They call this the 'principle of stratified diffusion'. This amounts to the generalisation that changes which occur first in upper- and middle-class families later come to be adopted in working-class families. This means that at any time in society, various patterns of family organisation can be found, each reflecting a stage of social change in the family. However, the principle of stratified diffusion is not independent of technological and economic change. The acceptance of the idea of smaller families among the working class was not widespread until the beginning of the twentieth century when the crushing poverty experienced by the working classes was beginning to recede and the possibility of an improvement in living conditions encouraged families to adopt family planning. By this time also the move for compulsory elementary education, first introduced in 1870, had become effective and children were no longer an economic asset to their parents. The use of contraception among working-class couples grew during the unemployment of the 1930s. However, after this time the use of birth control methods declined and the average size of working-class families has continued to be a little greater than those of middle-class families. In recent years, smaller family size has been accompanied by other changes; during the 1970s there was a marked increase in one parent families—most arising from broken marriages.

10.3   Parents and children

To the Victorians, 'Father' enjoyed a very special position in the family. He was head of the household and, as such, he commanded a great deal of respect. Of course, the image and the reality were often very different and it was only possible for this role to be played out to the full in wealthy middle-class households. The working-class father, however, was still head of his own particular family and he was expected also to have authority over the other members of his family.

In wealthier middle-class homes children might not see much of their parents, spending most of their time with nannies or governesses. It was usual for parents to send their sons to private boarding schools. In this way, middle-class families hoped to secure entrance for their sons into the professional occupations which had traditionally been confined to the sons of upper-class families. Daughters received some education at home, but usually with nothing particularly strenuous in mind, as the following quote from *Punch* indicates:

HOW TO 'FINISH' A DAUGHTER

1   Be always telling her how pretty she is.
2   Instil into her mind a proper love of dress.
3   Accustom her to so much pleasure that she is never happy at home.
4   Allow her to read nothing but novels.
5   Teach her all the accomplishments, but none of the utilities of life.
6   Keep her in the darkest ignorance of the mysteries of housekeeping.
7   Initiate her into the principle that it is vulgar to do anything for herself.
8   To strengthen the latter belief, let her have a lady's maid.
9   And lastly, having given her such an education, marry her to a clerk in the Treasury upon £75 a year, or to an ensign who is going out to India.
(*Punch*, 1852, cited in Charles L. Graves, *Mr Punch's History of Modern England*, Cassell.)

In working-class families children were an economic asset to the family as they were able to work in the factories and bring home money. These advantages began to disappear with the passing of the Factory Acts of 1833 and 1847. The Acts gradually became effective in limiting the

"GOT THOSE BOYS TO BED YET, HARRY?"

employment of young children, and the Education Act of 1870, by requiring children to attend elementary schools, also gradually had the effect of reducing the numbers of children employed.

Today relationships between parents and children have changed. In particular, 'Father' is no longer a stern and forbidding figure. Two psychologists, John and Elizabeth Newson, in *Four Years Old in an Urban Community* (Allen & Unwin, 1968) summarise some of their research into the relationships between parents and children in a sample of families living in Nottingham. In this, they describe the way in which fathers today help in caring for their children and how many of them join in playing with their children. Where both parents participate in the running of the home and in bringing up the children, the child is exposed to two role-models, neither of which performs exclusively 'feminine' or 'masculine' tasks. This is likely to socialise children into more flexible views of their roles as adults. Also, parents today spend more time with their children, treating them more as equals, taking an interest in their activities and providing them with new learning experiences. This contrasts with the nineteenth-century attitude that children should be 'seen but not heard'.

How have these changes come about? Today people cannot go out to work full-time until they are sixteen. Under these circumstances children are an economic liability. Also smaller, planned families allow parents the opportunity to give each child individual love and affection. The amount of time which parents can give their children has been affected by changes such as the shortening of the working week. In the nineteenth century this was between seventy and eighty hours for many members of the working class; today the forty-hour week is widespread. However, in *The Symmetrical Family*, Young and Willmott found that the distribution of these hours, and overtime hours, can create internal tensions in the family. For example, modern technology and industrial organisation has increased the use of shift work. This creates awkward timetables, limiting the hours a working-class family can be together. Thus the social and technological changes which have brought about the privatisation of some families, extending the time and money spent on children and the home, have also acted to limit the full realisation of this home-centred family.

Social relationships within the family between husband and wife, parents and children are more equal today than in the nineteenth century.

10.4   The woman's role

In the nineteenth century marriage was considered to be the right goal for every woman. Middle-class girls were brought up with this objective in mind and, once married, they passed from being under the authority of their father to being under the authority of their husband. In middle-class families it was thought to be a mark of refinement and wealth if a wife remained at home and did not involve herself in any kind of paid employment. Most married women therefore spent their time at home, either pregnant or recovering from pregnancy and supervising the running of the household with the aid of domestic servants, nannies and governesses. A middle-class woman who was not married would very often live with the family of a married relative. Many lower middle-class, unmarried women held positions as governesses.

In the working classes, wages were so low that every available member of the family had to work. Despite many pregnancies, married women worked as often as possible.

The dependent role of women in society was reflected in their lack of legal rights. For example, before the Married Women's Property Act of 1882 the wife's possessions became her husband's property when she married. Divorce was virtually impossible for a woman because of the legally complicated grounds that had to be established, the cost and the scandal. J. S. Mill, in his book *The Subjection of Women* (1869), summarised the married woman's position in the nineteenth century:

'There remain no legal slaves except the mistress of every house.'

About 40 per cent of all employees are women (1979). Of the 10 million women employed most of these (about two thirds) are married women. Forty seven per cent of women of all ages are in paid employment compared with 79 per cent of all men.

It can be seen that this proportion has been increasing. It is estimated that in the 1920s this proportion was just over 10 per cent.

The increase in the employment of married women in the workforce is partly to do with the increase in the proportion of women in the

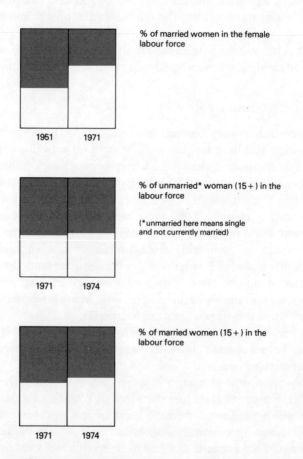

% of married women in the female labour force

1951   1971

% of unmarried* woman (15 +) in the labour force

(*unmarried here means single and not currently married)

1971   1974

% of married women (15 +) in the labour force

1971   1974

Figure 3.6   *The growth of the female work-force 1951–1974*
(Sources: Population Trends *HMSO*, 1975; Social Trends *CSO*, 1976)

population who are married. The percentage of single women has fallen from 15 per cent in 1900 to 5 per cent in 1970. The current proportion married at each age can be seen from Figure 5.9 in Chapter 5.

Today, women are getting married much sooner after they complete school or college, and therefore, there is less time in which they can be employed as single women. Typically, the first child is born shortly after marriage. Most couples have at least one child in the first five years of marriage. Smaller family size means that child-bearing is completed in a relatively short period. Figure 3.7 (below) shows that the employment pattern of a married woman reflects these years of child-bearing and family-raising in her married life. The times of lowest participation are when her family is young. Increased participation begins after the time her children are beginning to be self-reliant and entering the secondary school. From the graph it can be seen that, today, it is more common for married women to re-enter employment than it was in the 1950s. Now a third of all mothers are employed.

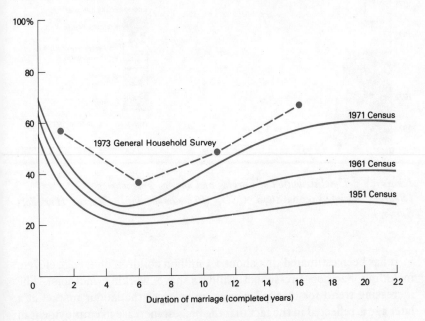

*Figure 3.7   Economic activity of women by duration of marriage
(Source:* Population Trends 1975, *HMSO)*

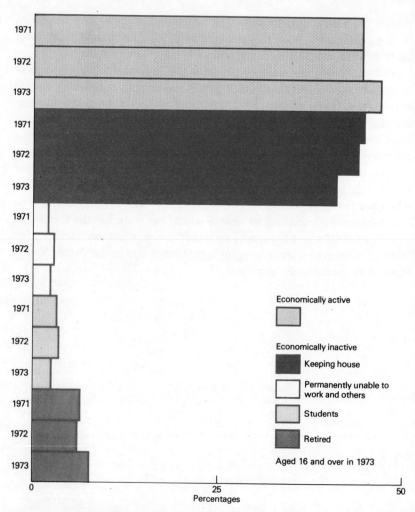

Figure 3.8   *The distribution of working and non-working women*
(*Source:* Social Trends 1976, CSO, *after sample data, General Household Survey*)

It has been estimated that about 2.5 million children under age eleven, including 820 000 pre-school children have working mothers. The increasing trend for married women to re-enter the labour market at a later age is reflected in the fact that the biggest increase in employment in recent years has occurred in the age group 45–59 years. In 1951, 22 per cent of this age group were working; by 1979 this proportion had risen to

61 per cent. B. N. Seear found that this pattern of employment is common in most OECD countries, but that employment rates are lower and re-entry less common in the Netherlands, Italy and France. In reviewing the opportunities for married women in OECD countries to re-enter the labour market, Seear has suggested that employers will have to make more provision for returning women employees, for example by providing training schemes.

Of course, we do not know the full extent of women's employment. For example, part-time work and such home-based work as copy-typing, addressing or filling envelopes, is often organised either on a very intermittent basis or is so casual that it goes undetected in official statistics and tax records.

In addition to the change in the proportions of married women working, there has also been some change in the type of occupations open to women since the nineteenth century. However, this change, in many ways, is less dramatic. For example, there is no particular reason why women should not be doctors, judges, lawyers, businesspersons, or MPs, but women are unevenly distributed in the occupational structure. According to Fogarty et al. in Women in Top Jobs (Allen & Unwin, 1971) the proportion of women in medicine is 16 per cent, in dentistry 7 per cent, among barristers 4 per cent, in architecture 2 per cent and among managers in large establishments only 12 per cent. According to PEP ('Women and Top Jobs: an Interim Report', Political and Economic Planning, 1967) where women are in managerial positions they 'tend to be in support roles rather than in line or general management'. Women make up less than 10 per cent of the employees in professions such as accountancy, engineering, veterinary surgery, surveying, and among solicitors and barristers. Women are disproportionately found in jobs such as primary school teaching, nursing, secretarial and clerical jobs, or working in industries such as food processing or clothing manufacture. It has been argued that this is because women are employed in occupations which are close to their traditional roles as wife and mother. Also, that it is because women participate in trade unions less than men. At present, about 20 per cent of employed women are in trade unions. But women have shown their willingness to strike in cases such as the Ford machinists' strike in 1968. Also, women have participated very effectively in strikes in the past, such as the strike movements in the 1880s and 1911–13, which were concerned with the sweated labour industries. However, in the postal workers' strike of 1970 the unwillingness of many female telephone operators to answer their union's strike-call led to the failure of the strike, since telephone communication still largely functioned. This lack of union support by so many women was criticised by the postal workers' union leadership at the time.

Why then are there these differences in the employment of men and women? Are women innately less intelligent than men and emotionally less suitable for responsible positions, as some people have argued?

These questions, in themselves, show how ready we are to overlook the part played by culture in affecting women's position in society today. What factors do affect women's role?

Socialisation

Early socialisation is called *primary socialisation*. In our society, the primary socialisation of girls encourages them to grow up thinking of themselves as less aggressive, ambitious and adventurous than their brothers. They are encouraged to play with dolls and tea sets and through this anticipatory socialisation learn to see themselves as future wives and mothers. As Richard Brown points out in 'Women as Employees' (in *Dependence and Exploitation in Work and Marriage* edited by Diana L. Barker and Sheila Allen, Longman, 1976), socialisation leads girls to 'a lower level of ambition, a lesser likelihood of staying on at school, less interest in a career and a tendency to regard marriage as a terminal state which it is more desirable to achieve than any occupational goal'. Of course, it could be argued that schools and colleges also contribute to this socialisation process by readily casting girls into these traditional roles.

Life-cycle and traditional roles

In society today, we continue to hold mothers most responsible for the welfare of their children. Consequently, as women rather than men remain at home to look after their young children, the course of the life-cycle becomes more important in influencing women's employment than men's. The pressures on women to remain at home with their children are immense and, according to Susannah Ginsberg (*New Society*, 6 January 1977), lead to conflict and guilt in mothers who, themselves, need to go out to work. Jack Tizard suggests (in the same article) that the importance attached to mothers being at home can be interpreted as an excuse for not providing more day-care services. Day-care services provided by local authorities fall short of the need for free places. For example, in 1970, the number of maintained places, in 453 day nurseries, for the whole of England provided facilities for only 0.5 per cent of the population under five. As Tessa Blackstone points out in *Education and*

Day-Care for Young Children in Need (Centre for Studies in Social Policy, National Council of Social Service, 1973), 'There are some families which can be kept together only by the provision of this service.'

Much of the pressure on mothers derives from the belief that the children of working mothers are emotionally deprived and that 'latch-key' children become truants and delinquents. In fact, the evidence indicates the reverse is true. For example, Pearl Jephcott, Nancy Seear and John Smith, in their study of women workers at the Peak Frean biscuit factory in Bermondsey (*Married Women Working*, Allen & Unwin, 1962) found no clear evidence of association between the incidence of local delinquency and working mothers, no evidence of child neglect and some preference on the part of children for their mothers to work. As one fourteen-year-old noted in her school essay, her mother was more 'interesting' than mothers who did not go out to work. The chart below shows the provisions made by working mothers in this traditional working-class neighbourhood for the care of their children. The importance of the extended family and close neighbourhood ties can be discerned from the diagram.

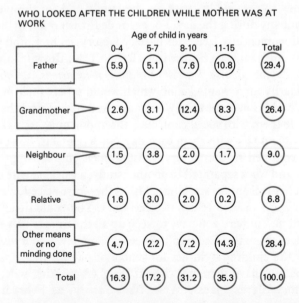

WHO LOOKED AFTER THE CHILDREN WHILE MOTHER WAS AT WORK

Age of child in years

	0-4	5-7	8-10	11-15	Total
Father	5.9	5.1	7.6	10.8	29.4
Grandmother	2.6	3.1	12.4	8.3	26.4
Neighbour	1.5	3.8	2.0	1.7	9.0
Relative	1.6	3.0	2.0	0.2	6.8
Other means or no minding done	4.7	2.2	7.2	14.3	28.4
Total	16.3	17.2	31.2	35.3	100.0

Figure 3.9   *Persons who looked after children while mother was at work*
(Source: 'Woman, wife and worker', *Problems of Progress in Industry*, No. 10, Department of Scientific and Industrial Research, 1960)

Since the 1930s adult women have earned about 45–55 per cent of men's weekly earnings. Although the Equal Pay Act (1970) and the Sex Discrimination Act (1975) are designed to make employment and pay more equal between the sexes and have narrowed the differential, however, many people still attach importance to the man's role as 'breadwinner'. This means that, for example, when time has to be taken off work to look after a sick child, typically it is the wife who does this, not the husband.

Dual labour market

Barron and Norris in 'Sexual Divisions and the Dual Labour Market' (in *Dependence and Exploitation in Work and Marriage* edited by D. L. Barker and Sheila Allen, Longman, 1976) suggests that there is a dual labour market, cutting across the different types of firms and industries. The primary sector contains well-paid, secure jobs, with promotional ladders. The secondary sector contains jobs which are boring and low-paid with no promotion prospects. The majority of women are confined to the secondary sector. Why is this? From what we know about socialisation it seems likely that many women do not aim for more demanding jobs. Also we know that married women tend to work for the extra money to provide luxuries for the family and for the pleasure of having company during the day. For example Brown *et al.*, in their study of married women in a Leicester hosiery factory: 'The Employment of Married Women and the Supervisory Role' (R. K. Brown, J. M. Kirby and K. F. Taylor, *British Journal of Industrial Relations*, 2, 1964) found that: 'primarily, they wanted a job which would satisfy their desire for a worthwhile addition to the family's income. At the same time they wished it to provide them with social contacts—the opportunity to make friends and to work and talk with them each day. Such contacts, however, were generally confined to the factory, most women emphasising that they kept home and work separate.' In another study, a working wife gives this account of her reasons for working: 'This is the worst place I ever worked in. . . . Where I was before it was piece-work. You could do as much as *you* wanted to, but here you have to keep up all the time . . . I've thought of going part-time. But I couldn't. I need the money. Otherwise I could never buy the children's clothes for school or pay for the trips they go on—I'd hate to have them go without that.' (A working wife, cited in 'The Factory Slaves', Jackie West, *New Society*, 24 February 1977.) This is not to say that all women work for instrumental reasons, or that these are any the less important than working, as many women do, in a career. However, secondary-sector industrial employment is a major component in women's employment and it has been suggested that in addition to socialisation the character of the work may have some effect on the fact that so many women are employed in these jobs. For example, Barron and Norris point out that the type of jobs available is responsible for creating a lack of ambition in women. The characteristics of the job tend to become the characteristics of the job-holder. From this point of view, high rates of absenteeism and job turnover are less a characteristic of women as employees than the type of jobs in which women are employed. Also, women's labour plays an important part in modern capitalism. Very often it is cheaper for an employer to employ women than to use machinery. Consequently, it is in the interest of many employers to support the idea that women employees are best suited to dull repetitive work.

B. N. Seear, in *Re-entry of Women to the Labour Market after an Interruption in Employment* (OECD, 1971) points out how, increasingly, this is likely to be the pattern of women's employment. In the future, the secondary types of jobs in which women are mainly employed will increasingly be automated. This will mean that new jobs must be created and that the areas of employment traditionally occupied by men will come to be open to both sexes. Seear raises the question: 'How many employers in how many countries are prepared to ask the key question posed by management in Sweden: "What jobs in this company can NOT be done by a woman?" and accept the answer they received: "Very few"?'

How have these changes come about?

Decline in family size

We have seen how, since the 1870s, beginning with the middle classes, family size has gradually decreased in Britain. R. M. Titmuss, in his book *Problems of Social Policy* (Allen & Unwin, 1950), estimates that in the 1890s a working-class mother spent about fifteen years in a state of pregnancy or nursing a baby in the first year of its life. Today, this time is in the region of three to four years. Earlier marriage, fewer children, and childbearing and nursing confined to the early years of marriage, have all contributed to making married women freer to go out to work today.

Social changes

Labour shortages during the First World War brought women into the labour force and their competence in jobs normally performed by men began to change attitudes previously resistant to working wives. The Second World War mobilised female labour in even greater numbers. In 1941 women were required to register under the Ministry of Labour and married women were under some pressure to take up part-time work. The trend for women to work has continued.

Education

The increase in women's education that has occurred since the nineteenth century has been important in extending opportunities for women. In the early nineteenth century, there were few schools for women and these were intended for the daughters of middle-class families. Much of the earliest efforts for women's education had to do with providing suitable training for governesses. For example, in 1848 Queens College in Harley Street was opened to teach and examine women who intended to become governesses. Two pioneers of secondary education, Miss Buss and Miss Beale, were amongst its early students. Miss Buss became headmistress of the North London Collegiate School in 1850 and Miss Beale, the Principal of Cheltenham Ladies' College in 1858.

By the end of the century, the Girls' Public Day School Company, whose schools were modelled on the North London Collegiate School, had opened thirty-three secondary schools, educating in all more than 7100 girls. Meanwhile, with the passing of the 1870 Education Act, elementary education was made free and compulsory for boys and girls from all social strata. However, it was not until well into the twentieth century and the passing of the 1944 Education Act that secondary education became free and compulsory for all boys and girls.

Higher education for girls began largely in the last half of the nineteenth century. Girton College, Cambridge began in 1869 at Hitchin and then moved to Girton in 1873. In 1880 Newnham College for Women in Cambridge was established. In 1879 Somerville Hall and Lady Margaret Hall opened in Oxford. In 1880 women were admitted as degree students to London and Manchester Universities. Women were admitted to full membership of Oxford University only in 1920 and Cambridge in 1948, although they had been able to receive degrees from the latter since 1921.

Today, all girls can stay on beyond the school-leaving age of sixteen in preparation for entrance into colleges, universities, business or professional worlds. Girls have generally been more reluctant than boys to continue education, and the influence of the home on this decision must not be ignored, since parents are often more interested in their sons having a career than that their daughters should. However, in the recent DES School Intention Survey (1975) a higher proportion of sixteen-year-old girls than boys stated that they intended to stay on in some form of full-time higher education. Interestingly, this proportion was mainly due to the high proportion of working-class girls intending to remain in full-time education. Much of this education takes place in institutions of further education, while some of the rest takes place in colleges and universities. Considerably more men are admitted to universities than women. For example, in 1978–9 there were 162 500 full-time male students in universities compared with 96 600 female. By comparison (1977–8) there were more than two-and-a-half-times more women (52 000) on teacher training courses.

Technology

Technology has affected the women's role in a number of ways.

1   Technology has affected the employment opportunities for women. For example, at the beginning of industrialisation working-class women were employed as unskilled factory hands and in domestic service. With the development of bureaucracies and the accompanying office work there was an expansion of clerical positions. The invention of the telephone and the typewriter in the nineteenth century gave jobs to many women. For instance, following the example of business, the Civil Service began to employ women typists in 1880. More recently the development of light industry and the location of this on industrial estates near new housing developments or in new towns has extended employment to many women unable to travel far to work.

2   Technology has brought new inventions and time-saving devices into the home. For example, inventions such as the vacuum cleaner and the fridge have made running a home less time-consuming. Community services such as the launderette take care of other domestic chores.

3   Developments such as 'the pill' have made contraception more reliable. This makes it more possible for a woman to plan her family and therefore continue in her career without unplanned interruption. Since 1974 family planning services have been available to all women through National Health Service hospitals and clinics, and from 1975 GPs have been able to provide free family planning.

Health

Improvement in health care has led to a greater expectation of life.

Combined with earlier marriage, and smaller families raised during about the ten years after the beginning of married life, this leaves a much longer time in which a woman is free to take up a job.

Legislation

Legal changes have affected the woman's role in a number of different ways:

(a) *Property* The first efforts to secure property rights for married women began in 1855. At this time, unless a woman was protected by a marriage settlement, customary among upper-class wives, then her property became her husband's at marriage. W. Thompson, writing in 1825, pointed out how:

Home . . . is the eternal prison-house of the wife. . . . The house is *his* house with everything in it, and of all fixtures the most abjectly his is his breeding machine, the wife.

(W. Thompson, *Appeal of One Half of the Human Race, Women, against the Pretentions of the Other Half, Men, to Retain them in Political and Thence in Civil and Domestic Slavery*, [his capitals] London 1825.)

The Married Women's Property Bill of 1855 met with a great deal of opposition which prolonged its life until 1857, when the Bill had its Second Reading. At that time, the resistance to the Bill is epitomised in the remarks of the Attorney-General, who saw the Bill as a threat to the 'social and political institutions of the nation'. What legislation there was, concerned the property of divorced and separated women. For example, legislation in 1858 following from a Government Bill on Marriage and Divorce, held that a woman who left her husband should have a right to property earned or inherited after the separation. The Married Women's Property Act of 1870 allowed a married woman the right to her own earnings and certain other limited possessions. It was not until the Married Women's Property Act of 1882 that a married woman had the right of independent ownership of her own property.

More recently, the Matrimonial Proceedings and Property Act (1970) created new provisions for the distribution of property after divorce. For example, where value has been added to property during marriage, this added value belongs equally to husband and wife. Also, in making a decision about financial provisions in a divorce, the court will take into account the wife's contribution in looking after the home and the children and her loss of any pensions rights following divorce. The Act became effective in 1971, at the same time as the Divorce Reform Act (1969).

(b) *Divorce*   Changes in the divorce laws since the Matrimonial Causes Act of 1857 and the provision of Legal Aid, which has been available since 1949, have made it increasingly possible for married women to obtain a divorce. This is discussed in more detail in Topic 10.5. These changes have been both a cause and an effect of women working. For example, greater independence may induce divorce, but at the same time, divorce might not be contemplated if women were not able to make their own way in the world.

(c) *At work*   In 1919 the Sex Disqualification Act allowed right of entry of women to most professions. In 1970 the Equal Pay Act made it necessary for employers to pay women equal wages where they are doing the same or broadly similar work to men. The effect of the Act can be seen in some reduction in pay differences between men and women. For example, between April 1970 and April 1974 the difference between average pay (with overtime) for men and women was reduced by 3.8 per cent. Between April 1974 and July 1975 this differential (excluding overtime) was reduced by a further 10.5 per cent. However, at present

There's certainly no discrimination between the sexes in this house. I let the women graduate from menial kitchen duties to concrete-mixing and so forth.

(1980) women's average weekly wage rates are only 60 per cent of men's earnings. The 1975 Sex Discrimination Act makes it illegal to discriminate against an individual on grounds of sex or marital status in employment, education, housing or other areas. This Act may have the effect of equalising men's and women's average earnings since part of the current difference can be seen as a reluctance on the part of employers to hire women in high-paying occupations. The Equal Opportunities Commission was also set up at this time to support the operation of both the Equal Pay Act and the Sex Discrimination Act. It may be too early to estimate the effectiveness of the Commission, but the Department of Employment's *Gazette* for December 1976 showed that there are many attempts to evade the legal requirements of the Equal Pay Act. For example, the DOE found several instances of management and trade union collusion in raising women's pay to only minimum salary scales, that is, below men's pay scales.

(d) *Political rights*   Before 1918 it was impossible for women to vote in general elections. In 1918 women over thirty were given the vote. The voting age for women was finally equalised in 1928, when all women over twenty-one were able to vote. The voting age was reduced, for both sexes, to eighteen in 1970.

The husband's role

We have seen that there has been a change in the husband's role since the nineteenth century. He is no longer the autocratic head of the household but increasingly a partner in marriage. However the change is not complete. Conjugal roles more closely resemble those described by Michael Young and Peter Willmott (in *The Symmetrical Family*, Penguin, 1975) where the husband has one demanding job outside the home while the wife has two demanding jobs, than the symmetrical pattern itself. For example, S. Cunnison notes how 'women carried on the work of running their houses and looking after their families, cleaning, washing, shopping and cooking, the married ones with little or no help from their husbands. Such matters were considered to be the responsibility and duty of women regardless of their position as wage earners' (*Wages and Work Allocation*, Tavistock, 1966).

Among families where both husband and wife have careers there remain differences in the way in which husbands and wives evaluate their roles. In *Dual Career Families Re-examined* (Martin Robertson, 1976), Rhona and Robert Rapoport quote a middle-class husband's view of his marriage: 'I would say both of us look upon it as an absolute fifty-fifty partnership. . . . Everything is done jointly, almost everything as far as possible, as a family.' His wife, with a career of her own, has a different interpretation of their conjugal roles: 'I think a wife must put her husband's career first. If you marry a husband who is a geographer or an archaeologist, you've just got to adjust yourself to the fact of living abroad if necessary and giving up one's own job.' Despite the cultural pressures on a wife to perform a deferential role, Rhona and Robert Rapoport show that some couples succeed in supporting each other in their personal careers. For example, one wife, in charge of a research unit in a large chemical and pharmaceutical company, describes her decision to carry on in her demanding career: 'We came to the conclusion that the (personal) cost would have been greater not to have done. . . . I've got twenty people now working for me. I organise their working day and then I come home and I've got a husband and two children.' In this example Rhona and Robert Rapoport note that both husband and wife felt that they had needed and benefited in their careers from being married to one another.

Employers

Labour shortages which encouraged employers to employ married women caused employers to make suitable provisions for their employees. For example, many firms organise their shift hours to coincide with the time that children return from school, so that mothers can get home at that time. Also, firms provide canteens for their workers. This is helpful for women themselves and for their husbands. Some firms, but not many, provide crèches for working mothers.

The women's movement

There are a number of specific formal and informal organisations in Britain today which are concerned with issues which affect women. The issues which concern these groups include enforcing the operation of the Equal Opportunities Commission with respect to the enforcement of the Equal Pay Act and the Sex Discrimination Act, pressurising for greater provision for pre-school play groups and nursery education, women's continuing education and career opportunities, and for eliminating sex stereotyping from educational materials, books, newspapers, films, plays and TV. At a more general level, these groups are interested in raising people's consciousness about the role of women in society and in ensuring that women's rights are protected. Their main publication, indicating the scope and nature of their activities, is *Spare Rib*.

10.5   Marriage and divorce

Marriage

Underlying the nineteenth-century idealisation of family life was the idea that family and marriage were inseparable. The image of marriage as an enduring, stable relationship, sanctified by God, was part of the middle-class idealisation of family life. Christian marriage implied a lifelong, faithful co-habitation of husband and wife, dutifully concerned with the procreation and rearing of children. However, as we have seen, marriage often deviated from this moral ideal, and allowed the operation of a double standard in sexual mores. Many women saw marriage as tyranny. As O. R. McGregor points out in *Divorce in England* (Heinemann, 1957), many middle-class women came to admire the heroine of a contemporary novel who rejected an offer of marriage on the grounds that it would lead her into servitude.

In the working classes and urban poor, marriage, where it occurred, did not approach the genteel institution envisioned by the middle classes. Low wages, constant pregnancies, poor hygiene and sanitation, and the uncertainties of daily life left fatigue, malnutrition, sickness and hopelessness, none of which were conducive to happy marriage.

Marriage has changed since the nineteenth century. Some of the problems faced by couples at that time have been alleviated by the services of the Welfare State and trade unions. Also, the development of more reliable forms of birth control, such as 'the pill', have made it possible for marriage to be separated from parenthood. It is possible for couples today to marry for other reasons, such as companionship. Also, social and personal attitudes towards the religious meaning of marriage have altered. For example, it has been argued that Britain is becoming a secular society. It is suggested that there is a decline in the importance attached to religious institutions in society and people's actions are less coloured by religious beliefs. In relation to marriage, the argument is that secularisation had led to a decline in the religious significance of marriage and that people no longer see their mutual responsibilities in terms of Christian duty. The recent increase in the proportion of all first marriages performed as civil ceremonies (a third in 1966, compared with a half in 1980) is taken as evidence favouring this argument. On the other hand, it is questionable whether religiously-based marriages, solemnised by church weddings, have always reflected religious commitment to marriage. For example, as Bryan Wilson points out, church ceremonies are used to signify important personal transitions, such as marriage, and so it is difficult to estimate the extent of religious commitment to marriage from changes in the proportions of church weddings when these may constitute no more than *rites de passage*.

Considering the altered circumstances of marriage, the greater range of opportunities available to women and the option of parenthood, the question arises, why do people choose to get married today? In fact, we have very little information on couples' reasons for getting married. In her book, *The Captive Wife*, Hannah Gavron notes that in her sample of middle- and working-class wives: 'The general impression was that they had not really got the most out of their youth before settling down. . . . In fact, what was revealed was a lack of foresight and of real thinking as to what marriage entailed.'

In our society the cultural idea of romantic love surrounds courtship and marriage. It is also commercially a very profitable idea, supporting a host of industries from cosmetics and fashions to sportscars and package tours. It has been argued that this distracts young people from recognising the seriousness of marriage and that it is lightly undertaken. In fact, recent statistics suggest that young people may be becoming more cautious about undertaking marriage than they were in the late 1960s and early 1970s. For example, from Table 3.4 it can be seen that marriage rates have been going down in recent years. Also, the total of 302 300 women marrying for the first time in 1974 was near to the lowest annual total of the post-war period, in 1954. In 1973 and 1974 there was a reduction in first marriage rates at all ages, but most noticeably amongst young people aged 20–24.

Marriage rate per 1000 of pop.	1965	1968	1969	1970	1971	1972	1973	1974
	7.8	8.4	8.1	8.5	8.3	8.6	8.1	7.8

Table 3.4 Marriage rate per 1000 of population in England and Wales (Source: UN *Demographic Year Books*)

When the marriage rates for England and Wales are compared with those for other countries this decline does not seem so pronounced. For example, in Sweden, marriage rates have been dropping very steeply for some time.

However, as with any statistics, marriage rates have to be interpreted. In fact, the recent decline in overall marriage rates could be looked at as more of a return to the normal level after a period of high marriage rates in the mid and late 1960s and early 1970s. Before jumping to the conclusion that these high rates reflect a greater popularity of marriage at this time, it is important to examine some of the factors which influenced these figures.

Demographic factors

1 One of these factors is the changes which have occurred in the proportion of the population entering the age groups at which marriage usually occurs. Most marriages occur amongst people between their late teens and mid to late twenties. Women tend to marry at earlier ages than men. When there are more people entering these age groups, this will send up the numbers of recorded marriages. In the mid and late sixties and early seventies, the growth in the number of marriages was partly a reflection of post-war baby boom children reaching marriageable age.

2 Another factor is the change in the age at which people marry for the first time. Where there is a sudden decline in the age at marriage, then every year for a while there will seem to be more people marrying than usual each year. This was happening in the 1960s in Britain. Table 3.5 shows how the average age at marriage has declined in this country.

First marriages

Average age of marrying (years)	1911	1931	1951	1961	1971	1972	1973	1974	1978*
Bachelors	27.3	27.4	26.8	25.6	24.6	24.8	24.8	24.8	23.8
Spinsters	25.6	25.5	24.6	23.3	22.6	22.8	22.7	22.7	21.5

Table 3.5   Average age at marriage in the UK
*Figures for England and Wales only

Real changes

Aside from demographic considerations, there may be real increases in the proportions of people marrying. This appears to have been the case in the late 1960s and early 1970s. So marriage appears more popular.

Legal changes and their effects

Marriage rates can also be affected by legal changes, such as changes in the age of consent. For example, in Britain the Family Law Reform Act took effect in 1969, lowering the age of majority to eighteen. At this time marriages at younger ages increased sharply.

Is marriage declining in importance?

Divorce has increased from two divorces on average per annum before 1857 to 138 000 in 1979. This looks like a startling increase and, it has been suggested, reflects the moral decay of marriage and the family that has occurred since the nineteenth century.

In examining this argument, it must be remembered that when comparing marriage and the family today with their nineteenth-century counterparts, much of what we think of as being family life in those times was, even then, idealisation. For example, as we have seen far from being warm, cohesive and stable, marriage and family life was often turbulent and unsettled in the working classes and urban poor. Given these circumstances it appears surprising that there should be so few divorces. Clearly, we need to look more closely at the figures for divorce.

Divorce

A. Divorce statistics

1 *Petitions for divorce* There are a number of different ways in which divorce is recorded, including on the one hand the number of people seeking divorce, that is by 'petitions' and, on the other, by the number of divorces granted. O. R. McGregor suggests that it is more useful to examine numbers of divorce petitions since these do not reflect differences in court procedures over time. The graph shows the increases which have occurred in divorce petitions from 1876 to 1974.

2 *Divorce rates* These are often used in order to compare divorce between groups, divorce from one time to another, and to compare divorce between different countries. Divorce rates are expressed as per thousand of the population (in the same way as birth and death rates) or per thousand of the married population. In many ways it is better to relate divorces granted, to the people who run the risk of being divorced, that is, the married population. Recent divorce rates per thousand married couples are shown in Table 3.6. From this it can be seen that the rates of divorces granted have gone up very sharply since the early 1970s.

1939–41	1944–46	1950–52	1960–62	1970	1971	1972	1973	1979
0.7	1.8	2.8	2.1	4.7	6.0	9.5	8.4	10.4

Table 3.6 Divorce rate per 1000 married couples in England and Wales

Table 3.7 below shows the divorce rates for some other countries. From this it can be seen that in the 1960s rates were highest in the USA.

Country and year	Rate	Country and year	Rate	Country and year	Rate
Australia		France		Norway	
1963	3.1	1961–63	2.9	1962	2.9
1960–62	2.8	1953–55	2.9	1959–61	2.8
1953–55	3.3	1945–47	4.9	1949–51	3.2
1946–48	4.4	1935–37	2.3	1945–47	3.2
Austria		Germany		Sweden	
1950–52	6.7	(Fed. Rep. of)		1962	5.0
1938–40	3.8	1963	3.5	1959–61	4.9
		1960–62	3.4	1949–51	4.9
Canada		1949–51	6.4	1944–46	4.2
1963	1.9	1946–47	6.3	1939–41	2.7
1960–62	1.7			1934–36	2.3
1955–57	1.7	Japan			
1950–52	1.7	1962	3.7	United States	
1940–42	1.1	1959–61	3.7	1964	10.7
		1954–56	4.4	1963	10.3
Finland		1949–51	5.3	1962	9.4
1962	4.4			1960	9.2
1959–61	4.1	Netherlands		1955	9.3
1955	4.2	1962	2.2	1950	10.3
1949–51	4.6	1959–61	2.2	1945	14.4
1939–41	2.2	1951–53	2.6	1940	8.8
		1946–48	4.5	1935	7.8

Table 3.7   Divorce rate per 1000 married couples, selected countries, 1935 to 1964
Source: *Marriage and Divorce: A Social and Economic Study*, Hugh Carter and Paul C. Glick, Harvard University Press, 1976 (after data from the UN *Demographic Yearbook* and other sources)

In order to understand fully the differences in the rates between countries, it would be necessary to examine the particular social and legal circumstances of each country. In addition to these countries Italy should now be included in the table. Divorce became possible there in 1970.

B. Factors influencing the incidence of divorce in Britain

1   Population structure and characteristics   The population has more than doubled since the nineteenth century. Also, a higher proportion of the population are married. The increase in the expectation of life that has occurred since the nineteenth century exposes marriage to a greater period of risk in which divorce can occur.

2   Legal changes   With the Matrimonial Causes Act of 1857, for the first time divorces began to be less costly and therefore accessible to more people. However, it has taken over a hundred years for divorce laws and other legal provisions to reach their present state which makes it possible for almost anyone to obtain a divorce. The most recent legislation is the Divorce Reform Act (1969), which became effective in 1971. Under this Act, a new approach to divorce was introduced. Rather than requiring the establishment of guilt on the part of one partner in causing marital breakdown, it is now enough to show that that 'irretrievable breakdown' has occurred. This is taken to have occurred if husband and wife have lived apart for two years and both of them want a divorce, or where the couple have been living apart for five years but only one of them wants a divorce. Also, where the behaviour of one or other of the parties is unreasonable or involves adultery which cannot be forgiven, then this constitutes proof of 'irretrievable breakdown' of a marriage.

Since 1973, a 'special procedure' has been instituted which speeds up and simplifies the granting of a divorce. This procedure allows a divorce to be granted on the evidence of irretrievable breakdown submitted in writing, without any court hearing. From 1 April 1977, this procedure became available for all undefended divorce proceedings.

3   Changes in attitudes towards divorce   It has been suggested that there is greater tolerance of divorce and this has encouraged more people to petition for divorce. Changes in private attitudes to divorce are difficult to gauge. William Goode, in his study of divorce in the USA (*After Divorce*, Free Press, 1956) found that people were not intolerant of divorce so much as confused about how to relate to the divorcee. This ambivalence encouraged divorcees to modify their role as ex-husband or ex-wife and adopt the stance of eligible future spouse. In this role, social relationships became easier since people could more easily relate to this familiar pattern of behaviour. According to Goode, the ultimate effect of this move was to propel the divorcee into re-marriage. At the time of Goode's study, divorce, while not infrequent, may have been sufficiently unusual

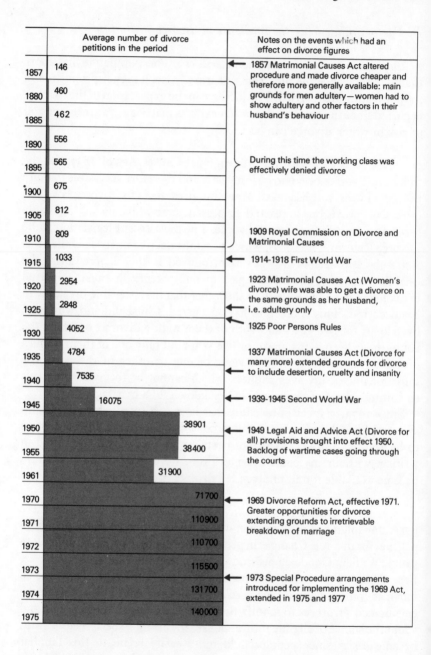

	Average number of divorce petitions in the period	Notes on the events which had an effect on divorce figures
1857	146	1857 Matrimonial Causes Act altered procedure and made divorce cheaper and therefore more generally available: main grounds for men adultery—women had to show adultery and other factors in their husband's behaviour
1880	460	
1885	462	
1890	556	
1895	565	During this time the working class was effectively denied divorce
1900	675	
1905	812	
1910	809	1909 Royal Commission on Divorce and Matrimonial Causes
1915	1033	1914-1918 First World War
1920	2954	1923 Matrimonial Causes Act (Women's divorce) wife was able to get a divorce on the same grounds as her husband, i.e. adultery only
1925	2848	
1930	4052	1925 Poor Persons Rules
1935	4784	1937 Matrimonial Causes Act (Divorce for many more) extended grounds for divorce to include desertion, cruelty and insanity
1940	7535	
1945	16075	1939-1945 Second World War
1950	38901	1949 Legal Aid and Advice Act (Divorce for all) provisions brought into effect 1950. Backlog of wartime cases going through the courts
1955	38400	
1961	31900	
1970	71700	1969 Divorce Reform Act, effective 1971. Greater opportunities for divorce extending grounds to irretrievable breakdown of marriage
1971	110900	
1972	110700	
1973	115500	1973 Special Procedure arrangements introduced for implementing the 1969 Act, extended in 1975 and 1977
1974	131700	
1975	140000	

Figure 3.10 *Divorce legislation and its effects on the divorce rate 1876–1974*

for people to find the situation difficult to handle. It is questionable whether his findings apply in the USA today. However, they may be illuminating in considering contemporary divorce in Britain, where divorce is not yet entirely commonplace in society.

Changes in the law tell us something about changes in publicly held social attitudes towards divorce, as do changes which have occurred in the Church of England's position on divorce. For example the Minority Report of the Royal Commission on Divorce and Matrimonial Causes in 1912 emphatically rejected extending the grounds of divorce beyond the existing grounds of adultery. This was agreed to by the Archbishop of York. By 1966, the Church of England had made clear its opinions on divorce by the publication *Putting Asunder*. In this, the Church of England supported the view which is now part of our law. That is, that irretrievable breakdown of marriage is the appropriate basis on which to grant divorce.

4 *Changes in women's role*   Earlier in this chapter it was noted that women's role has changed since the nineteenth century. Today, women are increasingly entering the labour force. It has been suggested that because women are freer to make their own way in the world, owning their own property, earning their own wages, divorce is not the daunting prospect it was in the nineteenth century. Of course, at that time few women could have afforded divorce anyway, but the social stigma attached to divorce and the lack of women's rights made divorce largely impossible. Legislation which has occurred in the twentieth century has equalised the grounds on which women may petition for divorce, and Legal Aid provisions have had the effect of benefiting women, many of whom would not otherwise have been able to afford the legal costs of divorce. At the present time many more wives than husbands petition for divorce.

C.   *Factors associated with divorce*

From an analysis of divorce statistics we know what characteristics tend to be associated with divorce. However, it must be remembered that this is not at all the same thing as saying that these features cause divorce. Colin Gibson, examining divorce statistics in the 1960s and early 1970s, found that the following characteristics were associated with divorce:

1 *Age at marriage*   Divorce was more frequently associated with marriages where the wife was below age twenty when she married. It has also been found that this is even more true where both spouses are under twenty at the time of marriage.

2 *Pre-marital pregnancy* Divorce is associated with marriages where the wife was pregnant at marriage. Since the proportion of marriages like this is greater where the wife married under twenty, the two things are related.

3 *Social class* Social class differences exist in divorce. Upper classes are less likely to divorce than the manual working class. However, in one white-collar class divorce is also high, so the relationship between social class and divorce is complex. However, social class can be considered a key variable in understanding some of the other factors associated with divorce. For example, early marriage and high rates of pre-marital pregnancy are more usual in the manual working class. Colin Gibson suggests the financial strains of coping with a baby, a wife unable to work and the difficulties of finding accommodation, must inevitably create difficulties for young people at a time when their earning capacity is not very great, and this leads to marital disharmony.

4 *Marriage duration* In 1974–5 the most common duration of marriage amongst divorced couples is four years. Where marriage began early, divorce often occurs sooner than where the couples married in their twenties. Because of the social class differences in the age at which couples marry, this means middle-class marriages tend to last a little longer before divorce. In 1970, among couples married before twenty and married for five years, the national divorce rate was 23.1 per 1000 marriages. In his sample, Colin Gibson found that 30 per cent of marriages where the bride had been under twenty lasted less than seven years. Presently there is an increase in the number of divorces occurring to older couples and among longer-lasting marriages. For example, in 1975, just over 20 per cent of divorces were to marriages of over twenty years' duration. The reasons for this increase are discussed later (see: Present-day trends in divorce).

5 *Children* Other researchers have examined the association between family size and divorce. O. R. McGregor found that divorce was more common where the couple was childless. Recent research suggests that there has been a decline in the number of divorces associated with childlessness (that is, where couples have no children, or the children have grown up and left home). But the researchers conclude: 'From the evidence at present available it is impossible to judge whether marriages with children are more, or less, prone to divorce than marriages without children' (*Population Trends*, No. 3, Spring 1976, HMSO).

6 *Age at divorce* The age at which most divorces occur today continues to be in the late twenties.

Present-day trends in divorce

At the current divorce level (1979–80), about one married person in a hundred is divorced in the course of a year. For couples aged 25–34 years old, it is nearly two in a hundred. Recent divorce statistics show the changes which have been occurring in the characteristics of the divorcing population. For example, in 1971 and 1972 there was a sharp increase in the number of divorces associated with marriages which had lasted a long time. The reason for this is that the new divorce law, effective since 1971, by introducing the 'irretrievable breakdown' grounds for divorce, has made it possible for many couples whose marriage had, in fact, ended many years ago, now to seek divorce. Also, this does not require them to prove the 'guilt' of one partner, an aspect of earlier divorce laws which probably deterred many people from petitioning sooner for divorce. The new divorce law therefore has changed the character of divorce statistics. However, it is likely that this effect will gradually disappear from the figures. The present divorce figures have also been affected by an increase in the number of people divorcing for a second time. If the divorce rate for the 1971–3 period were to continue in the same way, this would result in 22 per cent of all women being divorced at least once by the time they are forty-five years old.

D.   Divorce and the role of marriage in society

As we have seen, much of the increase in the number of divorces is an artifact of changes in the characteristics of the population, and of social and legal changes. The fact that the numbers have gone up reflects these considerations more clearly than the idea that there is a corresponding decline in the significance attached to marriage. Also, as McGregor points out, if numbers of divorces have gone up, divorce rates have not increased so strikingly. For example, the number of divorce petitions was thirty times greater in 1950 than in 1911, but the rate of divorce petitioning was only twenty times greater. For example, we saw that, before 1857, there were on average only two divorce petitions a year. This was at a time when marriage faced at least as much stress as it does today. However, at that time, social and legal considerations made divorce impossible. Today, rather than divorce terminating marriage entirely, it usually opens up the way to re-marriage. For example, in 1965 11 per cent of all marriages involved a divorcee; in 1972 this figure was 22 per cent and by 1978 it had become 33 per cent. The current marriage rates, therefore, while falling particularly at younger ages, mask this rapid increase in the re-marriage of divorced persons. This suggests that enthusiasm for marriage has not declined. Our high expectations for fulfilment in marriage may make young people today cautious of embarking on marriage without financial security, and perhaps, in general, make us vulnerable to disappointment. However, these expectations may also make us willing to seek satisfaction in marriage a second time, after initial disappointment. As Colin Gibson points out: 'modern morality . . . is opposed to the idea of continuing with a marriage long since dead but not to a rejection of the institution of marriage'. (Colin Gibson, 'Divorce and Social Class in England and Wales', *British Journal of Sociology*, Vol. XXV, No. 1, March 1974)

What has been considered here has been based on analyses of divorce statistics. We must remember that, at any time, there are going to be many more unhappy or broken marriages than ever reach the divorce courts. In fact, we really do not know the extent of marital breakdown in Britain. Also, rather than divorce signifying unhappiness, in many ways it may result in more equanimity for family members than unhappy marriages which continue. Much of the research which examines the effect which marital discord has on family members overlooks these considerations. For example, it is misleading to examine the amount of juvenile deliquency among children with divorced parents without also looking at the proportions of juvenile delinquents whose parents are not divorced and the proportion of non-delinquent children who have divorced parents. Very little research has been conducted into marital disharmony. However, in his book *Marital Breakdown* (Penguin 1971), Jack Dominian discusses some of the research findings of American sociologists. These indicate that happily and unhappily married husbands and wives tend to have the following characteristics:

Happily married	*Unhappily married*
Emotionally stable	Emotionally unstable
Considerate of others	Critical of others
Yielding	Dominating
Companionable	Isolated
Self-confident	Lack of self-confidence
Emotionally dependent	Emotionally self-sufficient

Table 3.8   Characteristics of happily and unhappily married partners (Source: *Marital Breakdown*, Penguin, 1971)

Of course, these findings are very general and changes in social and personal circumstances are likely to modify individuals' characteristics over time.

The family today and in the future

We have seen that the family today is a thriving institution. Industrialisation and urbanisation may have severed the direct economic links between family members, but their impact has modified rather than destroyed the significance of the family unit in society. New agencies, such as the National Health Service, have taken on many of the functions which were previously entirely the responsibility of the family group. The family has thus been freed to perform more efficiently and effectively its essential functions. As Ronald Fletcher points out, in *The Family and Marriage in Britain* (Penguin, 1966) 'it is perfectly clear that the modern family—entailing the equal status of wife and husband and their mutual consideration in marriage; the high status of children; and the improved standards of income, housing and household equipment—aims at, and achieves, a far more satisfactory and refined provision for [the performance of essential functions] than did either the pre-industrial family or the family of early industrial Britain.'

What will the family be like in the future? Will it continue to be a pattern of human association in society?

These are interesting questions to consider even though the answers will be speculative. The family is part of society and is therefore affected by and itself effects, changes in society.

In *The Symmetrical Family*, Young and Willmott suggest that, in accordance with their principle of stratified diffusion, families throughout the social structure will increasingly reach the stage of the symmetrical family, a pattern of family organisation they find in some higher classes today. This change will occur at the expense of the privatised home-centred family. Young and Willmott make this prediction partly on the basis of their 'principle' and partly on the basis of the effects of modern technology and modern feminism. Modern technology will take over boring, dull, repetitive jobs and release men and women for more fulfilling occupations and leisure-time activities; modern feminism will create opportunities for fulfilling jobs for women outside the home, equal to those of men. With appropriate education and economic conditions, these forces will result in husbands and wives each having two jobs, a paid occupation outside the home and joint responsibility for home life and the care of children.

Technology can affect the family in another way also. Recent developments in medical technology, such as abortion and improved methods of contraception, as well as new methods for encouraging conception, have extended the range of choices open to members of the family. In the long term it is likely that other scientific and technological developments will affect the family, possibly contributing to profound changes such as a move to adopt alternative forms of human association. Perhaps present experiments in communal living are forerunners of such fundamental changes in social organisation. For example, we may find ourselves in the situation where people no longer associate with one another in terms of family groups but instead relate to some new and, as yet, un-named principle of human association.

Terms used in this chapter

siblings	patrilineal	loose-knit
ascribed status	matrilineal	close-knit
achieved status	bilineal	stratified diffusion
bride price	peer group	cohort
socialisation	home-centred	community network

Further reading

R. Ash, *Talking about the Family* (Wayland, 1973)

M. Anderson (ed.), *Sociology of the Family* (Penguin, 1971)

D. L. Barker & S. Allen (eds), *Dependence and Exploitation in Work and Marriage* (Longman, 1976)

E. Bott, *Family and Social Network* (Tavistock Publications, 1957)

M. Farmer, *The Family* (Longman, 1970)

R. Fletcher, *The Family and Marriage* (Penguin, 1962)

R. Fox, *Kinship and Marriage* (Penguin, 1967)

H. Gavron, *The Captive Wife* (Routledge & Kegan Paul, 1966)

J. & E. Newson, *Patterns of Infant Care* (Penguin, 1963)

R. & R. Rapoport, *Dual Career Families Re-examined* (Martin Robertson, 1976)

E. Rosser & C. Harris, *The Family and Social Change*, (Routledge & Kegan Paul, 1965)

D. W. Winnicott, *The Child, the Family and the Outside World* (Penguin, 1964)

P. Townsend, *The Family Life of Old People* (Penguin, 1963)

C. Turner, *Family and Kinship in Modern Britain* (Routledge & Kegan Paul, 1969)

M. Young and P. Willmott, *Family and Kinship in East London* (Penguin, 1969)

M. Young and P. Willmott, *The Symmetrical Family* (Penguin, 1975)

Questions from GCE 'O' Level Sociology Examination Papers

1 What is a family? Describe some of the different kinds of family organisation you have read about and explain why they are all families. (AEB, June 1972)

2 To what extent is is true to say that the extended family no longer exists in Britain? On what evidence is your opinion based? (AEB, November 1971)

3 'Far from being the basis of the good society, the family is the source of all our discontents.' Discuss. (AEB, November 1970)

4 Imagine a country in which living in families was officially prohibited. Describe the difference this might make to that society. (AEB, Specimen Paper for New Syllabus, 1972)

5 Distinguish between an extended and a nuclear family. Is the latter more important than the former in contemporary Britain? (Oxford Local Examinations, 1970)

6 Account for some of the changes which have taken place in the pattern of family life in recent years. (AEB, June 1968)

7 In what ways have relationships within the family changed during the last one hundred years? What kind of evidence is there to support your views? (AEB, June 1973)

Great Britain

Number of live births	Proportion of women (per 1000) with specified number of births, who were first married in:		
	1870–79	1900–09	1925
0	83	113	161
1–2	125	335	506
3–4	181	277	221
5–9	434	246	106
10 or more	177	29	6
all	1000	1000	1000

(AEB, June 1970)

8 What does the table above tell us about family size in Great Britain since 1870? How would you explain this change?

9 What are the major social factors affecting family size in contemporary Britain? (Oxford Local Examinations, 1973)

10 A hundred years ago the average number of children in a family was about six; what is the corresponding average now? Explain this change. (AEB, November 1972)

11   Newspapers often refer to the generation gap. How acceptable or useful do you find this phrase (AEB, June 1972)

12 *a*   What reasons are there for mothers returning to work?

b   What factors have enabled mothers to return to work? (AEB, June 1976)

13   Monogamy without divorce, monogamy with easy divorce, polygamy. Describe how each of these three kinds of marriages would be likely to affect relationships within the family. (AEB, November 1972)

14 *a*   What factors have caused the changes in the divorce rate since 1900?

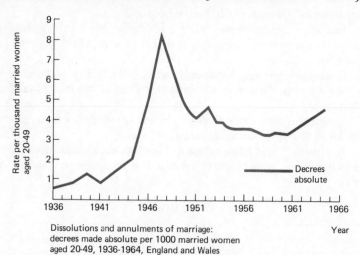

Dissolutions and annulments of marriage:
decrees made absolute per 1000 married women
aged 20-49, 1936-1964, England and Wales
                                                         Year

b   What effects, if any, have these changes had on family life? (You may find the above graph useful.) (AEB, June 1972)

15   Describe and account for changes in the divorce rate in Britain during this century. (Oxford Local Examinations, 1975)

16   What are the essential functions of the family? How does the State assist the family in fulfilling these functions? (AEB, June 1973)

17   Discuss the suggestion that the most important cause of the decline of the 'extended family' is geographical mobility. (Oxford Local Examinations, 1975)

18   How and why has the role of woman gradually changed in Britain during this century? (AEB, June 1977)

19   'Changes in divorce laws may create more broken marriages or may allow marriages which are already broken to be terminated.' Explain this statement. (AEB, June 1980)

20   'The family in modern Britain has experienced several important changes and this is sometimes seen as indicating a breakdown in family life.' What are these changes and how have they affected the modern family? (AEB, June 1981)

4 Education

Unit 11 The Development of Education

11.1 The functions of education

We have seen how the family is the first important agency of socialisation, but we live in a highly developed industrialised society, and the family alone cannot provide us with all the skills and knowledge necessary to prepare us for adulthood and earning a living in our complex society. The second major agency of socialisation is the school, which, as we grow older, gradually replaces the family by providing a formal environment for learning and training for work. Education does not begin and end with school, as the broadest meaning of the word is the whole continuous process of socialisation throughout life. Formal education through schooling is, however, an important aspect of our socialisation. Society recognises its importance: the law requires us to spend at least eleven years of our life at school, and we spend £10 000 million (1980) on all forms of education. There are about eleven million children of all ages, or one-fifth of the population, attending school in the United Kingdom.

The preparation of young people for earning a living is an obvious *economic function* of education, but education has other and perhaps no less important functions as well. The broad transmission of culture is more possible in the school than in the family. The school provides a *stabilising function* in that it usually endeavours to preserve the existing order of things from our cultural heritage. Culture, in this context, is used in the sense of being a way of life characterised by generally accepted standards of behaviour, beliefs, conduct, and morals. However, although each country has its own special culture, within the culture of a nation there are class differences which make for 'working-class' and 'middle-class' cultures. For the most part our education has been dominated by middle-class culture, mainly because the majority of our teachers and educationalists are themselves the products of a middle-class upbringing. Attitudes and opinions change, and as society has changed, schools have changed their values. For example, many schools no longer insist on school uniform for all their pupils; the curriculum is far wider and choices are much greater. To a lesser degree it is possible that schools themselves have been instrumental in bringing about changes. There is undoubtedly less conformity nowadays about the ideas that should be transmitted relating to topics such as law and order, marriage, sex and religion. So long as the way is left open for flexibility and gradual changes, several sound arguments can be put forward in support of education playing a more or less traditional role.

1   The attitudes, beliefs and customs of society have been formulated over a long period and there probably were good reasons why society adopted these ideas and ideals.

2   Our national heritage is preserved by conserving, to some extent, the patterns of existing society.

3   Whereas revolutionary attitudes may sweep away much that is out-of-place and wasteful in a modern society, it is possible that valuable cultural ideals may be lost at the same time.

4   We have a responsibility to transmit to posterity the best things that have been handed on by past generations.

5   It would be unfortunate if peculiar national traditions and characteristics disappeared under a cloak of dull uniformity.

The *political functions* of education have undergone radical changes. Until modern times our political leaders were drawn from an exclusive social background. Although it can be argued that too high a proportion of ministers and senior civil servants still come from certain famous public schools, nevertheless it is now recognised that everyone must be educated so that they may share and then take responsibility for the political leadership of society by using a vote. Ideally the educational system should be organised so that the best leaders in society emerge because their abilities and other qualities were encouraged through opportunities in all kinds of schools.

Until comparatively recently it was generally agreed that education had a *selective function*, meaning that because of the disparities of talent and ability among us all, some form of grading was necessary, for example, some children be selected for grammar schools at the age of eleven. There is now some debate as to whether this is either desirable or workable. Today all political parties subscribe to the belief of *equality of opportunity*; they differ, however, on what exactly is meant by 'equality' and 'opportunity', and part of this debate is examined in Topic 12.4.

All these functions may be summarised to three basics of a school:

1   the development of personal qualities
2   the teaching of the values and norms of society
3   the transmission of knowledge and learning.

11.2 The growth of education

The public education system in Britain dates from the nineteenth century when it became clear that an industrial society necessitated an efficient labour force. The governing classes realised that it was in their own interests to have a better-educated working class. A working class that could read, write, and understand simple arithmetic was able to operate machinery more efficiently as they understood written instructions and could calculate the dimensions of components. Earlier, particularly during the French Revolution, it was feared by those in power that a literate working class would be inspired to violence by reading revolutionary literature.

In 1837, Lord Brougham criticised the British Government for 'having done less for the Education of the People than any one of the more civilised nations of the world'. At this time only about one-tenth of the population of this country had any schooling, whereas in Germany about one-sixth went to school. Brougham went on to add that in Britain, 'the kind of education afforded was far more lamentably defective than its amount'. In 1833 the government initiated an annual £20 000 educational grant which went mainly to the National Society for the education of Anglicans, and to the British and Foreign Society for the education of non-conformists. These two voluntary societies were providing most of the schools. Thirty-seven years later the foundations for a national educational system were laid in Forster's Education Act of 1870. Although this Act was supposed to provide adequately for elementary education it would be a mistake to believe that Britain had a universal compulsory system from 1870. The new locally-elected school boards set up by the Act had great difficulty in getting the children to the schools and it took two more Acts to make education compulsory:

1   Sandon's Act of 1876 stated that it was the duty of parents of children aged between five and thirteen years, to see that they received elementary instruction.

2   Mundella's Act of 1880 made it the duty of every school board to get to school all its children of school age.

The next vital piece of educational legislation was Balfour's Act of 1902 which set up Local Education Authorities in place of the school boards. The provision of public secondary education was now in the hands of the LEAs: new maintained secondary schools were built and the old endowed grammar schools were also aided from the rates. A proportion of scholarship places were offered to the bright children from elementary schools—the 'educational highway' had not been built, but an 'educational ladder' was in the early stages of construction. The Fisher Act of 1918 abolished fees in elementary schools; it also gave LEAs the power to provide nursery schools and to raise the school-leaving age to fifteen. The Hadow Report (1926) and the Spens Report (1938) were investigations into secondary education. For their time, half a century or more ago, they were enlightened in their recommendations, stressing among other things an expansion of secondary education. The economic circumstances between the wars were used by the governments of the day as reasons for not implementing their proposals. During the Second World War the Norwood Report (1943) also considered a re-structuring of secondary education as being necessary. In 1944, R. A. Butler introduced the now famous Education Act which was to implement in large measure the proposals of the earlier reports, and to undertake a complete revision of all aspects of the educational system. This Act was the blueprint upon which most educational developments were based for the next twenty years. The 1944 Act laid down important principles:

1   There should be free education for all.
  2   Regard should be given, as far as possible, to the wishes of the parents.
  3   Full-time and part-time education should be provided for those over compulsory school-leaving age.
  4   Educational planning should be based upon local experience, interest and knowledge.
  5   There should be set up a three-tier educational system consisting of three stages:
a   *Primary* (2 to 11)
           nursery (2–5)
           infant (5–7)
           junior (7–11)—now often called 'middle' (8–12)
b   *Secondary* (11 to 15-plus) tripartite system
           modern ⎫
           grammar ⎬ now mainly comprehensive
           technical ⎭
c   *Further*
           technical colleges
           art schools
           agricultural institutes
           teachers' training colleges—now colleges of education
           universities.
  6   The school-leaving age should be raised to sixteen (implemented 1972–3).
  7   There should be equal opportunity for all.

The secondary or *tripartite* division of education into grammar,

secondary modern, and technical schools particularly interested
educationalists, and many aspects of it became the basis of much
sociological research.

11.3 The tripartite system

Much of the philosophy behind the 1944 Act was based upon firmly-held
Christian principles and requirements, such as compulsory religious
instruction and the 'corporate act of Christian worship' (morning
assembly) at the beginning of each school day. The basic assumption was
made that it was possible to categorise children by their abilities, either as
'academic' or 'manual' in their skills, and that provision of a particular
type of schooling should be made accordingly: the more academic
children should go to grammar schools, the less academic to secondary
modern and technical schools. The Spens and Norwood Reports,
together with the research findings of social psychologists, such as Sir
Cyril Burt, an eminent pioneer in intelligence testing, helped to provide
material for the notion that valid aptitude and intelligence testing could
be made. (Five years after his death in 1971, Burt was accused of

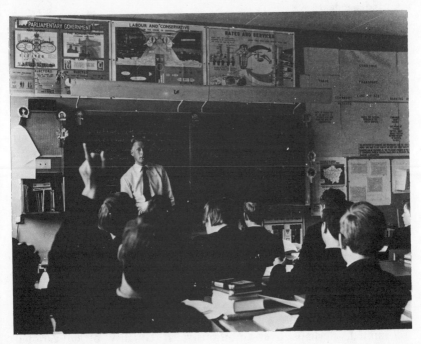

A formal teaching situation

falsifying his statistical findings in other research on intelligence testing.)

The separation of secondary schooling at the age of eleven was almost universally determined by pupils sitting the *eleven-plus examination*. This usually involved tests in English, arithmetic, and intelligence. The pattern of the examination varied slightly from one local education authority to another (some for example, gave an emphasis to the primary teachers' confidential reports), but for the most part the kind of school that children would attend after the age of eleven depended upon them either passing or failing this crucial examination in their last year in the primary school. It was possible under the tripartite system for a very few children who did particularly well in the secondary modern school to transfer at a later date, usually in the fifth or sixth form, to the grammar school. Table 4.1 shows the percentage of children attending the different kinds of school in 1958. As can be seen, just under one-fifth of children attended grammar schools, while almost two-thirds went to secondary modern schools.

	%
Grammar and direct grant schools	19.1
Secondary modern	63.0
Independent	5.1
Technical	2.8
Special	1.3
Unallocated	8.7
	100.0

Table 4.1   Distribution of twelve-year-old children in secondary schools in June 1958
(Source: J. W. B. Douglas, *The Home and the School*, MacGibbon & Kee, 1964)

There were also regional variations in the number of grammar school places. Table 4.2 shows that Wales awarded proportionately more grammar school places than England, and that children living in the South had the least chance of gaining a grammar school place. Some of the greatest regional variations were lessened slightly as there were more technical and private schools in some of those areas providing least grammar school places. To compare Wales with the South illustrates this point. Wales had the highest number of grammar school places, but a much lower proportion of the population were middle-class and there were fewer private schools. The South had a much higher proportion of middle-class people and a greater number of private schools. The 1944 Act aimed, perhaps over-ambitiously, at equality of educational opportunity for both sexes, and this was thought to have been achieved in regard to grammar school places. Slightly more girls obtained grammar school places than boys (20.2 per cent as compared with 18.0 per cent), but this was balanced by slightly more boys attending technical schools.

Region	Percentage of grammar school places, 1957
Wales	28.6
S. West	26.7
N. West	22.6
W. & E. Ridings	22.0
East	21.0
N. Midlands	20.0
Midlands	18.7
London & S. East	18.2
North	17.0
South	13.1

Table 4.2   Regional variations in the award of grammar school places
(Source: J. W. B. Douglas, *The Home and the School*)

Criticisms of the tripartite system

About a decade or so after the introduction of the tripartite system a growing number of teachers, educationalists and politicians began to have doubts about its fairness and efficiency, or whether it was matching the principle of equality of educational opportunity. Their criticisms were largely based on two arguments: firstly that the method of selection at eleven was unfair and possibly inaccurate, and secondly that there was inequality of opportunity since a disproportionately larger number of middle-class children gained grammar school places. We shall see in Topic 12.2 how middle-class children tended to perform much better at grammar schools than their working-class contemporaries at the same schools. Table 4.3 illustrates this point.

1   The eleven-plus examination was too rigid. Intelligence is not 'fixed' at eleven years and many children may be late developers. A poor performance on the day of the examination might determine a child's whole future career in an adverse way. Some bright people invariably perform badly under examination conditions.

2   There were wide regional disparities in the availability of grammar school places.

Occupation of father and social class	Occupation/social class as a per- centage of the national pop- ulation 1961	Grammar school leavers at 16 (%)	Grammar school leavers at 17 and 18 (%)
Professional and managerial (1 and 2)	19	17	39
Clerical and non-manual (3)	21*	17	20
Skilled manual (3)	30*	51	34
Semi-skilled manual (4)	21	9	5
Unskilled manual (5)	9	6	2
	100	100	100

* estimated

Table 4.3 Attendance at grammar school by social class and percentage of social class

(Source: *The Crowther Report*, Vol. II, HMSO, 1959)

3 The system heightened and perpetuated class differences as a much larger proportion of middle-class children obtained grammar school places and gained more qualifications there.

4 Local education authorities often provided better facilities for their grammar schools than for their secondary modern schools.

5 The assumption that children are either 'academic' or 'manual' in their skills is not true. There were not the facilities in many secondary modern schools for a number of children who would benefit from more 'academically-biased' courses. Similarly some bright 'academic' children would benefit from being taught 'manual' skills.

6 Very few children who showed promise at secondary modern schools were transferred to grammar schools.

7 A growing number of pupils attending secondary modern schools wanted to continue their education past the school-leaving age, but provision for them was not widely enough available.

11.4 The comprehensive system

As a result of the dissatisfaction that had developed over the tripartite system, and the weight of sociological evidence showing the perpetuation of class differences (two examples are given in *Further reading* at the end of this chapter: Jackson and Marsden's *Education and the Working Class* and Douglas's *The Home and the School*) a number of education authorities began to introduce comprehensive schooling as an alternative system in the 1960s. The term 'comprehensive' is a general one as there are many kinds of comprehensive schools: some are *all-through* comprehensives which means that pupils may complete their entire secondary education in the same school from eleven years to eighteen, others have pupils transferred from middle schools at the age of twelve to fourteen, and in other authorities pupils attend comprehensive high schools and may choose to go to sixth form colleges at the age of sixteen. Some comprehensive schools stream, band or set their pupils by general ability or subject ability, while others have little academic division in their classes. Some of the arguments about these different systems are discussed in Topic 12.3. The common feature of all comprehensive systems is that children of wide-ranging abilities attend the same secondary school. The introduction of comprehensive education has itself aroused as much controversy as the tripartite system. It has become a political football between successive Labour and Conservative governments and local authorities.

The Labour Government elected in 1964 decided to allow the development of comprehensive education by local authorities, who considered the needs of their own area and then put forward a plan to the Department of Education and Science. According to Circular 10 issued by the Department of Education in June 1965, LEAs were expected to submit a plan for a comprehensive system of secondary education, but by 1978 there was still a minority of local councils that had not complied, and no comprehensive education was available in their areas. The Conservative Government elected in 1970 back-pedalled over the question of extending comprehensive education. In its White Paper, *Education: a Framework for Expansion* (December 1972), very little was said upon the subject of secondary education and only an extra £10 million a year was allocated for spending upon the worst secondary schools in 1975–6 and 1976–7. The White Paper was followed by a letter to all education authorities requesting them to limit their bids for money for secondary school improvements to one project which the LEA regarded as outstandingly urgent. The main criterion suggested by the Department of Education was that improvements should be made where most of the teaching accommodation was constructed before 1903. The most important change in secondary education in recent years has been the growth in comprehensive education (see Table 4.4). The Labour

Government elected in 1974 expressed its determination to withdraw the State subsidy from direct grant schools.

Year	Percentage of secondary pupils in comprehensives
1950	0.3
1960	4.7
1968	20.0
1969	26.0
1970	30.8
1971	35.9
1972	41.1
1973	47.0
1974	57.4
1975	64.3
1979	80.0

Table 4.4   The expansion of comprehensive education in England and Wales

In 1980 eight out of ten secondary pupils in England, and nine out of ten in Scotland and Wales, were in comprehensive schools.

Advantages of comprehensives

1   The abolition of the eleven-plus examination took a great strain away from pupils who were being carefully prepared for this examination, often to the exclusion of more socialising influences. It also allowed the schools to enlarge their educational horizons, and not to concentrate such a large proportion of their resources upon securing eleven-plus passes.

2   Comprehensive schools are often able to provide greater resources and the *economies of scale* which accompany large institutions: a small secondary school might not be able to provide large, well-equipped laboratories. The distribution of pupils to teachers (*pupil–teacher ratio*) decreases as a school gets larger.

3   The expansion of the comprehensive school system has been accompanied by the concept of the 'Open Sixth' (or *new sixth former*) where young people are able to remain at school in voluntary attendance after the age of sixteen to increase their number of CSE or GCE 'O' Level passes, or to prepare for further educational advancement such as GCE 'A' Level.

4   There is not likely to be such a wastage of talent, particularly among working-class children and late-developers.

Disadvantages of comprehensives

1   It is often said that an individual pupil loses his or her identity in such a large institution. Although the comprehensives may attempt to overcome this difficulty by dividing into lower, middle and upper sections, and by having year tutors and form tutors, nevertheless there is difficulty in developing individuality.

2   There are also diseconomies of scale especially where a comprehensive school is not purpose-built: it may take some pupils ten minutes to travel from one part of the school to another.

3   It is contended that where there is no streaming and selectivity and all the pupils in one age group are taught as a unit, the brighter pupils are held back. In the early seventies it was apparent that in spite of substantial achievements the comprehensive schools were not securing as large a proportion of university entries (especially to Oxford and Cambridge) as were the traditional grammar schools.

4   In spite of their attempts to provide an egalitarian society, comprehensives have been accused of being just as meritocratic as the old selective schools. In an article in *Comprehensive Education* (Number 13, 1969) Marsden suggests that the continuation of streaming in a comprehensive school is damaging to pupils' morale and educational performance.

5   It is difficult to ensure the full recognition of parents' choice and still establish schools containing pupils from all the ability ranges; even when comprehensives are neighbourhood schools, they may be made up of pupils either from middle-class or working-class families, tending to create inequality in educational opportunity.

The secondary schools were faced with problems when the school-leaving age was raised in 1972–3. There were almost a third of a million more pupils between the ages of fifteen and sixteen in the mid-1970s. Many LEAs were unable to offer secondary schools any more financial help towards going comprehensive except from monies available for raising the school-leaving age. Therefore, the advent of the comprehensive schools and the raising of the school-leaving age to sixteen have both been retarded in their scope by the lack of financial resources. Secondary schools will have to broaden their outlook and change their methods to cope with the challenge of the raising of the school-leaving age. The Government Social Survey carried out in 1968 revealed that teachers' ideas of the aims of education were very different from those of their pupils and of their pupils' parents. It is still necessary for the schools to impart a general basic education, but young leavers will expect courses geared to their vocational and social needs and to the activities which are provided for them outside the school. Pupils leaving at fifteen, and their

On behalf of all your teachers, Ronald, I cannot express too deeply our sorrow that the end of term brings us to the parting of the ways.

parents, placed great stress, according to the Government's report, on the school's function to help towards a good job and teach them such useful aspects of life as how to handle money sensibly and speak easily. The teachers tended to place the greatest emphasis on developing character and personality, and thought that their pupils rated earning power above job satisfaction. The government survey indicated a gap here between the ideas of the school and the ideas of the pupil. The schools are not entirely to blame. When the school-leaving age was raised to fifteen in 1944, there were great hopes of clear-cut educational advancement especially in the secondary modern schools. Unfortunately, because of patchwork changes, lack of money and old-fashioned curricula, the expected progress has not been maintained. Secondary modern schools were not given the beneficial staffing ratios, laboratory and athletic facilities which would allow the potential benefits of the raising of the school-leaving age to be fully realised. There are cynics who believe that the Government raised the school-leaving age in 1972–3 as a cheap way of reducing unemployment. However, this is an unfair criticism because the schools had planned, or ought to have planned, for this move over a period of eight years from the time the scheme was announced. The Schools Council, which receives about £4 million from central and local government, commissioned a secondary school curriculum survey in order that methods of teaching should be rethought and the educational diet offered to secondary school-leavers should be more in tune with the requirements of society.

Unit 12 Education and Social Class

12.1 Socio-linguistics and early learning

Whilst most of the major developments in education over the past hundred years have been in the secondary and higher fields, over the past twenty years a quiet revolution has been taking place in the primary sector. When a child enters the secondary school it is expected that he or she will have acquired the basic skills of reading, writing and arithmetic so that the more specialised subjects of the secondary school curriculum can be undertaken. A child's performance in the secondary school will therefore be dependent to a large degree upon the kind of schooling received at primary level. However, before a child even enters the primary school home background will have played its part and will continue to be important in these earliest years at school. In the process of socialisation, mainly carried out between the home and the school, relationships with others are important. In school these are twofold:

1 *Pupil–teacher relationships* During the school day the teacher replaces the parent as the main adult influence on a child's life. The younger or more emotionally unstable a child is, the more important this relationship will become. For this reason children in primary schools have a class teacher who is with them most of the day, and remedial classes spend more time with their class teacher. Because a teacher must divide her or his time among the whole class, the role of the parent is never entirely duplicated. A teacher may have different standards from the parents, and because a school is an institution on a larger scale than the home there is a difference in the child's environment. A good teacher, especially of young children, tried to bridge the gap between home and

school as much as possible by contact with the parents. As we grow older and enter secondary education the specialist disciplines of the teachers do not always allow for the special relationship with the pupils, and this may be passed on to the form teacher or year tutor. In the secondary school situation the pupil learns to rely less directly upon the teacher and more upon himself to achieve success, thus the secondary school teacher has a different role from that of the primary teacher. Douglas's findings in *The Home and the School* stress the importance of the pupil–teacher relationship.

2   *Inter-pupil relationships*   The classmates, or *peer group*, usually form the basis of friendships in school. Sometimes groups of special friends develop within the class; this can be seen when sides are picked for a game of football, or by where children choose to sit. Each group has its own values and means of self-identification, sometimes with a special language or slang, or with the exchange of presents on birthdays or at Christmas. Very young children imitate their parents in games of 'mothers and fathers'; as they grow older boys will start to play tougher games, adopting a tougher masculine role. Because there are so many other children of the same age group around, school is an excellent place for this aspect of the socialisation process. The modern trend of smaller families means that the peer group in school has an increasingly important role to play in a child's socialisation.

Many studies have shown that children of working-class backgrounds are less successful in school than those from middle-class homes. One important study has been Brian Jackson and Dennis Marsden's *Education and the Working Class* (Penguin), but many other sources also reveal that working-class children start school with a disadvantage which is rarely overcome. This disadvantage has nothing to do with inherited intelligence (as children with working-class parents who have been adopted into middle-class homes at an early age achieve the same success as do middle-class children) but has much to do with the home background. This is not to say that there is anything wrong with a working-class background, indeed many working-class children enjoy advantages over middle-class children in other ways, but the values of society are largely middle-class values and success is often measured in terms of achievement at school and the kind of job that one has. Achievement at school we may term *scholastic achievement*. Home background is determined by the many *socio-cultural* factors. Why do middle-class children do so much better at school than working-class children? One explanation is given by Basil Bernstein in an article entitled 'Social Class and Linguistic Development: A Theory of Social

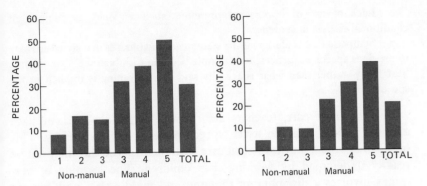

Figure 4.1a   Children with poor problem arithmetic score
Figure 4.1b   Children who have below-average oral ability
Source: From Birth to Seven, *a survey made in 1972 by the National Children's Bureau of 17 000 children born in the week 3 to 9 March 1958)*

Learning' (Chapter 24 of *Education, Economy and Society*, edited by Halsey, Floud and Anderson, Collier-Macmillan, 1961).

Bernstein maintains that it is a lack of ability in language on the part of working-class children that hinders their success. The ability to read and write is slowed down, and because so many intelligence tests are based on skill with words the middle-class children have a considerable advantage. Intelligence tests involving arithmetic do not show such a difference between children of middle- or working-class backgrounds (see Figure 4.1). Because language is so important in schools (we must be able to read and write as the first essential skill) middle-class children perform much better. Bernstein suggests that there are two kinds of language, the *restricted code* (public language) and the *elaborated code* (formal language). The restricted code is spoken in the homes of working-class children, and is characterised in a number of ways. The elaborated code is a middle-class speech pattern (this has nothing to do with accent) which can convey more complicated meanings. Even the thought processes are affected by the use of language, and a child who is able to use the elaborated code may think more clearly and grasp new ideas more readily.

Some examples of the restricted code are:

1   Short and simple, often unfinished, sentences.
2   Repetitive use of conjunctions, such as 'so', 'then', 'and', 'because'.
3   Little use of subordinate clauses.
4   Muddled information as there is digression from the subject.
5   Limited use of adverbs such as 'thoroughly', 'impatiently', 'hastily'.

6 Lack of use of impersonal pronouns such as 'one', as subjects of conditional clauses or sentences.

7 Sympathetic circularity: using statements and phrases that signal answers to previous speech sequences, for example 'wouldn't it', 'you see', 'you know', 'just fancy' rather than what is actually said. The meaning is implicit in the speech.

For the most part, teachers are themselves middle-class, or have adopted middle-class life styles, speech patterns and vocabulary. This means that unless they take great care with their speech they may not be readily understood by working-class children. The learning of new things involves a discipline of thought, and middle-class children are more often better prepared for such mental discipline at an earlier age.

In Britain a quarter of all homes have fewer than a dozen books. Middle-class children are more likely to enjoy the benefits of early reading books and hear a wider vocabulary. Often they are taught the advantages of *deferred gratification*: to put off immediate pleasure or satisfaction and to enjoy it more after something has been accomplished, for example not to watch television until the toys have been cleared up, or, when older, not to go out until homework is finished. Middle-class children are more concerned with achievement, as the virtues of education and a good career are emphasised by their parents. The middle-class child is more likely to understand some of the complexities of relationships. The following is an example of the difference between a working-class mother and child and a middle-class mother and child in a relationship which is changing as a child misbehaves:

Working-class mother: 'Don't jump in the puddles!' (Child continues jumping.)
Middle-class mother: 'Please keep out of the puddles, or you new shoes will be ruined.' (Child continues jumping.) 'If you don't stop, Mummy will get very cross.'

The working-class child is given a simple direct order; when the order is disobeyed the consequences are immediate and possibly painful. The middle-class child is, by way of contrast, informed why he should not jump in the puddles; when he still disobeys he is given a warning signal 'if' of the possible consequences. Reasons and consequences are given to the middle-class child, while the working-class child is simply given an order. This is a stereotype example, but in the school the middle-class child will have been prepared to expect reasons for, and consequences of, learning.

The primary stage extends from the age of two to eleven years and includes nursery, infant and junior (or middle) schools. Nursery schools have been very few in number until the 1970s; the Government's White Paper of December 1972, *Education: A Framework for Expansion*, promised that in the next ten years nursery education would be made available to the two-to-five year olds whose parents wished them to have it. Apart from the clamour for the extension of nursery education by the mothers of the pre-school age group and by such pressure groups as organisers of playgroups, the Plowden Report of 1967 and the Halsey Educational Priority Report of 1972 both recommended much more nursery education, since it is in these formative years that the basis of a good education is laid. As sociologists we may be interested in schemes which attempt to improve the achievement of children whose home circumstances handicap them when they arrive at school. Although the Government White Paper of 1972 pledged an increase of about 300 000 nursery school places, the Plowden target will not be achieved until 1981-2. The White Paper accepted several of the recommendations of Dr Halsey's Report and many of the nursery projects will be directed towards helping educational priority areas. The Government has not set out any hard and fast lines about the way in which nursery education is to develop; it is hoped that local authority plans will reflect local needs and social pressures. The increased scope of nursery education will help towards an earlier identification of children with social, medical and psychological problems. Most nursery expansion will be within the framework of the school structure with classes for the under-fives forming part of primary schools. Although there are many who would have wished to see more money spent upon pre-school playgroups, the National Children's Bureau which investigated twenty playgroups set up in Southwark in the 1970s found that the needs of the most severely deprived children were not best met by playgroups run by mothers. Participation in playgroup activity was often not possible for the most deprived and the mothers were the ones who were the least suitable to help. During 1974-5 £15 million was to be made available for the extension of nursery education. Most of the youngsters attending nursery schools will only be there part-time, but allowance has been made for about fifteen per cent to attend full-time, mainly for social reasons. It is expected that LEAs will take account of other provisions for the two-to-five year old age group, and prepare schemes which incorporate the contributions of voluntary playgroups, day nurseries and all other forms of day care with the school nursery classes. It will be necessary to establish the closest possible link between home and school, so mothers will be encouraged to give practical help in running playgroups and in assisting nursery teachers. There will be a great need to increase the

Young children investigating pond life in a classroom situation

Children using a gun clinometer to help them calculate the height of a church tower

recruitment of nursery assistants and to extend courses for training nursery teachers.

The rest of primary education will continue in much the same way. Compulsory education in Britain legally begins at the age of five years and usually at the age of seven children go on to their junior (or middle) schools. Some of the most exciting developments in educational practice during the last twenty years have taken place in infant and junior schools, where considerable attention has been paid to work of a creative nature and the fullest possible development of the individual child. In the past it has been frequently the practice for junior schools to concentrate upon pupils in the 'A' stream with the best teachers allocated for their tuition, while the children in the 'C' stream were left largely to fend for themselves. Although the 1944 Education Act made transfer at the age of eleven compulsory, there has been a growing feeling amongst educationalists that the transfer age of eleven was not necessarily the best, and certainly ought not to be so arbitrary. The Plowden Report recommended the ages of eight and twelve as far more suitable for transfer and many schools have been reorganised into two main age-ranges:

4-plus to 8-plus—first schools   8-plus to 12-plus—middle schools

It is not a good thing for children to experience too many changes in the learning situation during their early life: an extension of the first school period to four years gives them an opportunity to gain confidence in number ability and in reading before being moved to a different environment. The extra years in the first school gives them a continuity and greater social stability when they greatly need it and they are thus more capable of developing their *basic educational skills*. The exciting educational experiments which have been developed in junior schools have given encouragement to the extension of this period of education. It is thought by many educationalists that the children will gain considerably from an extra year in the middle school instead of being transferred to the secondary stage at eleven. It must also be borne in mind that the retention of pupils at the secondary stage from the age of eleven to eighteen or nineteen constituted an extremely long period in one educational institution.

12.2 Education and attainment

Earlier in this chapter we traced the development of the educational system and saw how the present structure evolved. The philosophy of equality of opportunity is still generally accepted, but whether this is really possible is a question still to be considered. It is perhaps true that whatever social system we live in, there will always be significant differences between us. These may be of a physical and mental nature: some of us will be taller and stronger than others, and in the same way it is accepted by most psychologists that we are born with different levels of intelligence. Professor Hans Eysenck suggests in his book *The Inequality of Man* (Maurice Temple Smith, 1973) that children born of intelligent parents are likely to be more intelligent than average, but not as intelligent as their parents; likewise, children born of less intelligent parents, although less intelligent than average, will tend to be more intelligent than their parents. If Eysenck's research is correct, there will be a movement towards an approximate average level of intelligence. It is possible to trace the intellectual progress of children (this is done regularly in many schools) as they make their way through the educational system and to measure this against common standards of achievement, such as GCE examinations. Further questions then arise:

1   Are children reaching their full potential in the school system?
2   Apart from the school, are there other factors which determine our performance in the educational system?

Already some evidence has been presented which has pointed towards the possible answers to these questions, and the underlying common factor appears to be social class. Middle-class children start school with an advantage over working-class children. Under the tripartite system the majority of grammar school places went to middle-class pupils. Public schools are inevitably the preserve of the middle class. Most students in higher education are of middle-class origin. Although comprehensive education is still comparatively new, some evidence seems to exist that middle-class pupils still perform better than working-class pupils.

$$\text{Intelligence Quotient (IQ)} = \frac{\text{mental age}}{\text{chronological age}} \quad \text{multiplied by 100}$$

If an IQ test showed a child's mental age to be 12, and his chronological age was 10, his IQ would be 120 ($\frac{12}{10} \times 100$).

Figure 4.2   *How Intelligence Quotient is reached*

Educational psychologists have long recognised the importance of preparation for learning and personality development before a child attends school. The human brain develops most rapidly in babies from being a quarter of adult weight at birth, to within 10 per cent of adult size by the age of five. In terms of our personality and facilities for learning the pre-school years are crucial. Some infant school teachers claim to be able to recognise potential delinquents at the age of six. Middle-class children enter school with a considerable advantage, and then go on to extend their chances of success inside the school system.

Jackson and Marsden in their study of eighty-eight working-class, grammar school boys in Huddersfield found a conflict between the different values of the home and school. Their achievement at school was seriously affected by such things as lack of homework facilities, and their parents' failure to understand its importance. Parental support was found to be important: only those boys who had some connection with a middle-class situation (such as having a middle-class mother) completed the course. The working-class, grammar school boys who did not have this connection rejected the grammar school values and sought support and identification with their working-class peers. Socio-cultural factors which tend to improve the chances of greater scholastic achievement of middle-class children are:

1   greater parental concern with education
2   books and speeech at home designed to help a child's vocabulary
3   middle-class speech patterns and norms of behaviour in school
4   more opportunity for travel and stimulation through educational visits
5   higher levels of parental expectation
6   the deferred gratification of 'study now and get a better job later'
7   economic provision to stay on at school after the age of sixteen
8   homework facilities (and even private tutors).

It is often thought that intelligence cannot be increased appreciably, although how to learn and accumulate knowledge can. The more middle-class the home background, teachers and schools, the better will be the pupil's response. We have been studying implications of educational ability, but the ability to pay for educational advantages cannot be ignored (see Figure 4.3).

Ability to pay still plays a part in the educational achievement of those who enter direct-grant grammar schools and public schools. At further education level, students' grants are not of a universal standard and those at universities have better provision than those at colleges of education, while some parents do not make the full parental contribution to the student's grant. Generally, a person with mediocre innate ability has

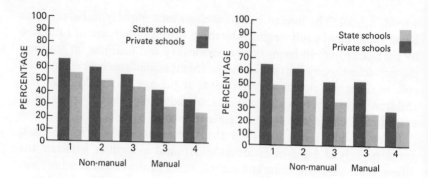

Figure 4.3 *Differences between State and private schools*
  a) *Percentage of 'good' readers at seven years old who are attending State and private schools*
  b) *Percentage of children with 'good' arithmetic ability attending State and private schools*
(Source: From Birth to Seven, *a survey made in 1972 by the National Children's Bureau of 17 000 children born in the week 3 to 9 March 1958)*

more chance of improving his position, and moving up the social-mobility class league, if he comes from a middle-class background.

Most infant and junior (or middle) schools are *neighbourhood schools* so that the schools in working-class areas are made up of pupils with a working-class upbringing, whilst those in middle-class areas consist of children with parents of middle-class status. The middle-class parents are frequently more enthusiastic about their children's educational achievements. Some working-class parents mistrust education. 'What good does it do you? Are you any better off (ie happier) as a clerk or as a teacher? . . . at the back is this vaguely formulated but strong doubt of the value of education.' (Richard Hoggart, *The Uses of Literacy*, Chatto & Windus, 1957). Dr J. W. B. Douglas in *The Home and The School* found that far more grammar school places were obtained (these were in the days when the eleven-plus examination was the yardstick) by middle-class children whose parents were anxious for them to succeed. (See Table 4.5.) Achievement then is closely related to social classes. Bernard Rosen, in *The Achievement Syndrome*, produced startling results, finding that only 32 per cent of a group of boys from the three lowest social classes scored high marks on an achievement scale, while 83 per cent of boys from the two top social classes scored high marks.

In the field of further education, highest educational achievement is found amongst the middle class. Table 4.6 shows a distinct bias in favour

	Grammar school places				
Social class	Academic record of primary school	Awarded %	Measured ability at 11 %	Teachers' comments %	Mothers' wishes %
Middle class	good	53.2	48.0	61.2	57.7
	fair	35.5	34.8	49.2	46.9
	poor	14.6	23.0	39.4	36.1
Manual working class	good	26.8	19.6	32.3	30.6
	fair	13.3	14.0	20.0	26.6
	poor	4.8	7.8	14.8	17.9

Table 4.5 Academic record of primary schools by social class: award of grammar school places, comparison of observed and expected results (Source: J. W. B. Douglas, *The Home and the School*, MacGibbon & Kee, 1964)

	% (approx.)	
Higher professional	19	
Other professional and managerial	41	Non-manual 71%
Clerical	11	
Skilled	17	
Semi-skilled	5	Manual 24%
Unskilled	2	
Not known	5	
Total %	100	

Table 4.6. Social class of students' fathers by occupation 1961–2 (Source: *New Society*, 5 November 1964)

of the middle and upper-middle classes.

Similarly, Table 4.7 indicates that students who achieve entry into Cambridge University (usually with high grades at 'A' level) number higher among those from the middle class. A similar pattern is found at a good 'redbrick' university such as Leeds, but not to the same extent.

	Cambridge %	Leeds %
Group A		
Professional, senior managers, company directors, teachers, writers, etc.	75	45
Group B		
Junior managers, business owners, shopkeepers, salesmen, clerical workers	15	25
Group C		
Foremen and manual workers	8	30
Not known	2	—

Table 4.7 Students' social class according to father's occupation, at selected universities
(Source: Peter Marris, *The Experience of Higher Education*, Routledge & Kegan Paul, 1964)

'Equal opportunity for all' seems an impossible goal while class divisions have so much bearing upon whether or not children can adjust to society (see Figure 4.4).

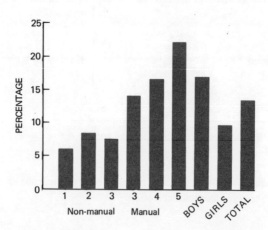

Figure 4.4 *Percentage of 'maladjusted' children in each social class, and the total percentage of boys and girls*
(*Source:* From Birth to Seven, *a survey made in 1972 by the National Children's Bureau of 17 000 children born in the week 3 to 9 March 1958)*

The third follow-up of the 17 000 children born in the week of 3–9 March 1958 (*Britain's Sixteen-Year-Olds*, ed. Ken Fogelman, National Children's Bureau, 1976) confirms the working-class/middle-class divisions in levels of educational attainment.

Nowadays, more skilled workers are required and the education system must be geared to provide highly qualified people. Although it is often feared that educational standards will decline with an extension of opportunities, there is no real proof that this happens, because the nature of educational processes may change. Kingsley Amis has complained about 'tapped untalent', suggesting that students have insufficient talent to take advantage of opportunities currently offered. However, King points out, 'There is an interesting cyclical relationship involved in which an industrialised society needs money to provide education and educated people to make money' (R. King, *Education*, Longman, 1969).

Social selection prejudicial to the working class is possibly the greatest single factor aggravating attempts to secure equal opportunities throughout society. Table 4.8 shows that only 25 per cent of male Oxford and Cambridge students had fathers whose occupations were classified as manual and agricultural workers, although 64 per cent of all employed males aged forty-five to fifty-nine years fall into these classes—forty-five to fifty-nine years being the likely age of the students' fathers.

Parental occupation	Applications %	Acceptances %	All economically active males aged 45–59 in Great Britain %
Administrators and managers	13	13	6
Professional, technical, etc.	25	27	8
Other non-manual	23	24	22
Manual and agricultural	28	25	64
Unidentified	9	6	—
Total	100	100	100
Number in sample:	7407	3625	

Table 4.8 Percentages of Oxford and Cambridge applications and acceptances by occupation of parents. (Percentages may not add up to 100 due to rounding.) (Source: *Cambridge Colleges: Statistics of Admissions for 1972 Entry*)

Great advances have been made, especially in the last hundred years: in 1861, according to the Newcastle Commission, only 5.4 per cent remained at school beyond the age of thirteen. Secondary education in Britain is now provided for everybody, and there has been a continual and rapid expansion in further education. But if this country is to compete successfully in a technological age, then a tremendous expansion of present opportunities at every stage is essential. The Robbins Report of 1963 stated that 'About everywhere we have travelled we have been impressed by an urge to educational development ... which has often been translated into plans for expansion far surpassing the scale of British plans.'

12.3   Arguments in education

At Ruskin College, Oxford, in October 1976, the Prime Minister called for a national debate on education to take place. What he meant was widespread public discussion on all aspects of schooling and educational standards. Following this lead, the Secretary of State for Education and Science took part in a much publicised debate with the Shadow Spokesman on Education, and attended several large public meetings up and down the country to hear the views of educationalists, teachers, parents, pupils and all interested in the subject. Many opinions and suggestions were made, but nothing really clear or conclusive emerged from the 'debate' except that it demonstrated a lot of concern for the subject. Education as a topic will always arouse argument, yet without an appreciation of the facts it will always be difficult to resolve such arguments. As sociologists we must be careful when weighing up the evidence on matters such as teaching methods, the changing attitudes of pupils, examination success rates, and the school system in general. We have already examined some of the arguments over the tripartite and comprehensive systems; this topic will consider briefly three further areas of controversy.

Should pupils be streamed according to ability?

Streaming means the selection of children for different classes on the basis of ability. The purpose is to make teaching more effective as children of similar levels of ability can be taught at the same pace. The eleven-plus examination is an example of streaming on a large scale. The critics of streaming argue that it is both harmful and socially undesirable, particularly for those children in the lower streams. They argue that once a child recognises his or her lower status by being in the bottom stream he or she will make little effort to improve that position. At the same time it is argued that the less able will benefit from being in the same class as the brighter pupils since they would learn from them. Brian Jackson in his book *Streaming: an Education System in Miniature* (Routledge & Kegan Paul, 1964) compared the reading progress of children in a school both when they were streamed and when they were unstreamed, and found that there were similar results. The 'top' group marginally improved in reading when unstreamed and the 'bottom' group made substantial progress when not streamed. J. W. B. Douglas, however, in *The Home and the School*, found that although the less able benefited from being with the brighter children, the bright children were held back—either by unsuitable teaching, or by lack of competition. He also found that a disproportionately higher number (11 per cent) of middle-class children were allocated to the upper streams compared to their actual 'measured ability', likewise disproportionately fewer (26 per cent) middle-class children were allocated by their teachers to the lower streams, compared to their measured ability. Most teachers would agree that it is easier to teach classes that have been streamed, particularly for mathematics and languages where the subjects require a step by step building-up on precise knowledge. Few secondary schools are completely unstreamed. Some schools operate a *setting* system whereby pupils are placed in different groups according to their ability in each academic subject, and they may come together for those subjects where ability differences hardly affect teaching methods and the pace of learning. According to Caroline Benn and Brian Simon (*Halfway There*, Penguin, 1970) the 'system of setting is a refinement of streaming, having the same objective, but attempting a more precise classification of pupils across the subjects'. *Banding* is 'a coarse, or modified form of streaming'.

Formal or informal teaching?

The basic classroom situation is that of the teacher and the class. How the teacher goes about teaching will depend not only upon the subject, but also on the teaching method preferred. In primary schools a more free and easy atmosphere usually prevails, based upon learning through discovery, spontaneity, and creative activity. In general this is termed child-centred *informal teaching*. When pupils remain seated and receive direct instruction from the teacher at the front of the class this is known as teacher-centred *formal teaching*, and is most commonly found in classes

Informal teaching to younger pupils

which are geared towards examinations in the secondary sector. The movement in recent years has been towards informal teaching, particularly in the primary and middle schools, and was the method thought most advisable in the 1967 Plowden Report. The Bullock Committee which reported in 1975 looked into the standards of literacy (reading and writing) in primary schools and found that there was almost no difference in standards whether the system of streaming or non-streaming was employed. They concluded that standards of literacy had not fallen, as many people thought, in recent years.

An interesting piece of research was published in 1976, entitled *Teaching Styles and Pupil Progress* (Lancaster University) by Neville Bennett. This was a thorough investigation of teaching methods employed in Cumbria and Lancaster primary schools by thirty-seven teachers. Their methods were placed in the categories of 'formal', 'mixed' and 'informal'. The children in the sample were tested in June before their entry into the fourth-year junior classes in September, and were retested the following June. Normal classroom conditions prevailed and the children were not placed in a 'test' atmosphere. It was found that teaching style proved to be highly significant in reading, mathematics and English. With only one exception (who was said to be an exceptionally dedicated lady teacher) the greatest progress in all three subjects, for both boys and girls, was made in the formal situation, the least progress in the informal situation, while the mixed situation came in between the other two. Bennett's findings were not, however, without critics. V. R. Rogers and Joan Barron in the *Times Educational Supplement*, 30 April 1976, pointed out that half the teachers in the survey felt the tests favoured formal teaching (one-third said there was no bias, and one-sixth said it favoured informal methods). They also pointed out that the formal teachers tended to be older and more experienced than the informal teachers; objective research should have had teachers of equal years with experience of both methods. Bennett's research team, they suggest, may possibly have been testing the effectiveness of teaching experience rather than teaching style.

Abolish the public schools?

In 1968 a commission on public schools under the Chairmanship of Sir John Newsom reported on the best way of integrating the public schools into the State system. The Commission's brief had a political background to it as many Labour Party members are opposed to the public schools, and this was a response to that pressure from the Labour Government. Page 8 of the First Report sums up the conclusions and recommendations:

Our general conclusion is that independent schools are a divisive influence in society. The pupils, the schools and the country would benefit if they admitted children from a wider social background. We recommend a scheme of integration by which suitable boarding schools should make over at least half of their places to assisted pupils who need boarding education. This change will take some time, and not all schools can be brought within the integrated sector simultaneously. The details should be worked out school by school, by a body we shall call the Boarding School Corporation.
(*Public Schools Commission*, First Report, Vol. 1, HMSO, 1968)

Public school pupils total just over 5 per cent of the school population, and yet one-fifth of university places go to students from the independent sector. Table 7.4 shows that 192 Members of Parliament, out of 514 surveyed, had been to a public school. David Boyd's study *Elites and their*

Education (National Foundation for Educational Research, 1973) shows that there has been little change over the past forty years in the proportion of public school people reaching the higher occupational groups. Attendance at a public school usually bestows distinct advantages (particularly from the oldest Headmasters' Conference Schools, such as Eton, Harrow and Winchester). Public schools are usually better equipped and have more favourable pupil–teacher ratios than state schools. Business and social connections (the 'old school tie') play some part in ensuring that better employment opportunities are afforded to public school leavers. Whether or not the prestige and influence of the public schools are declining is not the question at issue, although it is worth noting that in the ten-year period from 1961–3 to 1971–3, the number of officer cadets with a public school background attending the Royal Military Academy at Sandhurst declined from 59 per cent to 49 per cent. The main argument rests upon the desirability of having a privileged minority of school children in Britain. The supporters of independent schools maintain that everyone should be free to spend their money on whatever they wish, and that education should continue to be a purchasable commodity just as anything else. Also, they argue, why destroy something that is a success in educational terms? Independent schools are said to maintain some of the best and most traditional standards of education.

Opponents of the public school system argue that most people are not 'free' to purchase a better education for their children since it costs far more than the average family can afford. They argue that public schools *are* socially divisive, that their products exercise too much influence, and therefore this is reason enough for their abolition, or else integration into the State system, as the Public Schools Commission suggested. Simply by passing legislation to abolish or integrate the public schools may not necessarily destroy their influence, as many of the richer schools may then re-establish themselves abroad in countries such as Eire or on the Continent.

Unit 13 Further Education

13.1 Further education

Further education is a very exhaustive term covering all types of education that extend beyond the secondary stage. It may be:

1   full-time or part-time
2   vocational or non-vocational
3   academic, liberal or technical
4   social or scientific.

Further education includes a multifarious range of activities extending from the part-time day-release course of a sixteen-year-old youngster attending a technical college to the top levels of higher education including the universities. There are 700 major institutions of further education in England and Wales, including agricultural colleges, colleges of art, colleges of commerce, technical colleges, colleges of education, polytechnics and universities. There were 154 000 full-time and sandwich course students and 754 000 part-time and other (excluding adult education) students on non-advanced further education courses in 1978. We have already considered the courses that are provided mostly at technical colleges, eg Ordinary National Diplomas, Higher National Diplomas and the like. There are just over a hundred colleges of education in Britain, and their purpose is to turn out qualified teachers with a sense of vocation. The colleges of education normally take students at the age of eighteen, although their role has been modified by the Government's acceptance in 1972 of the six main proposals of the James Report:

1   a large expansion of in-service training for Britain's 400 000 teachers
2   a planned reinforcement of the process of induction during the teacher's first year at school
3   the progressive achievement of an all-graduate teaching profession
4   improved training for further education teachers
5   improved arrangements for the control and co-ordination of acceptance for teacher training
6   the whole-hearted acceptance of the colleges of education into the family of higher education.

In 1976 the Secretary of State for Education and Science announced plans to cut back drastically the number of places at training colleges. The decision was made on two grounds, the falling birth rate (see Topics 15.2 and 17.1) and the need to lower public expenditure. It does not now seem likely that the James proposals for expansion of in-service training will come about on the scale envisaged, but it is still possible that colleges of education will continue to move into a closer relationship with the other further education institutions and the period of their time devoted to pre-service training will gradually diminish.

In the seventies one of the most interesting developments in the field of

Lanchester Polytechnic

further education was the establishment of polytechnics. The first three 'polys' were designated in January 1969 and by 1973 all of the thirty proposed polytechnics were operational (see Figure 4.5). A polytechnic is similar to a university in many ways except that it puts stress upon the utilisation of knowledge as well as upon its generation, transmission and distribution. Therefore, although they can award degrees and range over the whole field of human knowledge in the same way as universities, polytechnic courses often tend to be more outward-looking so that a student's knowledge is applied in the fields of business, industry and science. The Secretary of State for Education has stated the polytechnics will be parallel in status to the universities; the main difference is that polytechnics are more orientated towards students' careers. Polytechnics have a more comprehensive student-body than the universities because they include full-time and sandwich-course students with part-time students from the surrounding areas. On successful completion of his course, a polytechnic graduate is often better qualified for a job in society than a university graduate because polytechnics afford extra practical training. Polytechnics are contributing to our society by offering the opportunity of further educational qualifications to students who may not have the necessary 'A' Level grades required by a university. The polytechnics believe that they can overcome the less high-powered academic background of students by more practical teaching methods geared closely to contemporary society and by offering longer courses of study in some cases.

There are forty-four universities in the United Kingdom offering 300 000 students (1980) a wide variety of courses at varying levels. Most however, were taking first degree courses. A useful division of the universities (though decreasingly important as the 'levelling up' in society continues), comprises the following three groups:

1   Oxbridge: the two old universities of Oxford and Cambridge established in the twelfth and thirteenth centuries.

2   The 'redbrick' or 'city' universities which began with the establishment of London University in 1836 and include such universities as Bristol, Durham, Manchester, Nottingham and Sheffield.

3   The 'new' universities such as East Anglia, Essex, Keele, Kent, Lancaster, Surrey, Sussex, Warwick and York.

The question 'What are universities for anyway?' was the title of Lord Annan's first Dimbleby lecture in 1972. Lord Annan believed the answer was simple: 'Universities exist to promote the life of the mind.' This definition may seem woolly to some people, but nevertheless it is argued

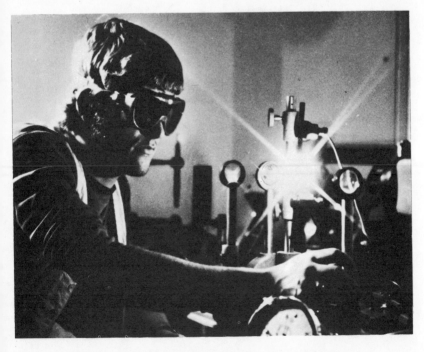

Student at Brighton Polytechnic working in a spectroscopy laboratory

that there should be a place in every society for people who are able to discover new knowledge through research or reflection. This knowledge will then be transmitted to society at large by teaching students whatever is considered to be intellectually important, so that the students themselves may ponder upon the knowledge, possibly adding to it in the pondering. Universities are not factories of knowledge. Their highest

1	Newcastle upon Tyne Polytechnic	16	Oxford Polytechnic
2	Sunderland Polytechnic	17	Hatfield Polytechnic
3	Teesside Polytechnic	18	Middlesex Polytechnic
4	Leeds Polytechnic	19	North-East London Polytechnic
5	Huddersfield Polytechnic	20	City of London Polytechnic
6	Sheffield Polytechnic	21	Polytechnic of North London
7	Preston Polytechnic	22	Polytechnic of Central London
8	Liverpool Polytechnic	23	Thames Polytechnic
9	Manchester Polytechnic	24	Polytechnic of the South Bank
10	Trent Polytechnic	25	Kingston Polytechnic
11	City of Leicester Polytechnic	26	Brighton Polytechnic
12	North Staffordshire Polytechnic, Stafford.	27	Portsmouth Polytechnic
13	Wolverhampton Polytechnic	28	Plymouth Polytechnic
14	City of Birmingham Polytechnic	29	Bristol Polytechnic
15	Lanchester Polytechnic	30	Polytechnic of Wales

Figure 4.5   *New polytechnics and college groupings*

mission is the seeking after truth so that society as a whole shall benefit from new wisdom and changing knowledge.

In 1971, the first 25 000 students were enrolled in the Open University, which awarded its first degrees in 1973, to students who had completed degree courses by using a combination of television, radio and correspondence courses together with a network of seminars, tutorials and short courses. It would be wrong to regard the Open University merely as a cheap substitute for more formal institutions of higher education. The learning process goes on throughout the whole of life, and the Open University offers opportunities to members of society who have missed opportunities at some point in the educational process: the latent potential of a generation that had fewer chances should not be lost for ever. Polytechnics and universities tend to reinforce the existing structure of society because middle-class youngsters are more able to take advantage of the opportunities offered, whereas Open University facilities allow increased opportunities to an older group and could marginally loosen the structure of society. The Open University should be regarded as an opportunity for learning 'between generations rather than within them' (Alan Hartley, 'Open Doors', *Guardian*, 26 September 1972).

Finally, there are the broad liberalising courses of adult education supplied by the Workers' Educational Association (WEA), local education authorities, certain residential colleges and the extra-mural departments of universities. The Russell Report of 1973 produced guidelines for transforming the rather patchwork Cinderella activities of the present adult education service into a more meaningful system. Maturity and motivation mean that those over the age of about twenty-two years often have more to offer to society provided their horizons are broadened. Adult education is seen both as a way of tempting people to spend their increasing leisure more fruitfully, and as a method of making them more useful members of society.

13.2 Youth culture

Since 'teenager' became a vogue word, a distinct youth culture has developed, especially in the affluent capitalist societies. It is difficult to assess the extent to which this distinctive culture has been artificially produced by commercial enterprises seeking the annual £4000 million (1980) which young people have to spend, or how far it is a natural phenomenon associated with the so-called generation gap. Many modern youngsters believe that parents ruin the first half of their life; perhaps they may find later that their own youngsters will ruin the second half. When the youth of society is given more freedom some will seek permissiveness and promiscuity, whilst others will decide to rebel against the imperfect society in which they find themselves, indulging in campus revolts or even deciding to drop out of conventional society altogether. It is not necessarily a bad thing for young people to challenge the very basis of society; a few years later they have so often settled down and accepted almost completely and apathetically the very ideals of the society which they once thought were so bad. There is little doubt that in a few years we shall be asking, 'Where have all the Hippies gone?'

The social implications of a *youth culture*, however temporary the phase, provide sociological problems. It is a time when a distinctive group are more separate from the rest of society than at any other time in their lives. The youth have their own groups, amusements, and other interests. They frequent the same discotheques, football matches, pubs and youth clubs. Youth clubs are going through a difficult period because they are stamped with the hallmark of so-called 'respectable society' from which the youth are trying to separate themselves. The increased affluence, especially of the young working classes, has been a significant factor contributing to a segregated youth culture; the middle-class youngster relying on a Government grant for further education and frequently dependent upon parental contributions, is often less able to indulge in the expensive activities of working-class counterparts. Business enterprises sponsor a distinctive non-adult culture by using the mass media to promote incessantly the sale of motor scooters, motor bikes, stereos, pop records, drinks, teenage magazines, youth gear, transistors and cosmetics. About a third of the average teenage boy's expenditure goes on cigarettes, drink and general entertainment whilst the average teenage girl spends about forty per cent of her money on cosmetics and clothes. 'This is distinctive teenage spending for distinctive teenage ends in a distinctive teenage world' (Dr Mark Abrams, *Teenager Consumer Spending*).

Perhaps it is wrong to think of a promiscuous younger generation without realising the part played by an apathetic and cynical older generation.

Our youth of today love luxury; they have bad manners, contempt for authority and disrespect for older people. They no longer rise when adults enter a room, they contradict their parents, chatter before company, gobble their food and tyrannise their leaders.

This statement was made by Socrates about 2000 years ago.

Nevertheless there are some undesirable traits shown by the youth of today that were not mentioned by Socrates, and they are far more dangerous to society than gobbling one's food. Problems such as petty crime, drug-taking, soccer hooliganism and vandalism are associated with young people. However, similar problems have always existed in some form or other, and the concept of *status ambiguity* may help to explain them. This means that some teenagers may go through a stage of not knowing whether they are children or adults when faced with certain social situations or roles to play. This may then lead to a 'conflict' situation.

The official Youth Service aims to encourage development of young people by helping them to broaden their interests, enjoy recreational pursuits and mix socially in their leisure time. The youth service does valuable work through local education authorities and in helping voluntary youth movements such as the Scouts and Girl Guides Associations (over 1 200 000 members), the National Association of Boys' Clubs (162 000) etc. The traditional youth movements provide opportunities for many young people, but more imaginative ideas are required if society is to cater adequately for today's youth. John Ewen (*New Society*, February 1972) and the Dennis Stevenson Report (*Fifty Million Volunteers*, HMSO, 1972) both advocated special co-ordinating machinery for youth work, attached to the Prime Minister's Office and under the control of a cabinet minister. Such is the importance that some sociologists attach to modern youth problems. Other ways to improve the present situation include:

1   more public funds
  2   providing activities more in keeping with the demands of modern youth
  3   'teach him how to promote change within established systems' (Harry Kidd, *The Trouble at LSE 1966-67*, Oxford University Press, 1969)
  4   encouragement for self-help. Pete and Suzie in *The Paint House* tell the story of London delinquents who came to smash up their self-programming youth club and then stayed to plaster and paint it before calling it their own. (*The Paint House*, Penguin Books, 1972).

Terms used in this chapter

stabilising function	status ambiguity
restricted code	deferred gratification
elaborated code	streaming
peer group	vocational
scholastic achievement	culture

Further reading

O. Banks, *The Sociology of Education* (Batsford, 1968)

C. Benn & B. Simon (eds), *Halfway There* (Penguin, 1970)

M. P. Carter, *Into Work* (Penguin, 1969)

E. Craft (ed.), *Linking Home and School* (Longman, 1967)

J. W. B. Douglas, *The Home and the School* (MacGibbon & Kee, 1964)

K. Fogelman (ed.), *Britain's Sixteen-Year-Olds* (National Children's Bureau, 1976)

J. Ford, *Social Class and the Comprehensive School* (Routledge & Kegan Paul, 1967)

D. H. Hargreaves, *Social Relations in a Secondary School* (Routledge & Kegan Paul, 1967)

J. Holt, *The Underachieving School* (Penguin, 1970)

B. Jackson & D. Marsden, *Education and the Working Class* (Routledge & Kegan Paul, 1962)

R. A. King, *Education* (Longman, 1969)

E. Midwinter, *Priority Education* (Penguin, 1972)

R. Pedley, *The Comprehensive School* (Penguin, 1969)

E. Reimer, *School is Dead* (Penguin, 1971)

Questions from GCE 'O' Level Sociology Examination Papers

1   In recent years what additional provisions have been made to secure better vocational training for young people at work? Explain briefly what further measures you would like to see, and why. (AEB, November 1970)

2   Explain carefully what is meant by tripartite and comprehensive systems of secondary education. What factors have tended to make English secondary education move towards various kinds of comprehensive schemes? (AEB, June 1970)

3   Boys and girls aged 15–17 day or block release for
                        further education, 1969

	Number (in thousands)	% of total age group in work
boys	200	40
girls	55	10

a   What reasons can you suggest for the sex difference in release for further education?

b   What changes would you expect during the next few years and why?
(AEB, November 1972)

4   'Every society is faced with the need to preserve and transmit its culture.'
What does culture mean in this context? What part does education play in this
process of preservation and transmission? (AEB, November 1971)

5   What are the major social factors affecting educational achievement?
(Oxford Local Examinations, 1972)

6   What, if any, is the connection between social class and educational
achievement? (Oxford Local Examinations, 1973)

7   'The importance of the relationship between home and school becomes
clearer as the child grows older.' What sociological evidence exists to support
this statement? (AEB, November 1976)

8   Give a sociological explanation of the important changes in secondary
education which have taken place during the last thirty years. (AEB, June 1972)

9   'During the nineteenth century ... public concern with elementary
education was ... the need to ensure discipline, and to obtain respect for private
property and the social order, and that kind of instruction which was
indispensable in an expanding industrial and commercial nation.'
               (*Educational and Social Change in Modern England*, D. Glass)
What are the functions of education in the United Kingdom today? (AEB, June
1973)

10   To what extent has the aim of equality of educational opportunity been
achieved? (AEB, November 1969)

11   What do sociologists mean by 'Youth Culture'? How do they account for
the growth of 'Youth Culture' in modern industrial societies? (AEB, June 1973)

12   Is the function of the educational system in this country mainly to train
people for future employment? (AEB, June 1969)

13   What contribution, if any, has the abolition of the eleven-plus examination
made to increasing equality in educational achievement? (Oxford Local
Examinations, 1974)

14   'The main factor in educational inequality is not the type of school
attended, but the child's home life before he or she even goes to school.' Do you
agree? (Oxford Local Examinations, 1975)

15   What difficulties do school leavers experience in making the move from
school to work? (Oxford Local Examinations, 1975)

16   'Innate ability is not always the most important factor in producing high
achievement at secondary school.'

a   What kind of evidence is there to support this statement?

b   State what other factors are also important and discuss them briefly.
(AEB, November 1974)

17   Summarise what the table overleaf tells us about differences in performance
at grammar school between the four groups of boys. How would you explain the
differences?

Performance at grammar school selection, during grammar school, and admission to university, by occupation of father (Boys, England and Wales 1955–1956)

Occupation of father	Top group at entry to grammar school %	Grammar school record of two passes at 'A' level %	Students admitted to university from all grammar schools %	Students admitted to university from all (incl. public) schools %
Professional, managerial and clerical	33.5	52.5	63.5	74.0
Skilled manual	45.3	32.8	30.3	21.7
Semi-skilled manual	16.3	7.1	4.9	3.4
Unskilled manual	4.9	1.6	1.3	0.9
	100.0	100.0	100.0	100.0

Source: R. K. Kelsall, *Report on an Inquiry into Application for Admission to University*, London 1957.

(AEB, Specimen Paper for New Syllabus, 1972)

18 (a) 'Education and the qualifications it may bring is one of the few ways open to the offspring of the manual working class to obtain a measure of control over their life chances . . .' Explain what is meant by the above statement.

(b) '. . . There is, however, a tendency for the children of the manual class to leave school unqualified.' What explanations do sociologists offer for this tendency? (Source: Adapted from *Discovering Society*, National Extension College) (AEB, June 1980)

19 To what extent is a child's educational future still influenced by the social background from which he/she originates? (AEB, November 1978)

5 Population
Unit 14 Demography

14.1 The study of population

In those days a decree was issued by the Emperor Augustus for a general registration throughout the Roman World. This was the first registration of its kind. (Luke 2: 1–2)

The study of population, sometimes regarded as a discipline of social science on its own, is termed *demography*. Sociologists are concerned with many aspects of demography, especially those which tell us about *social structure* and *social change*.

From the earliest times of civilisation, governments have wanted to know the size of populations, perhaps to calculate the number of fighting men available or to find out how much they might raise in taxation. The Bible records that the Emperor Augustus issued an order for a *census* of the number of people in the Roman Empire to be made. It was because of this census that Bethlehem was Christ's birthplace and not Nazareth. After the Norman conquest, William the Conqueror sent investigators throughout Britain to record details of land use and where people lived: these details were recorded in the famous Domesday Book. In the modern world demography has become more important: a knowledge of the changes in population allows governments to plan ahead. Some of the things that a government may wish to find out from a census are:

1   whether more children are being born, in which case more schools will have to be built
2   whether there are to be more elderly people, so that more money must be set aside for pensions
3   places where the population is increasing, which will need more housing, factories, roads and other amenities
4   whether people are living in overcrowded housing conditions
5   where unemployment exists, and what kind of jobs are in short supply
6   where immigrants have settled, and where emigrants have gone
7   how many people are getting married and divorced.

Once the Government and local authorities have the statistics they are able to make provision for the changes that have taken place in the population.

14.2   The census in Britain

Every ten years since 1801 the Government has appointed investigators to gather information about every inhabitant of the United Kingdom. The last census was conducted in Britain in 1981, and was one of the most detailed surveys ever carried out by a government. This survey was conducted by the Registrar General's department, which appointed several thousand temporary civil servants (mainly local government workers and teachers) known as *enumerators*. Each enumerator was assigned a certain number of households in his locality. Although computers and the most modern techniques of processing are employed, it takes several years for all the information to be processed and analysed by the Registrar General. Today the changes that are taking place in the population and in society as a whole are so considerable and rapid compared with those of a century ago, that it has been found necessary to conduct a small census of ten per cent of the population every five years: this is known as a *mid-point sample survey*. Owing to economic circumstances the mid-point survey in 1976 was not taken.

In April 1981, every householder was bound by law to give details of everyone staying in their household on the night of the census (see Figure 5.1). Included in the census were people in hospitals, hotels, prisons and ships in British ports. The police sought out vagrants to prevent people being omitted, for if each enumerator missed just one household from his list the numbers unrecorded from the census would, it is estimated, equal the inhabitants of a town the size of Nottingham.

There was some concern expressed in Parliament at the time of the 1971 census about the kind of questions that were asked. Some people felt that it represented an intrusion into their private affairs. In particular, the questions relating to a person's country of origin and their parents' country of origin were thought by some to be a potentially dangerous statistical exercise, as the information might be used later against the coloured immigrant community and their children. Yet the personal details and results of the census are to be kept strictly confidential by the Census Office, and not even other government departments may have access to the individual forms.

Census data is one of the most precise forms of demographic material, but other sources of information on population are available to the

Government. Since 1837 the registration of births, deaths and marriages has been compulsory. These figures do provide some guide to population trends, but all sources need to be supplemented by the census material. In some countries, particularly those under totalitarian regimes, registration goes much further than in Britain. In most countries in Europe, citizens are required by law to register their address with the police, and in some countries all adults must carry an identification card which contains some demographic data. The controversy that accompanied the last census was over whether Britain was becoming too 'continental'. Was the individual citizen's freedom being eroded by the introduction of questions of an economic nature, such as those about car ownership and housing conditions? There are very few people, however, who do not recognise the importance of gaining statistical information from a census; much of our knowledge of society in Britain today and in the past has been obtained from the census as well as from other government departments.

Unit 15 The Size of a Population

15.1 The population of Britain

It has been estimated that at the time of the Norman invasion in 1066 the population of Britain was 1.5 million. An increase of one million each century would bring us to the figure of 10.5 million when the first national census was conducted. The official mid-year estimate for 1979 put Britain's population at 55.9 million: one hundred years ago it was 28 million, so our population has doubled during the past century. After the 1971 census demographers estimated the population would be 63 million by the year 2001. We are likely to see some variation in this number as different trends have occurred since the last census was taken: currently 58 million is projected.

In 1798, Thomas Malthus advanced one of the first important theories of population. Malthus believed that the population increased at a faster rate than a nation's ability to produce food; consequently the population increase was threatened and limited by periodic famine. The high birth rate meant that in theory a population would double itself every twenty-five years, increasing at a *geometric rate*, but food production could not match this increase as it only rose at an *arithmetic rate*. According to

PART B

Complete a line in Part B for **every person present,** that is every person wh
a spends Census night 25/26 April 1971 in this household
or b joins this household on Monday 26 April and has not been included as pre

For any other person who usually lives in this household complete a line in Part C on the back page.

B1 Fill in this column first for **every person present.** (see note above) Write **name and surname.** Begin with the head of the household (if present). *For a baby who has not yet been given a name write 'BABY' and the surname.*	B2 Write the **date of birth** of the person.			B3 Write the **sex** of the person, (M for male, F for female).	B4 If the person usually lives here, write 'HERE'. If not, write the person's **usual address.** *For boarders write 'HERE' only if they consider this their usual address. For students and children who are away from home during term time give their home address. For persons with no settled address write 'NONE'.* BLOCK CAPITALS PLEASE	B5 Write 'HEAD' for the head of the household and **relation-ship** to the head for each of the other persons; for example 'Wife', 'Son', 'Daughter-in-law', 'Visitor', 'Boarder', 'Paying Guest'.	B6 Write 'SINGLE' 'MARRIED', 'WIDOWED' o 'DIVORCED' a appropriate. *If separated and not divorced write 'MARRIE*
	Day	Month	Year				
1st person JOHN CITIZEN	6	3	39	M	HERE	HEAD	MARRIED
	Day	Month	Year				
2nd person JANE CITIZEN	20	11	41	F	HERE	WIFE	MARRIED
	Day	Month	Year				
3rd person ALAN JOHN CITIZEN	12	6	64	M	HERE	SON	
	Day	Month	Year				
4th person MARY JANE CITIZEN	7	10	68	F	HERE	DAUGHTER	
	Day	Month	Year				
5th person EMILY MAY SMITH	22	9	14	F	10, LONG ROAD NEWTOWN LANCS.	MOTHER-IN-LAW	WIDOWE
	Day	Month	Year				
6th person							

If there are more than six persons present continue on a new form.
(The enumerator will supply you with one if he has not already done so.)   2

Figure 5.1   Part of a Census Form

s form elsewhere.

job last week (the week ended 24th ote B7)		B8 Will the person be a **student** attending **full-time** at an educational establishment during the term starting April/May 1971? (see note B8) *This question need not be answered for children under 15 years of age.*	B9 *a* If the person was born in England or Wales or Scotland or Northern Ireland tick the appropriate box. or *b* If the person was born in another country, write the name of the country (using the name by which it is known today) and the year in which the person first entered the United Kingdom (that is England, Wales, Scotland and Northern Ireland).	B10 Write the country of birth of: *a* the person's **father** *b* the person's **mother** *This question should be answered even if the person's father or mother is no longer alive. (If country not known, write 'NOT KNOWN'.) Give the name by which the country is known today.*
on had a job even if it was only part-time temporarily away from work, on holiday. off.				
have a job tick whichever of boxes 2, 3, 4 if box 5 is ticked state the reason; for 'Student', 'Permanently sick'.				
ot be answered for children under 15 years				

---

a job at some time during the week
eking work or waiting to take up job
ending to seek work but sick ☐ YES
holly retired
t seeking work for some other reason, namely ✓ NO

a Born in ✓ England 01 ☐ Scotland
02 ☐ Wales (incl. Monmouthshire) 03 ☐ Northern Ireland
or b Born in .... (country)
and entered U.K. in .... (year)

a Father born in (country) **ENGLAND**
b Mother born in (country) **ENGLAND**

---

a job at some time during the week
eking work or waiting to take up job
tending to seek work but sick ☐ YES
holly retired
t seeking work for some other reason, namely **HOUSEWIFE** ✓ NO

a Born in ✓ England 01 ☐ Scotland
02 ☐ Wales (incl. Monmouthshire) 03 ☐ Northern Ireland
or b Born in .... (country)
and entered U.K. in .... (year)

a Father born in (country) **ENGLAND**
b Mother born in (country) **SCOTLAND**

---

a job at some time during the week
eking work or waiting to take up job
tending to seek work but sick ☐ YES
holly retired
ot seeking work for some other reason, namely ☐ NO

a Born in ✓ England 01 ☐ Scotland
02 ☐ Wales (incl. Monmouthshire) 03 ☐ Northern Ireland
or b Born in .... (country)
and entered U.K. in .... (year)

a Father born in (country) **ENGLAND**
b Mother born in (country) **ENGLAND**

---

a job at some time during the week
eking work or waiting to take up job
tending to seek work but sick ☐ YES
holly retired
t seeking work for some other reason, namely) ☐ NO

a Born in ✓ England 01 ☐ Scotland
02 ☐ Wales (incl. Monmouthshire) 03 ☐ Northern Ireland
or b Born in .... (country)
and entered U.K. in .... (year)

a Father born in (country) **ENGLAND**
b Mother born in (country) **ENGLAND**

---

a job at some time during the week
eking work or waiting to take up job
tending to seek work but sick ☐ YES
holly retired
ot seeking work for some other reason, namely **PRIVATE MEANS** ✓ NO

a Born in ☐ England 01 ✓ Scotland
02 ☐ Wales (incl. Monmouthshire) 03 ☐ Northern Ireland
or b Born in .... (country)
and entered U.K. in .... (year)

a Father born in (country) **SCOTLAND**
b Mother born in (country) **SCOTLAND**

---

a job at some time during the week
eking work or waiting to take up job
tending to seek work but sick ☐ YES
wholly retired
ot seeking work for some other reason, namely ☐ NO

a Born in ☐ England 01 ☐ Scotland
02 ☐ Wales (incl. Monmouthshire) 03 ☐ Northern Ireland
or b Born in .... (country)
and entered U.K. in .... (year)

a Father born in (country)
b Mother born in (country)

3

PLEASE TURN OVER TO THE NEXT PAGE ➞

Malthus, no normal increase in food production would be sufficient to sustain a population at a constant rate of growth.

Apart from the Irish potato famine of 1845–7 the population did maintain a steady growth rate (Figure 5.2), and people are better fed now than ever before in Britain. Although Malthusian theory has not applied in this country, it has some validity in countries like Bangladesh or Puerto Rico where food supplies barely keep pace with the population increase. Many demographers accept the broad principles of Malthusian theory for the underdeveloped countries, yet advanced industrial nations have

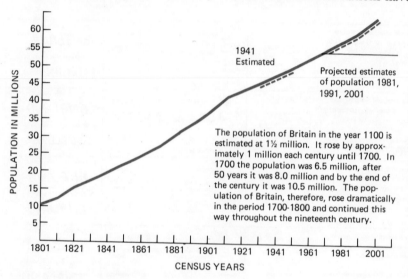

Figure 5.2   Population of the United Kingdom 1801–2001

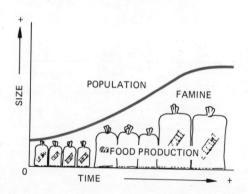

Figure 5.3   Malthus's projection of food production and population growth in theoretical terms

been able to match population increase with sufficiency in food
production through imports, and in some cases have obtained a surplus of
agricultural products. The demographic factors of birth rate, death rate,
immigration and emigration will affect the size of a population. Social and
economic conditions influence these four factors and help to explain why
Malthus was wrong in his predictions when they are applied to the
technologically advanced countries of the world.

15.2   The birth rate

Demographers usually express the birth rate in numbers of live births per
thousand of the population. This is termed the *crude birth rate* because it
is only an approximate measure of fertility: a more accurate figure would
be obtained if only the numbers of women of child-bearing age were
considered. The crude birth rate (see Figure 5.4 and Table 5.5) will tell
demographers and sociologists something about family sizes in a
country: a decline in birth rate will mean that the size of families is
decreasing, although the overall population may be increasing due to
people living longer, or more people entering the country than leaving it.
The effect of family size on the socialising function of the family has been
mentioned in Chapter 3, but its wider importance in demographic terms
must also be understood.

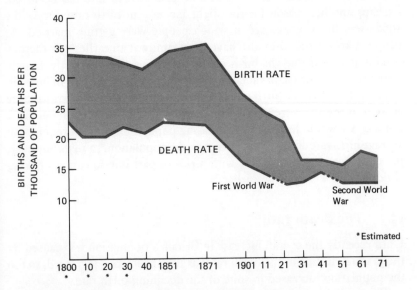

Figure 5.4   *Crude birth and death rate in Britain 1800–1971*

During this century the birth rate in Britain has declined steadily, except during the periods which followed war-time in 1920 and 1947, when servicemen returned to their wives from whom many had been separated for some time. The birth rate remained fairly constant at sixteen live births per 1000 in the inter-war years; after the last war it rose slightly but the latest figures (1979) show an uneven decline to a rate of 13.0 per 1000 live births. It would be difficult to give precise reasons for the stability of the birth rate this century, yet we may reasonably assume a number of factors:

1   The general rise in standards of living has been attributed to, and recognised as being made more possible with, smaller families.

2   As women have improved their status and have gone out to work in greater numbers they have not wished for large families and constant child-bearing.

3   Improved contraceptive techniques and the greater availability of these devices have allowed better family planning.

4   The provisions of the Welfare State have meant that parents need not rely upon their children to support them in old age.

The slight rise in the birth rate during the 1960s may have been due to improved economic conditions: the upper professional classes have always tended to have larger families, and better material circumstances and upward social mobility for some could have caused them to follow this trend, yet most recently a decline in the birth rate has occurred. Perhaps another reason for the slight increase in birth rate during the 1960s was the younger age at which people were getting married. As people marry earlier they also have their family at an earlier age, thereby making it appear that the birth rate is increasing. Very recently, largely owing to economic factors such as the dramatic rise in the cost of housing in the early 1970s, the birth rate fell low enough to give a zero growth rate in 1976. If the 1970s trend had continued, with the lowest birth rate since the war, we would have had a decreasing population, since it requires an average birth rate of 12 per 1000 to renew the population. In 1978, however, the trend was reversed again, with a rise in part due to couples having children that were put off earlier.

15.3   The death rate

Until recently the overall increase in Britain's population was caused by the gradual decline in the death rate: as life expectancy increased, so too the population increased in spite of the declining birth rate.

The *crude death rate* is the number of deaths as a proportion (per 1000) of the total population in a given year. A century ago the crude death rate was twenty-two per 1000; by the turn of the century it was sixteen per 1000; since 1960 is has remained more or less constant at just over twelve per 1000, as can be seen in Table 5.1b below.

The reasons for the decline in death rate may be directly attributed to such things as:

1   advances in medical science
2   improved hygiene and sanitation
3   better feeding
4   improved living conditions and housing.

Advances in medical science and better social and economic conditions have helped to raise the life expectancy of people from fifty years in 1900 to an average of seventy-four years today (see Table 5.1a).

			per 1000
1841	41 years	1930–32	17.2
1871	43 years	1950–52	14.1
1901	50 years	1960–62	13.1
1931	61 years	1966	12.9
1971	71 years	1972	12.6
1977	74 years	1975	11.8
1979 (males: 70 years		1978	12.0
females: 76 years)			

Table 5.1a Life expectancy in the United Kingdom

Table 5.1b Crude death rate in the United Kingdom

Four stages in Britain's population growth

Stage one: until 1750 Until about 1750 the rate of growth was slow. This period was one with a high birth rate and a high death rate. Poor agriculture and diet, lack of knowledge of medicine and hygiene, and occasional plagues were the principal factors influencing the slow population growth of about one million each century from the year AD 1000. After 1750 the brown rat predominated over the black rat, leading to the elimination of plagues.

Stage two: 1750–1870 During this time Britain's population trebled owing to a high birth rate and a falling death rate. Agriculture improved with higher yields and better stock through breeding. The discoveries of the industrial revolution and the development of the factory system

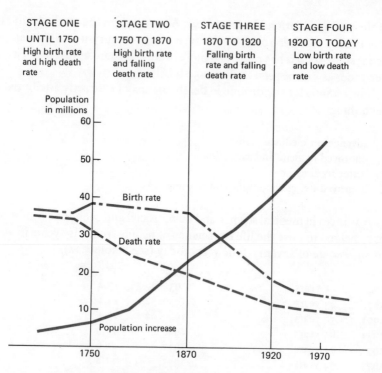

STAGE ONE | STAGE TWO | STAGE THREE | STAGE FOUR

UNTIL 1750 | 1750 TO 1870 | 1870 TO 1920 | 1920 TO TODAY

High birth rate and high death rate | High birth rate and falling death rate | Falling birth rate and falling death rate | Low birth rate and low death rate

Population in millions

Birth rate

Death rate

Population increase

1750 · 1870 · 1920 · 1970

Figure 5.5   Four stages in Britain's population growth

brought people to the towns. From 1840 onwards public health measures controlling sanitation and water supplies were beneficial as people lived in cleaner conditions with less risk of disease.

Stage three: 1870–1920   A falling birth rate and falling death rate slowed down the rate of population growth. Plentiful food from imports as well as home production ensured adequate feeding for most people. Bye-laws and government control of hygiene and sanitation became more stringent. Medicine made significant advances and life expectancy increased. Family sizes fell as birth control became widely practised. Living standards rose.

Stage four: 1920 till today   The modern period has a low birth rate and a low death rate. Infant mortality is negligible, and life expectancy has greatly increased. A gradual, slow increase in population has occurred, due primarily to the increased life expectancy. The Welfare State and higher living standards have meant a minimum provision of welfare for all and better material well-being. Epidemic diseases have been almost eradicated, while concern about the environment has grown.

15.4   Infant mortality

Infant mortality is the death rate of children born alive but who die before the age of one year, normally expressed per thousand live births. The considerable decline in infant mortality is an important factor of increased life expectancy. The infant mortality rate is used frequently as an index of social and economic progress. Although social and economic advances were made in late Victorian times, the infant mortality rate remained around the figure of 150 per 1000. The failure to apply knowledge of medical science and the poor living conditions of a great number of the working class did not help to alleviate conditions until the first decade of the twentieth century. Only when poverty decreased, standards of hygiene improved, and the midwifery services were extended, was there a noticeable decline in infant mortality (see Table 5.2).

Boys have a higher infant mortality rate than girls. In 1978 14.8 boys per 1000 died under the age of one year. The rate for girls in the same year was 11.7 per 1000.

The introduction of penicillin, and the development of more effective vaccines during the war further lowered the infant mortality rate. Since 1945 the figure has continued to fall, but not so dramatically.

Date	Rate	Date	Rate
1851	154	1941	49
1891	153	1951	30
1901	128	1961	22
1921	72	1980	15

Table 5.2   Infant mortality in the United Kingdom per 1000 live births, 1851–1980

Other industrial countries have experienced similar trends in their infant mortality rates; Britain lags behind certain European countries, but is better than others:

Italy	26	France	15
West Germany	23	Canada	15
Eire	18	Japan	11
Belgium	17	India	139

Table 5.3   Comparison of infant mortality rates
(Source: UN Demographic Yearbook, 1974)

In South Africa there are marked differences in the approximate rates for different races:

Whites: 20   Blacks and coloured: 100   Asians: 60

These figures reveal the importance of social and economic conditions to survival in infancy. The poorer nations have the highest infant mortality and the lowest life expectancy. In most countries of Africa, Asia and South America it is estimated that half the children die before reaching fifteen years, while in Europe the average figure for child deaths before fifteen years is about five per cent. The situation in India today can be compared to Britain a hundred years ago in terms of infant mortality.

15.5   Emigration and immigration

During the nineteenth century, and for the first thirty years of the present century, the number of people leaving Britain (an estimated 20 million) exceeded the numbers entering. Over the twenty-year period of 1931–51 some 465 000 immigrants entered Britain, and since 1951 there has been an excess of about 250 000 emigrants over immigrants. Some controversy has arisen over the actual numbers of immigrants in Britain, particularly those coming from Commonwealth countries since 1945, and it is important therefore to establish as accurately as possible the amount of migration to and from Britain.

For almost four centuries Britain welcomed migrants from other countries. Most of these immigrants were refugees from religious and political persecution in Europe, such as the Huguenots from France in the seventeenth century and Jews since the time of Oliver Cromwell. Since the middle of the last century, Irish immigrants have come in an almost constant flow to England and Scotland. Precise figures of immigration from Eire do not exist since the creation of the Republic some forty years ago when free access was granted together with immediate economic and political rights on entry; it is estimated, however, that there is an inflow of some 10 000 Southern Irish immigrants each year. Jewish migration occurred in two main phases, during the 1880s and 1890s when the Jews escaped from the pogroms in eastern Europe, and during the 1930s when they were refugees from Nazi persecution in central Europe. Various other national groups, such as Poles and Czechs, came to Britain to serve with British forces during the war and remained afterwards. After the war a number of Europeans returned to Britain as former colonial countries were given their independence.

To many people the term 'immigrant' is synonymous with the coloured immigrants from Commonwealth countries in the Caribbean, India and Pakistan. According to the Institute of Race Relations, 620 000 immigrants from India, Pakistan and the Caribbean entered Britain between the years 1955 and 1967 (see Figure 5.6). An Act of Parliament in 1962 gave the Government power to restrict the number of people entering Britain from the Commonwealth: this and subsequent restrictions have reduced the number of Commonwealth immigrants to a tiny fraction of the numbers that entered Britain on British passports before 1962. The coloured population of Britain is less than four per cent of the total population: increasingly this percentage is made up of the

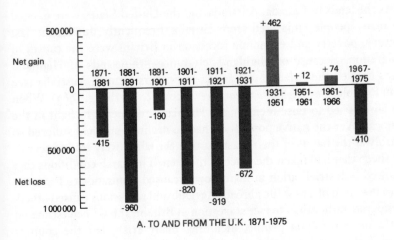

A. TO AND FROM THE U.K. 1871-1975

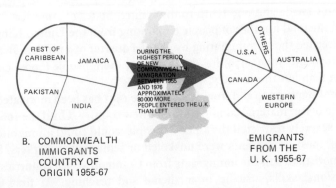

B. COMMONWEALTH IMMIGRANTS COUNTRY OF ORIGIN 1955-67

EMIGRANTS FROM THE U.K. 1955-67

Figure 5.6   *Migration*

children of New Commonwealth parents who were born in the United Kingdom. Not as immediately recognisable as Commonwealth immigrants or their descendants are several thousands of immigrants of European origin and those from Australia, Canada, New Zealand and South Africa who have entered Britain in the past thirty-five years. Excluding those on the diplomatic staff and in the armed forces, some 25 000 United States citizens are resident in the United Kingdom, and a further 75 000 citizens of other European countries. In 1973 Britain entered the European Economic Community, membership of which provides for the free mobility of labour throughout the nine member countries, so the number of European migrants to and from Britain may fluctuate more than in previous years.

As the lands of Canada, Australia and the United States were opened up many people emigrated from Britain. Frequently during the last century, poverty and economic recession in Britain were the causes of emigration. Because of Highland 'clearances' thousands of Highland Scots crossed the Atlantic to Canada and others went to Australia (see John Prebble, *The Highland Clearances*, Secker & Warburg, 1963). When the lairds tried to raise men for the Highland regiments to fight in the Crimean War the native population had so declined and had suffered so terribly at the hands of their masters, that the lairds were told to recruit the sheep that had taken the place of the men. The harsh conditions that followed industrialisation in many towns caused thousands to leave the cities in search of a new life abroad. Agricultural recessions caused others to emigrate rather than to face starvation in Britain. It has been estimated that some 20 million people, including many Irish, left the country between the years 1830 and 1930. Most remained abroad.

Thousands have left Britain since World War II, about one-third emigrating to Australia, one-third to Western European countries, one-sixth to Canada and one-tenth to the United States of America. In this period the total number of people emigrating from the United Kingdom has exceeded those immigrating by about a quarter of a million. Between June 1978 and June 1979, for the first time, more people (6000) entered Britain than left the country.

Most migration to and from Britain since 1951 has been motivated by a belief in better material conditions in the new country. Until the 1962 Act which severely restricted the kinds of people would could immigrate into Britain, most immigrants were unskilled or semi-skilled workers. Since 1962 more than half the immigrants from Commonwealth countries have professional skills, usually in medicine and teaching. At first Commonwealth immigrants undertook work, which was often poorly paid with few chances of promotion, in industrial areas. The National Health Service could not function without the large number of Commonwealth doctors and nurses, some of whom were originally recruited in accordance with National Health Service policy when Mr Enoch Powell was the Conservative Minister of Health.

Migrants from Britain now tend to be skilled workers and many are professionally qualified. While many of the doctors in Britain come from the Asian Commonwealth countries, several hundred doctors leave Britain annually for the United States. In terms of the qualifications of those entering and leaving Britain, the balance is roughly even. The United States too operates a restriction upon numbers of immigrants, but it has been calculated that America has gained far more in economic terms from European migrants with skilled and professional qualifications who were trained in Europe than the United States has ever spent or loaned in peaceful foreign aid.

Unit 16 Population Distribution

When a government conducts a census it is concerned to find out not only how many people there are, but where the population is spread or distributed. Distribution also means the proportion of males to females, and the proportion of different age groups within the population. Where people are concentrated and live is a *geographic distribution* (Figure 5.7); distribution by age or sex is *demographic distribution*; if the census records the occupations and such things as the housing conditions of people an *economic distribution* can be calculated.

16.1 Sex distribution

For every 100 girls born in Britain today there are on average 106 boys born. As boys are often weaker than girls at birth and in infancy (page 155), in earlier times the numbers evened themselves out as more infant boys died. The advances in medical science have ensured that more boys survive than in former times, but there are more females in Britain than males. There are a number of reasons why there is a greater proportion of females: the most important one is that the expectation of life for women is, at seventy-six years, seven years more than for males at sixty-nine years (Figure 5.8 and Table 5.1a).

In 1979 there were 27.3 million males and 28.7 million females. Non-biological reasons for the greater longevity of females, which causes

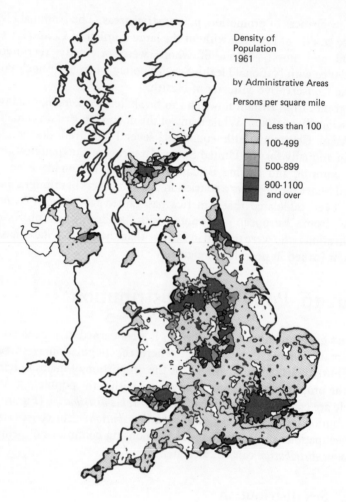

Figure 5.7 *Geographical distribution of population in the United Kingdom*

women to outnumber men in the fifty-year and older age groups (Figure 5.9), may be the more hazardous lives that men lead. To give some examples:

1 In World War I three-quarters of a million men were killed serving in the armed forces, and in the last war some 250 000 died.

2 Men are engaged in more dangerous occupations such as mining, deep-sea fishing or the building industry.

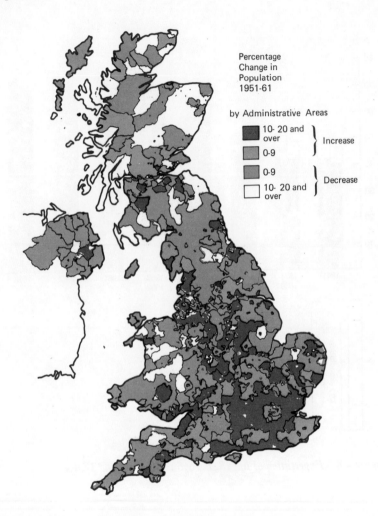

Percentage
Change in
Population
1951-61

by Administrative Areas

10- 20 and
over
} Increase
0-9

0-9
} Decrease
10- 20 and
over

Reproduced by courtesy of the Central Office of Information

3 Men are the majority of drivers: in 1975 six and a half thousand people
died in road accidents.

4 Because they smoke more than women, men are more prone to diseases
associated with smoking such as lung cancer which claims eight times as many
men as women.

The risks to women in pregnancy and child-birth have been greatly
decreased: in 1950 just under one woman in a thousand died in

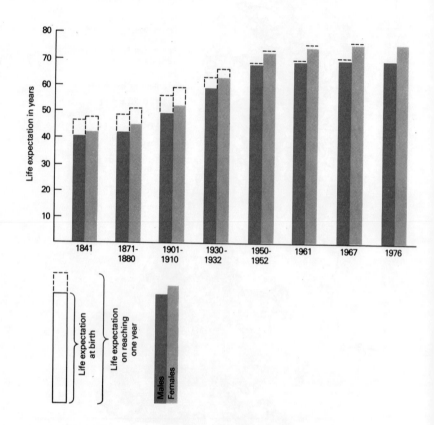

Figure 5.8   *Expectation of life 1841–1976 in England and Wales*

childbirth; today the risk is one in ten thousand. A possible cause for this
tenfold improvement is that almost all (97 per cent) births are in hospitals
and private nursing homes, yet in 1961 one in three mothers had their
babies at home.

16.2   Age distribution

Age distribution is of considerable importance to demographers,
sociologists and economists in the prediction of future trends, and in
planning for governments.

In 1979 the mid-year estimated age distribution in Britain was:

Age Group	percentage
under 15	21.6
15–64	63.7
65 and over	14.7

Those under fifteen are either infants or at school and people over the age of sixty-five are usually retired, therefore most of the working population is between the ages of sixteen and sixty-five. It is the working population who undertake the task of providing the elderly with economic goods and services and of providing for the needs of dependent young people: society always has the job of looking after those at the top and lower ends of the age scale.

Since 1871 older people have formed a growing proportion of the population as a result of increased life expectancy. In 1900 the number of

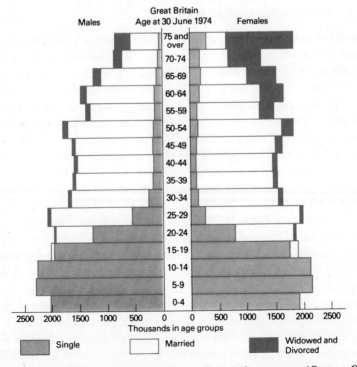

Figure 5.9   Population structure by age, sex and marital status 1974 (Source: Office of Population Censuses and Surveys)

people over the age of sixty-five was about five per cent of the population; today the figure is over thirteen per cent, and this percentage is expected to be the same at the end of the century.

Until very recently the fastest growing proportion of the population has been the under-sixteen age group, ie there has been a slightly higher birth rate. But this trend has been reversed and we shall have a more balanced population in terms of age distribution by the end of the century, as about two-thirds of the population will be of working age and the rest will be infants or of school age, or those of retirement age.

When estimates of the working and non-working sectors of the population are made, factors such as the raising of the school-leaving age and developments in education (such as more people taking advantage of higher education) must be taken into account. Improved technology and automation may mean that people will work fewer hours and choose to retire earlier. (These matters will be discussed in Chapter 9.)

16.3   Geographical distribution

One of the most important features of Britain's population is that most of us live in towns, cities or other urban areas. The reason is simple: most of the jobs are in the towns and most of us like to live near our place of work. More than a third of the population live in just seven areas: Greater London, Manchester, Birmingham, Leeds, Liverpool, Newcastle and Glasgow. Because some urban areas may not be separate local government units, but a mixture of different authorities which border one another, we refer to them as *conurbations*. Some 16 million people live in conurbations, and 22 million in other urban areas: forty per cent of the population live on just four per cent of the land area. If a line were drawn from Chester to Hull the land area of Britain would be divided in halves, but two-thirds of the population live south of that line. This concentration of population within a defined geographical area is termed *density*, usually expressed in terms of the number of people living within a square kilometre. England, which has four-fifths of the United Kingdom's population, in 1978 had a density of 355 to the square kilometre; Scotland with a tenth of the population (5.2 million), had a density of 66, and Wales with 2.7 million inhabitants, had a density of 133 per square kilometre. Northern Ireland's population is 1.5 million with a density of 109 per square kilometre. The average density for the United Kingdom is 228 persons per square kilometre (1979).

Some international statistics are given in Table 5.4.

	Persons per square km (1974)
United Kingdom	228
Netherlands	412
West Germany	247
France	98
United States	24
Canada	2
Hong Kong (1968)	3797

Table 5.4   Population densities
(Source: *Social Trends, 1981*, CSO)

16.4   Internal migration

Demographers are often concerned with the movement of population within a country. The numbers involved and rate at which this internal migration takes place have important consequences. In some places there has been considerable depopulation, while elsewhere the population has risen considerably within a short space of time. The principal motive for internal migration, as for immigration into and emigration from Britain, is an economic one. Where traditional industries such as mining or shipbuilding have lowered production or closed down, people have chosen to move away to where there are jobs in places where industry is expanding. Because the data on internal migration has been rather inadequate in the past, the 1971 census sought to remedy this deficiency by asking a question on the movement of home within the past five years.

The North of England, Scotland, Ireland and Wales are places where the highest losses through migration have occurred since the 1930s. In some of the highland areas of Scotland and Wales a considerable depopulation has resulted from a failure of the birth rate to match the outward flow of people: because the migrants are often young adults the decline is even more marked because they have not stayed to bring up children. The Midlands and South of England have gained in population through migration from other parts of the country and also from the natural increase in population. This trend was most marked during the economic depression of the inter-war years as unemployment caused many to move to the newer light industries of the Midlands and South. After the war the drift to the South continued, although it has been government policy to encourage investment in depressed areas.

Britain is one of the most densely populated countries in the world

Movement of population to the towns and cities began in Britain in medieval times. London's population more than trebled during the reign of Elizabeth I. This movement to the towns accelerated considerably in the industrial revolution of the last century. In the 1920s *suburbanisation* occurred around many of the larger towns: residential suburbs grew up where housing estates were built within easy travelling distances of the cities and larger towns. Since 1945 some thirty-two towns have been built or are being built to carry 'overspill' city populations and thereby relieve the overpopulation pressure in the cities. These new towns were planned to give their inhabitants the pleasures and benefits of living close to the countryside together with the facilities of town life. The movement to suburbs and new towns is known as *urban dispersal*. After the war the planning of urban dispersal by central and local government authorities ensured that the countryside was protected from excessive exploitation and at the same time provided accommodation. Before the war suburbanisation was often a haphazard affair as builders spread the houses along routeways into the towns and cities. This 'ribbon development' is much better organised and planned today, although there are still exceptions. Of late, the demand for housing has grown considerably, particularly around London, so that some local authorities

Modern urban development

are faced with the problem of either protecting the green belt around cities or of providing more homes. Some commuters to London have been known to travel up to a hundred miles to get to work each day. The number of inhabitants of Greater London has declined by about a million and a half since the war, half a million Londoners having left between the years 1970 and 1975. People have left the city centre mainly for the home counties of Essex, Hertfordshire, Surrey and Kent. The old centres of many of the large cities have been left almost to decay. The poorer housing conditions of these places are often inhabited by the elderly and the less well-off, and in many places New Commonwealth immigrants have moved into these central city parts. Government policy was to discourage industry in city centres but this is now being reconsidered.

Unit 17 The Future Population

17.1 A population policy for Britain?

From the beginning of this century until the mid-1950s demographers, economists and politicians were expressing some concern that Britain's population was ageing. This was due to increasing life expectancy and a declining birth rate; in the 1950s and 1960s life expectancy continued to increase, but the birth rate began to increase as well. It was then suggested that Britain's population would become too large by the end of the century. In 1961 a population of 70 million was projected as likely by the year 2001. For an already densely populated country, a further increase in population would perhaps cause many problems: environmental problems such as pollution and the loss of natural amenities; economic and social problems such as diminishing natural resources, lack of housing, strain on education and welfare services. The 1971 census revealed a decline in the birth rate and the population projection for 2001 was lowered to 63 million. After 1971 the birth rate continued to decline still further but began to rise again in the late 1970s. Demographers are now projecting a very slight increase in overall population by the end of this century to 58 million.

Date	Rate per thousand	Date	Rate per thousand	Date	Rate per thousand
1961	17.8	1972	14.8	1975	12.4
1966	17.8	1973	13.8	1976	11.9
1971	16.1	1974	13.1	1979	13.0

Table 5.5   Crude birth rate, United Kingdom 1961–1979
(Source: Social Trends 1981, CSO)

A number of reasons may account for this recent decline in the birth rate. One answer must be the greater knowledge and availability of family planning. Local authorities and the National Health Service run family planning centres where advice on contraceptive methods and devices are available. Since the Abortion Act of 1967 (see Topic 36.2) many unwanted pregnancies have been terminated legally. Economic factors, particularly the dramatic rise in housing costs in the early 1970s, or high unemployment in the mid-1970s, will also affect the birth rate. The Family Planning Association estimate that as many as one pregnancy in three is unplanned; this would suggest that with ever increasing knowledge of contraception and the introduction of simpler and more reliable methods, the birth rate and overall population will continue to decline.

We have seen how demographers have been surprised in the past, but the size and structure of a population has far-reaching social and economic consequences. Governments and local authorities may often have to take long-term planning decisions costing millions of pounds on the basis of projected population statistics. The decision to reduce by one-third the number of places in teacher training was made in 1976 on the evidence of the declining birth rate of the previous five years. Most economists and sociologists would agree that the present decline in population will be ultimately beneficial for the nation. At mid-1977, the overall population of England and Wales was 49 million, a decrease of 23,000 on the previous year's estimate and the third successive annual drop. In 1978 the slight rise in birth rate reversed this trend.

Another aspect of the recent decline in population that has interested sociologists is that the largest proportion of the fall in birth rate is among social classes 4 and 5. The number of children born in the year 1975 into these social classes has declined by thirty-three per cent compared to the average for the previous five years. In comparison the proportion born to social classes 1 and 2 has only declined by four per cent over the same period. People from social class 3 had fewer children than all other classes in 1975. This means that working-class families are getting smaller. In 1971 about one in five families with four or more children were in the manual worker group compared with one in eight from the non-manual groups. According to a report for the Office of Population Censuses and Surveys by David Pearce and Malcolm Britton in March 1977, the biggest single factor in this very substantial fall in working-class births was a marked reduction in pre-marital illegitimacies (see Topic 36.1) from the previous five-year average of 37 000 to 30 000 in 1975. Three out of four illegitimate children were born to mothers from social classes 4 and 5.

The experience of other countries such as France after the war has shown that it is fairly easy to encourage population growth, if this is desired, through generous state benefits and allowances for people who have large families, but to achieve the reverse poses many more problems. If benefits and child allowances were not given to large families, then the poor, who tend to have the larger families, would suffer more and it would be harder for them to escape the poverty trap than at present. Only a few extremists seriously suggest compulsory family limitation through sterilisation. Fortunately the latest population trends in Britain indicate a favourable balance in size and structure.

17.2 World population trends

The world population is currently estimated to be 4000 millions, and this figure is expected to reach 6000 by the end of the century, giving therefore a growth rate of just under two per cent annually. Astonishingly there are more people alive today than have ever died. This massive increase has been a fairly recent phenomenon in terms of world history, and it creates problems (primarily for the poorer nations of the world). Although the populations of advanced technological countries in Europe and the United States stabilised during the inter-war years, the populations of the underdeveloped nations continued to increase. In the richer, developed nations there is a fairly even age distribution with about a quarter of the population under fifteen years, but in underdeveloped countries the percentage of children is much greater at forty to fifty per

Abandoned children in Bogata

cent. This is one of the reasons why there will be a high population growth rate over the next generation.

The reasons for the growth in world population are similar to those which caused Britain's population to rise a century ago. The death rate is falling due to a better knowledge of hygiene and medicine, and particularly as epidemic diseases today can be controlled, through immunisation and vaccination, at relatively low cost. The lower infant mortality and higher birth rate in underdeveloped countries have resulted in many more children surviving to adulthood, but contraception is not nearly as widely practised as in developed countries. There may be many reasons for this: ordinary people are often unaware of the advantages of family limitation (in many of these countries the desire to have sons outweighs all considerations of family size); contraceptive techniques may be expensive or unknown; possibly there are religious objections to contraceptive devices, as in Roman Catholic countries; to some extent improved farming methods have helped to feed some of the growing numbers, for example a 'miracle rice' which yields twice as many grains has been successfully introduced to some countries (although periodic famines do still occur).

Whether the world's resources of minerals and foodstuffs will be able to support such a large increase in population is still in doubt. Some economists and scientists maintain that there are not enough resources to give even half the world's population a standard of living equivalent to that of the average European at the present time. Feeding and controlling the world's population growth are perhaps the greatest and most urgent problems facing mankind today, but there is also the difficulty of distribution of resources which may bring problems of ecology and environment. Malthus's dreadful predictions of a century and a half ago are a reality in some parts of the world today, and many more may suffer in the future.

Terms used in this chapter

census	distribution	geometric rate
enumerator	demography	arithmetic rate
life expectancy	ageing	crude birth rate
infant mortality	conurbation	suburbanisation
migration	density	urban dispersal

Further reading

D. Hay, *Human Populations* (Penguin, 1976)
T. H. Elkins, *The Urban Explosion* (Macmillan, 1973)
R. K. Kelsall, *Population* (Penguin, 1975)
T. K. Robinson, *The Population of Britain* (Longman, 1968)
Social Trends (CSO, 1976)

Questions from GCE 'O' Level Sociology Examination Papers

1 How useful is the population census to the sociologist? (Oxford Local Examinations, 1972)

2 The population of the United Kingdom is now about 56 million. Describe some of the important differences it would make if the population rose to 80 million. (AEB, Specimen Paper for New Syllabus, 1972)

Vital statistics

3 United Kingdom (per 1000 population)

	1902	1932	1967
Birth Rate	28.6	16.3	17.5
Death Rate	17.3	12.2	11.3

(*Source*: Registrar General U.K.)

a What are the causes of the changes in the birth and the death rates since 1902?

b Discuss the important consequences of these trends. (AEB, June 1973)

4 The projected increase in the population of the United Kingdom 1969 to 2001

	Increase due to	Per cent change	Change in millions
a	declining mortality rates	$+2\frac{1}{2}$	$+1\frac{1}{2}$
b	excess of births over deaths	$+17$	$+9\frac{1}{2}$
c	effects of immigration and emigration	nil	nil
Overall increase		$+20$	$+11$

i What is the most important cause of the increase in population projected?

ii Explain clearly what is meant by the three kinds of increase *a*, *b* and *c*.

iii What are the most important consequences that may result from an increase in population in the United Kingdom? (AEB, June 1972)

5   What social consequences would you expect from a rise in the proportion of elderly people in the population? (Oxford Local Examinations, 1975)

6   Give a sociological explanation for the following figures:

Deaths of infants under one year of age in England and Wales

Year	Deaths per 1000 legitimately born	Deaths per 1000 illegitimately born
1918	91	186
1935	56	89
1945	44	65
1955	25	32
1965	19	25

(Source: *Registrar General's Statistical Review*, HMSO)
(AEB, June 1970)

7   What are the major factors affecting fertility in contemporary Britain? (Oxford Local Examinations, 1974)

8   Suggest some causes that could account for a marked increase in the population of:
a   a simple agricultural society
b   a modern industrial society.
(AEB, November 1969)

9   *Infant mortality rates per 1000 legitimate live births, by 'social class' 1921, 1939 and 1950*

		1921	1939	1950
i	Professional and managerial	38	27	18
ii	Intermediate (clerical and lesser professionals)	55	34	22
iii	Skilled	77	44	28
iv	Semi-skilled (manual)	89	51	33
v	Unskilled (manual)	97	60	41

Discuss the above figures and explain
a   why there are differences between one group and another and
b   why changes have taken place since 1921. (AEB, June 1971)

10 Describe the main changes in the geographical distribution of the population in Britain during this century. (Oxford Local Examinations, 1975)

11 What do you understand by the phrase 'population explosion'? What are its causes and possible consequences? (AEB, November 1970)

12
*Changing distribution of the population of
England and Wales (percentages)*

	Age groups		
Year	0–14 %	15–64 %	65+ %
1851	35	60	5
1901	32	63	5
1951	22	67	11
1964	21	67	12
1979 (estimate)	20	65	15

a Account for changes in the distribution of population by age-groups since 1851.
b What effects do such changes have? (AEB, November 1970)

Country	Population	Birth rate	Death rate	Infant mortality	Expectation of life	
					Male	Female
UK	55 million	18.4	11.5	19.0	68	74
USA	200 million	19.4	9.4	24.7	67	74
India	500 million	38.4	12.9	139.0	42	41
Brazil	80 million	43.0	11.1	170.0	39	46

13 *a* Explain briefly the precise meaning of the following: birth rate, infant mortality, expectation of life.
b In which country on the Table is the population likely to be increasing most rapidly? What problems are often aggravated by a rapid increase in population? (AEB, November 1971)

14
*Population of Great Britain
People born overseas*

Birthplace	1931	1951	1961	1966
Number of people (thousands):				
Foreign countries	347	722	842	886
Canada, Australia, New Zealand	75	99	110	125
Other Commonwealth	137	218	541	853
Irish Republic	362	532	709	732
Total born overseas	921	1571	2202	2596

Population of Great Britain
People born overseas

Birthplace	1931	1951	1961	1966
As percentage of population:				
Foreign countries	0.8	1.5	1.6	1.7
Canada, Australia, New Zealand	0.2	0.2	0.2	0.2
Other Commonwealth	0.3	0.4	1.1	1.6
Irish Republic	0.8	1.1	1.4	1.4
Total born overseas	2.0	3.2	4.3	5.0

(Source: *Social Trends, 1972*, CSO)

Make use of the above figures in writing an essay on immigration and population in the UK. (AEB, November 1974)

6 Communications and the Mass Media

Unit 18 Communications

18.1 The importance of communicating

Clearly if we are to participate in the society in which we live we must communicate with other people. A great deal of communicating is performed on a person-to-person basis by the simple means of speech. We have already seen the importance of socio-linguistics in Topic 12.1 in the socialisation and development of the child. If we travel in buses, stand in football match queues, or eat in restaurants, we are likely to engage in conversation whereby we impart information or ideas, receive news or comment, and very likely have our opinions challenged by other members of society.

One of the first sociologists to appreciate the importance of communications in society was Charles Horton Cooley. He directed attention to *primary groups* and *secondary groups*. Primary groups, such as families, have very close relationships between their members; secondary groups, such as casual acquaintances, communicate infrequently and therefore have less influence upon each other. No doubt you have more acquaintances than friends, but the friends exert the greater influence upon you because of frequent personal confrontation.

Face-to-face contact is by no means the only form of communication and during the last 200 years the art of *mass communication* has become one of the dominating factors of contemporary society. Two things, above others, have promoted the enormous growth of the communication industry:

1 Inventiveness has led to advances in printing, telecommunications, photography, radio and television.

2 Speed has revolutionised the imparting and reception of communications so that local news often takes a back seat to national news, which itself is often almost eclipsed by international news. The Israeli raid on Entebbe airport, Uganda, in 1976 was followed by six books about the subject and two films within months of the event.

No longer is the possession of information the prerogative of a privileged minority. In the last century the wealthy man with his own library was indeed fortunate, but today the public library provides a free service. Forty years ago people flocked to the cinema, but at the present time far more people sit at home watching a programme that is being channelled into millions of homes. Technological progress in the field of mass communication has given rise to many social problems such as:

1 a dull uniformity of programmes that pander to majority tastes
2 the *conditioning* of people *en masse*
3 a frequent neglect of minority groups
4 an excess of power wielded by controllers of the means of communication
5 the possibility of political interference by the rulers of the day.

18.2 What do we communicate?

Communication is no longer merely concerned with the imparting of information. The modern communications industry influences the way people live in society and broadens their horizons by allowing access to:

1 information
2 education
3 entertainment.

The printing, broadcasting and advertising industries are all involved with informing, educating and entertaining. Although it is not possible to establish exact proportions, nevertheless it is fairly certain that the largest sector of the communications industry is devoted to entertainment. It is no accident that the *News of the World* is the only newspaper in the United Kingdom to top the 5 million circulation mark.

A great deal of the material which is communicated by the mass media is very valuable to the individual and to the society of which he is a part, but the vast modern network of communications is open to abuse. Some of the advantages and disadvantages have been tabulated below. No doubt further additions to the list can be made.

Advantages		*Disadvantages*	
1	People are much better informed than ever before	1	People are conditioned by the controllers of the media
2	Experiences previously enjoyed by the minority are available to the masses	2	Standardisation by mass production has meant a dull levelling down
3	A wide variety of material is available to cater for all tastes	3	Much synthetic and trivial material is communicated

Table 6.1 Advantages and disadvantages of mass communication

Sociologists distinguish two main ways by which the communications media can influence society. The mass media can be used to produce either:

1 a *cultural class system*, or
2 a *cultural democracy*.

A cultural class system tends to emerge when the media encourage class distinction, for example between:

1 classical and pop music
2 learned commentaries and human-interest stories
3 high-brow and low-brow tastes

A cultural democracy arises when the voice of the people prevails and the demands of the masses dominate the channels of communication for most of the time. Thus a continuous diet of pop-music may be provided on Radio 1, but in Britain we pride ourselves on a natural ability to compromise, so that neither a cultural class system nor a cultural democracy develops. An attempt is made to gear the system of mass communications to *the tastes of the majority*, without *minority interests* being neglected. We can see this compromise at work when we study our next topic (the press). The quality and popular newspapers provide for all tastes so that no one is forced to read one side of a case. With all communication and mass media there are two sides of a reciprocal relationship at work (see Figure 6.1).

Unit 19 The Press

19.1 What is the press?

The term 'the press' is used frequently as being synonymous with important daily newspapers; it is most probable that these newspapers exert more influence upon people's knowledge, opinions and attitudes than all the other forms of communication that are produced by the printing presses. But in the broadest sense, the press includes:

1 national daily newspapers
2 Sunday newspapers
3 provincial newspapers
4 press agencies
5 periodicals, magazines and journals
6 books of reference and fiction.

The *Willings Press Guide* of 1981 recorded that 123 daily newspapers and 14 Sunday newspapers are published in Britain. In proportion to its population, there are more newspapers bought in Britain than by the citizens of any other nation.

However, the choice of papers in Britain is relatively limited owing to the modern tendency for press mergers and closures. (The *Sun* is the only new national daily paper to have built up a large enough circulation to enable it to survive, with a successful formula of the kind found daily on its page three.) There are several principal newspaper publishing groups in Britain. They include:

1 Associated Newspapers
2 International Publishing Corporation

3 News Group Newspapers
4 Mirror Group Newspapers

All the media of communication are closely linked. For example, most of the major newspaper proprietors have shares in independent television contracting companies and are influenced by the advertising industry. The main national daily and Sunday newspapers are given in Table 6.2.

Title	Controlled by	Circulation average (in thousands) Jan-June (incl.) 1980
DAILIES		
Daily Express (1900)	Express Newspapers Ltd	2 325
Daily Mail (1896)	Associated Newspapers Ltd	1 984
Daily Mirror (1903)	Mirror Group Newspapers Ltd	3 650
Daily Telegraph (1855)	Daily Telegraph Ltd	1 445
Financial Times (1888)	Pearson Longman Ltd	197
Guardian (1821)	Guardian Newspapers Ltd	375
Sun (1969)	News Group Newspapers Ltd	3 837
The Times (1785)	Times Newspapers Ltd	315
SUNDAYS		
News of the World (1843)	News Group Newspapers Ltd	4 472
Observer (1791)	The Observer Ltd	1 017
Sunday People (1881)	Mirror Group Newspapers Ltd	3 856
Sunday Express (1918)	Sunday Express Ltd	3 100

Title	Controlled by	*(cont.)* Circulation
Sunday Mirror (1963)	Mirror Group Newspapers Ltd	3 856
Sunday Telegraph (1961)	The Sunday Telegraph Ltd	1 031
Sunday Times (1822)	Times Newspapers Ltd	1 418

Table 6.2 National Newspapers (Source: *Benn's Press Directory* 1981, Vol. 1)

19.2   Who reads what?

It is perhaps too easy to make simple distinctions between types of newspapers, between a popular and a quality paper.

The popular papers are frequently of the tabloid type and are likely to concentrate upon sensationalism, human interest stories, sport, prominent headlines and many photographs, while the quality press is of the large broadsheet format and concerns itself with informative journalism and commentaries upon politics, economic problems, literature and the arts. A suggested division into popular and quality newspapers is given below.

Popular	Quality
Daily Mirror	*Daily Telegraph*
Daily Express	*The Times*
Sun	*Guardian*
Daily Mail	*Sunday Times*
News of the World	*Sunday Telegraph*
Sunday People	*Observer*
Sunday Mirror	
Sunday Express	

These popular newspapers may find their largest readership among people of working-class origins, nevertheless it would be too sweeping a statement to say that the popular press is confined to working-class readers or that only the middle and upper classes read the quality papers. This can be seen from Table 6.3, prepared with the help of a survey conducted by the Joint Industry Committee for National Readership Surveys (JICNARS).

	Upper Middle Class and Middle Class	Lower Middle Classes	Skilled Working Classes	Lower Working Classes
Estimated per cent of	%	%	%	%
adult population	14	22	33	31
Daily Mirror	5	18	42	36
Daily Express	14	27	32	27
Sun	5	17	44	37
Daily Mail	16	30	29	24
Daily Telegraph	42	34	15	9
Daily Record	3	15	44	38
Guardian	42	34	15	8
The Times	51	27	13	9
Financial Times	53	29	12	5
News of the World	5	16	41	38

	Upper Middle Class and Middle Class	Lower Middle Classes	Skilled Working Classes	Lower Working Classes
Sunday People	5	19	41	36
Sunday Mirror	6	20	43	31
Sunday Express	22	31	28	19
Sunday Post	8	19	36	37
Sunday Times	43	30	19	8
Observer	36	34	20	10
Sunday Mail	5	19	40	36
Sunday Telegraph	40	32	18	11

Table 6.3 Readership profiles by social grades (based on July 1974 to Dec. 1974 data) (Source: Joint Industry Committee for National Readership Surveys)

Whether or not a person takes a certain newspaper will depend a lot upon his own attitudes and interests and upon the coverage given to those interests in his or her paper.

Unit 20 Radio and Television

20.1 Radio

In 1972, the BBC celebrated fifty years of broadcasting. The organisation began as a company but was established as a public corporation in 1927 when J. C. W. Reith, who had been managing director of the previous company, was appointed Director-General of the BBC.

In *Only The Wind Will Listen: Reith of the BBC* (Hutchinson, 1972) Andrew Boyle describes how, from the moment Reith took over at the BBC, he was a law unto himself. He was an authoritarian who was determined that the BBC should give what he called 'a conscious social purpose to the exploitation of this medium' and that broadcasting in Britain should be a public service, not dominated by commercial interests or government control. These views are expressed in his autobiographical books, *Into The Wind* (1949) and *Wearing Spurs* (1966).

Controversy still rages about whether it was right for Reith to encourage programmes aimed at an upper middle-class culture, in an attempt to raise standards of taste according to criteria that he alone established. Also, is it desirable or ethical to use a monopoly in broadcasting to shape the pattern of listening in accordance with what one man, or a small group of people, regard as the best public interest?

Until the establishment of local commercial radio stations in 1972, radio broadcasting in Britain had been the monopoly of the BBC. Although a public monopoly, the BBC remains comparatively free from interference by the Government of the day. The Queen appoints the twelve governors of the BBC, including the chairman, on the recommendation of the Government, but from this stage on government influence takes a back seat and the Governors are responsible for the entire broadcasting system, including the content and culture of the programmes. The Governors appoint the Director-General as the BBC's chief executive officer: he is chairman of the BBC's Board of Management and discusses all major policy matters with the Governors. Antagonism to the monopolistic position of the BBC in radio broadcasting was first expressed in tangible form when pirate radio stations, such as Radio Caroline and Radio London, took to the air. Although they were made illegal in 1967, the pirate stations proved:

1   that there was an enormous demand for non-stop pop music
2   that many firms were willing to pay to advertise on commercial radio.

Pressure from this competitive source had three main results:

1   the introduction in 1967 by the BBC of a fourth network to supply a continuous service of pop music
2   the division of the BBC's service into four main channels catering mainly for
pop music (Radio 1)
sports coverage and light music (Radio 2)
classical music (Radio 3)
speech programmes—news, drama, talks, etc. (Radio 4)
3   the establishment of local commercial stations operating under the control of the Independent Broadcasting Authority (previously the ITA).

20.2   Television

The main pattern of television services in Britain was established in 1954 when the Conservative Government authorised the setting-up of the Independent Television Authority (ITA) to provide an additional television service to that provided by the BBC. The Television Act of 1964 extended the life of ITA to 1976 and authorised the BBC to run a second television channel called BBC 2.

In 1936 the BBC launched the first regular television service, but this was suspended during the war. The earliest regular European colour television service was transmitted in 1967 on BBC 2; in 1969 BBC 1

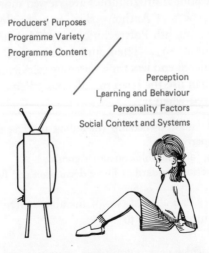

Producers' Purposes
Programme Variety
Programme Content

Perception
Learning and Behaviour
Personality Factors
Social Context and Systems

Figure 6.1   *Communication is double-edged*
(Source: J. D. Halloran The Effects of Mass Communication, *Leicester University Press)*

went into full colour. About 18 million households are equipped with television sets capable of receiving BBC and ITV programmes; half of these are colour sets. The BBC has to take the utmost care that it is not influenced by any commercial interests nor expresses political bias.

Commercial television is now controlled by the Independent Broadcasting Authority (IBA). Whereas the BBC is financed by government grants related to licence fees, the costs of independent television are met entirely from advertising revenue. The overall responsibility for administering the independent part of the television system is in the hands of the IBA appointed by the Minister of Posts and Telecommunications. The independent television programmes and the accompanying advertisements are provided by separate programme companies. The IBA performs four main functions:

1 selects and appoints the programme companies
2 transmits the programmes
3 determines the programme output
4 controls the advertising.

It is sometimes assumed that the working classes are more inclined to watch commercial television programmes than are the middle classes. There is some evidence that comedy and light entertainment programmes appeal more to the working-class audiences whilst informational and educational programmes are viewed more by the middle-class. Anthony Piepe and Anthony Box, two sociologists engaged in research at the Portsmouth Polytechnic, reported their findings in *New Society*, 25 September 1972. Their study of 272 families indicated that *home-centred* families spend less time watching television than *traditional* families. Rather than use the term middle-class, Peipe and Box called a family home-centred when it:

1 was involved in home ownership (including mortgages) compared with living in rented property
2 owned at least four durable consumer goods
3 enjoyed a superior standard of home decoration and furnishing.

Traditional families had at least two of the above attributes.

The IBA is required by law to:

1 provide services which cover information, education and entertainment
2 ensure that programmes are of a satisfactory standard and properly balanced
3 control the frequency, amount and nature of the advertisements.

	United Kingdom							
	February				August			
	1968	1970	1973	1976	1968	1970	1973	1976
Average weekly hours viewed								
Age groups:								
5–14	19.4	21.9	29.5	22.0	14.8	17.0	22.7	19.0
15–19	15.6	16.7	16.8	18.4	12.0	13.4	13.0	13.9
20–29	15.6	16.6	18.1	19.1	11.2	13.9	13.7	14.0
30–49	17.4	18.4	18.4	19.0	11.4	13.2	13.4	13.2
50 and over	17.5	18.4	19.0	20.4	11.6	14.3	14.3	14.5
Social class of adults *(15 and over):*								
A (top 5%)	13.9	14.6	15.0	16.6	10.2	11.4	11.2	11.3
B (next 25%)*	15.9	16.5	16.8	17.7	10.7	12.5	12.8	12.5
C (bottom 70%)	17.9	19.0	19.3	20.3	11.8	14.4	14.4	14.6
Overall average weekly hours viewed by all persons aged 5 and over	17.6	18.7	19.3	19.9	12.0	14.2	15.3	14.7

Table 6.4   Television viewing in the United Kingdom
(Source: *Social Trends, 1976*, CSO)

* Inserted by the author.

The IBA has the responsibility for the moral standards of its programmes. It is important that public taste is not unduly offended but it is also important that modern works should not be excluded from the TV screen because they are considered daring or incomprehensible by contemporary standards. Clearly the rights of the minority must be protected but the majority also have their standards and attitudes, and whether or not they are prepared to accept new ideas can only be determined by subjecting these ideas to their scrutiny. The members of the IBA cannot be expected to see every programme and must inevitably trust their appointed executives to use initiative in making some important but controversial decisions.

In March 1977 an official committee headed by Lord Annan reported on all aspects of broadcasting. Among their main recommendations were:

1 A fourth television channel independent of both the BBC and ITV companies should be established, run by an Open Broadcasting Authority when the economic situation allows for it.

2 Both BBC and commercial radio should be taken over by a Local Broadcasting Authority with the availability of at least one service for everyone.

3 A Complaints Commission to be established for people who feel they have been misrepresented or unjustly treated.

4 No advertising on ITV children's programmes, and the overall number of commercial breaks to be reduced.

5 There should be no obligation to show party political broadcasts on all channels, except during General Elections.

6 Some cooperation between BBC and ITV to avoid the televising of popular events such as major sports matches at the same time.

As sociologists we are concerned with the proportion of TV time devoted to the various facets of social life (education, religion, documentaries, etc.) and with the general pattern of programmes. See Table 6.4 (see also Topic 30.2 on Leisure).

One aspect of the influence of television which has been much publicised is the influence of television upon crimes of violence. In spite of all the subjective 'guesstimates' that are made about the adverse effect of television and cinema programmes, comparative studies 'lead us to doubt very strongly whether screen violence has any *direct* effect on the real behaviour of young people' (*Violence on the Screen*, by André Glucksmann, British Film, 1971). The world in which we live may be no more violent than the world of yesteryear; it is merely that through the medium of television in particular, the horrors of modern wars and

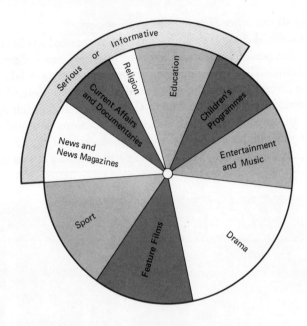

Figure 6.2   *Division of ITV programmes*
(Source: ITV, *Independent Broadcasting Authority, 1973)*

disasters are on our television screens often within a few hours of their happening. Mrs Shirley Williams, as Secretary of State for Education and Science, pointed out in April 1977 that the average young American had witnessed 35 000 killings on television by the time he had grown up. She also believed that television had a bad effect on children, particularly the very young, as they often stayed up too late watching television and were too tired for their lessons the next day. This was a cause of poor reading and writing standards.

As sociologists we must be objective and therefore be wary of those who continually stress, usually without research or evidence, the supposedly bad effects of television especially upon young people. Sociological research has suggested that 'any connection between the mass media and overt behaviour will be indirect' (L. Bailyn, *Mass Media and Children*). Perhaps the soundest contribution to the controversy about the influential effects of television has been made by James Halloran in *Television and Delinquency* (Leicester University Press, 1970); Halloran's approach to the research into the importance of television in shaping social values has been to place TV's influence in relation to all the other factors in modern society.

It does seem likely that the more a person is exposed to television, the less likely that person is to be much moved by what he sees. Certain of Dr Hilde Himmelweit's investigations (*Television and the Child*, Oxford University Press) suggest the more used a child is to films, the less he seems alarmed by them. The Annan Committee felt that television has more of an impact where attitudes and opinions are uninformed, particularly on children. They criticised the showing of violence between 9 and 10 p.m., as too many children were still watching at this time; and

Making a TV documentary

they rejected the idea that viewing violence had a 'cleansing' effect, considering that the reverse was more likely as violence may arouse passions in some people which could cause harm. Dr Himmelweit, who was a member of the Committee, said: 'A stream of violent programmes conditions children to accept violence as an effective and necessary way of solving problems and to remove their inhibitions about resorting to violence.'

Unit 21 Influence of the Mass Media

21.1 Advertising

The sociologist is interested in all forms of persuading people, from the brutal brainwashing described by George Orwell in *Nineteen Eighty-Four* to subtle methods of propaganda such as *subliminal advertising*. (Subliminal advertising is the fast flashing of information introduced into cinematic or televised programmes so that the subconscious mind registers what the eye does not.) The most obvious persuasion to which

The caption underneath this photograph reads 'The Ormarin Bath is for ladies who want to do a little more than keep clean.'

the ordinary citizen is exposed is the medium of advertising.

Although it is not possible to determine the percentage of advertising which is solely *informative* (giving details of an article's price, use, size and colour), it is almost certain that in a modern sophisticated society there is far more *persuasive advertising*. The advertisers appeal to such motives as sex, snobbery and status in their endeavour to expand the sales of their products. Expenditure upon advertising is steadily increasing in almost all countries.

As would be expected, the developed nations of western Europe and North America spend far more on advertising than do the poor underdeveloped countries of Asia and the Middle East. Table 6.5 lists the countries spending over 1.25 per cent of their GNP upon advertising in 1970. Contrast these with Indonesia (0.01 per cent), Iraq (0.06 per cent) and Pakistan (0.08 per cent) which are examples of less developed countries with very low percentages of advertising expenditure.

In Britain over £1000 million (1980) is spent annually upon advertising. Newspapers still lead in advertising expenditure, followed by television.

Country	Advertising expenditures as a percentage of Gross National Product
Eire	2.23
Switzerland	2.18
United States	2.11
New Zealand	1.65
Denmark	1.64
West Germany	1.56
Australia	1.44
Netherlands	1.38
Sweden	1.32
Austria	1.30
Argentina	1.28
Canada	1.25

Table 6.5   Countries in which advertising expenditure exceeded 1.25 per cent of GNP in 1970

21.2   The power of the press

Everyone has an opinion or point of view on almost any subject, and these opinions may range from those which are strongly felt to those of almost indifference. In a free democracy we are entitled, within reason and libel laws, to express our points of view publicly. For most of us the expression of an opinion will be to a limited audience within hearing range, whereas the mass media can reach out to millions. It is generally accepted that the mass media must remain 'free' in a democracy as they are important bastions of our individual liberty. Invariably one of the first acts of a newly imposed totalitarian regime is to impose censorship on the mass media, and then to convert it into a propaganda vehicle for the regime's point of view. In Britain, as in other western democracies, we pride ourselves on the freedom of our press and the political neutrality of all forms of broadcasting. Are we however, too uncritical of our free press and neutral broadcasting services? An analysis of the political viewpoint of our national newspapers, found mainly in the editorial columns, will show that more than two-thirds, and three-quarters in terms of circulation, of the newspapers listed in Table 6.2 consistently express political opinions to the right of centre. (It is useful exercise to look at the editorials and political commentaries from a sample of newspapers across the political spectrum over a brief period and see how they interpret a particular political event.) The explanation may lie in the ownership of most newspapers by a handful of millionaires or wealthy shareholders. Yet every national newspaper proclaims its political neutrality and independence. Furthermore, it is expected that mature adults can distinguish between bias and the deliberate distortion of facts. After all, C. P. Scott, the famous editor of the *Manchester Guardian*, declared that news was sacred but comment was free. By this he meant that although he did not think that newspapers should be untruthful and tamper with the news, nevertheless they should comment fearlessly upon the news.

A great danger to unthinking readers is that it is so easy for a reporter to begin an article with a simple factual statement and then to insidiously introduce biased comment so that readers hardly know where the news ends and the comment begins. News and comment may be cunningly interwoven; merely one word can cause the reader to be unwittingly influenced. A correspondent who begins an article '*Even* the Con-servative Party', or '*Even* the Labour Party', may be endeavouring to suggest that the Party has a low standard of morality, but that even the members of *this* party are capable of showing a small measure of virtue on some particular issue.

The opinions and views that we hold are gained from somewhere. For the most part they will be derived from a lifetime of experience, but a large area of our thinking will have developed from what we have heard, viewed or read via the mass media. We may, for example, have an opinion on the forms of treatment necessary for various kinds of criminals, but how many of us have experience of the police service, the courts, or prisons? Of course we are entitled to our point of view, but the best opinion is surely *informed* opinion, yet how much of our opinion comes from the mass media which may itself be biased in some way, and not from our own experience? We may have firm opinions on schooling today, and ninety-nine per cent of the population has been to school, but might not schools have changed since we were taught? Is one school the same as another in all respects?

Sociologists and social psychologists are interested in the effects of the media upon opinion forming (for example the University of Leeds Research Unit carried out surveys on the General Elections of 1959 and 1964 to assess the impact of party propaganda), and commercial organisations are keenly interested in the success of advertising. One of the problems associated with all such investigations is that the most profound influences and effects will be long-term, and therefore difficult to assess. Very few of us buy several newspapers reflecting different political viewpoints, therefore day after day our daily newspaper may reinforce our prejudices or gradually and subtly change our previously-held viewpoints, but we may be unaware of the influence the newspaper is having upon us. Newspapers, rather more than broadcasting (which is subject to stricter controls of 'neutrality' by the ITA and BBC governors), will for the most part claim to reflect readers' opinions and tastes, yet perhaps occasionally it might be honest, although rude, to tell someone that when we want their opinion on a matter we will read the *Daily* ——. The power of the press is considerable, while the Press Council, its watchdog for complaints set up in 1953, now adjudicates on average less than fifty complaints a year and upholds only a quarter of them. At the same time it is fair to say that much of the recent success of consumer complaints against retailers and manufacturers of inferior goods has been achieved by the backing of the press, but this might possibly be considered of less importance against the background of the very considerable political influence that newspapers can exert.

Terms used in this chapter

conditioned	quality papers
cultural class system	minority interests
cultural democracy	majority interests
class distinction	informed opinion
popular papers	subliminal advertising

Further reading

J. G. Blumler & D. McQuail, *Television and Politics, Its Uses and Influence* (Faber, 1968)
J. A. C. Brown, *Techniques of Persuasion from Propaganda to Brainwashing* (Penguin, 1963)
J. D. Halloran, *Television and Delinquency* (Leicester University Press, 1970)
J. D. Halloran, *Mass Media and Society* (Leicester University Press, 1974)
H. Himmelweit, A. Oppenheim & P. Vince, *Television and the Child* (Oxford University Press, 1958)
V. Packard, *The Hidden Persuaders* (Penguin, 1970)
J. Tunstall, *Media Sociology* (Constable, 1970)
R. Williams, *Communications* (Penguin, 1962)

Questions from GCE 'O' Level Sociology Examination Papers

1   What do you understand by the words 'mass media'? Why are sociologists interested in the mass media? What kind of work have sociologists done in this field? (AEB, November 1971)

2   Newspapers often refer to the generation gap. How acceptable or useful do you find this phrase? (AEB, June 1972)

3   Make use of the following figures to help you write an essay on the influence of newspapers in Britain today.

Average daily circulation of national newspapers

	1960	1964	1968
Daily Express	4 270 000	4 190 000	3 787 000
Daily Mail	2 825 000	2 400 000	2 039 000
Daily Mirror	4 649 000	5 085 000	4 949 000
Daily Sketch	1 075 000	847 000	886 000
Daily Herald	1 418 000	—	—
Sun	—	1 414 000	1 009 000
Guardian	212 000	278 000	270 000
Daily Telegraph	1 206 000	1 324 000	1 379 000
The Times	260 000	255 000	415 000

(AEB, June 1970)

4   Discuss the sociological arguments for and against introducing commercial radio in this country. (AEB, June 1971)

5   Do you agree with the statement that radio and television represent the single most important factor in the formation of opinions and attitudes? (AEB, November 1969)

6   If you wanted to conduct a survey in your school or college to find out more about the students' television viewing habits, how would you go about this? Describe what preliminary work would be necessary, what methods you would use, and what kinds of conclusions you would be justified in coming to. (AEB, June 1970)

7   What evidence is there to support the view that the mass media are influential in forming or changing attitudes? Make quite clear what kinds of attitudes you are discussing. (AEB, June 1972)

8   'Media of communication which were at one time limited in their impact can now reach almost a whole population and may exert a tremendous influence upon people, their opinions, their attitudes and their way of life. . . . At one end of the scale mass media can be used to provide sober factual information, and at the other can become a vehicle for political propaganda.' (Adapted from A. Hancock, *Mass Communications*, 1968)

What evidence has been put forward by sociologists concerning the effects of mass media? (AEB, November 1976)

9   The effect of any kind of mass media is determined by the audience it reaches? What factors have sociologists suggested are important when considering the effects of mass media? (AEB, June 1976)

10 Sociologists are interested in whether the mass media shape or reflect the views of their audience. Discuss the sociological evidence as to the effects of mass media in any *two* of the following areas:
(a)   Youth culture
(b)   Consumer behaviour
(c)   Behaviour of young children
(d)   Religious behaviour.   (AEB, June 1978)

7 Government and Politics

Unit 22 Government

22.1 The meaning of government

Government is the means by which different societies or groups are led and organised. When we talk about the Government we usually mean the people who control the affairs of the nation. The kind of government that we have in power is important because it can directly change our lives and the way in which society is organised. People who have various ideas about what should be done to lead and organise society become involved in another discipline of social science, the discipline of *politics*. Politics, therefore, is the study of people who have power or who seek to exercise power in society and the way in which they are able to influence events.

Many of the words used in government and politics are taken from the language of the Ancient Greeks, whose civilisation was one of the first to experience many different kinds of government and to produce writing about political ideas. The word politics comes from the Greek *polis* meaning a city; the ways in which different city-states were governed introduce us to some of the concepts of politics. When Athens was at its highest point of civilisation and power in the fifth century BC it was governed by an assembly of male citizens who decided all matters of policy and leadership by vote. Because Athens was governed by the citizens (even though women and slaves were excluded) it was known as a *democracy* from the word *demos* meaning people. In the rival city-state of Sparta a small group or *élite* made most of the decisions in government; since this was rule (*archia*) by a few (*oligos*) Sparta was known as an *oligarchy*.

Just as Athens and Sparta were traditional enemies, so too there is a constant conflict between the political philosophies of democracy and élitism in the writings of political theorists. In ancient Athens it was possible for all the citizens to gather in one place, for each to be heard, and for them all to take decisions, but in modern states with populations numbering millions no such direct participation in democracy is possible. In democracies today representatives are chosen to conduct the affairs of government on behalf of the electors. The method of choice the electors exercise, and the composition of the representatives, is the subject of the study of *political sociology*.

Who are the electors?

Who are the representatives?

Why and how do people vote in a certain way?

The answers to these questions can be categorised and analysed in a sociological manner, but first we must understand the workings of our Government.

22.2   Government in the United Kingdom

Government in the United Kingdom (see Figure 7.1) has evolved during the course of our history. The central Government meets in the Houses of Parliament at Westminster. Parliament is divided into two chambers: the House of Commons, and the House of Lords; of these the House of Commons is the more important as the Lords have had their powers considerably reduced since 1911.

The House of Commons comprises 635 Members of Parliament who have been elected by the adult population. Each MP represents an area or constituency in the United Kingdom which contains an approximate average population of some 60 000 electors. Since 1872 voting for MPs has been by secret ballot. Almost all the MPs belong to one of the three major political parties: Labour, Conservative, or Liberal. The party

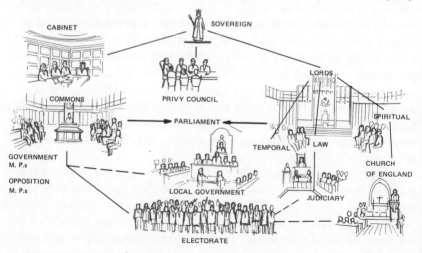

Figure 7.1   Diagrammatic representation of government in Britain

which has the largest representation in the Commons usually forms the Government because, being in the majority, it is most able to secure the success of its policies. After an election the leader of the party which has the most MPs is asked by the Queen to become Prime Minister, and to select members of his party to form the Government.

The Government consists of MPs who have been chosen by the Prime Minister to run various ministries or departments of state. Each minister or secretary of state is responsible for introducing any new laws in the form of Acts of Parliament (known as bills until they have passed through Parliament) concerning his department, and for carrying out the wishes of Parliament with the help of civil servants in his department. Ministers and their Civil Service departments are termed the *executive* because they execute the wishes of Parliament. Parliament is known as the *legislature* because it makes changes in the law and may introduce new legislation. If there is any dispute about the interpretation of the law the *judiciary* or judges decide the dispute. The highest court in the land is found in the House of Lords.

The second largest party in Parliament is known as the Opposition, since its members seek to criticise and oppose many of the measures that the Government may introduce. Although they rarely succeed in defeating the Government in a straight vote, they are constantly ready to take over and form a government should they win in an election. As an alternative government their leaders are sometimes referred to as the Shadow Cabinet.

The House of Lords contains three types of peer (lord): the Lords Spiritual, who are the two Archbishops of the Church of England and another twenty-four senior bishops; the Lords Temporal who hold hereditary titles (dukes, marquesses, earls, viscounts and barons), or who are people who have been given peerages for life only, under the Life Peerages Act of 1958, and who do not pass their title on to their heirs. The third group of peers are the Law Lords who are the most senior judges of appeal. Altogether about a thousand hereditary peers are entitled to sit in the Lords, yet only a minority choose to attend. Most of the business in the Lords is conducted by the life peers who are usually elder statesmen and who came to prominence in political life when they were MPs in the Commons. The principal function of the Lords is to have a second look at legislation from the Commons and to suggest constructive amendments to it. All financial measures pass through the Lords without a vote, and they are unable to hold up any matter approved by the Commons which has been passed in two successive sessions; the Lords have the power to delay a bill for only one year, but this is rarely used.

22.3   The passage of legislation

Almost all new legislation originates from the *Cabinet*, which consists of the Prime Minister and his most senior colleagues. Not all members of the Government form the Cabinet, but only some twenty or so of the most important ministers and secretaries of state who meet regularly at 10 Downing Street to discuss important matters of policy under the chairmanship of the Prime Minister. It is possible for an individual MP (known as a private member) to introduce new legislation, but he has little chance of success unless the Government is prepared to lend its support to the measure.

Before a bill becomes an Act it is considered on three occasions, known as *readings*. The first reading is just a formality; at the second reading the general principles of the bill are debated in the Commons; then it passes to a committee of MPs for further examination before it passes back to the Commons for a third and final debate. If the measure has been approved in all its three readings in the Commons it goes to the Lords where the same procedure is employed. Finally it is sent to the Queen for

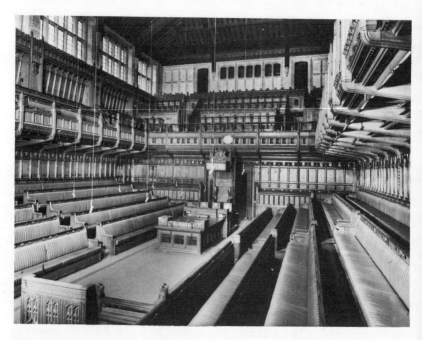

The Chamber of the House of Commons

formal signature (known as the Royal Assent), when the bill becomes an Act of Parliament and hence law.

The Monarch plays very little part in government. The Sovereign is the symbolic Head of State, whose most important governmental function today is the selection of the Prime Minister and the right to advise and warn governments on various aspects of their policies.

22.4   The separation of powers

Eighteenth-century political philosophers on the Continent often admired the system of government in Britain, although by modern standards we should have regarded it as corrupt and undemocratic. The reason for their admiration was the way in which the three branches of government (legislative, executive, judicial) were at once complementary and yet distinct. Although Parliament (the legislature) is theoretically supreme, the Government (executive) is able to function efficiently because it commands a majority of supporters in the Commons. The judiciary is technically independent of the legislature and executive, and therefore we are free from tyranny—for if there were no legislature (or just a puppet parliament) the executive would be answerable to no one, and would in all likelihood control the judiciary. In other words, we would have a dictatorship. As it is, while the executive is given considerable power to govern it is, nevertheless, ultimately answerable to the legislature, the Sovereign, and possibly to the judiciary. For the most part majority government has meant efficiency in government. Should a government seek to extend its authority and become no longer answerable to the legislature (ie to members of Parliament and, hence, the electorate) it would become undemocratic. A general election *must* be held every five years, though rarely do governments remain in office for the full period. The electorate, therefore, is able to express its approval or disapproval of the Government's policies at regular intervals.

22.5   Local government

The central government at Westminster directs and controls the affairs of the nation as a whole, but a large number of the functions of government are either shared with local authorities or directed entirely on a local level. Not only does this make for greater administrative efficiency, but the variations of regional and local needs are met by local democracy. The basic functions of local government may be divided into three categories:

1   personal: education, health and welfare
2   environmental: planning, housing and roads
3   protectional: weights and measures, the police and fire services.

Under the Local Government Act of 1972 a major reorganisation of local government took place in England and Wales in 1974 (Scottish local government was changed a year later). Greater London which had been reorganised ten years earlier was not affected by this Act. The changes in population distribution, together with the desire to spread more evenly the administrative tasks, led to this reorganisation, and a two-tier system of local government has now been introduced in England and Wales. The top tier consists of some fifty-two county councils, the lower tier of 333 district councils. The six largest conurbations, apart from London, were formed into units known as metropolitan county councils, these are Newcastle (Tyneside), Leeds (West Yorkshire), Sheffield (South Yorkshire), Liverpool (Merseyside), Birmingham (West Midlands), and Greater Manchester. The responsibilities of the top and lower tier are broadly:

a   *county councils:* overall planning, education, personal social services, refuse disposal, libraries, police, roads, fire service
b   *district councils:* housing, environmental health (sewerage, drains, hygiene, food, clean air), museums, playing fields, public transport.

There are several sources of income to meet the costs of local government: more than a third of the revenue comes from government grants, a quarter from the rates, another quarter from loans, and the rest is made up from services that councils provide and charge for, such as car parking. By far the greatest proportion of expenditure is on education, which accounts for half of local government spending. Although local government expenditure was £18 000 million in 1980 (out of a total of £68 000 million for all public expenditure), and so much of our daily lives is affected by the decisions taken in council chambers, very few people seem to take much interest in local politics and government. The average percentage of the local population voting for the councillors, who serve for four years, is between thirty and forty per cent: in some places it falls to as low as ten per cent. This may be compared to France where three-quarters of the electorate of Paris voted in the 1977 municipal election. A survey conducted for the Committee on Management of Local Government found that a quarter of the electorate were unable to name just one service provided by their local authority, while more than a third felt indifferent about influence on their local council.

Lack of interest in local affairs is coupled with a lack of knowledge about local government. The better informed may be aware of the functions of local government, but many feel that all the real decisions taken in government are made in Whitehall and not the Town Hall. A healthy democracy requires that there is public interest and participation in all levels of government, both national and local.

Unit 23 The Electorate

Subjects of the United Kingdom over the age of eighteen years who are not serving prison sentences, who have not been certified as insane, and are not peers, are entitled to vote in parliamentary and local government

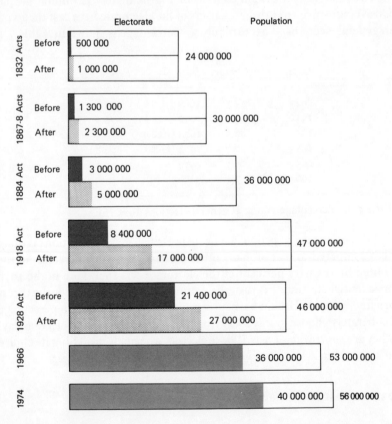

Figure 7.2   Electorate and population, 1832–1974 (after 1918 the figures do not include the Republic of Ireland)

elections. Over the past 150 years the right to vote (franchise) has been gradually extended from a few male property holders before the Reform Act of 1832, to the present electorate (Figure 7.2). In the nineteenth century the electorate divided its support between the Conservative and Liberal Parties; since World War I the Labour Party has gradually replaced the Liberal Party as the main contender for power against the Conservatives.

The study of the way in which people vote is also a minor discipline of social science, known as *psephology*. The techniques of psephological analysis of voting behaviour have become quite refined since World War II, with various ways of surveying and sample analysis in opinion polls, while a considerable degree of accuracy in prediction has been achieved for some elections since 1945.

The electorate in Britain consists of approximately 42 million people. On average since 1945 three-quarters of the electorate have cast their vote in general elections. This turnout as a percentage is shown in Table 7.1.

Date	Percentage	Date	Percentage
1945	73.5	1966	75.8
1950	84.0	1970	72.0
1951	82.5	1974 (Feb.)	78.7
1955	76.7	1974 (Oct.)	72.8
1959	78.7	1979	75.2
1964	77.0		

Table 7.1   Percentage voting at general elections 1945–79

The percentage of people who vote in British general elections is quite high compared to that of many other parliamentary democracies: in the United States sixty per cent of the electorate cast their vote in the 1976 presidential election. In Australia, voting is compulsory under the threat of a fine. As we in Britain have no compulsion to vote a certain percentage deliberately choose to stay away from the polling stations on election day. They are *positive abstainers*. Those electors who made no deliberate choice to abstain but who fail to vote are known as *negative abstainers*.

23.1   Abstentionism

Over the past twenty-five years the margin between the major parties has been narrow in terms of votes cast at general elections:

	Conservative	Labour	Liberal	Others
1955	13 287	12 405	722	346
1959	13 750	12 216	1639	255
1964	12 002	12 206	3093	349
1966	11 418	13 066	2327	453
1970	13 144	12 179	2117	900
1974 (Feb.)	11 928	11 661	6056	1695
1974 (Oct.)	10 458	11 458	5348	1909
1979	13 700	11 510	4310	1700

Table 7.2   Votes cast at general elections 1955–79 (thousands) '

Because the difference is often so small (eg 20 400 votes difference between Labour and Conservative out of an electorate of 36 million in 1964) the rate of abstentionism can have a profound effect upon the outcome of the election. Mr Wilson's Labour Government had a majority of four in 1964, and one seat, in Brighton Kemptown, had a majority of only seven votes. The much lower turnout in local elections makes the effects of abstention even more marked.

Under our system of election the candidate who gains a simple majority wins, even if the combined votes of his opponents total more. For example, we may have three candidates Smith, Brown and Jones; on election day the results are: Smith: 12 000; Brown: 11 750; Jones: 11 500. Smith wins with a majority of 250 even though Brown and Jones have a combined anti-Smith total of 23 250. The Liberals argue that this was the reason they were only able to elect thirteen MPs in 1974 although nationally they polled more than 6 million votes. In 1951 more Conservative MPs were returned than Labour, although the Labour Party polled nationally 231 000 more votes than the Conservatives. In February 1974 the Conservatives polled 267 000 more votes than Labour. Although there was no clear majority for either party then, the difference between more votes polled nationally yet less seats in Parliament is explained by the differences in size of majorities obtained in the constituencies. Even if a candidate gets just one more vote than his nearest opponent he is still elected. Four-fifths of all the seats in Parliament are considered safe, ie the sitting member's majority is high enough more or less to guarantee his return at the next election. Where the majorities are below four figures the seats are *marginal* and it is in

A politician seeks to persuade the voters

these constituencies where a swing of five per cent or so in the other direction can unseat the sitting member; naturally psephologists usually concentrate their studies in these marginal constituencies. According to Jean Blondel in *Voters, Parties and Leaders* (Penguin Books, 1969), about eighty-five per cent of those who vote show a continuous allegiance to the same party at each election. The remainder are known as *floating voters* who change their vote or who abstain, and who usually make the difference in outcome in a general election. Because a one or two per cent abstention rate of a party's supporters may put the other party in power, the abstainers and floating voters merit further attention.

Positive abstainers are thought to be a smaller group than negative abstainers. The positive abstainer may choose deliberately not to vote for a number of reasons. These usually are:

1   He may not be able to vote for the party that he supports in his constituency (for example if he supports the Liberal Party and there are only Labour and Conservative candidates).

2   He may have a personal dislike of the candidate standing for the party of his usual choice.

3   There may be some aspect of the policy of the party that he usually supports that he has considerable disagreement with, but he cannot bring himself to vote for one of the other parties.

4   He may be cynical about the whole idea of elections.

5   Possibly he may think that the result is a foregone conclusion anyway, particularly in a safe seat.

The negative abstainers are perhaps more numerous. They tend to be the least interested and least informed about political matters. They are usually found among the youngest, oldest and poorest members of the community. There may also be practical reasons for abstaining. If the polling stations are in remote places, as in some rural areas; if a mother

'Ullo. Which public-spirited party has come to nurse us in the art of wise government this time?

cannot leave her very young children to vote; or possibly if someone is ill and has not got a postal vote, then abstentionism is inevitable.

If we assume a failure of twenty-five per cent of the electorate to vote, from this figure between five and eight per cent are not true abstainers: they are people who have died since the electoral register was compiled; people who are on holiday or away on business at the time of the election, or people who have moved out of the constituency and have not obtained a postal vote. This leaves a real abstention rate of just under twenty per cent, or on average about one-fifth of the electorate in general elections since the war.

The *floating voters* who change their allegiance from one election to another, and who are thought to number about fifteen per cent of the electorate, are similar to the abstainers: they tend to be the least politically minded and are easily swayed by election propaganda. It is remarkable that the outcome of such an important thing as a general election in the United Kingdom is usually decided by the rate of abstentionism and the fickle floating voter who is often unaware of the serious issues involved, simply because the two major parties are so evenly balanced. Psephologists are often amazed, if not amused, by the high degree of political ignorance found among floating voters and negative abstainers: for example many such people are unable to name three cabinet ministers nor could they name the candidates in their constituency.

23.2 The voters

Male and Female

If women were still without the franchise it is quite possible that we should have had a succession of Labour governments over the past three decades; certainly the proportion of the labour vote would have been much higher. Blondel suggests that women tend to vote Conservative more than men, in a ratio of about 60:40, and there are more women electors. The main reason for the Conservative bias of women, particularly those who do not go out to work, is thought to be that they are less influenced by industrial conditions and trade union activity. In an industrial situation the differences between the classes are often more noticeable: women, who often work in offices, are in a more middle-class situation and do not experience conflicts of the kind found on the factory floor. It has also been suggested that women are more passive than men and therefore more conservative in temperament.

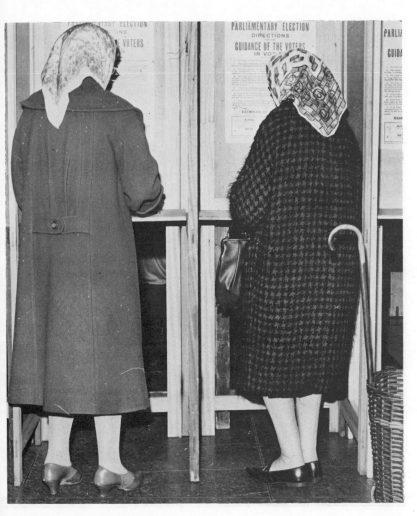

Women tend to vote Conservative

Age

Another factor linked to voting behaviour is that of age. The young tend to be more radical in outlook and the old more conservative: this may be because the young are more idealistic, while the middle-aged are more complacent about matters. The young, particularly the young married couples with small children, are more likely to have problems establishing themselves economically and thus tend to seek more immediate political solutions for their problems and be more radical.

The eighteen-year-olds vote for the first time (April 1970)

Religion and Region

Compared to most other European democracies, religion plays very little part in Britain's politics—with the significant and tragic exception of Northern Ireland. Communicant members of the Church of England tend to vote Conservative, but Labour draws much of its strength from the non-conformist areas of England as well as from Scotland and Wales.

On the results of previous voting figures, if Scotland and Wales had their own parliaments Labour would have held power there for half a century. In England, where most of the population is concentrated in the southern half of the country, the Conservatives usually hold the majority, except in the heart of industrial towns and cities. Catholics in England and Scotland usually vote Labour as most are of Irish descent and have an historical antipathy towards the Conservatives. This is reflected in some constituencies in Liverpool, Glasgow and London.

Class

The greatest determining factors of voting behaviour are the environment and social class of the elector. In simple terms, the higher up the social scale someone is, the more likely they are to vote Conservative. Three-quarters of the middle class vote Conservative, and two-thirds of the working class vote Labour. More than seven-eights of voters (ie those who vote Labour or Conservative) identify their class-interest with the two major political parties. There are of course exceptions: the working-class Conservative voter has greatly interested political sociologists (such as Mark Abrams, *Class Distinction in Britain*) who found in 1958 that thirty per cent of the solid working class voted Conservative. It has been this group who have sustained the Conservative Party since the war (the working class is greater than the middle class numerically, therefore the working-class Conservative vote is of considerable significance). Most working-class Conservatives are found in the more prosperous middle-class areas and regions of England, such as the Midlands and the South East. In the predominantly working-class industrial towns and conurbations of the North East there is a more solid Labour vote as is shown in Figure 7.3.

E. A. Nordlinger, in *Working-Class Tories*, offers two explanations to account for the large Conservative working class vote; he summarises them as the *deferential* and the *pragmatic* voters. Many of these voters are from the lowest economic level: the deferential voters consider that the country is best run by those who were born to it and who received the best (ie public school) education; the pragmatic working-class Conservative voter admires someone who has achieved a position of power through his own efforts and ability, and like the deferential voters he has a good deal of respect for political leaders of high social status. Many of the more extreme views associated with the Conservative Party are held by their working-class supporters and concern such groups as strikers, students and coloured immigrants.

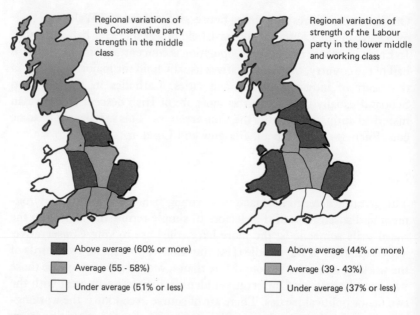

Figure 7.3   *Regional variations of voting behaviour in two social classes, General Election 1959*
(Source: Blondel, Voters, Parties and Leaders, *Penguin, 1969)*

Unit 24   The Political Parties

24.1   The Conservative Party

The Conservative Party was born in 1834. Originally the *Tories* were the party who opposed the Hanoverian succession in the eighteenth century. Before the 1867 Reform Act extended the franchise, the political groupings in Parliament were loose: MPs frequently changed sides on one issue or another, and this did not really matter as MPs were usually of the same upper and professional classes and were responsible only to a small wealthy·section of the population: as long as the interests of the voters were not seriously threatened, a loose political association with one party or another was sufficient. After 1867 the working-class voter was able to exercise some influence, and it was recognised by the Conservatives that a tightening up of party discipline was needed in Parliament and that a national organisation was necessary to secure the

Lady Douglas-Home and Mrs Reginald Maudling at a Conservative Women's Conference

election of their MPs. At the beginning of this century the Conservative politicians were primarily concerned with two aims: to keep Ireland as part of the United Kingdom, and to protect British industry from ever-increasing foreign competition. Today the Conservative Party is identified with the interests of businessmen and property owners. Its basic philosophy is to support business, and to keep state interference to a minimum in economic matters.

24.2 The Labour Party

The Labour Party was officially formed in 1906, although various socialist groups combined together five years earlier to provide trade union and socialist representation in national and local government. The first Labour Government, although not possessing an overall majority of MPs, held power for nine months in 1924. Despite a split in the party in 1931, when the leadership found itself at odds with the mass of its supporters, Labour began to replace the Liberals as the second major party in the inter-war period. The Labour Party's philosophy differs from the Conservatives' in its belief in more state intervention to alleviate any stress caused by the economic system. Socialists believe that the wealth of the nation should be distributed more evenly among all sections of the population through a progressive taxation system and the nationalisation of certain major industries. Clause 4 of the Labour Party's constitution perhaps best sums this up:

To secure for the workers by hand or by brain the full fruits of their industry and the most equitable distribution thereof that may be possible, upon the basis of the common ownership of the means of production, distribution and exchange, and the best obtainable system of popular administration and control of each industry or service.

The Labour Party held power immediately after the war from 1945 to 1951, from 1964 to 1970, and from 1974 to 1979.

24.3   The Liberal Party

The Liberal Party grew out of the eighteenth-century Whig faction and transformed itself at about the same time as did the Conservative Party in the nineteenth century. By and large it can be said that the Liberal Party stands somewhere between the Conservative and Labour parties in terms of its political philosophy. Since World War I the Liberals have until recent times declined in strength. Liberal candidates have now polled 6 million votes since 1945, but their representation in the Commons has been limited to under a dozen because the mechanism of our electoral system does not favour minority third parties. Ironically, however, when the minority Labour Government fifty years ago proposed a system of proportional representation it was the Liberals who voted the measure down. If membership of the House of Commons were to be shared out proportionally to the number of votes cast for each party, the Liberals would usually have more than 100 seats. From February to October 1974, and from 1977 to 1979, when the Labour Government no longer had an overall majority, the thirteen Liberal MPs (and the Nationalist parties) had an influence in politics far beyond their numerical strength in the Commons.

Recently, the Liberal Party has attracted attention particularly by its alliance with the new Social Democratic Party (SDP) formed from disenchanted members of the Labour Party. A joint statement, called 'A Fresh Start' was issued in June 1981 in which the aims of the alliance were set out as viable alternatives to the goals of the other two main parties.

24.4   Membership of political parties

Membership of political parties is divided between those who are active in their party's affairs, and those who give only limited support — usually merely providing a financial contribution. Unless a trade unionist has deliberately chosen to opt out of a political levy (known as 'contracting out') part of his union contribution goes towards the Labour Party. For this reason membership of the Labour Party is apparently high as indirectly very many trade unionists in the Trades Union Congress are affiliated members of the Labour Party. The Conservatives obtain financial support from some businesses and from their claimed party membership of three million. If trade unionists are included, the Labour Party numbers some six million members; of these less than half of a million are individual party members. About two-fifths of the Labour membership participate in their party's activities, whereas something between a quarter and a third of the members of Conservative associations participate in their party's activities.

Most of the business conducted by the constituency parties is concerned with local politics. At election time, agents (who in marginal constituencies are often full-time, paid officials) and volunteers seek to persuade the voters to come to the polls in support of their party. Each of the political parties holds an annual national conference, usually in the autumn, to debate issues of national policy. The influence that constituency parties and associations have upon MPs, the Government and the Opposition, will vary from party to party, issue to issue, and according to the strength of demands. The parliamentary party, consisting only of MPs, elect their own leadership, and naturally will have a considerable influence on party policy as most of the leading politicians in a party are MPs or members of the Government. Yet the parliamentary parties cannot really afford to ignore the wishes of the ordinary constituency members on too many issues. In the first place, the candidate is selected by the local organisation, and there is always the threat that he will not be re-adopted, although this is a very rare occurrence. When elected, the MP must pay some attention to the party workers in his constituency if only to maintain their enthusiasm and support, just as he must look after the people in his constituency who may or may not have voted for him.

Blondel in Chapter 4 of *Voters, Parties and Leaders* points out that even in solid working-class areas more than half the officers of the Labour Party are middle-class, and in the Conservative Party more than three-quarters of the local associations' officers are middle-class. Of the ordinary membership more than half are middle-class, while in the Labour Party the proportion is somewhat lower. This will mean of course that people of middle-class origins and occupations predominate in all the major political parties. The MPs are even more solidly middle-class: more than half of them have been to university and only a very small minority have not received a secondary education at a grammar or public school.

24.5 Political motivation

Because our political parties are mass parties they must contain members with quite widely differing views within the same party. On almost every issue there will be some who disagree with the majority of their political colleagues. Disagreement does not mean that they will leave the party, unless they consider the issue to be extremely serious, as there are many more issues on which they share a common approach. The voting on whether Britain should join the Common Market provided an example of this: several prominent Labour politicians, including the then Deputy Leader, Mr Roy Jenkins, voted with the Conservative Government and Liberals; on the other side a number of prominent Conservatives, including Mr Enoch Powell (now an Ulster Unionist), voted with the Labour Opposition. Obviously, if the issue is felt to be very important, or if there arise many other matters where someone is not happy with the way in which his party is going, then resignation may be the best course. Mr Dick Taverne resigned his seat in Lincoln when he disagreed with the Labour Party's policy on the Common Market; he fought and won the seat again, holding it from 1972 to 1974 with his own Democratic Labour Party; yet resignation is rare. Most party members and party politicians hold strong convictions, or believe in a basic ideology which commits them to their particular party; indeed, that is why most of them entered politics in the first place. Voters too show a strong sense of loyalty to one party, usually for life; we have already given the figure of eighty-five per cent for loyal voters. Young and first-time voters largely follow their parents' lead in voting for the same party. Why is there this strong party-allegiance?

The principal reason for this consistency in voting behaviour is that, rightly or wrongly, the parties are identified with self and class interest. As has been explained, a large number of working-class Conservative voters apparently choose a party which would appear to contradict their class interests, or at least what are regarded as being against their class interests by two-thirds of their fellow working class. At the same time a fifth of the middle class vote Labour, which would seem to be against their own interests. There is perhaps no specific reason for the way in which someone votes. Most probably it is primarily an identification of class interest, combined with approval of the policies of the party, feelings about the leadership of the party, and finally respect for the qualities of the candidate who is standing. The voter has his or her image of the party and its politicians constantly reinforced favourably, or disillusioned gradually, over a period of time. The role of the mass media in determining attitudes and opinions may be considerable in this process.

H. J. Eysenck's scale of political attitudes is interesting from a psychological as well as a political viewpoint (Figure 7.4). In the Conservative, Labour and Communist parties, the working class have a *tougher* attitude on political matters than other classes. As we can see from chapters dealing with socialisation and class, simple and direct solutions are to be expected from members of the working class, and politics are no exception. Of the middle classes, the Socialists have the *tenderest* attitudes. The Labour Party may be described as being a coalition of trade unionists and intellectuals (there is a high proportion of teachers

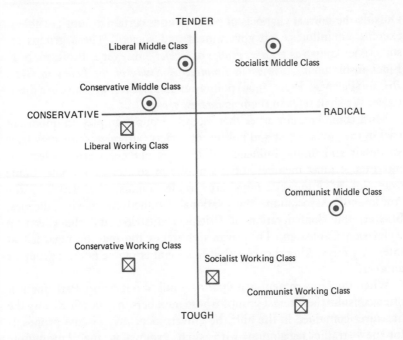

Figure 7.4 Party supporters and the two scales of political attitudes, 1950 (Source: H. J. Eysenck, Sense and Nonsense in Psychology, *Penguin, 1957)*

and academics in the party), and intellectual opinion usually favours moderation and compromise on issues. The position of the Communist middle class, nearest to mid-point on the tough-tender scale, is perhaps due to the rather curious situation of *being* a middle-class Communist. Certainly this scale does reveal the connection between the socialisation process, environment and the choice of political party. At first sight there may appear to be some anomalies, for example the Liberal working class is more 'Conservative' than the Conservative middle class. Also the Liberal working class is far more 'tender' than the other working-class groups. Although interesting, Eysenck's scale (Figure 7.4) is now more than twenty-five years old. It would be a useful exercise to draw a similar scale today and compare it with the old one, seeing which positions have changed and why, over the past quarter of a century.

Unit 25 Politics Outside the Parties

25.1 Interest groups

Outside the normal channels of party politics certain groups are able to exercise an influence on government and society. These groups are sometimes known as *pressure groups* or *lobbies*, however as Professor S. E. Finer in his book *Anonymous Empire: A Study of the Lobby in Great Britain* (Pall Mall Press, 1966) points out, not all exert pressure in a direct sense. We shall refer to them as *interest groups*.

Most commentators agree that interest groups can play an important part in the government and politics of society, although some may have an unfair and undue influence which does not necessarily reflect the interests of most members of the public in society as a whole. Some examples of interest groups are: trade unions, the RSPCA, the Automobile Association, the National Council for Civil Liberties, Shelter, the Confederation of British Industries, and the Clean-up Television Campaign. The various churches too may be regarded as interest groups. Almost every adult is a member of one interest group or another.

When the Government is preparing a bill to put before Parliament it often consults the interest groups whose members may be affected by the measures contained in the bill: the Government may discuss proposals for new traffic legislation with such groups as the Automobile Association, the Royal Automobile Club, the Royal Society for the Prevention of Accidents, and the Motor Manufacturers' Association. If a private Member of Parliament is fortunate enough to be allowed time to introduce a bill, he may well seek the advice of an interest group concerned with his proposed legislation: a private member's bill to regulate conditions in private zoos might be drawn up by the RSPCA, who will then seek to persuade other MPs to attend the Commons on the day of the bill and vote for it. Interest groups may choose a variety of methods to win support for their cause. They may make direct appeals to MPs by writing to them and inviting them to attend functions where they will put their case. Sometimes interest groups will seek to win over public opinion by placing advertisements in newspapers or by writing to the press. Demonstrations and marches are another means of gaining publicity for their cause.

Interest groups may be divided into two kinds, those who act in a defensive manner to protect their members' interests if these appear threatened, and those who are seeking to promote a cause. The *protective groups* are trade unions, professional associations, and groups who may seek to protect individuals unable to look after themselves, eg the NSPCC was created to prevent cruelty to children. *Promotional groups* are more concerned with getting things done, to promote or amend legislation which they feel will benefit society, or more directly, themselves. The people of Wing village ran a successful promotional campaign to prevent the siting of London's third airport near their homes. The Campaign for Nuclear Disarmament seeks to persuade people that Britain should not have nuclear weapons. Broadly, therefore, protective groups are concerned with the interests of individuals, and promotional groups seek a wider appeal for their causes. Sometimes the protective groups undertake a promotional role (for example, the Automobile Association ran a campaign to reduce motor taxation by getting its members to send postcards to MPs) yet their principal function is to keep a constant watch over the interests of their members.

As in the political parties, the membership of interest groups may be people drawn from many different walks of life. The difference between interest groups and the political parties is that they have limited aims and do not seek power at Westminster.

A criticism of interest groups is that they may be undemocratic: protective groups do not claim to represent anyone but their own members; and an interest group which is well organised and well financed is more likely to be successful than one which is poorly led and has a small budget. This means that there is an inequality in the representation of various interests. The motorists are well represented, but pedestrians, who are in the majority, are not able to exercise as much influence upon governments. A strong trade union in a key sector of the economy can make its strength felt very rapidly, but an old age pensioner has only the power of the ballot box and not the strike weapon at his disposal. As in political parties, only the interested (usually meaning the middle class) members participate in the group's affairs, thus a sectional interest is put forward as being the group interest.

There has been some dissatisfaction expressed at the way in which MPs may allow business or trade union interests to prevent them taking an objective view of political affairs. There is no suggestion that MPs are corrupt if they hold directorships of companies or are sponsored (ie have a proportion of their election expenses paid) by a trade union or professional association, yet some concern has been voiced that an MP may be placed in the morally unsatisfactory position of being the unofficial parliamentary spokesman for, say, the drugs industry or the National Union of Mineworkers.

	Lab	Con	Lib	Others
Barristers	33	48	2	—
Solicitors	10	11	—	3
Journalists	27	22	1	1
Publishers	—	3	—	1
Public relations	1	2	—	—
Teachers, lecturers	76	8	1	5
Doctors, surgeons	6	3	—	—
Farmers, landowners	—	21	2	1
Company directors	3	72	2	1
Accountants	4	7	1	1
Underwriters and brokers	1	16	—	—
Managers, executives and administrative	29	20	1	2
Other business	25	22	—	3
Clerical and technical	17	1	—	—
Engineers	29	3	1	—
Trade union officials	19	—	—	—
Party officials	3	4	—	—
Mine workers	17	—	—	—
Rail workers	4	—	—	—
Other manual workers	7	—	—	—

Table 7.3 Occupations of MPs elected October 1974
(Source: *The Times*, March 1974)

On the other hand, in an age of a mass public and a developed technology and bureaucracy governments are informed of matters and sensitive issues which might have escaped their attention had there not been the intervention of an interest group. Interest groups are thus participating in the wider democratic process. Because an elector does not vote specifically for each item on a political party's manifesto, it may be said that his membership of an interest group looks after his needs and enables him to press for action on matters which were not covered in the election manifesto.

There are thought to be some 6000 national interest groups (national in that any citizen may join these groups) and despite the inequalities of representation, this does mean greater public participation in government, which is not a bad thing for democracy. The Government is able to prevent the excessive influence of any one group by questioning whether its interests coincide with the public interest.

25.2 The Establishment

Mention was made at the beginning of this chapter of the conflict throughout political history between élitism and various forms of democracy. We have also outlined some of the theories of élitism in Topic 7.2. The underlying suggestion of most of these theories is that there can never be a true democracy, or that although people may vote every four years or so they do not have any real power. Others suggest that élites are necessary, if not inevitable, in the governing of a nation. In some countries a ruling élite is clearly identifiable: they are members of a military junta or of a single permitted party where there is no opposition. It has been suggested that we have an élite of a kind in Britain: this élite, termed the *Establishment*, is not immediately recognisable as a ruling class, but there are people who, because of their birth, wealth, or position in government are able to exercise considerable power.

One definition of the 'Establishment' is: those circles who are able to exercise considerable influence over the lives of others but who are not democratically answerable in their positions of power.

The Establishment is composed of a number of top people from important institutions, such as financiers from the City, senior civil servants, high-ranking officers of the armed forces, judges, and the directors of the mass media and nationalised concerns. The aristocracy too is part of the Establishment; but as they are insignificant in numbers they do not on their own constitute a ruling class. The Government may exercise power by directly implementing political measures; the

Establishment exercises power indirectly (an example might be if the City were to direct investment out of Britain on a massive scale, thereby destroying a government's economic policies). The Establishment does not have any political aims, except those of maintaining its permanence. The Establishment favours a Conservative administration since the Conservatives are least likely to threaten its position; but a Labour Government is usually unable or unwilling to effect much change upon its powers.

	Lab	Con	Lib	Others
Oxford	60	80	2	1
Cambridge	24	73	2	3
Other universities	106	56	1	12
	190	209	5	16
Service colleges	—	9	—	—
Technical colleges and colleges of technology	34	2	2	1
	34	11	2	1
Eton	1	48	1	—
Harrow	—	10	—	—
Other public schools	11	116	3	2
Grammar	161	58	6	10
Secondary or technical	27	4	—	—
Elementary and adult elementary*	54	2	—	—

* Including Ruskin College and National Council of Labour Colleges

Table 7.4 Educational background of MPs elected October 1974
(Source: *The Times*, October 1974)

The public schools have been described as the nurseries of the Establishment. Contacts made at school and university are often useful later on, particularly in business. These contacts between members of the Establishment may be reinforced through marriage. This is not to suggest that the Establishment is some kind of conspiracy (indeed, many of its members would not even recognise its existence) because the Establishment is not interested in rule, only with maintaining its own existence. Perhaps we may describe the Establishment as the most powerful informal interest group in Britain. It may be argued that it is a good thing to have an Establishment, as the only alternative is greater State domination. Equally it can be said that the Establishment is too strong and some form of democratic control is needed in many of its spheres of activity.

25.3   Politics in Britain

After the French Revolution in 1789 the National Assembly sat in a semicircle with the more extreme revolutionaries on the left and the more moderate politicians ranged towards the right, where the supporters of the *ancien régime* were seated. At Westminster the MPs sit on either side of an aisle, as the chamber was originally a church: the Government and their parliamentary colleagues sit on the right-hand side of the *Speaker* (chairman) the Opposition on his left. When political attitudes are discussed we use the words left and right, which originated with the National Assembly, to denote how radical or how conservative these attitudes are.

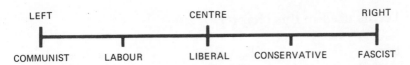

Figure 7.5   A theoretical representation of the wings of the British political parties

Just as there are constant changes in party policies, so too do politicians move along the left-right axis, sometimes ahead of their party and on other occasions behind it. In general terms the parliamentary politicians adopt attitudes which are more to the centre than those of the rank and file membership of the political parties. Politics is sometimes said to be the art of compromise, and when the reality of power is felt many politicians tone down their views. Where free debate is allowed, less extreme opinions will usually prevail. Democracy can only really survive when the media are free to comment upon and criticise the actions of all politicians. Although public opinion may be against one or other of the parties on certain issues at different times, the overwhelming majority of the public are in favour of maintaining the present political system. As governments are answerable to the people at each general election they cannot afford to ignore public opinion too often on too many issues. The principal difficulties in maintaining democracy in a country of 56 million people with only 635 representatives are to ensure participation through the existing system and to enable the public to make its voice heard. We have seen how such participation may take place within the political parties, or through the medium of interest groups.

Until May 1979 the Scottish and Welsh Nationalist parties had increased their strength. In October 1974, Plaid Cymru (Welsh Nationalists) gained 11 per cent of the votes cast in Wales and three seats in Parliament. In the same election the Scottish Nationalists obtained 30 per cent of the votes cast in Scotland and eleven seats. Both these parties have a younger-than-average membership and a growing number of supporters. Although the Labour Government's Devolution Bill was technically defeated in February 1978, there is the possibility of a break-up of the United Kingdom, particularly if in Scotland the Nationalists obtain more than half the Scottish seats in another General Election. A referendum which showed a majority of the people in Scotland and Wales in favour of political independence would make this inevitable. In the meanwhile, through Britain's membership of the Common Market, there is a trend towards larger political units with Britain sending eighty-two representatives to the new directly elected European Assembly.

Terms used in this chapter

democracy	dictatorship	psephology
marginal seat	socialist	Establishment
floating voter	interest group	radical
deferential voter	promotional	devolution
franchise	oligarchy	executive

Further reading

J. Blondel, *Voters, Parties and Leaders* (Penguin, 1963)
J. H. Goldthorpe, D. Lockwood, F. Bechofer, J. Platt, *The Affluent Worker: Political Attitudes and Behaviour* (Cambridge University Press, 1968)
W. L. Guttsman, *The British Political Elite* (MacGibbon & Kee, 1965)
H. Eckstein, *Pressure Group Politics* (Allen & Unwin, 1960)
G. A. Jones, *The Political Structure* (Longman, 1969)
E. A. Nordlinger, *Working-Class Tories* (MacGibbon & Kee, 1967)
R. Rose, *Politics in England* (Faber, 1965)
R. Rose, *Studies in British Politics* (Macmillan, 1966)
P. Stanworth & A. Giddens (eds), *Elites and Power in British Society* (Cambridge University Press, 1974)

Questions from GCE 'O' Level Sociology Examination Papers

1   What are the respective functions of central and local government? (AEB, June 1968)

2   Outline some of the most important ways in which an individual can have an influence on the government of this country. (AEB, June 1970)

3   'Generally speaking, social class and the way one's parents and neighbours vote both have a very strong influence on political leanings. Until quite recently it was usually supposed that people who saw themselves as manual workers, or as coming from a working-class home would vote Labour, and those who considered themselves as middle-class would vote Conservative. . . . One of the key facts of British politics is that about one-third of *those who think of themselves as working-class* usually vote Tory.'
(Source: Crick & Jenkinson, *Parliament and the People*)

a   What is the importance of the phrase 'who think of themselves as working-class'?

b   What explanations do sociologists offer for the working-class Conservative voter? (AEB, November 1976)

4   To what extent is it true that the Conservative Party is an upper class and middle class party, whereas the Labour Party is supported by, and represents the interests of, working class voters? (AEB, November 1971)

5   *Voting intention by region and class 1963–66*

		London and S.E. England	S.W. England	E. Midlands	N.E. England	Wales
	Voting					
Class	*Behaviour*	%	%	%	%	%
Middle }	Conservative	74.1	77.4	83.2	72.7	58.0
Class ∫	Labour	13.0	9.9	8.9	18.6	30.8
Skilled }	Conservative	33.6	38.2	33.5	26.5	15.2
Working ∫ Class	Labour	56.0	46.9	59.0	69.2	79.9

Source: Table adapted from 'A Sociological Portrait: Politics' by Anthony King in *New Society*, 13th January 1972.

Explain clearly what the table tells us about the relation between social class and voting behaviour. (Point out what information is missing from the table.) (AEB, June 1973)

6   Does social class determine the way a person votes? (Oxford Local Examinations, 1972)

7   What are pressure groups? Give two examples of influential pressure groups in this country, describing their aims and how they try to get what they want. (AEB, November 1974)

8 *a*   What is the role of pressure groups in our society?

b   Describe, with the examples, two *types* of pressure groups, showing how they differ from each other. (AEB, June 1975)

9   Is there any connection between social class position and voting behaviour in contemporary Britain? (Oxford Local Examinations, 1974)

10 What are the major social factors which influence how people vote in Britain? (Oxford Local Examinations, 1975)

11 Outline briefly the part played by *two* of the following in politics in Britain:

a   political parties
b   pressure/interest groups
c   opinion polls
d   mass media.
(AEB, June 1976)

12 'Democracy involves more than just the right to vote.' Explain. (AEB, June 1978)

13 Do pressure/interest groups play an important part in enabling people to influence government in modern Britain? (AEB, June 1979)

8 The Welfare Society

Unit 26 The Background to Welfare

26.1 Poverty through the ages

The Welfare State grew out of the needs and miseries of those people in society who suffered from great *poverty*. From the beginnings of human life there have always been some people forced to live in poverty, lacking sufficient food, clothes and shelter.

Before the State intervened it was left to voluntary groups to help the poor. Those living in squalor often combined to help themselves and unless rich benefactors were moved to compassion it was largely the poor who helped the poor. Sometimes the poor acted together in violent social revolt as in the Peasants' Revolt of 1381, or sometimes they made peaceful, communal efforts such as Robert Owen's villages of co-operation in the nineteenth century. In the middle ages the monasteries helped to relieve poverty, but after the dissolution of the monasteries by Henry VIII poor relief passed to the State; the 1601 Poor Law placed the responsibility for relieving poverty upon local government and it was largely the parishes who looked after the poor, but they did this in a harsh and cruel manner.

As the State failed to provide adequately for the poor, it was left to individuals to help relieve poverty. After the Great Plague of 1665, many of the poor were without work and in danger of starving. Thomas Firmin believed that the poor should be given the means to help themselves so he provided them with raw materials to enable them to work and escape from their poverty. The *self-help* idea has continued throughout the centuries and Samuel Smiles in his book entitled *Self-Help* (which ran to four editions in the first months of its publication in 1859) echoed thoughts in keeping with the aims of the great friendly societies. These societies did more than anyone else in the late nineteenth and early twentieth centuries to encourage the poor to assist themselves. From 1872 to 1874 alone membership of Friendly Societies (such as the Oddfellows and the Foresters) rose from two to four millions.

Urban poverty began in the growing industrial towns of the early

One hundred years ago—Gustave Doré's picture

nineteenth century, and has lasted to the present day. The nineteenth-century towns with back-to-back houses and the terrible squalor so vividly depicted in Gustave Doré's pictures, were places of horror and deprivation. The death rate increased considerably from 1821 to 1831 in some of the expanding industrial towns, even though the overall population of these towns was increasing rapidly: according to Chadwick's Report of 1842 the average expectation of life amongst the working classes in Manchester was seventeen years, compared with thirty-two years in rural Rutland. In Manchester the average expectation of life amongst the gentry was thirty-eight years.

The Speenhamland System of 1795 had provided poor relief by small money payments but the deterrent Poor Law of 1834 forced the able-bodied poor to endure the atrocious conditions of the Victorian workhouse. The Speenhamland System of poor relief was not really *State welfare* because it arose from a local decision made by magistrates meeting at the Pelican Inn in the village of Speen, Berkshire. The system was adopted in most counties, but the 1834 Act established a State system intended to give paupers the least possible help based upon the principles of 'less eligibility' and 'the workhouse test'. The only help for the poor was to be provided in the workhouse. Investigations and reports of conditions in towns after the passing of the 1834 Act revealed a state of overcrowding, filth and fever never before witnessed in Britain. These reports included:

1   1838: Dr Southwood-Smith, Dr Arnott and Dr Kay's report on London
2   1840: report of the Health of Towns Committee
3   1842: Edwin Chadwick's report on an Inquiry into the Sanitary Conditions of the Labouring Population of Great Britain
4   1844/5: report of the Health of Towns Commission.

The various reports on early Victorian life threw light upon the worst period of English poverty. In part of Leeds all the streets and dwellings in one area were:

. . . deficient in sewerage, unpaved, full of holes, with deep channels formed by the rain intersecting the roads, and annoying the passengers sometimes rendered untenantable by the overflowing of sewers and other more offensive drains, with ash-holes, etc. exposed to public view, and never emptied;

In Westminster, water was so short that in Snow's Rents:

On the principal cleaning day, Sunday, the water is on for about five minutes, and it is on also for three days in the week for one half-hour, and so great is the rush to obtain a modicum before it is turned off, that perpetual quarrelling and disturbance is the result.

The origins of a welfare society sprang from the poverty revealed by these reports. Southwood-Smith and Chadwick were not termed sociologists but some of their investigations and research work followed the best traditions of modern sociological surveys and were directly responsible for measures such as:

1   Public Health Act 1848
2   Sanitary Commission 1869
3   Public Health Act 1875.

The last Act, passed a century ago, made local councils responsible for the general health of their areas including control of diseases, drainage, sanitation, sewerage, water, etc.

Charles Booth, in *Life and Labour of the London Poor*, showed that one

Providence Place, Stepney, 1908

Londoner in three lived in continuous poverty, while about one person in ten lived perpetually on the edge of starvation. Charles Booth started his inquiry in 1886 and published accounts between 1889 and 1907. He covered an exhaustive field of sociological topics including employment, health, housing, religion and wages. Booth vividly described London's slums: the back-to-back houses thrown up by speculative builders, the sunless courts and the insanitary tenements. The people who existed under these conditions 'lived the life of savages, with vicissitudes of extreme hardship and occasional excess'. When they were able to get work it was very lowly paid and of the most unskilled nature, such as occasional labouring or street-selling, but many were just 'loafers, criminals and semi-criminals'. Charles Booth's most important contribution was to study social problems not as disconnected subjects, but to indicate the extent to which bad health, disabilities, poverty, slums, unemployment and working conditions were related. Practical social workers such as Lord Shaftesbury, General William Booth of the Salvation Army, and Dr Barnardo, accomplished much but it was clear that no permanent universal solution to the problem of poverty was possible without massive *State support*. The whole of society had to accept

Unemployed man, Wigan, 1939

the ideals of welfare provisions. From these origins the Welfare State arose.

Acceptance of welfare principles and efforts to establish a Welfare State have not yet led to the disappearance of poverty. The world wars of this century and the sufferings of the poor in the inter-war depression have been major setbacks to the advance of the welfare society. World wars have rendered people homeless and destitute and have led to the mass migration of unfortunate people. The poor condition of the low-paid British working class after World War I culminated in the General Strike of 1926, soon to be followed by the Great Depression of 1929–33. Three million British people were unemployed in 1933 and street corners were littered with discontented, hungry men many of whom had given up hope of ever having a job again. The families of these men were deprived as the dole in 1930 only amounted to £1.50 for a married man with two children. The poverty was aggravated by a means test whereby if someone in the family found work then the State unemployment pay was reduced. Great masses of unemployed marched upon London demanding work rather than charity. The comparative affluence of the middle classes in the 1930s made the lot of the poor even harder to bear. During the war mass bombing rendered people homeless, particularly in the more densely concentrated working-class areas such as London's East

	No. of live illegitimate births as % of all births %	No. of children in care per 1000 population under 18 years %	No. of children supervised under 1958 Children Act per 1000 population under 18 years %
England & Wales	7.9	5.2	0.08
Greater London	11.4	7.9	0.12
Brent	14.6	8.2	1.3
Camden	17.1	14.0	1.0
Hackney	15.6	11.8	1.1
Hammersmith	16.7	15.8	2.1
Islington	14.2	15.0	1.0
Lambeth	17.0	12.2	1.5
Lewisham	13.2	9.8	1.6
Southwark	13.1	11.2	0.6
Tower Hamlets	13.5	26.1	0.5
Wandsworth	14.3	12.4	2.0
Birmingham	11.3	7.4	0.9
Bradford	8.3	9.1	0.4
Cardiff	10.8	5.1	0.5
Coventry	9.0	5.1	0.6
Liverpool	10.3	5.4	0.4
Manchester	16.5	9.6	0.4

Table 8.1 Special need groups (Source: R. Holman, *Socially Deprived Families in Britain*, Bedford Square Press, NCSS, 1970)

End. There were genuine attempts by the Coalition Government in Britain to secure equality of sacrifices: rationing, which was not abolished completely until 1954, aimed at fair shares for all at least in the bare necessities of life.

Since World War II pockets of real poverty have remained. Pensioners, the low-paid and widows have all suffered great hardship. Television plays such as *Cathy Come Home* and *Edna, The Inebriate Woman*, have brought to the mass of the people the plight of the unemployed, the vagrants, the homeless and the unfortunate misfits who exist even in our so-called Welfare State.

Poverty is a relative concept. Even a condemned cottage in Britain would be paradise to those people in Hong Kong who are dwelling in shelters made of petrol tins. People are poor because they are deprived of the opportunities, comforts and self-respect regarded as normal in the community to which they belong. It is therefore the continually moving *average standards* of that community that are the starting points for an assessment of its poverty (Social Science Research Council, *Research on Poverty*, 1968). Compare the percentages in Table 8.1. Note carefully how certain London boroughs and some conurbations have many more *cases of special need* than the average population of England and Wales.

> My song is of that city which
> Has men too poor and men too rich;
> Where some are sick, too richly fed,
> While others take the sparrows' bread.
> (W. H. Davies, writing about London)

Why does poverty still exist in advanced industrialised societies? Some possible reasons are given below. They are deliberately controversial. Try arranging them in order of importance and see if you can add to them.

1   There are great inequalities of wealth and income combined with a constant battle to keep up with inflationary conditions.

2   Some people find it difficult to adjust to a modern society. The pace of advanced industrialised societes means that there is a lack in the quality of life so that many become misfits or drop-outs.

3   Government ministers, who are largely products of the middle classes, are unable sufficiently to appreciate or sympathise with the poor.

4   Not enough welfare is provided; eg in some EEC countries family allowances are two or three times as high as in Britain.

5   The welfare services provided are often badly-managed or bureaucratic:

too much money may be spent in administering schemes rather than in actively relieving poverty.

6 Many people, especially the elderly, do not receive social security payments to which they are legally entitled because they are unaware of their rights or incapable of making applications. Some are too proud to apply for what they consider to be charity.

7 More research into conditions of poverty is required, and the findings of surveys which reveal severe social deprivation should be acted upon speedily. Often social survey reports are shelved or not acted upon for many years.

Table 8.2 suggests that low wages and old age are the two most important causes of poverty experienced by the estimated seven million people on or below the poverty line.

Cause of Poverty	1899	1936	1953–4	1960
	%	%	%	%
old age	1*	15	49	33
sickness	2*	4	7	10
unemployment	2	29	5	7
low wages	55	38*	30*	32*
large family (5 or more children)	22	5*	5*	8*
single-parent family	12*	8	5	10

* Estimated figures.

Table 8.2 Percentage of those in poverty (Source: *New Society*, 1 March 1973)

There is a bare minimum of subsistence recognised by most people, and modern industrial societies (with problems of increasing populations, overcrowding and a large proportion of elderly people because of the longer expectation of life) find it difficult to maintain this minimum standard for everybody in spite of the affluence enjoyed by the many. An often-used standard level for the poverty line is based upon the national assistance (or supplementary benefit) scale. This standard has the advantage that the rates paid 'conformed closely to the Beveridge Standard which in turn bore a close resemblance to the standard used by Rowntree', ie in 1899 (B. Abel-Smith and P. Townsend, *The Poor and the Poorest*, G. Bell & Sons, 1965).

26.2 The origins and development of the welfare society

The term *Welfare State* did not come into common usage until after World War II, but we have seen the State responsibility for the welfare of society *as a whole* developed gradually over many centuries. The nineteenth century gave great impetus to welfare provisions as urban slums forced people into the *poverty trap* and as *national economic growth* supplied the financial means for poverty to be more vigorously tackled. The idea of a Welfare State suggests social measures imposed from above so that citizens shall be entitled to reasonable conditions of education, housing and employment and to receive State aid when their conditions fall short of a certain level. A welfare society 'recognises its collective responsibility to seek to achieve the maximum welfare of each and every individual citizen and not only to relieve destitution or eradicate penury'. (*The Welfare Society*, ed. Joan Eyden, National Council of Social Service, 1971.)

The real origins of the Welfare State were established by the reformist Liberal Governments of 1906 and 1910 and especially in the period from 1906 to the beginning of World War I. The fuller development of the Welfare State started with the Beveridge Report of 1942 ('Report of the Committee on Social Insurance and Allied Services', Cmd. 6404, HMSO) and was put into legislative form by the Labour Governments of 1945 to 1951. Some minor erosions of welfare principles have been made since, but generally, Britain has enjoyed Welfare State conditions for about thirty years, although there are always new areas into which social services may be extended.

In Britain the Liberal Government of 1906 began zealously to improve the lot of the poorer classes. Charles Booth had advocated old age pensions and in 1908 pensions of one shilling (5p) to five shillings (25p) a week were given to those over seventy years old, subject to a means test. The most important Liberal measure was the 1911 National Insurance Act based largely upon Bismarck's scheme which had proved successful in Germany. Contributions were made by the Government, employers and employees, and covered all workers between the ages of sixteen and seventy who were not receiving more than £160 a year (ie well above the average wage for this period). The 1911 Act provided for disablement, maternity and sickness benefits, and for some medical services including those of a general medical practitioner. By 1914 nearly 14 million people contributed to, and received benefit from, the National Health Insurance Scheme.

Very slow progress was made in the inter-war years. Orphans' and widows' pensions were started in the 1920s, while the Education (Provision of Meals) Act of 1926 permitted a limited distribution of meals and milk to children at State schools. Local authorities were given further responsibilities for working-class housing including slum clearance and for providing welfare services for particular groups such as the blind, the mentally defective, mothers and young children. The Poor Law Relief (or Public Assistance) was made the responsibility of county and county borough councils. The depression and its aftermath brought a reduction in welfare services and in 1931 unemployment benefits were cut by ten per cent with a means test which many people regarded as a humiliating inquisition. When the war came in 1939, a Welfare State did not exist but Britain was advancing very slowly towards it.

The development of the Welfare State as we know it began with the Beveridge Report of 1942. Beveridge advocated welfare services aimed at 'the destruction of Want, Disease, Squalor, Ignorance and Idleness'. A new face was given to welfare because 'the scheme as a whole will enhance, not certain occupations and income groups, but the entire population'. This last quotation is taken from the Government's Social Insurance White Paper which was one of four that followed the Beveridge Report. The other White Papers put forward schemes for improvements in Workmen's Compensation, a full employment policy and a free health service. The principles set out in the survey reports of this period gave rise to:

1 Family Allowance Act 1945
2 National Insurance Act 1946
3 National Insurance (Industrial Injuries) Act 1946
4 National Health Service Act 1946
5 New Towns Act 1946
6 National Assistance Act 1948
7 Children's Act 1948.

The Labour Government of 1945–50 passed more social legislation in five years than had been enacted in the previous 500 years; the State was committed fully to the policy of working towards a society where each citizen would have the right to be cared for by the State from the cradle to the grave.

In its broadest context the term welfare state includes a modern government's responsibility for:

1 social services, including all social security measures (see Topic 27.1)
2 comprehensive health service
3 safeguarding the environment
4 full employment
5 equality of educational opportunity
6 special provision for the socially handicapped.

There are those who believe that welfare principles have been taken too far: workers are able to strike knowing that real economic suffering may be long delayed; thrift is less of a virtue and the spirit of enterprise is sapped; foreigners are able to come to Britain to take advantage of the National Health Service. But welfare services available to the community as a whole cannot be curtailed because the services are abused by a few; there are not many who would be prepared to go back to the pre-1945 system of selective State help of a minimum standard. In the long run, a *welfare society* has some advantages over a *welfare state* in the sense that the former term recognises a sense of caring by the whole of society. We should all be concerned that members of society should have all possible facilities to develop to the utmost, and be looked after if they fall upon bad times. Millions of pounds are paid out in welfare services, but many of those entitled do not claim benefits.

Unit 27 The Modern Welfare State

27.1 Social services

Social services and benefits are provided by the State literally from the womb to the tomb. An expectant mother receives a maternity allowance, while a maternity grant of £25 (1978) is payable on the birth of the baby. The maternity allowance starts eleven weeks before the baby is expected and goes on for eighteen weeks. Eligibility for maternity allowance depends upon the woman being a contributor to National Insurance and having twenty-six stamps on her national insurance card during the previous twelve months. A mother-to-be can get help and advice from an ante-natal clinic; after the child is born the mother usually takes the baby regularly to a post-natal clinic for cheap foods and a check-up, while health visitors go to the child's home to see that mother and baby are progressing satisfactorily. Where a child is left without parents, guardians' allowances are paid to those who bring up the child. Child benefit is £5.25 for each child under 16 and those under 19 receiving full-time non-advanced education at a college or school (since November 1981). In addition, since November 1980, there are cash provisions for certain people who are bringing up children alone (One Parent Benefit).

The Government announced in 1972 that there was to be a

considerable extension of nursery education (see Topic 12.1) so that schooling is possible from the age of two, although compulsory education does not begin until the age of five. While at school, youngsters receive help from the Welfare State in the form of such services as dental and medical examinations, subsidised school meals and, near the end of school life, the Youth Employment Service.

The transition from school to work is made easier by the Factory Acts which control the hours and conditions of work, while the Government sponsors training schemes at technical colleges. Apart from further education opportunities, councils set up youth committees which appoint youth officers to organise LEA youth clubs and help voluntary youth organisations.

On starting work a young person contributes to the National Insurance Scheme. The majority of workers have a contribution deducted from their wages and to this contribution the employer adds more money. National Insurance Scheme benefits are available (so long as certain conditions are upheld) to people who are:

1 unemployed
2 injured at work
3 sick
4 disabled
5 guardians
6 widows
7 expectant mothers
8 retirement pensioners
9 war pensioners
10 dependants of the dead (Death Benefit).

From the beginning to the end of life, the Welfare State watches and cares. Help and advice is offered in the way of legal aid and citizens' advice bureaux.

27.2 The National Health Service

Britain has developed an excellent, comprehensive, free national health service (see Figure 8.1), but there will always be improvements that can be made.

The NHS has suffered from:

1 The initial opposition of the medical profession, a minority of whom were preoccupied with the higher remuneration gained from the better-off private

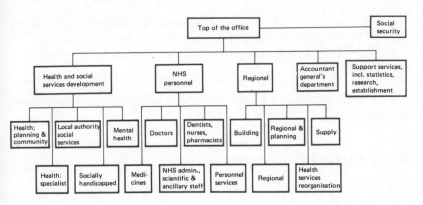

Figure 8.1 *New work-structure for the Department of Health and Social Security, from 1974*
(*Source:* New Society, *28 December, 1972*)

patients. There is still resentment from some people who think that the individual's personal relationship with his doctor is lost in a national system.

2 A lack of adequate financial resources so that staff have been underpaid, while there has also been a shortage of modern buildings and equipment.

3 The 'Brain Drain' which has meant the loss of many good doctors, especially to the USA, so that the NHS would not have survived without immigrant staff.

4 It has not been possible to undertake large-scale preventive medicine (except for a few illnesses such as tuberculosis) involving screening whole communities so that disease can be checked. Curative treatment is more expensive in the long run.

5 The existence of private patients able to secure priority in treatment.

6 A large growth of bureaucracy since reorganisation in 1973; there are today as many administrators, clerical and other workers, as there are qualified medical staff in the NHS.

The achievements of the NHS include:

1 The establishment of a comprehensive service where hospitals, general practitioners and local authorities combine so that more resources are available.

2 The provision of some well-equipped modern hospitals particularly in specialised medical fields: expenditure on health and welfare services amounts to over £7000 million a year (1975).

3 The removal of financial worry about the cost of treatment provided by hospitals, doctors, dentists, opticians, chemists, etc. (Although some charges have been imposed since the NHS was started, the bulk of the cost still comes from public funds.)

4   The acceptance by the majority of the medical profession that it is better to work for the service of the whole community than for private gain.

5   The supply of medical attention to all members of society regardless of social classes.

The services provided by the NHS may be divided into three main categories.

The hospital and specialist services

The Department of Health and Social Security, under the Secretary of State for Social Services, is ultimately responsible for the hospital service, although the day-to-day running is controlled by area health authorities and administered through regional health authorities. The NHS inherited a large proportion of nineteenth-century hospitals, but plans made in 1962, and revised in 1966, allowed for about £1000 million to be spent on hospital building in the ten-year period ending in 1977. There are nearly 3000 hospitals in Britain including about forty teaching hospitals, twenty-six of these being famous London hospitals: in actual practice teaching hospitals include groups of hospitals so that very many hospitals are involved in specialised teaching. A very high standard of medical training has been established by the NHS. There are specialised services in all fields of medicine and rehabilitation aids, including physiotherapy, artificial limbs, hearing aids, invalid chairs and vehicles, and surgical supports. Social workers help patients with socio-economic difficulties which may arise from their illness, resettlement or disability. Other specialised services include abortion (permitted since 1968), bacteriological laboratories, blood transfusion, chest radiography, drug dependence treatment, psychiatric help, etc. There is an increased urgency about the need to provide up-to-date mental hospitals.

The general practitioner services

The Minister of State for Health has overall responsibility but, since 1 April, 1974, effective administration is conducted by forty regional health authorities and ninety area health authorities. An individual citizen is allowed to choose his own doctor. More than three-quarters of the 26 000 general medical practitioners work in group practices or partnerships because this arrangement has the advantages of always ensuring that there is a doctor available, sharing expenses of surgery, receptionists, etc. and the pooling of medical experience. It is becoming a

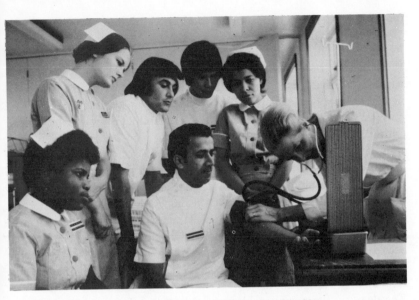

Training to be a nurse requires dedication to the patients' welfare

more general practice for midwives, health visitors and home nurses, employed by the local council, to be attached to doctors' practices. Almost all GPs in Britain play some part in the NHS. The maximum number of patients allowed to be on a doctor's list is 3500 and the average number is about 2500 (1980). The family doctor is usually the one to recommend a patient to other parts of the National Health Service, eg hospital, specialist or optical treatment. The health service in Britain also involves about 13 000 dentists, 1000 ophthalmic practitioners and 7000 ophthalmic and dispensing opticians. About 14 000 retail pharmacists dispense NHS prescriptions.

Local authority services

Local councils play a vital role in promoting the general welfare of their community. Four groups of people are looked after by local authority health services:

Mothers and young children More than three-quarters of babies receive checkups, vaccination, and innoculation, etc. at health centres. Theoretically there is a compulsory follow-up on newly born babies, and advice and education is given to mothers by health visitors. Local authorities make provisions for family planning advice, unmarried mothers and their babies, distribution of welfare foods and the organisation of day nurseries.

The mentally disordered   Local authorities have a statutory duty in the Welfare State to help the mentally disordered members of society. It is current practice for those with mental illness to be discharged from hospital, where possible, more quickly than in years gone by. It is necessary for social workers to do much rehabilitation work and for the authorities to provide occupational centres for the mentally ill and training centres for the mentally handicapped.

The physically handicapped   Local authority welfare services are available to the blind, deaf, disabled, educationally sub-normal and all who are permanently handicapped. This is a sphere where there is intensive co-operation between local councils and voluntary social workers. Assistance given to the handicapped includes social clubs, occupational centres and the provision of various aids to cater for individual needs (such as the provision of guide rails, special toilets and ramps).

The elderly   The social problems of old age are of a very special nature, and there are almost nine million people on a retirement pension today. As the expectation of life will probably increase while the birth rate may decline further (see Topic 17.1) a greater proportion of the population will be retired and elderly people.

Some particular problems of the elderly may be:

i   As so many live on their own they may need special welfare provisions, eg home nursing, domestic helps.

ii   The poor diet and living conditions of so many on a low income make for bad health: hence the demand for meals-on-wheels and special centres where the elderly may be provided with a substantial meal.

iii   The elderly often lack sufficient warmth: even in January 1978 some medical opinion believed that about half a million were suffering from hypothermia.

iv   Special housing is required to cater for the needs of the elderly, especially as they are so easily injured by falls.

v   There is often an inability to communicate with the outside world when medical and other welfare aid is required.

vi   Old people need to feel that some people really care about them.

vii   Elderly people ought not to be classified *en masse*. There are some whose mental health is improved if they are able to disengage from their contemporaries. They are entitled to privacy, but their well-being needs constant checking.

viii   On retirement those over sixty-five years may believe that they have lost their main purpose in life, so there is a need to provide hobbies of an active type.

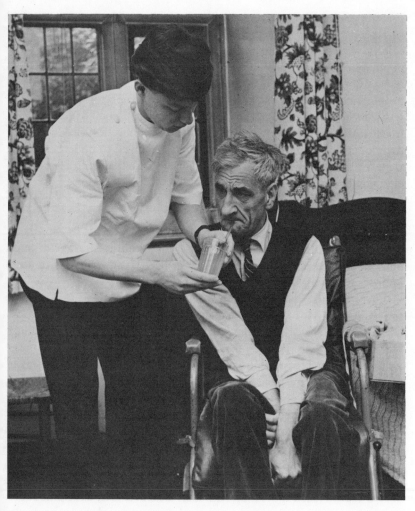

The elderly need to feel that people really care about them

ix   Loneliness is not just a case of being self-pitying and introspective.
'There are signs that loneliness is now being recognised as one of the major
causes of social disaster, and that severe mental illness often has its roots in
loneliness.' (*The Times*, 19 July 1971.)

x   As we get older we tend to lose our faculties, especially hearing and sight.
Social workers employed by local authorities are often the only contact that an
old person has with the outside world.

Local authorities provide facilities such as nursing, domestic help and
special laundry services. Under legislation passed since 1962 councils

provide clubs, day centres, meals for old people and recreational workshops. Social workers are increasingly engaged in helping the elderly, especially as the proportion of old people to the rest of the population is growing. The majority of old people needing special help receive it in their own homes, but local authorities provide about 2500 old people's homes (1975). These homes usually cater for thirty to fifty residents and house about two per cent of the population over sixty-five. Local authorities also provide special small dwellings for the elderly and the modern concept is for a warden to be employed to undertake social welfare duties in a housing complex especially designed with the needs of old people in mind.

27.3   Housing

Although a Housing Act of 1890 gave local authorities power to build houses for those in the lower income groups, very little was done to improve the housing situation until after World War II.

There are just over 20 million dwellings in Britain and they may be conveniently divided into three main groups.

Owner-occupied houses account for just over one-half of all dwellings which were mainly built in the inter-war and post-war years. A large number of them are in suburban developments and are bought by way of building society mortgages with repayments extending over fifteen, twenty, twenty-five or thirty years. These houses are owned largely by the middle classes because working-class people find it difficult to save the customary minimum ten per cent deposit or to keep up payments with the interest rates.

Housing owned by local authorities consists mostly of well-maintained modern dwellings the majority of which have been constructed since World War II (see Figure 8.2). Although local authority accommodation units allow working-class and lower-middle-class people to be housed in better conditions than would otherwise be the case, the tendency for the people from the two or three lowest social classes to be separated on to council estates had many disadvantages. Compare such an estate with a village where agricultural workers, retailers, teachers, farmers and businessmen all live in close proximity and share a communal life. The standard of local authority housing is continually improving and over ninety per cent of council dwellings built in 1978 had central heating.

A high proportion of council house tenants have incomes below the national average and include many old age pensioners. Local authorities give preference to those living in overcrowded conditions and to large

Housing since the war

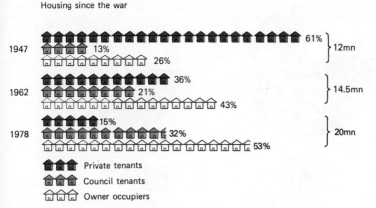

Figure 8.2 *Housing since World War II*
(*Source*: Social Trends, 1976, *CSO*)

families. Most councils have waiting lists and require applicants to have lived in the area for a specified time.

Privately rented housing now only accounts for about fifteen per cent of dwellings compared with over fifty per cent in 1947 (see Figure 8.2). Privately rented accommodation forms a very high proportion of the older property in Britain and about three-quarters is over fifty years old. Major reasons for the decrease in the proportion of rented dwellings are:

1 Increased availability of local authority accommodation.
2 More people are able to buy their own homes.
3 Many old rented properties have been demolished by slum clearance.
4 Rent restrictions originally introduced in 1915 as a temporary measure have been more severely controlled since the Rent Act of 1965.
5 The Housing Act of 1974 meant that private and public sector tenants are now treated on almost the same basis. In many cases this means that private tenants cannot be given notice to quit so easily by the owners, and many owners have become reluctant to let accommodation as a consequence of the 1974 Act.
6 Many local authorities encourage their tenants to purchase houses they are living in by giving favourable discounts on the market value.
7 Income tax allowance on the interest of mortgages makes it worthwhile to purchase a property rather than rent one.

Conclusion

There is still a severe housing problem in Britain. Apart from the three

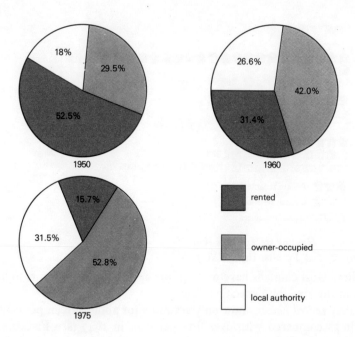

Figure 8.3   *Ownership of dwellings in the United Kingdom, 1950, 1960 and 1975.*
(Source: Social Trends, 1976, *CSO)*

main categories (see Figure 8.3) of owner-occupier, local authority and
private dwellings, there is also the work of *housing associations, house
improvement schemes, slum clearance* and *urban renewal*. A slum is a
property which has reached the end of its useful life and cannot be
reinstated at a reasonable cost. Where it is possible to use the existing
structure and improve a dwelling, then urban renewal is very worthwhile.

In 1972 a Housing Act was passed that left the then 8 million owner-
occupiers in a highly privileged position. They were excluded from the
provisions of the Act, but were receiving over £300 million a year in tax
relief. House purchasers received far more aid (about £70 per head in
1972–3 compared with an average of just over £50 for a council tenant),
and yet owner-occupiers are mainly in the top three of the five generally
recognised social classes. The 1972 Act was an ambitious piece of
legislation to restructure Britain's fragmented and often unfair housing
system, but it involved stiff increases in council house rents and
consequently was repealed by a Labour Government in 1974. The new
Act too has given rise to problems as there is a reluctance to let private
accommodation (particularly to people like students who require short-

Urban renewal—Arlington Development, Norwich

stay accommodation) as security of tenure is so much stronger. Building costs and the higher standards demanded by local authority and government regulations now mean that new council housing is on average much more expensive to build than new private housing.

27.4   Voluntary organisations

The following are some reasons why voluntary bodies still exist in a welfare state:

1   There is less administrative cost involved.

2   Volunteers give willingly of their own time and this is essential when people are lonely or feel they need someone who really cares.

3   Unpaid workers may be less patronising than professionals.

4   Voluntary organisations are not over-organised and have less rigidity and bureaucracy than agents of the State.

5   Small organisations may be better able to deal with local welfare problems.

6   Volunteers are deeply interested:

a   they may have had experience themselves of a certain problem (eg Gamblers Anonymous)

b   they are free to act as pressure groups against the Establishment (eg Society for the Aid of Thalidomide Children)

c   they are willing to listen patiently to other people's problems (eg Samaritans).

The Welfare State has always encouraged voluntary organisations. It arose out of the voluntary principle and past charitable work mostly conducted by various religious bodies. In the nineteenth century, William Booth left the Methodist Church in order to establish the Salvation Army which recognised that spiritual comfort needed backing by practical Christian charity to the starving and homeless. William Booth's *In Darkest England and the Way Out* described the conditions of the down-and-outs in 1890 and several of Booth's suggestions, which were way ahead of their time, are now part of the Welfare State services, eg aid for released prisoners and lawyers' advice to the poor. Orphans brought up in good conditions in a local authority's children's home owe much to the pioneering efforts of Dr Thomas Barnardo who worked for the welfare of the poverty-stricken homeless waifs of London, and opened his first home for children in Stepney in 1867. The non-conformist churches were in the fore of voluntary work of a welfare nature: the Methodists concentrated upon the large cities and used their central halls as social missions; the London Missionary Society was mainly supported by the Congregationalists and helped people to start life afresh in British colonies; the Baptists did much social work among the deprived and under-privileged. The religious bodies and individual philanthropists laid the foundations of the Welfare State and gradually in the twentieth century the Government began to take over institutions organised on behalf of the orphans, the poor, the old and the sick.

There are probably over 100 000 voluntary organisations in Britain. The Charity Commissioners were faced with over 70,000 applications for registrations when they began compiling a register in 1960. It is very difficult to classify voluntary bodies because of their numerous organisational structures and frequently inter-related aims. There are organisations whose main work is involved with:

1　Religious motivation: Church Army, YMCA, Toc H, Society of Friends.
　2　Helping those with personal problems: National Council for the

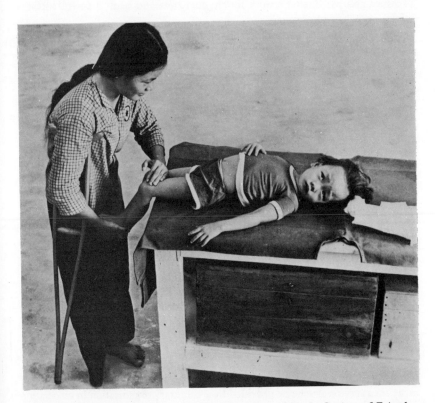

First Vietnamese Physical Therapy Service, organised by the Society of Friends

Unmarried Mother and Child, National Society for the Prevention of Cruelty to Children.

3　Family problems: Family Welfare Association, National Marriage Guidance Council.

4　Providing services for the sick: British Red Cross Society, St John Ambulance Brigade.

5　Looking after the special needs of the disabled: Royal National Institute for the Blind, National Association for Mental Health, National Society for Mentally Handicapped Children, Royal National Institute for the Deaf.

6　Caring for those who suffer from similar problems: Alcoholics Anonymous, Narcotics Anonymous.

7　A wide range of services: Women's Royal Voluntary Service assists in hospitals, does relief work in emergencies, provides residential clubs for the elderly and supplies meals-on-wheels.

8　Administering the funds of self-supporting organisations: Carnegie United Kingdom Fund, Nuffield Foundation, Wolfson Foundation.

9　Help for special groups of people and acting at the same time as modern pressure groups: Shelter's work for the homeless and badly housed, PROP's efforts on behalf of prisoners.

10　Supplementing the central and local government's own services: Central Council for the Disabled, National Society for the Prevention of Cruelty to Children.

11　Filling a gap in services provided by the Welfare State: Royal National Lifeboat Institution.

12　Improving the quality of life: Friends of the Earth.

13　Maintaining world peace: United Nations Association, CND.

14　International problems such as aid to the under-developed countries: Oxfam.

15　Providing a central link between voluntary organisations: National Council of Social Service, National Institute for Social Work Training.

The National Council for Social Service brings together most of the principal voluntary associations for consultation and joint action. It is very important to avoid duplication of services with subsequent wastage of resources and additional administrative expense.

The Beveridge Report saw the need for the enlistment of voluntary workers. In the *Voluntary Worker in the Social Services* (Bedford Square Press of the NCSS) five ways in which volunteers may work are suggested:

1　as members of a voluntary body undertaking a particular type of work

2　in a service or scheme provided by a voluntary organisation in association with a local authority or other public body

A Shelter photograph of some contemporary housing in Birmingham

3 as members of an organisation recruiting volunteers for work of a variety of different kinds within public services such as hospitals

4 as volunteers directly recruited by and attached to a hospital, school, local authority department or other public body.

5   in a service provided and staffed by a public body, but operating from premises unconnected with that body and working as a separate entity.

There will always be a need for voluntary organisations to pioneer and experiment in paths of welfare which the state has yet to travel.

27.5   The Welfare State and the family

The Welfare State provides the family with greater security. If the breadwinner is temporarily out of work, then unemployment benefit is available; if the unemployment is of a long-standing nature, such as structural unemployment, then the State provides redundancy payments or the opportunity to learn a fresh job at a Government Skill Centre. When there is sickness in the family, then the free services of the general practitioner or the hospital are available and there is sickness benefit to help the family at a time which could be one of financial hardship. If the family has been relying upon the earnings of the wife, then if she becomes pregnant they can fall back upon maternity allowances and the lump sum grant. Retirement pensions and death grants are entitlements under the National Insurance Scheme. The State pays widows' pensions (however inadequate) and industrial injury benefits. So the Welfare State has helped to make the family more secure.

Yet in many ways the family is less of a unit because the State has usurped, or at least partly taken over, many of the family's original functions. For centuries it has been the responsibility of the father to find a home for his wife and children. Husband and wife together were expected to bring up their children without interference or help, to educate them especially in the vocational sense when it was customary for a son to follow his father in a trade. The family provided guidance on morals and behaviour without the help of State or school. Recreational activities took place within the framework of the family.

However, the modern Welfare State has an influence upon the family from the beginning. Marriage requires legislation by the State even if the marriage ceremony is performed by the Church. Divorce needs the State's acceptance and the parties to the divorce have rights which the State protects. Family planning advice and devices are provided by the State; the expectant mother and the young mother can use the assistance provided by the State. It is most likely that confinement will take place at a State hospital.

The extension of nursery education in the 1970s, saw an increasing tendency for the mother to get back to work earlier and therefore her influence upon the child may have been lessened. Religion plays little part in most family life today: it is perhaps left far more to the State school to implant beliefs, ethics and good standards of conduct. With more educational and library facilities, the culture of society is transmitted to some extent outside the family circle.

Young people tend to leave home at an earlier age, especially since legal adulthood has been reduced from twenty-one to eighteen years. If young people go away for further education they may only return for fleeting vacational visits to the family; at the age of about twenty-two it is common to secure a job in a different town so that contact with the family is almost relinquished. As the age of marriage has decreased, the young people of the family of origin soon start families of procreation. As another family begins, it is likely that the Welfare State will have more influence upon this new family than will the family of origin. Working-class children are more inclined to stay within the family atmosphere after leaving school at sixteen, until they get married in their twenties, but much of their leisure time, especially in their late teens, will be spent away from the home, possibly at youth clubs or at night school. The middle-class young person of a similar age may have a study where he can disengage from family life, and it is likely that the State school may play at least as great a part in his life as will his family. When a father and mother are elderly, they frequently receive more assistance from the local council's paid domestic help than from their own children, and they may finish their days in an old people's home provided by the State rather than being cared for by their own children, as was customary in previous generations. Even though the Welfare State provides further education at colleges, polytechnics and universities, a parental contribution, depending upon the parents' income, is expected towards a student's grant. The State encourages the young person to remain at educational institutions and provides most of the financial means to allow him to do so: many young people are not an economic asset these days. Apart from youngsters who go out to work and who may be expected to pay about £10 a week for their keep, young people of today are more likely to be an economic burden to other members of the family who are gainfully employed.

So the contemporary family is, in many ways, less of an *economic unit*. Nowadays about sixty per cent of married women are in employment, while the children are cared for at school by school welfare officers, school counsellors and the teaching staff generally. There may be nobody at home during the day so the likelihood of parents not knowing of truancy is greater, and if the child becomes unwell during the day responsibility falls on the staff, and not on the parents. A large proportion of juvenile delinquency takes place between 4 pm and 6 pm when many children are expected to return to an empty home, and then other servants of the Welfare State (eg police officers or probation officers) have to sort out the problems and exercise guidance which otherwise should have been the responsibility of the parents.

Terms used in this chapter

poverty	slum clearance	welfare society
social security	urban renewal	voluntary organisations
Beveridge standard	fair rents	housing associations
urban slums	under-privileged	self-help
poverty trap	national insurance	average standards

Further reading

B. Abel-Smith & P. Townsend, *The Poor and the Poorest* (G. Bell & Sons, 1965)
A. B. Atkinson, *Poverty in Britain and the Reform of Social Security* (Cambridge University Press, 1970)
E. Butterworth (ed.), *Social Welfare in Modern Britain* (Fontana, 1975)
C. Coates & R. Silburn, *Poverty: The Forgotten Englishman* (Penguin, 1971)
J. Kincaid, *Poverty and Equality* (Penguin, 1973)
P. Marris & M. Rein, *Dilemmas of Social Reform* (Penguin, 1967)
P. Morris & M. Rein, *Social Services in Britain* (HMSO, 1976)
D. Marsden, *Mothers Alone* (Penguin, 1969)
D. Marsh, *The Welfare State* (Longman, 1970)
F. Parkin, *Class, Inequality and Political Order* (Paladin, 1972)
W. G. Runciman, *Relative 'Deprivation' and Social Justice* (Penguin, 1966)
R. M. Titmuss, *Essays on 'The Welfare State'* (Allen & Unwin, 1963)
P. Townsend, *The Concept of Poverty* (Heinemann, 1970)
D. Wedderburn (ed.), *Poverty, Inequality and Class Structure* (Cambridge University Press, 1974)

Questions from GCE 'O' Level Sociology Examination Papers

1 What do you understand by 'poverty'? To what extent has poverty been reduced in the UK since 1945? (AEB, November 1974)

2 What do you understand by 'the Welfare State'? (AEB, June 1968)

3 What do you understand by 'the affluent society'? To what extent, if any, do welfare services contribute to 'affluence'? (AEB, June 1971)

4 'The development of the Welfare State has made voluntary associations

irrelevant to present-day problems.' Discuss. (Oxford Local Examinations, 1971)

5   Assess the contribution made by Sir William (later Lord) Beveridge to the development of the Welfare State. (Oxford Local Examinations, 1970)

6   What do you understand by a 'slum'? Why are slums usually found in central urban areas? (Oxford Local Examinations, 1970)

7   Explain carefully what you mean by the term 'welfare society'. What effect, if any, has the provision of welfare services by the State had on the family, religious bodies and voluntary organisations? (AEB, November 1971)

8   'However comprehensive the services provided by the State there will always be a need for voluntary organisations.' Do you agree? (AEB, November 1969)

9   Is there a housing problem in Britain? Give reasons for your answer. (Oxford Local Examinations, 1973)

10   What are the major social problems of old age? Are present services adequate to meet these problems? (Oxford Local Examinations, 1971)

11   What are the major social consequences of urban renewal? (Oxford Local Examinations, 1972)

12   Is the function of the family being affected by the increasing activity of the Welfare State? (AEB, November 1969)

13   Give a brief account of Charles Booth's *Life and Labour of the London Poor*. (Oxford Local Examinations, 1971)

14   'What counts as poverty varies from time to time and place to place.' Discuss. (AEB, June 1975)

15   Outline briefly the development of the National Health Service in Britain. What have been its major achievements and limitations? (Oxford Local Examinations, 1975)

16   Examine the contribution of Charles Booth and Seebohm Rowntree to the study of poverty. (Oxford Local Examinations, 1975)

17 (a) What is the difference between absolute and relative poverty?
    (b) Why do those in poverty in industrial societies tend to remain poor?
    (AEB, June 1979)

18   'The cause of poverty in our society is the unequal distribution of society's resources.' Why do some groups always have only a very small share of our society's resources? (AEB, June 1978)

19   'Once in poverty a family tends to have great difficulty escaping from it.' Why is this so? (AEB, June 1980)

9 The Economy and Employment
Unit 28 Work and the Economy

28.1 Why do we work?

We work to satisfy our needs. In any society man must work hard enough to satisfy his three basic needs for food, clothing and shelter. People in a primitive society are able to manage with very basic foodstuffs. In 1971, a party of social anthropologists and sociologists discovered a group of about twenty-five Tasaday people living in caves in the Philippines on a diet consisting mainly of natek, which was prepared from the pith of the palm tree, plus tadpoles, frogs and crabs that were caught by hand and wrapped in leaves and roasted. Some researchers think that the Tasaday people have been cut off from communication with other human societies for about 2000 years but yet they survived. Admittedly, the clothing and housing needs of the Tasaday society were very sparse: the men's only clothing was a pouch of orchid leaves worn as a kind of loin cloth whilst their shelter was a bare cave.

As societies become more civilised, so their needs increase and it becomes very difficult to distinguish between a *need* and a *want*. A man does not *need* a car in order to live, but he *wants* one so that he can carry on the type of life to which he is accustomed and which may include commuting every day from a village some miles from where he works. So although we work to produce the essential things which we need, we are also often striving to obtain things that we want, ie things we should like to have if we had a little extra money. Some people would call these things *luxuries* and consider the essential things as *necessities*. It is a simplification however to separate economic goods into necessities and luxuries, for not only is the luxury of today the necessity of tomorrow, but things which some people believe they need so desperately that they regard them as being necessities, other people would consider as luxuries. Is a telephone a necessity or a luxury to an elderly, sick woman living on her own? Is a radio necessary for a blind man living in a modern society? Some welfare workers would regard both the telephone and the radio, in these cases, as real needs that ought to be supplied by the State. Decisions about which goods and services should be supplied by the individual and which by the State are political decisions depending to some extent upon whether capitalism or communism is accepted as the best way of organising the production and distribution of economic goods.

We work to produce goods and services; the more complex the society the more complicated will be the methods of production and the channels of distribution. Professor J. K. Galbraith in *The Affluent Society* (Hamish Hamilton, 1957) suggests that law and order constitute a basic requirement of production. In any society, men will not be encouraged to work if the goods they produce are destroyed through theft, violent acts, civil strife or arson. So law and order are essential if people are to work to fulfil their needs and wants. The product of man's work will also be increased by improved educational standards, a good health service and an efficient transport system.

The simpler the society, the easier it is to see a close relationship between a man's work and his needs and wants. If a man tills the soil or works as a hunter, then he and his family (or tribe) will consume the produce of the land or wear the skins of the animals killed in hunting expeditions. It is very easy to see that he works to provide his family (or tribe) with satisfactions.

In a modern industrial society the relationship between work and need or want is not so obvious. Consider this discussion between a lorry driver and an acquaintance whom he has not met for a long time.

Lorry driver: I thought it was you.
Friend: It must be a few years now.
Lorry driver: Yes, I'm not around here much these days.
Friend: What job are you doing now?
Lorry driver: Driving heavy goods vehicles for sixty hours a week.
Friend: How much do you get?
Lorry Driver: £75 a week.
Friend: Do you like it?
Lorry driver: No. It's just a means to an end.

What is the end that the lorry driver has in mind? He is presumably thinking of earning money and spending it upon food, rent, clothing and other necessities for his family and himself, with something left over for his leisure pursuits. He admits that he does not get any enjoyment from the work; he is often not aware of any direct relationship between his work and his wants. He works merely for his wage, because the money which he is paid enables him to satisfy his wants.

He goes to work
to earn the cash
to buy the food
to get the strength
to go to work
to earn the cash,
           and so on.

In a modern society money is essential so that people can satisfy their needs and wants. A clerk cannot be paid in ledger sheets nor can a policeman be allowed to keep as slaves the criminals that he catches. So money is used as a medium of exchange and as a yardstick (or *unit of account*) by which the value of all work and wants are measured. Unfortunately money sometimes acts as a veil which hides the relationship between the reason why a man works and the wants that he is working to satisfy, but the relationship exists even though it may not be apparent to the worker. Where a person is not working for money it is usually easier to see why he works. If a man digs his own vegetable garden he is working to produce vegetables to satisfy needs. If a young lady

Factory work is often monotonous

makes a dress she is working to provide herself with an article which will give satisfaction. Even if a person indulges in a hobby which costs him money he is still working to provide satisfaction. There are two main reasons why man will always have to work to satisfy his desires:

1   The goods that he makes will be used up. A cigarette is made to be smoked and as soon as a new car is driven the tyres and other components will begin to wear.

2   Man's wants can never be satisfied. It is true that 'keeping up with the Joneses' makes man chase his own tail; he becomes involved in a consumer-orientated society which brings higher living standards but not necessarily a greater degree of happiness. This constant endeavour of man to improve his lot should not necessarily be viewed with disparagement, because it is a motivation which raises man above the higher animals.

We work to make things to use, so we are both *producers* and *consumers*. An automobile worker helps in the production of motor cars and he probably drives a car himself. When man works he merely changes the location and shape of things; he is not able to produce something from nothing. So in an economic sense man does not create goods. He may take iron ore from the ground and work upon it until, when it is combined with other things, he has produced aircraft, bicycles, cars or cutlery. Society is supplied with the things which it demands by man combining his *labour* with things from the land (*raw materials*) and with *capital* (factories and machinery). Economists call labour, raw materials and capital the *factors of production*. Most modern economists believe that the organiser (or *entrepreneur*) is a fourth factor of production; it is he who decides what shall be made and how the other factors of labour, raw materials and capital shall be combined.

28.2   Employment and unemployment

We saw in Topic 28.1 that people work to produce goods and services. These goods and services may not necessarily be beneficial to society: cigarettes, drugs or guns are made because they are demanded by members of society who are willing to pay money for them. These people are prepared to give some of the value of their work (ie money they have earned) in order to pay for goods and services. In a *capitalist economy* the variety of goods offered will be determined in the long run by the *effective demand* of the people. Economics is concerned with effective demand because a person's desire to possess something can only be satisfied if he has the ability to pay the price demanded.

Industry or Service	Great Britain	N. Ireland	Total
	Thousands		
Employees:			
Agriculture, forestry and fishing	421	53	474
Mining and quarrying	361	2	363
Manufacturing industries:			
Chemicals and allied industries	424	2	426
Metals, engineering and vehicles	3957	49	4006
Textiles	555	39	594
Clothing and footwear	418	23	441
Food, drink and tobacco	728	26	754
Other manufactures	1582	27	1609
Total: manufacturing industries	7664	164	7828
Construction	1338	49	1387
Gas, electricity and water	335	9	344
Transport and communications	1501	24	1525
Distributive trades	2690	63	2753
Professional, financial, scientific and miscellaneous services	6327	141	6468
National government service	583 }	40	1583
Local government service	960 }		
Total: employees	22 182	477	22 659
Employers and self-employed persons (all industries and services)	1820	71	1891
Total in civil employment	24002	548	24550

Figures may not add up to the totals shown because of rounding.

Table 9.1   Total in civil employment in Great Britain (1973)
(Source: *Britain 1975*, HMSO)

Not everybody in society works. The number of employed in Britain
totals about 26 millions out of a population of 56 millions (1981). There
are four groups of people who do not work (ie whose work is unpaid):

1   children of pre-school age and those undergoing full-time education
2   housewives: married women who stay at home to do housework and/or
look after children.
3   retired people: usually women over the age of sixty and men over the age
of sixty-five
4   those unemployed because they are physically or mentally handicapped,
plus people who are unable (or unwilling) to get a job.

There are also almost 3 million unemployed (2 998 800: Sept. 1981) and over a quarter of a million in HM Forces, making a total *working population* of roughly 26 millions. Those registered as unemployed are included by the Department of Employment in the total working population. The working population may conveniently be divided into three groups:

1 *Primary workers* engaged in the first stages of production such as agriculture, mining and fishing
2 *Secondary workers* who mostly work in manufacturing industries
3 *Tertiary workers* who provide services and in a modern affluent society make up about half the work force, eg over 6 million people are engaged in professional, financial, scientific and miscellaneous services, apart from those working in the distributive trades, transport or for the Government.

The first half of the 1970s saw a large movement of labour from manufacturing into the public sector, ie local and central government employment. The economic recession since the mid-1970s highlighted the shrinking industrial productive base of the economy and, together with cuts in public expenditure, has caused all parties to agree that regeneration of manufacturing industry is of prime importance.

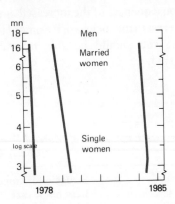

Figure 9.1 Women provide the main source from which new labour can be drawn

The effects of the Equal Pay Act and Sex Discrimination Act have been discussed in Chapter 3. Most of us would agree that women should have more scope for entry into the professions: according to *Planning for Women at Work* (a document presented to the National Conference of Labour Women, 1969) less than five per cent of those engaged as actuaries, architects, chartered accountants, engineers and solicitors were women. After all, as the Royal Commission on Trade Unions and Employers' Associations, 1965–1968 (the *Donovan Report*) pointed out, women will provide the only substantial source from which extra labour, and particularly skilled labour, can be drawn. (See Figure 9.1.) The unequal social and economic position of women is seen in the opportunities afforded to boys and girls. Apart from the fact that less money is spent upon the education of girls, the number of girls' training opportunities is far fewer than those offered to boys. About forty-three per cent of the boys who entered employment in 1970 were indentured for apprenticeships compared with seven per cent of girls. On the other hand, nearly forty per cent of girls entered clerical work, much of it of a routine nature, compared with nine per cent of boys. Three important reasons for these unequal training opportunities are:

1   Girls are less willing to undertake long apprenticeships because they do not look upon the job as a lifelong career.

2   Employers are reluctant to accept girls for apprenticeships because they are likely to get married and not stay the course.

3   Some trade unionists have been prejudiced against females in the past, especially in trades traditionally reserved for males.

The causes and consequences of the increased employment of married women is of great interest to the sociologist. Some of the possible effects are given in Table 9.2; you should be able to add to the causes and consequences suggested.

| *Increased Employment of Married Women* | |
Causes	*Likely Consequences*
Emancipation of women	Struggle for equal pay
Increased demand for female labour	Less home care for children
	More women trade unionists
Nursery education for under-fives	Less time spent in looking after the home
More female career opportunities	
Time-saving domestic gadgets	Delinquency amongst children who return to an empty house
Inflation erodes the husband's pay	
Smaller families	Husband helps wife with the domestic chores
Desire for 'pin money' to supplement the family income	Family dependent on joint income

Table 9.2   Increased employment of married women

Since World War II there has been a remarkable change in the employment situation in Britain. In 1931, unemployment was twenty-one per cent and until the outbreak of war in 1939 the percentage of unemployed was nearly always over ten per cent; since the war until 1975 Britain has had an almost permanent state of *full employment* using this term in the Beveridge sense that more than ninety-seven per cent of those registered for jobs are employed (Lord Beveridge, *Full Employment in a Free Society*, Allen & Unwin). A Government White Paper entitled *Employment Policy* was published in 1944 and since then successive governments have succeeded in maintaining a state of full employment, until 1972 when the unemployed numbered over one million (see Figure 9.3) for the first time since the war and rose to 1.6 million in 1978. It is usually possible by economic planning and by following principles first laid down by Lord Keynes to see that 'full employment is maintained'. Lord Keynes advocated that extra government spending when necessary should be directed towards useful public works. 'Even three per cent appears as a conservative, rather than an unduly hopeful, aim to set for the average unemployment rate of the future under conditions of full employment.' (Lord Beveridge, *Full Employment in a Free Society*.)

A state of full employment has sociological consequences. A state of *over-full employment* may arise where workers find it so easy to obtain jobs that instead of an employer being in the position to say to a worker, 'If you do not work, there are other people ready to take your job,' a worker is able to say to the boss, 'If you don't want me, it will be very easy for me to find work elsewhere.' It is when workers have taken this attitude that some people have argued that a measure of unemployment is good for a society: they have argued that men will work harder if there are unemployed people willing and waiting to take their jobs. So although unemployment over a long period is very bad for an individual, over-full employment may be bad for society in general if it leads to persistent industrial unrest and indiscipline at work.

Full employment may also adversely affect *labour mobility*: a dynamic economy requires that some workers should be willing to move between areas and between occupations. Certain older industries (such as coal, cotton, shipbuilding, wool and railways) are declining and can only use a smaller labour force, whilst expanding industries such as chemicals, computers, electronics, plastics and vehicles may be crying out for a larger work force. Where the staple industry is established in a traditional and localised setting then it is very difficult to get workers to move their homes, leaving old associations and familiar surroundings to take their families to a different area.

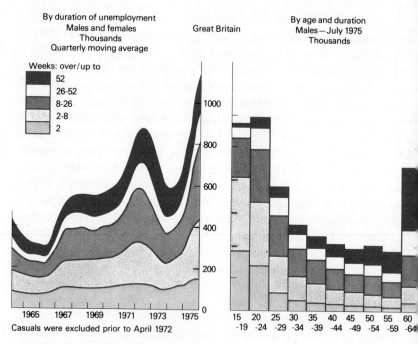

By duration of unemployment
Males and females
Thousands
Quarterly moving average

Great Britain

By age and duration
Males — July 1975
Thousands

Weeks: over/up to
52
26-52
8-26
2-8
2

Casuals were excluded prior to April 1972

Figure 9.2   Unemployment 1965–1975
(Source: Social Trends, 1976, CSO)

Until recently full employment has also led to a more affluent working class and the subsequent expansion of the advertising industry (see Topic 21.1), and of credit purchases. Workers may be unduly influenced by advertisers and the tempting hire purchase offers so that 'the consumer is by no means the key factor in the situation. Rather, it is the producer who as a rule initiates economic change . . .' (S. R. Parker, *The Sociology of Industry*, Allen & Unwin). Modern youth culture (see Topic 13.2) is both a cause and consequence of the very favourable market position in which most young people have found themselves in recent years, at least until the economic recession from the mid-1970s. Those in their late teens had been able to get jobs relatively easily and demand high wages, especially as the proportion of those going on to further education had increased. In this respect girls aged over sixteen were in a slightly more favourable situation than boys of a similar age because:

1   there are more males than females in the population in this age group
    2   a greater percentage of males than females go on to further education. (Only just over a quarter of British students are females.)

Young wage-earners have found themselves in a favourable position in recent years

Intensive advertising campaigns and instalment buying (over £3000 million in 1980) have led to:

1   some families spending beyond their means and then being subjected to adverse social pressures
2   manufacturers imposing rapid changes in fashion and *planned obsolescence* with goods not made to last
3   an increase in the employment of married women and teenagers
4   workers choosing to do overtime rather than have more leisure time.

Unemployment is a social scourge, but nevertheless no society can secure 100 per cent employment because there will always be some who:

1   are unable to work because of sickness, either temporary or chronic
2   do not want to work because they find social security benefits sufficient for their particular needs
3   are out of work because of weaknesses or changes in the economic structure.

Eight causes of unemployment which arise from the economic system itself are given below.

Type of *unemployment*	*Main cause*
1 Casual	Employment offered cannot always be steady and some workers are unspecific, such as manual labourers who move from one unskilled job to another.
2 Cyclical	Trade cycles have brought mass unemployment, eg about 3 million in Britain from 1931–3; these cycles have largely been replaced by milder yet still serious recessions.
3 Frictional	Unemployment is caused by workers with a special skill not being able to get work in one area, but a shortage of the same type of worker existing in another area.
4 International	Unemployment can spread between countries as was seen after the Wall Street crash of 1929. About 20 million workers were out of work in the USA and the effect of their decreased purchasing power on imports caused unemployment to spread throughout the world.
5 Regional	Workers in some regions, such as NE England, suffer from long-standing unemployment because of the decay of old staple industries upon which they had come to place complete reliance; they are loath to move to another area or learn another job.
6 Residual	There will always be a hard core of people who are unable to work: even laziness may be regarded as a disability, especially if it is caused by some deep-rooted psychological upset.
7 Seasonal	A man may find work at a seaside resort in the summer and at a sugar beet factory in winter, but unemployment will be caused by the lag between these seasonal jobs.
8 Structural	Unemployment is caused by the changes in demand for products, eg more people might decide to travel by air, with a consequent increase in unemployment in the shipbuilding industry.

From the sociological aspect unemployment for whatever reason is bad for an individual although obviously long-term mass unemployment is far worse than temporary unemployment from casual or seasonal causes. Long term unemployment, even when State assistance staves off financial worries and material suffering, can lead to a feeling of inadequacy and, if widespread, may result in social unrest. Mass unemployment before World War II led to misery and despair for the one-time breadwinner and for his family. Children suffered deprivation in their home life which was reflected in educational handicaps. Worry over lack of income is a common cause of quarrels within a family and entire families from babies to dependent relatives suffer from a man's inability to hold down a job. In desperation he may drown his sorrows at the pub, or gamble away his unemployment benefit, while his wife and children go hungry and badly clad. In the worst cases the unemployed may be tempted into crime to augment the social security benefits received from the State. After years of unemployment a man may lose his job skills and become filled with despondency as he regards himself as a reject from society.

Modern problems of redundancies brought about by rationalisation, mergers, automation and other technological changes have forced Governments to take measures to alleviate some of the subsequent social problems. Three Government aids for help and retraining are:

1   Twenty-seven Industrial Training Boards that encourage firms to develop training programmes and make grants to promote special technical training in depressed parts of the country such as Development Areas and Intermediate Areas (see Figure 9.3).

2   Fifty Government Skill Centres with courses especially arranged for skilled apprenticeship training.

3   Lump-sum payments to redundant workers from a Central Redundancy Fund.

28.3   The distribution of income and wealth

In 1969 nineteen people died leaving estates of over a million pounds, an amount it would have taken the average manual worker a thousand years to earn. The distribution of wealth is much more unequal than the distribution of before-tax incomes. A Royal Commission headed by Lord Diamond reported on income and wealth in Britain in 1976. The disparities of income and wealth are indicated in Tables 9.3 and 9.4.

THE ASSISTED AREAS

Special development
areas

Development areas

Derelict land
clearance areas

Intermediate areas

Glenrothes
Glasgow
Edinburgh
Livingston

Newcastle

Leeds
Skelmersdale
Manchester
Liverpool
Sheffield
Nottingham

Cardiff

London

Plymouth

Figure 9.3   Development Areas and Intermediate Areas (1972)

Share owned by:	Share of total income	
	Before tax	After tax
	%	%
Top 1 per cent	6.4	4.4
2–5 per cent	10.8	9.8
6–10 per cent	9.7	9.4
11–20 per cent	15.8	15.8
21–80 per cent	51.8	53.9
81–100 per cent	5.8	6.8

Table 9.3a Distribution of personal income before and after tax (percentage shares of total personal income in 1972/73)

Shared owned by	1949	1959	1964	1967	1972/3
	%	%	%	%	%
Top 1 per cent	6.4	5.3	5.3	4.9	4.4
2–5 per cent	11.3	10.5	10.7	9.9	9.8
6–10 per cent	9.4	9.4	9.9	9.5	9.4
11–20 per cent	14.5	15.7	16.1	15.2	15.8
21–50 per cent	31.9	34.0	32.8	33.7	33.9

Table 9.3b Trends in the distribution of personal income (percentage shares of total personal income, after income tax) (Sources: Ivor Morgan, *The Social Science Teacher*, November, 1976, and *Royal Commission on the Distribution of Income and Wealth*, HMSO, 1976)

A mere five per cent of the population of the UK hold about half the country's wealth. The economist regards income as a *flow* which is received usually weekly or monthly, whereas wealth is the *stock* of goods held at a certain time. Wealth includes all things with a money value such as land, houses, cars and furniture. The very unequal distribution of both wealth and income has been brought about mainly by the capitalist nature of our society: one would expect a collectivist system to result in a more egalitarian state if communistic principles were really applied and a new wealthy class was not allowed to emerge and replace the old.

Years	%
1911–13	65–70
1924–30	60
1936–8	55
1946–8	50
1951–6	42
1960	42
1966	32
1976	25

Table 9.4a Percentage of total personal wealth owned by top one per cent of adults

Adult population	1962	1966	1976
	%	%	%
Most wealthy 1 per cent	36.6	32.2	25.0
Most wealthy 2–5 per cent	25.6	26.3	21.0
Most wealthy 6–10 per cent	13.2	14.6	14.0
Most wealthy 11–25 per cent	18.3	20.1	18.0

Table 9.4b Percentage of marketable wealth owned by adult population
(Sources: S. Crossley and D. W. Pollard, *The Wealth of Britain.*, Batsford 1968 and *Everyman's Report on the Royal Commission on Income and Wealth*, HMSO)

It can be argued that some disparities of wealth and income are justified; the necessary saving required by any progressive society will come mainly from the rich. According to the costs and surplus theory, there is a certain minimum cost of keeping alive and the rest is surplus which can be ploughed back in the form of investment. But it is impossible to determine exactly what are an individual's costs and what is his surplus, especially as in an affluent society expenditure tends to rise to exceed income. We have long shelved Micawber's simple rule that a man who receives £20 a year and spends £19.97½ is a happy man, whereas if he spent £20.02½ he would be an unhappy man. The idea that if the great inequalities of wealth and income are evened out we shall kill the goose that lays the golden egg, has been replaced by the realisation that it is not only the individual within society who can invest; the State as a whole can invest, eg in nuclear power stations or in automated steel plants.

Tables 9.3a and 9.3b, indicating the unequal distribution of income, may lead us to consider ways of mitigating the inequalities of the social structure. The comprehensive social services available in Britain help to ease the lot of the less well-to-do. The National Health Service, social security benefits, and housing subsidies all help to alleviate poverty. Incomes are evened out to a limited extent by progressive direct personal taxation (see Table 9.3b) whereby the greatest burden of tax falls on those who are more capable of bearing it and Britain has one of the highest maximum rates in the world. Some would say that these measures are only tampering with the sociological problems of inequality and that the real answer is a radical change in the structure of society, from a capitalist one motivated largely by private profit to a communist society motivated (one would hope) by the principle of service. Human nature being what it is, ideals are often not practised; it is very difficult to organise society along unselfish and less acquisitive lines.

Given the existence of inequalities of wealth and income, some of the important sociological problems that arise include:

1   the deprivation suffered by a large proportion of the population in terms of educational opportunity and good health
2   the temptation for crime to increase as the have-nots attempt illegally to bring about a more equitable society
3   the environmental problems of poor housing and undernourishment and the fact that inertia tends to continue the inequality rather than correct it.

Although sociologists had hoped that the extension of the social security services, combined with progressive taxation, would have brought about a far more equal distribution of income and wealth, investigations have suggested that great inequalities still remain.

There is more than a hint from a number of studies that income inequality has been increasing since 1949 whilst the ownership of wealth, which is far more highly concentrated in the United Kingdom than in the United States, has probably become more unequal and, in terms of family ownership, possibly strikingly more unequal, in recent years. (Richard M. Titmuss, *Income Distribution and Social Change*, Unwin University Books, 1962.)

Unit 29 The Organisation of Work

29.1 The division of labour

In a very primitive society where needs were simple it would have been possible for a man to be self-sufficient. Robinson Crusoe was able to survive on his lonely island before Man Friday arrived. Crusoe was able to grow his own corn, milk goats, and make clothes from skins, while his shelter was a rough wooden hut surrounded by a defensive stockade. However, his life was made easier because he had tools, rescued from the ship, and which had been made by a specialist craftsman. If Robinson Crusoe had been shipwrecked with his family it is likely that he would have divided up the labour: a wife could have prepared the meals, made or mended clothes or cleaned the house. Man and wife would have divided the work between them each according to their several abilities. If there had been any children they would have been allotted tasks depending upon their ages, abilities and aptitudes. In primitive societies it was customary for the very young to be given the job of ensuring that the fire was kept alight, whilst elder children might have looked after a flock just as David looked after the sheep in Biblical times. The more numerous the group, the more specialised the tasks of the members. A commune in China or a kibbutz in Israel may be almost self-sufficient, although goods from outside the community will be required if living standards are to be comparable with other societies, eg they would need new seeds, fertilisers, farm implements and more complex machinery. The *division of labour* is concerned with workers concentrating upon one task or perhaps a few tasks. In medieval times a village community would have its own blacksmith, carpenter, tailor and wheelwright.

It was in eighteenth-century Britain that the division of labour was employed for the first time in an industrial setting with workers specialising in some small part of the productive process. Division of labour of an industrial nature began in workshops that used some means of mechanical power: 300 workmen were employed in a silk mill at Derby in 1719. The credit for organising factory production based upon the division of labour is usually given to Richard Arkwright and Jedediah Strutt, who established the first cotton spinning factory at Cromford in 1771. These workers were assisted by water power and the factory on the river Derwent still remains as a fine example of industrial archaeology. In *The Wealth of Nations*, Adam Smith described an eighteenth-century pin factory where ten persons manufactured 48 000 pins a day, whereas if the workers had 'all wrought separately and independently, and without any of them being educated to this peculiar business, they certainly could not each of them have made twenty, perhaps not one pin a day'. Mass production by the conveyor belt system has resulted in the division of labour being operated so intensively that a worker's task may take only a matter of seconds. Production of the famous Ford Model T motor-car was divided into 7882 different pieces of work so that the simplicity of each job was such that '670 jobs could be filled by legless men, 2638 by one-legged men, two by armless men, 715 by one-armed men and ten by blind men'. (Henry Ford, *My Life and Work*, Heinemann.)

It has been said that most of the advantages of the division of labour are economic, whereas most of the disadvantages are social. It is true that the division of labour has the great economic advantage of enabling output to be increased while piece-work rates of pay can be used to encourage workers to speed up their production, but some of the advantages are also social. Some of the social advantages are listed below:

1 Jobs can be found for people who would otherwise not find employment because of limited mental or physical ability.

2 Although the tasks performed may be automatic, workers quickly acquire skill at a particular task and can even take pride in mastering a job which would seem uninteresting to the majority of people.

3 Working with others on a conveyor belt system or an assembly line may bring a worthwhile feeling of co-operation at work.

4 Some workers regard long periods of training as tedious and unremunerative, so they are pleased to learn their task quickly and get on with the job of production.

5 Employers can use aptitude and vocational tests to see that each worker finds a job that suits his particular talents.

6 Some firms, on the other hand, move workers from one task to another so that they do not become too bored.

7 Apart from not having to learn to use different tools, workers are saved the bother of setting aside one tool whilst they select another tool for the next task.

8 There are some people who do not want to exercise responsibility or take on work which requires mental effort, so they are quite happy to perform very simple tasks and be able to chat or listen to music while they work.

9 Workers are able to purchase goods which would be beyond their means were it not for the decreased costs made possible by division of labour.

10 The woman's role has been changed greatly by mass production because she has gadgets that could not be cheaply produced without the division of labour, and these time-saving devices decrease her household chores so that she can find work, money and companionship at the local factory.

However, there are serious social disadvantages of the division of labour causing *alienation* (see Topic 29.2):

1   There is a loss of job–satisfaction because the worker is not involved with all processes that lead to the finished product.

2   The work is so repetitive that it is difficult to take much pride in the task itself, and the worker may rarely see the finished article.

3   Boring work may destroy creative abilities, so that even non-work time is spent passively and the employee is unable or unwilling to express any individuality in his leisure activities.

4   Monotonous work leads to fatigue.

5   There has been a decline in individual craftsmanship and many unskilled factory hands have no opportunities of displaying any artistic talents or merit at work.

6   Standardisation leads to dull uniformity both of products and producers.

7   The class gap between employer and employee widens as the old personal relationship between master and man is whittled away.

8   The large-scale employment of married women may lead to the neglect of children and increases in juvenile delinquency.

9   Workers may have a high risk of unemployment, because they may be replaced by modern machinery, or a large work-force may have to be stood off if a few key workers come out on strike.

10   Although 'economic sociologists are currently at loggerheads over the relative merit of the basic causes of strikes' (N. J. Smelser, *The Sociology of Economic Life*, Prentice-Hall) strikes are apparently more frequent when a large number of workers are employed under one roof, eg in a motor car factory.

29.2   Alienation

Émile Durkheim was the first to draw attention to the sociological importance of the division of labour. Durkheim linked the use of this specialised industrial process with social differentiation and social evolution. He stressed that the division of labour enhanced the significance of social relationships in occupational groups and thus influenced the moral ideas of an industrial society.

The division of labour and grim industrial conditions of the nineteenth century led Karl Marx to develop further his idea that the individual's or the class relationship to the means of production influenced and determined all other relationships within society. The concept of *alienation* was developed by Marx as a means of describing a worker's attitude and sense of frustration with his purely repetitive part in the industrial work process. To perform a routine task for many hours each

Excessive alienation can lead to industrial conflict

day in a factory meant that the worker was little more than an appendage
to his machine, and having no other economic resources to sell other than
his labour, he was simply a wage slave. Alienation therefore means a
separation of the individual from the process he is engaged in as it
becomes meaningless to him. He may also become separated or cut off
from his fellow workers. The worker has almost no interest in the work
that he is doing, and views his job purely as an instrumental means of
supporting and enjoying himself and his family outside the factory.
Alienation is mainly applied to the industrial work situation, but a sense
of alienation might well be found in other spheres of human activity and
life; for example, Jackson and Marsden found evidence of alienation
from parents when working–class boys went to university (*Education and
the Working Class*).

Improvements have been made in working conditions in factories over
the past hundred years, and the working class has gained considerable
material benefits. Sociologists have shown considerable interest in the
work situation in their attempts to obtain an understanding of society.

Car workers in particular have been the focus of attention for many sociologists (such as Goldthorpe, Lockwood, Bechofer, and Platt, *The Affluent Worker*) possibly because of the monotony of the assembly line, invented in 1910 by Henry Ford. The high incidence of strikes, particularly unofficial strikes, in the motor industry is often thought to be primarily caused by the work situation: alienation being increased by the assembly-line type of working. R. Blauner in his book *Alienation and Freedom: the Manual Worker in Industry* (University of Chicago Press, 1967) identifies four types of alienation: *powerlessness*, when decisions are made over which the worker has no control; *meaninglessness*, in that they see only their own small part of the manufacturing process and not the whole, thus there is little or no sense of purpose other than the weekly wage packet; *isolation* occurs when a sense of community is absent in a large factory with a high labour turnover and frequent job switching, friendships become harder to form (there is neither the time for conversation nor is it often possible to speak without shouting above the noise); *self-estrangement* is when there can be no personal expression put into work, such as a craftsman is able to do, and there is no satisfaction in the task to be done. Strikes are not the only symptom of alienation; other industrial problems such as absenteeism, lateness, labour turnover, and even accidents are often much higher in those jobs where alienation is most apparent.

Émile Durkheim was also interested in the connection between occupation and social relationships. He linked the use of the specialised process caused by the division of labour with social differentiation and social evolution. Durkheim stressed that the division of labour enhanced the significance of social relationships in occupational groups and thus influenced the moral ideas of industrialised societies.

29.3   Technology and automation

Changes in technology such as the use of automation or computers have an important impact on social relations. Technical changes in methods of production have made possible what Dr James Burnham has referred to as the managerial revolution, whereby paid managers are able to control vast business enterprises and those who work for these enterprises. Burnham predicted that the main holders of power in future societies would not be communists, socialists or capitalists, but rather people who possessed expert technological skills.

Some of the classical sociologists of the nineteenth century realised that the change to industrialised production played a vital part in the evolution of society. 'The mode of production of material life conditions the social, political and intellectual life process in general.' (K. Marx and F. Engels, *Selected Works*.) A modern French sociologist distinguishes three stages in the development of technology:

1   the disintegration of a worker's skill, eg by division of labour
2   the mechanisation of productive techniques and the development of an integrated system of production
3   the advent of automation whereby the worker merely controls and superintends
(A. Touraine, *An Historical Theory in the Evolution of Industrial Skills*, McGraw-Hill).

The economist J. K. Galbraith has taken up the theme that power has passed to the *technostructure* and that technological planning by-passes the market (J. K. Galbraith, *The New Industrial State*, Hamish Hamilton). It is almost as if advanced technology has brought some realism to the once discredited Say's Law that supply creates its own

Automation involves the use of complex machinery which performs many tasks with a minimum work-force. The main control room of a CEGB power station.

demand. The ultimate in productive technological changes is a robot-controlled automatic factory with articles produced without human participation: raw materials would be fed automatically in at one end of the factory and the finished products would emerge at the other end. The ultimate in automation is rarely reached and there are so many stages in automation that one may include many technical developments that make production simpler. The ultimate state of a completely automatic factory or office is described as *full automation* (*Automation*, HMSO).

Automation may be considered as the reversal of the division of labour because whereas the latter divides up work into many parts to be performed by a large work-force, automation involves the use of complex machinery which performs many tasks with the minimum work-force. The social consequences of automation will depend on the extent of the automatic processes but certain general social gains and losses are inevitable.

The social advantages of automation may include:

1   the lessening of the soulless nature of work that is so much a cause of alienation.

2   more time available for leisure pursuits (this will be more advantageous to those who are capable of using their leisure in a worthwhile way: in ancient Greece menial chores were performed by slaves, leaving the élite to pursue artistic and intellectual activities)

3   more opportunities for full-time education in a technological age demanding greater expertise and high qualifications

4   more economic goods available so that the standard of living can be raised

5   an expansion of service industries (such as catering, holiday agencies, entertainment and sport) especially as less work-time will be spent in manufacturing and people will look for new ways in which to spend their increased leisure-time

6   a shorter working week and longer holidays in which to relax

7   more resources available to keep the sick and the aged: 'within twenty-five years automation will have made the old concept of charity obsolete' (Sir Leon Bagrit, *Automation*)

8   the expansion of the do-it-yourself (DIY) movement as people seek satisfaction from using their hands.

Some of the unfortunate social consequences of automation are likely to be:

1   an even greater gap between the rich and the poor because the means of production will be controlled by the wealthy technocrats

2   a large increase in the number of unemployed in the short run, especially

amongst less qualified workers who will be faced with redundancy

   3   a shortage of purchasing power for those who cannot find work

   4   an inability by trade unions to protect members who are unskilled

   5   the extension of synthetic and artificial entertainments (we have already had boxing matches by computer)

   6   over-production of goods, consequent upon under-consumption by the unemployed

   7   social revolutionary tendencies brought about by a lack of a purposeful life for those unable to adapt or find a place in a technological society

   8   *white-collar workers* gaining at the expense of the rest of society with subsequent trade union quarrels.

So technological advances are bringing radical changes to our society. There is a continual trend towards increased industrialisation and urban living, together with a decline in rural activities. The work-force is becoming more skilled and mobile; occupational structure is inevitably altering. Changes are far more rapid than they have ever been before; it is best to make the most of the technological advances that generally appear advantageous to society, but to attempt to control the pace of these changes. In what ways can man establish a more enlightened morality in keeping with rapid technological advances so that the social problems which accompanied earlier industrial revolutions are avoided?

29.4 Relationships between employer and employee

Relations between employer and employee generally become more strained in an industrial society. When firms are large, and labour relationships impersonal, a 'them' and 'us' atmosphere develops. However the interests of employers and employees are not necessarily fundamentally opposed: if the firm is a going-concern and productivity is increased, then it is more likely that employees will enjoy security of employment and improved earnings. Good employers are concerned that their workers should be well-paid, happy people. In societies where slavery was permitted, many slave owners appreciated that they would get more work if their slaves were well fed rather than emaciated. In a capitalist society, a philosophy of high wages may be conducive to more work and greater output. In any society it is preferable that there should be mutual respect between bosses and workers. The interests of employers and employees may sometimes be divided in a capitalist society, when the employer class is preoccupied with the maximisation of profit without regard for the welfare of their workers. Even in a *mixed economy* such as that found in Britain, strikes and other forms of unrest still occur in the public-sector industries that are controlled by the State and where profit is not the main motivating influence. Some of the reasons for industrial strife include:

1 employers attempting to secure labour on the cheap

2 workers believing that they are not securing their fair share either of the industrial organisation's initial profit or of extra profit brought by increased productivity

3 some workers believing that they are a special case and not receiving a just award for their labour

4 day-to-day frictions which arise when communications break down and one side of industry does not give full consideration to the other side's point of view

5 quarrels between workers' organisations such as:

a craft unions versus industrial unions

b manual workers versus white-collar workers

c demarcation disputes over who should do a particular job

6 a lack of effective *negotiating machinery* so that causes of dissatisfaction cannot be adequately discussed and eradicated.

7 income differentials for skill and responsibility may become eroded.

Effective negotiating machinery between employers and employees in a modern society pre-supposes the existence and acceptance of trade unions. Where trade unions and employers are able to arrange a system of successful co-operation then industrial disputes will be minimised. The main functions of trade unions are:

1 to improve the standard of living and increase the *real earnings* of their members (real earnings are not just monetary earnings, but rather the goods and services that can be bought with money earned)

2 to work for better peripheral money benefits such as higher overtime rates, piecework rates and bonuses

3 to strive for subsidiary *socio-economic benefits* such as shorter working hours, longer holidays and workers' amenities

4 to attempt to safeguard the jobs of their members especially where redundancies can be avoided

5 to be concerned with industrial education and especially with the adequate training of apprentices

6 to provide occasional benefits similar to the old friendly society benefits when trade union members experience industrial accidents, sickness, strikes, temporary unemployment or retirement

7 to work for the reform of industrial legislation possibly by participating

Engineering apprentices at work, Rowntree Mackintosh Ltd, York

indirectly in political matters (eg by contributing to the finances of the Labour Party)

8   to co-operate with employers and the Government in the establishment of effective bargaining machinery.

Bargaining machinery in Britain may be considered in three stages; each stage is of a slightly more serious nature although strikes may occur at any stage, if bargaining procedures break down. The stage at which bargaining between employer and employee may cease to operate depends upon the industrial climate and the amount of goodwill, or lack of goodwill, that exists between the two parties. The three stages are:

1   negotiations by employers and unions to secure a settlement to a dispute without calling upon outside help

2   conciliation by Department of Employment officers in an effort to draw the parties closer together

3   arbitration by a third party that gives an independent decision although often employers and unions will not agree to be bound by the findings of an arbitration board.

Strike action is usually the last resort by a trade union: even in a society that provides reasonable social security benefits, workers are likely to suffer most from a strike; employers may lose business, goodwill and profit while shareholders may suffer from a loss of dividends, but it is unlikely that they will have to cut down on foodstuffs or have a rental firm reclaim the TV set. Before strike action takes place trade unions are likely to use other bargaining weapons. Workers may deliberately *go slow*, or *work to rule* by rigidly adhering to an employer's rule-book. Relationships between employer and employee depend to a considerable extent upon the type of trade union to which employees belong. There are five main types of trade unions in Britain today:

1   *General unions* are the largest unions representing workers in a number of jobs. These include the three largest unions, ie the Transport and General Workers' Union (2 000 000 members), the Amalgamated Union of Engineers and Foundry Workers (1 400 000 members) and the National Union of General and Municipal Workers (800 000 members). The general unions have great financial strength but their power is often not so great as their membership would suggest because their members are engaged in different occupations.

2   *Industrial unions* represent workers in one industry and their power derives from the common interest of their members. The National Union of Mineworkers and the National Union of Railwaymen have displayed their unity by national stoppages during the 1970s.

3   *White-collar unions* are becoming more important as the service industries expand and more people work in the sphere of administration, finance, government, science and the professions. Nearly forty per cent of all trade unionists could be classified as white-collar workers by 1975.

4   *Craft unions* are the oldest and most numerous unions, but their membership figures are decreasing. About 450 craft unions represent less than 5000 members each.

5   *Confederations of unions* are organisations of unions that join in a loose way to give workers the strength that comes with unity. Their main importance, so far as the relationships between employers and employees are concerned, is that they enable workers to face the large confederations of employers with something approaching equal strength. An example of such a confederation of trade unions is the Confederation of Shipbuilding and Engineering Unions.

The Royal Commission on Trade Unions and Employers' Associations (the Donovan Report) drew attention to the fact that, although Britain's number of day lost through breakdowns in relationships between employers and employees was not excessive up to 1968 (compared with countries such as Australia, Canada, Italy and the USA, which had far worse records), about ninety-five per cent of strikes in Britain were unofficial strikes. These *wildcat strikes* were to some extent caused by a double system of industrial bargaining: the informal system of negotiations between individual employers and shop stewards often clashed with the formal system of official associations of employers and workers.

In 1977 the *Bullock Commission* on industrial democracy recommended that the shareholder representatives on boards of management in industry be matched by an equal number of representatives elected by recognised trade unionists in the firm. To avoid possible deadlock, a third group of joint nominees would be chosen from neither side.

Whether or not this will be successful in improving industrial relations will only be seen if the Bullock Committee's proposals are implemented.

The Industrial Relations Act of 1971 attempted to eliminate the double system of bargaining, but the Act was comparatively unsuccessful because of friction between the Government and the unions, culminating in the Trades Union Congress advising unions affiliated to the TUC not to register under the Act. Unregistered unions lost their legal protection, but the Conservative Government, elected in 1970, was forced to negotiate with these unregistered unions in an attempt to establish harmonious industrial relations. In 1972 the Government was accused of preventing the operation of its own 1971 Act when an almost unknown official called the Official Solicitor secured the release, against their will, of five dockers imprisoned by order of the National Industrial Relations Court set up under the 1971 Act. Their continued imprisonment could have brought a national dock strike and probably a complete breakdown of industrial relations in Britain. So a stalemate arose and the singular lack of success of the Industrial Relations Act of 1971 was indicated by the 1972 strike record of about 24 million workdays lost. The 1971 Act was replaced in 1974 by the Labour Government's Trade Union and Labour Relations Act which restored the privileges of the unions. It would seem that the most successful industrial relationships are found where employers and employees are left to negotiate freely without the Government attempting to force industrial co-operation by legislation. After this Act there was a period of four years when Britain enjoyed fewer strikes than at any time since 1960. This was due in part to the economic recession and an agreement between the Government and the TUC on the need for pay restraint at a time of high inflation. Since the beginning of 1979 the situation has worsened again.

Unit 30 Work and Leisure

30.1 Occupations

We have seen in Chapter 2 how important someone's occupation is in telling us something about him, and how the Registrar General divides occupations into five classes (see Figure 2.2). If you were conversing with a stranger it would probably not be long before you asked him about his occupation. If you found out what job he did, then you would be likely to make some pretty shrewd assessments about his life, interests, income and position in society.

The five classes used are necessarily arbitrary and it is sometimes very difficult to decide in which class, according to his job, a person belongs. As occupations change so classifications must be modified, eg the *Classification of Occupations*, 1970, omitted some groups previously included: boiler scalers; chimney sweeps; coopers, hoopmakers and benders!

Some examples of the groups in which various occupations are placed are given in Table 9.5 below, and in Table 2.1, in Chapter 2.

Social class		
1	Professional	architects, chemists, surveyors
2	Intermediate	farmers, social welfare workers, physiotherapists
3	Skilled	plumbers, turners, woodworkers
4	Partially skilled	fishermen, counterhands, waiters
5	Unskilled	charwomen, office cleaners, window cleaners

Table 9.5 Examples of occupations according to social classes
(Source: *Classification of Occupations*, 1970, HMSO, Appendix D)

As our society becomes better qualified there is a tendency for the percentage of workers in the professional, managerial and skilled classes to increase, and the less skilled to decrease (see Tables 9.5 and 9.6). The two main reasons for these percentage changes are the improved educational opportunities available, and the greater demand for higher-grade workers in an affluent modern society.

There are close relationships between occupations and the way in which non-work time is spent. There is a double-pull involved because a

A postman clearing a pillar box. In which group would he be placed in the classification of occupations, and why?

Socio-economic group of head of household	1971	1972	1973	1974
	%	%	%	%
Professional	3.9	4.1	4.2	4.3
Employers and managers	14.6	13.5	13.2	15.0
Intermediate and junior non-manual	19.8	21.4	19.9	20.0
Skilled manual (incl. foremen and supervisors) and own-account non-professional	33.3	33.3	33.9	31.9
Semi-skilled manual and personal service	19.5	18.2	19.4	19.8
Unskilled manual	6.6	6.8	6.5	6.4
Never worked	1.9	2.2	2.3	2.0
Full-time students	0.4	0.5	0.6	0.5
Total sample size, households (=100%) (numbers)	11 591	11 319	11 349	10 852

Table 9.6 Changes in the social class distribution of head of household, UK, 1971–4
(Source: General Household Survey, *Social Trends*, 1976, CSO)

person's occupation will influence his attitudes, but the opposite may also be true because specific occupations attract people with certain attitudes. Although less time is spent at work than was the case fifty years ago (largely because of shorter hours and longer holidays) nevertheless the average person is more involved with his occupation than people were centuries ago. In 1978 the average *actual* hours worked was forty-four, but the average *basic* week in Britain was forty hours. This is a longer working week than those of most continental countries such as Germany and France. Before 1761 there were forty-seven recognised holy days (often holidays) in England, and in the thirteenth century the skilled artisan worked only '194 days a year'. (H. L. Wilensky, *The Uneven Distribution of Leisure : The Impact of Growth on Free Time.*) The average person is in many ways more occupationally-orientated nowadays. Greater involvement in one's occupation means that it is increasingly difficult to distinguish between work and non-work activities. This is especially true of the professions and higher grades of work. A doctor may get great satisfaction from delivering a baby, even though it may be late at night. At home a teacher may study background material related to his subject, mark school exercises and prepare lessons for the next day. A professional footballer might be very willing to enjoy a game and display his skills even if no remuneration were involved. Where does work stop and non-work begin in these occupations and in the case of architects, farmers, nurses and scores of other jobs? Indeed, for many people the time spent outside their main occupational role may be considered subconsciously as the hardest work of all. The university professor might be asked by his wife to spend an evening putting up a shelf, but to a non-technical, academically-minded man this might be one of the most difficult occupations of all. In an economic society based upon mechanisation and division of labour, there are millions who work merely because they get paid for it, but the most satisfying occupations are those that people would be willing to do even if they were not paid. Work is any productive activity whether one is paid or not. The housewife who is proud of her home and the mother who looks after her baby with loving care, are both fulfilling worthwhile unpaid occupations. But in the economic world we are concerned with occupations in market situations. A man's place in society is governed not merely by his type of occupation but by the amount of goods and services he can command because of the money he receives for carrying out his occupation.

Some of the occupations that have been the subject of special studies by sociologists have been jobs which have a great socialising influence upon those engaged in the occupation: these workers are employed as a team and their very lives may depend upon each other. Thus Jeremy Tunstall's study *The Fishermen* (MacGibbon & Kee, 1969) shows how a trawlerman sees himself as a member of a class drawn together by occupation so that 'he has indelibly printed on him certain habits, reflexes, patterns of spending, attitudes to life . . .' Similarly, the coal miner faces a life of occupational hazards; he could not work alone and he spends his free time in the pub with his mates (Dennis, Henriques and Slaughter, *Coal is Our Life*, Tavistock Publications, 1969). But the schoolteacher spends much time in a classroom and a research scientist in a laboratory, often separated from colleagues doing similar work, so that in these occupations there is little socialisation. In the latter cases it is less likely that people with similar occupations will spend their leisure time together: they work separately and they play separately. 'A knowledge of the ways in which work and leisure are inter-related helps us to understand that the problems of leisure are not likely to be successfully tackled without some consideration of the quality and meaning of working life.' (S. R. Parker, *The Sociology of Industry*, Allen & Unwin.)

30.2 Leisure

We have seen that there is a close connection between work and leisure. If two men are watching a cricket match they may be at work, at leisure or participating in both work and leisure. One man might be paid for writing an account of the match for the press, or for scoring or umpiring. Another man might write and describe the match to an absent friend, or he might be very happy to score or umpire if he were asked, and he might be quite willing to do these things voluntarily for pleasure. The difference between work and leisure in these cases is very difficult to distinguish. If the first man, who was being paid as a journalist, scorer or umpire, would rather have been doing something else such as sailing or gardening, then work becomes more clearly discernible from leisure. But is gardening work? It can be work or leisure depending upon the person, place and time.

Yet having established this close relationship between leisure and work, it is clear that there are many cases where the two pursuits can be separated with greater clarity. The *Concise Oxford Dictionary* defines leisure as 'opportunity *to do*, *for*, afforded by free time, time at one's own disposal, . . . not occupied, without hurry'. It is this opportunity to do what one wants to do, indulging in one's chosen pursuits, having free time at one's own disposal, that is the real substance of leisure. In the past it was common for people to spend their spare time in an unhurried way, but modern leisure pursuits may include flying, motor racing, running 10 000 metres in the fastest possible time or playing twenty simultaneous games of chess against the clock. Dr Parker has pointed out that we cannot comprehend the problems of leisure without considering a man's working life, but the contrary also applied because a man's work may affect his leisure in different ways. A man who enjoys his work will want it to carry over into his spare time, whereas another man may wish to have a complete change of activity.

It should be clear why we are considering leisure in this chapter entitled The Economy and Employment. Firstly, a man must have leisure time if the economy is to be efficient and work is to be done well. Secondly, there are a whole series of leisure activities upon which a large number of people in the tertiary or service industries are employed; the provision of leisure by the organisation of bingo halls, professional football matches, package holidays etc. is an industry in itself. In the broadest sense, those engaged in providing library or museum services are part of the leisure industry, although their primary purpose may not be to provide pleasure pursuits. Need leisure coincide with enjoyment? Can leisure be spent upon activities that a person would rather not do?

If a person is engaged in mass production at work then he may well seek mass pleasures of a synthetic nature because his work has left him so dried-up that his creative abilities are nullified. The affluent society has provided the possibility of greater indulgence in leisure pursuits. The Duke of Wellington was worried that poor people might move about too much and get ideas beyond their station, but the growth of railways and other means of travel has popularised holidays away from home with the provision of many facilities for enjoyment. Transport has had a great influence upon leisure. Today there are about 18 million motor-cars in Britain and apart from providing a facility for pleasure, the motor calls for so many other ways of spending one's spare time: the car has to be cleaned and maintained. Other methods of travel such as aircraft and boats have extended leisure opportunities.

Dr Mark Abrams classified five ages of leisure, the first of these is the teenage period which is considered in Youth Culture (Topic 13.2). The young are the most concerned with out-going pursuits and with people of their own age. The young and the old (ie retired people) have more free time to spend than other members of society, but the young have more money and energy than the old. The normal teenager is less inclined to spend time in passive or home-based pursuits such as watching television. Table 9.7 sets out the five main stages of leisure.

Table 9.7 is over-simplified, but gives a generalised picture of leisure pursuits such as watching television. The table gives some of the main compensations and limitations: the teenager should be full of life and energy but may be easily bored; newly-weds often find it difficult to

1st Age	2nd Age	3rd Age	4th Age	5th Age
Teenager/Youth Culture	Young Marrieds	35 to 45 years	45 to 64 years	Over 65 years
Much time spent outside the home in company with peer group; working classes have more spending money than middle classes in many cases.	Set up home and have children; 70% women and 55% men married before they reach 25; essentially home-centred.	Home ties decrease as children are less demanding; more time spent outside the home.	Most affluent age; very few have responsibilities of children; less physical energy; status seeking.	Retirement of women at 60 and men at 65; physical and mental decline; little spare cash.
Mass sports; sexual freedom; luxury spending on non-essentials; search for danger to ease boredom.	Purchase of home and car; child caring; TV, reading; DIY and hobbies; home and car maintenance.	Public houses; visiting friends; dinners and dances; church and small group activities; camping and caravanning.	Eating and drinking more expensively; golf and bridge; colour TV; Continental holidays.	Inexpensive pursuits such as reading; gardening; knitting; whist; bingo; walking (often cannot afford pubs and cinemas).

Table 9.7   The Five Ages of Leisure

manage financially but they are wrapped up in each other, and young children give much pleasure; the thirty-five to forty-five year olds have time and money to spend outside the home, although they are probably still struggling to get 'established'; the forty-five to sixty-five year olds have most to spend and fewer financial worries but it is often a time of frustration and cynicism; the over sixty-fives have more time for leisure after retirement but usually have not the money to get the best from their spare time. All the various ages of leisure are influenced by a search for *status* as Thorstein Veblen argued in *Theory of the Leisure Class*: the young man wants a high-powered motor bike; the young marrieds are proud of their home and children; the middle-aged show their home movies or their car of the latest model; the old still have their pride and resist charity, but as Ronald Fletcher maintains, 'If old people could be made materially secure, there is no reason why the period should not be regarded in a positive, constructive way.' (*The Family and Marriage*, Penguin Books, 1962.)

Terms used in this chapter

factors of production	full employment	primary workers
entrepreneur	white-collar workers	division of labour
capitalist economy	wildcat strikes	automation
working population	mixed economy	negotiating machinery
labour mobility	alienation	technostructure

Further reading

H. Benyon, *Working for Ford* (CP, 1973)
T. Burns, *Industrial Man* (Penguin, 1967)
M. Carter, *Into Work* (Penguin, 1966)
N. Dennis, F. Henriques, C. Slaughter, *Coal is Our Life* (Tavistock, 1969)
R. Dore, *British Factory—Japanese Factory* (Allen & Unwin, 1973)
A. Flanders, *Collective Bargaining* (Penguin, 1969)
J. Goldthorpe *et al.*, *The Affluent Worker* (Tavistock, 1969)
T. Nichols & P. Armstrong, *Workers Divided* (Fontana, 1976)
S. Parker, *The Future of Work and Leisure* (MacGibbon & Kee, 1971)
S. Parker *et al.*, *The Sociology of Industry* (Allen & Unwin, 1967)
D. Weir (ed), *Men and Work in Modern Britain* (Fontana, 1973)
F. Zweig, *The Worker in an Affluent Society* (Heinemann, 1961)
Economic Trends (CSO)

Questions from GCE 'O' Level Sociology Examination Papers

1 In what ways does a person's work influence his non-work behaviour? (AEB, November 1969)

2 Some areas have high unemployment rates whilst jobs are available in other parts of the country. What factors tend to prevent unemployed workers moving into others areas where there are jobs? (AEB, Specimen Paper for New Syllabus, 1972)

3 What are the major social problems of unemployment? (Oxford Local Examinations, 1972)

4

		1911	1966
1	Employers and proprietors	6.7	3.4
2	White-collar workers	18.7	38.3
i	Managers and administrators	3.4	6.1
ii	Higher professionals	1.0	3.4
iii	Technicians and lower professionals	3.1	6.5
iv	Foremen and inspectors	1.3	6.0
v	Clerks	4.5	13.2
vi	Salesmen	5.4	6.1
3	Manual workers	74.6	58.3
i	Skilled	30.5	28.1
ii	Semi-skilled	43.4	26.1
iii	Unskilled	9.6	8.5
4	All occupied	100.0	100.0

The occupied population of Great Britain by major occupational groups 1911–66 (Source: D. Weir (ed.), Men and Work in Modern Britain)

a What changes in the occupational structure are indicated by the above table?

b How would you explain these changes? (AEB, November 1975)

5 What is the difference between automation and industrialisation? What effect is automation likely to have on the lives of employees? (AEB, November 1974)

6 Would you prefer a white-collar or a manual job? Why? (Oxford Local Examinations, 1972)

7 What do you understand by the term 'division of labour'? Illustrate your answer with reference to any *one* industry or occupation. (Oxford Local Examinations, 1974)

8 What are the major sources of 'alienation' in industry? (Oxford Local Examinations, 1974)

9   Distribution of wealth by groups of owners

Percentage of wealth owned by:	1962	1974
Most wealthy 1%	36.6	26.0
2%	46.6	34.9
5%	62.2	51.1
10%	75.4	67.5
25%	93.7	92.8

(Adapted from *The Wealth of Britain*, 1968 and *Inland Revenue Statistics*, 1975)

Discuss the argument that Britain is now a classless society, making some use in your answer of the above figures.

10   What are the most important social consequences of automation? (Oxford Local Examinations, 1973)

11   'It has been suggested that automation will bring a new golden age of leisure and plenty for everybody. It has also been suggested that automation poses the greatest threat to our standard of living and way of life since the Industrial Revolution.' (Adapted from E. Kristenson, *Automation and the Workers*) What are the possible consequences of automation? (AEB, November 1976)

a   Explain why there should be more boys than girls entering employment in 1967.

b   Account for the sex differences in the figures for apprenticeships and clerical work. (AEB, November 1969)

12   What do you understand by the term 'automation'? What effects does automation have on job satisfaction? (Oxford Local Examinations, 1975)

13   What are the causes and consequences of the increased employment of married women? (AEB, November 1969)

14   What are the major causes of industrial disputes? (Oxford Local Examinations, 1972)

15   What is a 'shop steward'? What part does he or she play in the British system of industrial relations? (Oxford Local Examinations, 1975)

16   Occupation has a marked influence on leisure. Discuss. (AEB, 1968)

17   Two men are watching a cricket match: one of them is working, the other is enjoying his leisure time. Explain how this might be true and say exactly what you mean by work and leisure. (AEB, June 1971)

18   'There is a growing literature tracing the ways in which the kind of work men do influences their pattern of life. Studies of leisure which have hitherto focused on social class differences are now developing the theme that there are occupational differences within class and status groupings which play a large part in determining the style of leisure, family behaviour, political orientations, as well as more general values.' (S. R. Parker)

19   Outline the major changes which have taken place in the distribution of trade union membership since 1945. (Oxford Local Examinations, 1974)

a   Explain this passage in non-technical language.

b   Give some examples of the class differences referred to. (AEB, June 1972)

20 What do you understand by leisure? Describe some of the different ways in which various groups spend their leisure time. How could you account for these differences? (AEB, Specimen Paper for New Syllabus, 1972)

21 'The kind of work a man does influences his whole way of life.' Discuss this statement giving examples wherever appropriate. (AEB, November 1972)

22 Describe and account for the changing pattern of leisure activities during the last fifty years. (AEB, June 1969)

23 Explain, with examples, how the occupation which a person follows affects many areas of his life outside work. (AEB, June 1979)

24 It is sometimes suggested that work is a central fact of life—its influence on our behaviour outside work is often very extensive. Show, with examples, the ways in which this happens and attempt to explain why. (AEB, June 1981)

10 Social Control

Unit 31 Social Order and Social Control

31.1 Social Order

To begin thinking about the term *social order*, we will start by looking at a school, which is something close to everyone's experience. In a school there are a great many pupils and staff, each with different backgrounds and interests. Despite this variety, we can think of individuals grouped together in clusters because they share the same interests and identify with one another. For example, pupils and staff who share a primary interest in sport make up one group in the school; those interested in sociology, another; a third group could be those students whose main interest is in leaving school at the earliest opportunity. Of course, a pupil could be thought of as belonging to all three of these groups at the same or different times in his school career.

In society there is a wide variety of people, with different backgrounds, involved in different activities but clustered together in groups because of their shared interests and goals. For example, there are many people in our society, from widely differing backgrounds, who are parents. However, even though they do not know one another, their common experience as parents allows them to be considered as a group. The men and women who are teachers in a school or a college are another example of a group. These groups, parents and teachers, share a concern with bringing up children, so we can think of social groups as being broadly interested in the same activity.

Not all groups in society have interests in common and this can lead to disagreements. For example, one of the most pressing jobs of town planners is to think of ways of coping with the increased number of private cars brought into city centres. One scheme has been to build multi-storey car parks in or near town centres. The goals and schemes of town planners, however, are not always thought of as such good ideas by other groups in the town who wish to preserve old buildings or scenic views in preference to providing multi-storey car parks.

These are small, local issues, but there is also conflict on a much wider scale in society between large and powerful social groups. One of the most conspicuous examples of this in Britain today is the basic differences of interest which exist between workers and management in industry.

Our society, then, is made up of many different social groups some of which co-operate with one another while others compete or conflict with one another. Why is it that groups do not merely seize what they want? Of course, force is used in society and groups do succeed, by fair means and foul, in furthering their own interests. The feudal barons of England furthered their schemes for getting more land by driving out neighbouring barons and force, though usually of a more subtle sort, is just as much a part of the society we live in today. The surprising point is not that force is sometimes used, but that we so often employ more peaceful means, such as discussion, to settle differences of interest.

Despite these varied interests, society does not collapse under the strain of their conflicting pressures. We know this because, generation after generation, society changes but endures. Sociologists therefore speak of there being an underlying unity and order in social life. It is this order that makes it possible for everyday life to carry on. For example, we go to school or to work and know that there will be someone to drive the bus, heat the building, help us with our work and cook lunch. We assume that the bus driver will stick to the route, the caretaker will not burn down the building, the schoolteacher or the boss will not scream at us and

The goals and schemes of town planners are not always considered good ideas by everybody

throw our work out of the window. In fact, we never think about these things because we take responsible behaviour for granted to an extent. This is because individuals perform social roles and their everyday behaviour conforms to their roles as bus driver, school teacher, mother, child. In general, people act in ways which we expect from them in their roles, and so social interaction is, to a considerable degree, predictable. This means we are able to plan and organise what we do to achieve our objectives. For example, hire purchase companies assume that their customers will continue to pay for their goods and the customers themselves use hire purchase arrangements because they are confident that they will be able to continue paying.

Social life is carried on according to rules, rather like a game of chess. For instance, the player himself decides how he will move his chess pieces but every move will obey the rules for the game of chess. The match can be played because each player knows and understands these rules; this allows both of them to plan their game and reach their objective of winning the match. If a player should suddenly invent his own rules his opponent would be confused and the game could not go on.

In the same way there are rules which control how we act in social groups and in society; if the rules are broken the situation becomes confusing, no one can be sure what anyone else is going to do, and social order is threatened. Imagine what driving a car would be like if there were no rules of the road.

31.2 Formal social control

There is a wide range of rules in society: rules about where to park the car; how to claim a tax refund; what to do if you are late to school; and how to treat other people. Some rules are considered to be more important than others. The sociologist distinguishes several different types of social rules. The most evident rules in society are those which constitute the law.

Over the centuries, laws have been decided upon by powerful social groups, written down, reviewed, altered and added to, so that now there is a vast body of material which is called the law and which applies to almost every aspect of social life. In order to ensure that everyone abides by these laws there are specific penalties, such as fines or imprisonment, for anyone found guilty of breaking the law. Breaches of the law are of two sorts: civil offences, which are offences against only the wronged individual, and crime, in which an offence has been committed against social order. A civil offence would be letting your dog bite the postman; a criminal offence would be stealing the postman's registered letters. The authority of the law in society is backed up by a complex system of agencies such as the police, the courts, the legal profession and the prisons, which ensure that the law is enforced and that those who break the law are punished.

The law is a means of social control: by the threat of punishments it affects what people do. However, the law also controls our actions in a less obvious way: there is widespread belief that the law is morally right and therefore should be obeyed. This respect for the justice of the law is one other way in which the law acts as a means of social control.

The sociologist refers to the law as a *formal social control*. This is because the law, unlike other types of social control, has special authority in society, and a complex system exists to ensure that the law is enforced. Laws are set out in writing and specific penalties have been drawn up to punish people who break the law. The police and courts are dependent on the law being set out clearly, otherwise it would not be possible to enforce it. In Britain, laws have been formally drawn up and administered since Roman times, but in England the law is not rigidly defined as it is in the USA (Codified Law and the Constitution). It is open to very flexible interpretation based upon Common Law, ie the accepted interpretation of the law arrived at by High Court Judges, whose decisions have become part of the Common Law.

31.3 Informal social control

Norms

Not all social rules are written down and there are many types of unwritten rules which exist in society. For example, one of these is that parents spend time playing with their children. An unwritten rule such as this is called a *norm* (it should be noted that 'norm' in this sense is entirely different from a *statistical norm*). A norm is a standard or pattern for the way we expect people to act and behave. Such a standard must be generally accepted by two or more people in society before it can be called a norm. It is not written down, and the individual who breaks the rule is not subject to specific constraints and penalties enforced by police or courts, although, as we shall see later, some norms are bound up with the law; the sociologist therefore refers to norms as *informal social controls*.

A norm, like a law, is part of the culture of a society and is passed on from one generation to the next through socialisation. An individual, as he grows up, will learn the norms of his particular society. For example, in our society we think it is right that children should grow up living at home with their parents, at least in the first few years of life. By contrast, until quite recently, it was a norm that children growing up in the kibbutzim of Israel should live, from the first months of life, almost entirely in the company of other children and in the care of specialised nurses and teachers.

We are so familiar with the norms of the society we grow up in that they are almost second nature to us; we take them for granted, seldom reflecting on them, questioning their importance or considering whether there may be better alternatives.

Mores

Some norms are particularly important in society; for example, those that refer to the way we should behave towards one another, treating each other justly and honestly. These are norms which have embedded in them the idea that it is morally wrong to treat people unjustly or to be dishonest. The sociologist calls such norms *mores*. Some of the most widely-held mores in our society are concerned with respecting the lives and the property of other people. Although there is variation between the mores of different societies, western industrialised societies have many fundamental mores in common. For example, in these societies it is considered morally important that a man should have no more than one wife at a time.

Mores are important in society because of the *moral values* they maintain. For example, men and women think it is morally important not to steal, to kill or to deliberately injure. Values are part of the culture of society and there are sometimes differences between the values of one society and another. This must be taken into account when considering the mores of societies different from our own and should make us wary of judging the merits of the mores of other societies. For example, in a polygynous society a man is expected to have more than one wife at a time. The moral values here are different from western societies which have traditionally favoured monogamous marriage. On the other hand, values such as the right of human beings to life and dignity are widely accepted in many different cultures and the violation of these values, as happened, for example, in Nazi Germany, elicits moral condemnation.

Mores play an important part in maintaining social order and many have been written down and incorporated into our laws. We can now understand why the law is usually thought of as being morally right. This does not mean to say that the law always reflects the social mores.

Sometimes the law is at variance with popular social mores and it becomes regarded as more moral to break the law than to observe it. For example, in the USA, many young people thought that it was wrong for the country to be involved in the war in Vietnam and they therefore illegally evaded the draft by which young men were sent to fight there.

How norms affect behaviour

Even though people cannot be made to obey norms in the same way that the threat of punishments may make us obey the law, norms do succeed in controlling what we do. How is it that they are effective? The reason is, we control each other. This can be seen if we think of someone learning a new role, for example as a student, a secretary, a wife or a motor vehicle mechanic. In every case we are socialised into the role through the reactions of other people: a shop assistant who gives a customer the wrong change learns from the agitation of the customer, or the manager, that it is part of his role to maintain the accuracy of money transactions in the shop. Of course, most people already know something about a particular role before assuming it because, besides being directly influenced by other people, we are also influenced indirectly through films, magazines and television.

We control one another's actions in other ways besides showing agitation: for instance, praise and reward encourage us to go on behaving as we are. Showing surprise, disappointment, disgust or completely ignoring someone are some of the other ways in which we bring people's actions in line with perceived social norms.

Folkways

The norm that people should form a queue when waiting for the bus is not usually one that is taken so seriously that there are heavy penalties for ignoring it. This is for two reasons: first, standing in line when waiting for a bus has little to do with being a morally right thing to do, although we often feel it is the fairest way to cope with this problem; secondly, there is no widespread agreement that forming a queue is so important that people should be made to conform. This, then, is an example of a type of norm which the sociologist calls a *folkway*. Other examples include: eating with a knife and fork; celebrating birthdays; and exchanging greeting cards at Christmas. Folkways are norms which are observed throughout society by particular social groups but breaking them is not considered to be morally wrong.

Customs are folkways which have existed for a long time in society. The use of holly and mistletoe at Christmas is a custom. Fashion is also a folkway and differs from custom because it is less permanent. Fashions in dress, such as mini or maxi skirts and studded leather jackets, are examples of this type of folkway. Do we control each other in any way so that we will conform to styles of dressing?

Folkways are part of the culture of a society and therefore we must remember to view them in the context of the society in which they arise. Often, folkways which at first sight seem better or worse than our own, are in reality different simply because of the cultural differences between the societies. Take, for example, customs about the way we greet one another. In this country we shake hands; in Italy or Greece it is not at all unusual for good friends to embrace one another.

Norms and values are part of the culture of society and like any other aspect of culture, they change. For example, in Britain in the mid-nineteenth century, it was considered right that middle-class married women should remain at home and devote themselves to being wives and mothers. Today, there is little objection to married women going out to work. Of course, technological inventions such as the washing machine and the fridge have helped to change the woman's role, but these by themselves would have made little difference if there had not also been changes in such norms and values as the one to the effect that 'woman's place is in the home'.

Norms and values are not always the same for everyone in society. Different social groups have different norms and values. We can see this if we think of the different ways in which people spend their leisure time. For example, it is a middle-class rather than a working-class norm to spend time off at the theatre, the ballet, the opera, at evening classes or taking part in amateur dramatics.

Unit 32 Religion: Another Type of Social Control

32.1 Beliefs and belief systems

What an individual does, makes sense to him. This is because there are reasons behind what we do; we usually know what these are and they seem sensible to us. They are perfectly natural.

Suppose that a man puts money in a charity collecting-tin; he may do this for any number of reasons: he knows the person who is making the collection and cannot refuse; he has a relative who works for the charity or who benefits from its care; his wife or children want him to make a donation; his neighbour is looking on; he cannot get into the shop unless the collector comes out of the doorway; he thinks it is his Christian duty; he thinks it will keep away the Evil Eye. The list is incomplete, but the point is that there are factors controlling his actions. In every case his reason for putting money in the tin is the result of informal social controls affecting what he does. We can never know for certain which of these reasons made him act this way.

We hold *beliefs* and these affect what we do. For example, if a man believes that there is an evil power in the world called the Evil Eye and that putting money in charity collecting tins will help to keep this away then this belief is the reason behind his putting money in charity collecting tins. Beliefs affect our actions and are another important type of social control.

What are beliefs?

A belief is an idea that we hold about what is true or factual. For example, some people think it is true that walking under ladders will bring them bad luck and a person believing this will deliberately avoid walking under ladders.

The beliefs that people hold vary from ideas about 'the fish that got away' to very serious and complicated ideas about such things as life after death. Some we can test to see if they are true or not: for example, men have found out by experiment that germs are responsible for many forms of illness. Some we cannot test to see if they are true or not. For example, beliefs about the Evil Eye, the existence of God and the purpose of life cannot be tested using any of the methods used by scientists to see whether they are true or not. This is because these beliefs are of a different sort from those concerning the physical world around us.

Belief systems

At any moment in the day we usually have several beliefs in our minds. Some of these will be about everyday things, such as whether school will close early because of the bad weather, which group makes the best music, whether the Channel Tunnel will ever be built. These ideas are not so important to us that they affect us over a long period of time. More important and deeply-held beliefs, however, may affect us for most of our lives. These are beliefs about such things as our spiritual nature, our relationship with a god, or with other human beings.

Religious beliefs, such as Christianity and other world religions, come into this category of deeply-held beliefs and have a great deal of influence on the actions of the people holding them. Religious beliefs are reinforced by symbolic actions, and participation in these rituals has the effect of binding together the believers into a moral community.

The sociologist looks on religious beliefs as examples of *belief systems* rather than as isolated beliefs. This is because a religion is made up of a number of related ideas and it is impossible to hold just one belief without also believing in several others.

Religious belief systems serve to relate the worldly affairs of life with a sacred sphere. The sociologist is not interested in the philosophical problems of whether the particular beliefs are valid or not: what he wants to find out is how people holding these beliefs are affected by them in their day-to-day lives. If he can understand more about the reasons for a person's actions by looking more closely at the particular doctrines of a religion, the sociologist will study the content of a religion. For example, doctrines that hold out the hope of a heaven or a better existence in a future life, affect the way people live out their daily lives in this life. In the same way, the threat of punishment for ignoring religious doctrines can also affect how people act in their day-to-day lives.

Belief systems are not confined to religious beliefs. There are other ways of thinking about man's place and purpose in the world. For example, a Marxist holds certain beliefs, about what is happening in the world, which depend on ideas about history and economics. His beliefs include no reference to any 'god'.

Belief systems are part of the culture of a society. Children learn the religion of their society. For example, many of us have grown up learning little or nothing about Buddhism, Hinduism or Islam. Children growing up in Asia are more likely to learn about one of these major religions. Asian families coming to live in this country continue to hold their religious beliefs even though they are many miles from home. This is because Hinduism or Islam is an important and familiar part of their daily lives and continues to have a meaning for them in this country. A Christian living in India or Pakistan would continue to practise his religion because, in the same way, it remains an important part of his way of life. Both Weber and Durkheim were concerned with the way in which social experience related to religious expression and belief.

32.2   What part does religion play in society?

Sociologists have suggested that religion serves functions which are broadly similar in most societies.

1   Religious beliefs give an explanation of uncertainties like failing crops, human life and death: these are problems which would otherwise be difficult to explain. In modern western industrialised society we have many scientific explanations which help us to understand the causes of such things, but these explanations cannot help in the same way as religion in explaining for example, why there are such things as life and death.

2   Religions are carried on in ways which can be seen and understood: for instance, by rites and rituals. Religious rites, such as the Christian Communion service, help people to express their religious beliefs and reinforce their social behaviour. Religious ritual helps to bring the believers together to participate in some common activity. In this way, religious rites help to strengthen the believers, uniting them into a moral community.

3   Taking part in religious rites gives the believers a feeling of well-being and comfort.

4   The ceremonies which are carried out by different religions carry on generation after generation. To the people who take part in religious rites such as Holy Communion, this event affects their actions and serves to link them with the past, present and future actions of members of society. In this way religion has implications for individuals' understanding of who they are, what they are, and where they stand in relation to on-going society.

5   Religion adds sacredness to the norms and values of society. This has the effect of emphasising the importance of group objectives over the wishes of individual members. From this point of view, it can be seen that religious beliefs can contribute to the stability of society, maintaining the status quo and encouraging conformity amongst believers.

6   Having encouraged members to conform, religious beliefs also offer some way of coping with the problem of not conforming. For example, breaking group rules is likely to arouse a sense of guilt in the believer. Religious beliefs include methods of coping with this problem, such as forgiveness, and with reintegration of the individual back into the social group.

7   Religions also perform what has been called a *prophetic* function. Although religions may encourage believers to conform to the norms and values of society, these may sometimes be interpreted by believers as being at variance with religious principles. Under these circumstances it is incumbent on believers to challenge the established authorities and even band together to overthrow them if this seems appropriate in bringing about a society more in line with the tenets of their religion.

8   In the course of life an individual matures physically and mentally, and must change his role in society many times. Through all these experiences he

encounters different problems and strains which can make confusing personal demands on him. It has been argued that religious beliefs provide the individual with a mental framework within which he can interpret and make sense of these personal maturation experiences.

We can see that, where everyone in society holds the same religious beliefs, and these permeate all social groups as in many traditional societies, religion plays an important part in unifying society and maintaining the existing social order.

32.3   Secularisation

Broadly, *secularisation* refers to the process whereby individuals, or society in general, becomes less religious, that is, more secular. Although a general definition has been given here, secularisation is really a somewhat complex phenomenon and not all sociologists agree that there is one all-embracing process involved. For example, in *The Religious and the Secular* (Routledge & Kegan Paul, 1969), David Martin suggests that there are at least four meanings which have been associated with the term secularisation. First, a decline in the sphere of influence and power of some ecclesiastical body, such as the Church of England. Second, an increasing disregard for the importance of religious customs, practices and rituals. Third, a decline in religiously conducted living, reflected in such things as a higher divorce rate. Finally, a widespread view of the world as understandable and controllable, that is, the adoption of a scientific view in place of a religious view of the world. David Martin notes that: 'Secularisation [involves] a large number of discrete separate elements, loosely put together in an intellectual hold-all', and concludes that the term has no real meaning. Another sociologist, Roland Robertson, considers the difficulties of examinining secularisation are tied up with problems of its own definition, and with measuring something as vague as 'de-religionisation' (R. Robertson, 'Sociologists and Secularization', *Sociology*, September 1971). In order to illustrate some of these difficulties concretely, the question of secularisation and its causes are examined in relation to Britain.

32.4   Religion in Britain

In many towns in Britain today, sights similar to the one in the photograph can be seen. Does this mean that religion is no longer important in Britain? This is a tricky question as we have seen

It is not uncommon to see churches for sale these days

secularisation is really several questions wrapped up in one and each needs to be looked at very carefully before we can set about giving an answer.

1   Has religion been important in Britain?
2   How are we going to find out how much religious belief there is in Britain today?
3   Has religious belief declined?
4   Does religion play any part in the life of Britain today?

These questions will be looked at in turn. In each case only the Christian religion will be considered, although it is recognised that other religions such as Judaism and, more recently, Hinduism and Islam are part of British culture.

Has religion been important in Britain?

Television programmes, films and, perhaps even Christmas cards seem to have conspired to present a picture of nineteenth-century Britain as a time when everyone attended church regularly. Although nineteenth-century statistical material is not always reliable, the results of a mid-nineteenth-century survey are useful and would seem to disagree with this picture. In 1851, the results of the only English Census of Religion ever taken showed that only thirty-nine per cent of the total population had gone to church or chapel on a particular Sunday in the year. Of this percentage, the majority were undoubtedly from the middle classes.

In his *Notes on England*, published in 1861, the Frenchman, Taine, describes a typical middle-class English family at Sunday prayers:

On Sunday evening he [the head of the household] is their spiritual guide, their chaplain: they may be seen entering in a row, the women in front, the men behind, with seriousness, gravity, and taking their places in the drawing room . . . The master reads aloud a short sermon—next a prayer; . . . lastly, he repeats the Lord's Prayer and, clause by clause, the worshippers respond.

By the first decades of the twentieth century, religious activity had reached a peak in this country. Even then, however, it was still a predominantly middle-class activity, the efforts of organised religious groups such as the Church of England, the Methodists and, after 1878, the Salvation Army, to bring the poorer working classes into the church, having generally failed to make any widespread impact on this social group.

How are we going to find out how much religious belief there is in Britain today?

So far, we have used statistics giving the percentage of persons attending church as a means of finding out how much religious belief there is in society. The 1851 survey can be used as a rough guide to the extent of religious belief in nineteenth-century England, but, in general, statistics of religious activities like going to church must be used with care as a source of information on religious beliefs in society. What, then, are the limitations of such statistics?

First, most of us have heard people say: 'I don't need to go to church to be a Christian'. Whether this is true or not is not important to the sociologist, but these people go unrecorded in statistics of religious behaviour, such as going to church, and he can never be sure of the numbers of people in society who think of themselves as Christians and yet who never take part in church activities. D. A. Martin in *The Religious and the Secular* notes the difficulty of really finding out what religious

I think it's a lovely name for a boy. But I still can't see why they have to christen it on the day of our last match of the season. (Going to church may be the result of family pressures.)

beliefs are held in Britain, by giving the example of research conducted during the period 1964–5, which showed that eighty-five to ninety per cent of people believe in God and call themselves Christians, while only fifty per cent believe in the related idea of the life to come. There are many sociologists who are doubtful if the figure for the numbers of people calling themselves Christian and believing in God are really as high as this research suggests. David Martin himself points out that many people think of being a Christian as the same as being respectable.

Secondly, the people who go to church and take part in other religious activities, like prayer meetings, may be doing this for a number of reasons, none of which have anything directly to do with religious belief. For example, going to church may be a habit, a way of passing time, or the result of family pressures.

Sociologists suggest that the statistics of the number of christenings, weddings and burials performed, for example in the Church of England, are not reliable guides to religious belief. We will return to this point later.

Thirdly, the biggest limitation of religious statistics is that in each religious group, such as the Church of England or the Baptists, the statistics are really recording different things. For example, to look at membership figures for the Roman Catholic Church and to compare these with figures from the Church of England or the Methodists is misleading. In the Roman Catholic Church membership means everyone baptised as a baby into the Roman Catholic Church, and some of them will have drifted away from the church as they got older. To look at membership in the Church of England gives us a choice between figures for Baptism, Confirmation, the Electoral Roll and Easter Day communicants. The sociologist is wary of using the first three. This is because being baptised or confirmed does not necessarily mean that a person has continued to join in church activities in his adult life. The Electoral Roll is a list of lay persons, over seventeen years old, who are eligible to take part in committees to do with some of the parish's affairs. This often has a lot to do with the personal ambitions of people rather than religious beliefs. Sociologists, therefore, make use of the figures of Easter communicants. A person who does not usually go to church but continues to think of himself as a member of the Church of England will almost certainly try to get to the most important event in the Church's year, the Easter Day Communion. The numbers of people attending this service can therefore give us the best idea of the practising membership of the Church of England. In the Methodist Church, membership figures refer to the men and women who, as adults, have joined the Methodists by attendance at a membership service.

From this account of what membership means in three different churches, it is possible to see how misleading it would be to make comparisons without first finding out the most appropriate statistics by which to look at church membership. Also, in trying to discover the extent of religious belief we must select only statistics about activities relevant to providing a reliable guide to belief.

Has religion declined?

Now we know something about the problem of using statistics of religious behaviour as a guide to religious belief in Britain, we can look at Figure 10.1 knowing that it must be interpreted carefully. In the figure, selected categories of statistics have been used which are appropriate indices of religious belief in each group.

From Figure 10.1 it can be seen that in the Church of England there has been some falling-away in the numbers of people attending Easter Day Communion. In other religious groups, the Methodists, the Congregationalists and the Baptists, there has been a gradual falling-

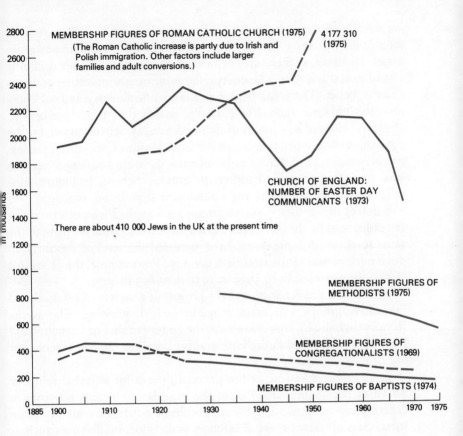

Figure 10.1   *Changes in 'membership' of some British religious groups, 1885–1975*
(Sources: Church Information Office; Church of England Year Book; Baptist
Handbook; *Minutes of the Methodist Conference*; Congregational Year Book; The
Catholic Directory; *Yearbook of the International Bible Students' Association*;
Yearbook of the Jehovah's Witnesses)

away in membership, from the first decades of the twentieth century to
the present.

The decline in the numbers of people interested in religious activities
can also be seen in such things as the decline in the numbers going to
Sunday service and Sunday school and in the numbers of magazines
published by religious groups. The decline in attendance at Sunday
services in groups such as the Methodists is a useful statistical trend to
look at in terms of estimating the extent of real religious belief in these
churches. This is because if someone belongs to such a group then they

are usually expected to attend services regularly and a falling-away in attendance has been construed as indicating genuine falling-away in belief. However, as there may be other factors responsible for declining attendance, this must not be interpreted as inevitably indicating a falling-away in belief. There has been a substantial decline in Sunday School membership since 1900. For example, at that time thirty per cent of children belonged to Church of England Sunday Schools alone, but by 1960 this had dropped to thirteen per cent. However, these data are less useful as an index of decline in belief since there are a variety of reasons why parents send their children to Sunday School, including non-religious factors such as having a quiet time at home on Sunday.

Some of the smaller religious groups such as the Plymouth Brethren are called *sects* by the sociologist. These have managed to keep about the same level, or, in some cases, have increased the level of membership during the course of the twentieth century. For example, the Jehovah's Witnesses increased from 5033 in 1931 to 65 693 in 1972.

Apart from smaller sects and the growth of a variety of mystical and meditative groups, one other religious body is growing. This is the Roman Catholic Church. However, the larger families of Catholics and the effects of Irish and Polish immigrants in swelling these numbers must not be overlooked.

In addition to looking at the national figures for different religious activities, sociologists also look at the records of religious activities in different communities. The overall decline on a national scale covers up social class differences, age differences and regional differences such as the continuing importance of religion in parts of Wales, Scotland and Northern Ireland. By examining religous statistics and survey results from the 1950s, Argyle and Beit-Hallahmi observe that church attendance and professed religious belief is higher amongst the middle and lower middle classes than the working classes. In general, the latter do not participate in organised religion. It has been suggested that the very poor and members of minority groups constitute the congregations of small sects. Argyle and Beit-Hallahmi contrast the British situation with the USA. Here middle-class religious participation is widespread but has been interpreted as conventional behaviour, religious belief being more strongly rooted in the working class. Argyle and Beit-Hallahmi found that attendance at church services was less common among young people, and congregations were more often composed of the elderly, many of whom were single and women. In his book *The Religious and the Secular* David Martin calls these places 'the last bastions of majority religious practice in the United Kingdom'.

Does religion play any part in the life of Britain today?

In order to answer this question we can look at two things. First, we must consider the importance of religion in the personal lives of men and women. Secondly, we must assess the importance of organised religious groups, such as the Church of England, in influencing what other groups, such as the Government, do in society.

We have seen that it is not necessarily possible to find out how people feel about Christianity by looking at the statistics of organised religious groups. Many people think of themselves as Christian without ever going near a church or chapel. However, there are occasions in the life-cycle of the individual when he or she may well attend a church service. These are times such as baptisms, weddings and funerals. For example, in 1967, over fifty per cent of all infants born in that year were baptised and over ninety per cent of burials were conducted with religious rites. In 1965 fifty-one per cent of all first marriages were solemnised in the Church of England; by 1974 this figure was forty-six per cent. In some cases, these figures may reflect religious beliefs, or a change towards more secular beliefs, but it is difficult to assess what they indicate. Many sociologists think that, with the exception of burials, for which very few people make prior arrangements, these religious events have taken on an importance in marking stages and changes in the role of the individual in the course of his life-cycle. For example, the change from being single to being married is a significant one for the individual and in the eyes of society. The event is well-marked by a solemn ceremony in a church. Because of the importance of these religious rituals in marking stages in the individual's life-cycle, the sociologist calls services such as baptisms, weddings and burials *rites de passage*. In *Secularization and Moral Change*, Alasdair MacIntyre suggests one of the characteristics of working–class religious practice is a high level of participation in these solemn religious ceremonies. This may indicate enduring religious beliefs in the working class which exist independent of formal, regular churchgoing. Bryan Wilson, in his book *Religion in Secular Society* (Watts, 1966) suggests that the churches are thought of today almost as an additional department of the Welfare State, to be used as and when required. The Salvation Army certainly appears to fulfil this function. It is the largest provider of sleeping accommodation for homeless single men in the country. It has been suggested that the Salvation Army copes with a section of the community that nobody else wants. Its practical, working-class ethos gives the Salvation Army an advantage over other organisations in that it does not alienate the very poor.

The Salvation Army copes with those sections of the community that nobody seems to want

Looking at the part played by religion in society in terms of the influence which groups, such as the Church of England, can have on the course of events in society, we can see that these bodies continue to have much wealth, power and influence. In terms of wealth, the Church of England continues to hold a great deal of land and property in the country. Its power can be seen in its close association with the Government. For example, Bishops sit in the House of Lords. However, as Bryan Wilson points out (*Religion in a Secular Society*, Watts, 1966) the days are long past when, in Lloyd George's famous statement, the Church of England was 'the Tory Party at prayer'. The influence of the Church can be seen particularly in matters that are to do with the family and with education. For example, the Church of England, as the established church of England, voices the Church's concern over issues such as birth control, divorce and abortion when it seems current practice or changes in the law may threaten Christian marriage and family life. In 1908, the Lambeth Conference passed the following resolution: 'The Conference regards with alarm the growing practice of the artificial restriction of the family'. Currently, the Church of England is not opposed to the use of birth control by married couples. In 1966, the Church of England produced the report *Putting Asunder*, in which the Church recommended that irretrievable breakdown of marriage should be substituted for the then existing grounds for divorce. This constituted a radical departure from the Church's position of moral condemnation of divorce earlier in the century. Acceptance of the authority of the Church in such matters has dwindled. Bryan Wilson suggests that this is partly to do with the general compartmentalisation of life that has occurred in the twentieth century: 'All of these developments, together with the earlier distinctions of the political and judicial areas of social life, and the more recent separation of recreational facilities from the community and the family, have tended to leave religious agencies very much less associated with the other social institutions than once was the case ... religion which once had a general presidency over the concerns of men ... has increasingly lost this pre-eminence and influence.' Despite this, the Church can still affect the individual's freedom of action. For example, in the case of remarriage, the Church may refuse to marry a divorcee in church. However, in general, there has been a decline in the extent to which the Church directly influences family affairs, and it has been suggested that its earlier authority on these matters is now being delegated to spokesmen from the social sciences. The decline of the authority of the Church of England has not been matched by all religious groups. The Roman Catholic Church, for example, is strongly against abortion and these views are also represented in pressure groups such as 'Life' and the Society for the Protection of the Unborn Child, which campaign in order to change the 1967 Abortion Law.

In terms of education, some background to the Christian religion is taught in schools, although this is not such a central part of school curricula today as it was a century ago. The Church of England, the Roman Catholic Church, the Methodists and several other religious groups were among the first social groups to set up schools and colleges in the nineteenth century. In 1900 there were more Church schools than State schools. However, the number of religiously-based schools and colleges has reduced substantially and they are no longer so free from Government control. It is a sign of the decline in the importance of religion in modern society that religious knowledge is not so highly valued in society as other types of knowledge, scientific, for instance. As Bryan Wilson points out, colleges do not usually ask prospective candidates to be proficient in religious knowledge, nor do they value it as a predictor of a candidate's likely success in subjects requiring rigorous analytical inquiry. Similarly careers in the Church may carry less social standing today. In some churches today clerics have jobs as paid workers in industry and are actively engaged in the same work as other employees.

The activities of the churches themselves have sometimes been constructed as acknowledging the marginal role played by religious institutions in Britain today. For example, in *Religion in Secular Society*, Bryan Wilson suggests that the current ecumenical movement in some churches reflects 'the turning in on itself of institutionalised religion, as its hold on the wider social order has diminished'. At the end of April 1977, the Archbishop of Canterbury, Dr Donald Cogan, met with Pope Paul VI to discuss matters of relevance to the Anglican and Roman Catholic Churches, such as mixed religious marriages and the common sharing of the Eucharist. Both pledged greater efforts towards unity of the two worlds of Roman Catholics and Anglicans.

Unit 33 The Law

33.1 Law and morality

We have already seen some of the points which are common to formal laws and informal social rules, such as norms. Both are types of social control. We know also that important mores, such as those about deliberately injuring or killing someone, or stealing property, are formalised and become laws, which can be enforced by the threat of punishment. However, morality and the law do not always go hand in hand.

People's opinions about what is right and wrong change. The problem is that the law involves all sorts of procedures. So although it can be altered, often it is not quick to change and reflect the ideas current in society. For example, ideas have changed about how right or wrong it is for married couples to be able to divorce (see Chapter 3). By the 1930s ideas about the morality of getting a divorce had changed more quickly than the law. A. P. Herbert, in trying to introduce a bill to change the divorce laws of the time, gave many accounts of how couples were forced to contrive ridiculous situations because adultery was virtually the only grounds on which they could get a divorce. Men and women were having to plan something that either looked like, or was, adultery, in order to get a divorce. This made a mockery of the existing laws, which were changed in 1937 to include other grounds for divorce. There is only one ground for divorce in England now, ie that the marriage has irretrievably broken down (Divorce Reform Act 1969).

The law can also sometimes try to pave the way for changing popular opinion about what is right and wrong. Acts of Parliament are sometimes designed to bring about a change in public opinion. For example, the use of the death penalty as punishment for murder has been a very controversial issue for a long time. In December 1969 the death penalty for murder was finally abolished in the Murder (Abolition of Death Penalty) Act, despite a widely publicised result of a public opinion poll which showed that eighty-four per cent of the population wished to bring back hanging. One MP gave this view of the difference between public opinion and the role of Parliament: '. . . one must pay regard to public opinion but that does not mean that we must be bound by public opinion . . . Parliament has the duty to make up its own mind . . .' (Hansard, December 1964 — S. C. Silkin, MP for Dulwich). However, public acceptance of abolition of the death penalty has not followed. Since recent IRA activities the public have increasingly demanded its restoration. A poll conducted for ITN in April 1977 showed over 85 per cent of those questioned favoured its restoration, but two years earlier Parliament rejected such a move.

We have seen that norms are not always the same for everyone in society, but whose views do laws reflect? Many sociologists would agree that the law reflects the views of those people who have enough power in society to make sure that their ideas are put into effect. For example, laws which punished by death anyone found guilty of stealing cattle were in existence in this country until 1832. We may be sure that it was the people who owned cattle and not the poor people who stole them who introduced that law. It is no coincidence that before 1832 it was only male landowners who had the vote and who were therefore able to influence legislation. Since then the franchise has been extended (see Fig. 7.2) and other social classes influenced legislation.

33.2 The police

There are forty-seven police forces in England and Wales and each of these has two basic departments, the uniformed branch and the CID. In some forces, such as the Metropolitan, these incorporate such different branches as the mounted and river police; but each is concerned with the same job, making sure that the laws are enforced.

The strength of each police force varies from district to district, but most forces are at present very understaffed for the work they have to do: in 1980, the ratio of police to the general public was one police officer to every 500 in Britain. The ratio has not altered appreciably in recent years. In 1978, the strength of the regular police force in England and Wales was 100 500 men and 8600 women.

In the course of their training, policemen learn that it is the primary duty of the police to prevent crime. Police duties also include the preservation of life and the maintenance of public tranquillity.

Actual or suspected offences may be reported to the police, or the police themselves may discover that an offence has been committed. All criminal acts which come to the attention of the police are called 'crimes known to the police' and this is an important category used in the collection of criminal statistics. These statistics are sometimes used as a

The Police are concerned with making sure that laws are enforced

measure of the success or failure of the police. However, it is important to remember that the statistics cannot record the absence of those crimes which the police may have prevented.

The success of the police in enforcing law and order is affected by the type of contact that there is between the police and public. In recent years this relationship has been influenced by several factors. The police force increasingly looks on itself as a profession: that is, skilled in the prevention of crime. However, at the same time, the police force in some cities, notably Glasgow and London, is understaffed. For the individual police officer this often means that he is under pressure to provide his superiors with suspects in the hope that this will lead to the solution of crimes and swell the total number of crimes known to the police which are cleared up annually. The police officer today usually works in an area which he does not live in: this presents problems because he does not know the people of the area, their way of life or their difficulties. Under these circumstances, he is forced to fall back on any means he knows by which to identify suspects and these tend to involve the ideas formed by his upbringing, his family and, most influential of all, his fellow officers. The typical suspect is often seen as an individual who has been in trouble or who comes from a problem locality, known to have produced offenders in the past. Young working-class lads in noisy groups are more likely

Watcha, Bertie—considering there is only one policeman for every 500 people in Britain you're a very lucky man. I am about to give you my undivided attention.

suspects than well-mannered, respectful middle-class youths; boys and men are more likely suspects than girls. An experienced policeman develops a sense of whom a suspect may be and will act upon his accumulation of knowledge.

In a study called *Crime, Police and Race Relations* (Oxford University Press, 1970), John Lambert describes police relationships with immigrants, with particular reference to the situation in Birmingham. He makes the point that Irish immigrants are not confronted with the same problems as Asians or West Indians in their relationships with the police. The difficulties appear to arise from the fixed ideas that each group has about the other. For instance, Lambert describes how a police officer talking to a mainly West Indian class at a London girls' school found that most of the children thought that everyone who went inside a police station was beaten up, this idea coming largely from the culture of the West Indies. This belief, however, was not found everywhere: children in Birmingham had a much more favourable impression of the police. Lambert suggests that in the case of Asian immigrants the problem arises because they see the police as corrupt and corruptible, an image which does not go down too well with the police. In the case of West Indians, the ideas of some of the police force about the excitability of West Indians does not help to improve relations between the two groups.

The relationship between the police and the public has been affected by the problem of motoring offences, which are not always seen by the general public as offences. According to the report of the 1962 Willinck Commission on Police, this problem has strained relations between members of the middle classes and the police. This observation is notable since, traditionally, the middle classes have good relations with the police. However, it must not be construed from this that strained relations deriving from motoring offences are confined to the middle classes. The 1976 Police Act aims to improve relations by setting up a new independent Police Complaints Board which will hear grievances against the police.

The ideas of the police about some groups in society being more likely offenders than others influence the way in which law and order is enforced in this country. For example, the police make decisions about whether or not an offence has been committed, whether to caution an individual or to issue a summons, whether or not to prosecute and, in all these instances, the judgement and views of the individual police officer about who are the guilty will affect the way in which these matters are decided. Strictly constitutionally, however, the police are answerable ultimately to the Home Secretary and Parliament.

33.3   The judicial system

The judicial system is the system of courts that exists in Britain to deal with civil and criminal offences.

What do we hope to do by punishing people who break the law?

There are four main ways of thinking about this:

1   We want to get our own back: that is, 'an eye for an eye'. This explanation is called the *retributive* reason for punishment. Today this seems a rather barbaric way of going about things and the other reasons for punishment are usually seen as being more appropriate.

2   By carrying out the threat to punish persons who break the law we hope to deter other people and make the offender think twice before committing any offences in the future. This is called the *deterrent* explanation of punishment.

3   By removing the offender from society and putting him in prison, or by limiting his actions by some other means such as a fine, we are restricting his opportunities to commit more offences and also protecting the public at the same time. This is called the *preventive* explanation of punishment.

4   By punishment we make the offender repent what he has done in the past. If the punishment takes time, such as a period of imprisonment, the prisoner is given a chance to reform. By this we mean that through some form of treatment the offender can be helped to think in a new way about himself and society, so that he will not want to commit any more offences. This type of explanation is called the *reformative* theory of punishment.

Of these four main explanations, the last three are now usually considered to best justify why we punish people who break the law. However, there is no reason to suppose that the first explanation has disappeared from modern society: for example, many people think that, for retributive reasons, it would be a good idea to bring back the death penalty for convicted murderers. Also, some sociologists suggest that by reforming a person through treatment we are really doing no more than disguising the old retributive reasons for punishment.

Breaking the Law

Actions which break the law are called offences and are of two sorts: *indictable* and *non-indictable*.

Indictable offences are those which at one time were triable before a jury, but most may now, by consent of the accused, be tried by magistrates. Ninety per cent of indictable offences in Britain are tried by magistrates but some, for example, murder, must still be tried by jury. In 1975 just over two million indictable offences were reported to the police, almost four times as many as twenty-five years earlier.

A non-indictable offence is one which is heard in a court such as a magistrates' court, which does not make use of a jury. In deciding the guilt or innocence of the person involved and in passing sentence, such courts are carrying out what is called *summary jurisdiction*. Most criminal offences are decided in the courts of summary jurisdiction. Trial by jury, then, is the exception rather than the rule.

The judge and the jury

Criminal cases which are not settled in the courts of summary jurisdiction are brought to trial in other types of courts where there is a judge and a jury. The jury is responsible for deciding whether a person is innocent or guilty of the crime of which he has been accused; it is up to the judge, within certain guidelines, to decide on the sentence which should be given to the convicted offender. The bench is the term usually used for people such as magistrates and judges who have the responsibility for making the decision on behalf of society as to the sentence which should be passed on a convicted offender.

Table 10.1   Courts which are concerned with civil offences

Many civil cases never reach the courts and are settled 'out of court' through the solicitors of the persons concerned. The Courts Act, 1971 centralised the resources of the higher courts of the two systems.

A *County courts*	These are courts which deal with smaller civil offences. There are about 300 of them throughout the country, grouped in districts. Cases of libel, slander and defended divorce cases are not dealt with at this level but go to the next higher courts.
B *High Court* Queen's Bench Chancery Family Division High Court of Bankruptcy	The Administration of Justice Act, 1970 altered the organisation of the High Court, so that there is now a separate new division of the High Court called the Family Division which deals with cases involving family and marriage. The Act also made provision for a Commercial Court to be set up within the Queen's Bench Division of the High Court.

The courts

In considering the court systems of England and Wales it is important to bear in mind the statement of the 1969 (Beeching) Report of the Royal Commission on Assizes and Quarter Sessions that in giving a brief

Table 10.2   Courts which are primarily concerned with criminal offences

Part 1

A   *Magistrates' Courts**
These are of two types: those presided over by stipendiary magistrates, sitting alone or with lay magistrates; and those presided over only by lay magistrates. Stipendiary magistrates sit mainly in the Greater London area, but may also be found in larger cities. Lay magistrates predominate in more than 900 magistrates' courts in England and Wales. Magistrates' courts are able to send a case on to be tried at a higher court (see Part 2 in the Table). Today magistrates receive some training for their work.

B   *Juvenile Courts*
Juvenile courts can deal with any criminal offences (except homicide) committed by young persons aged from ten to seventeen. They also deal with all children and young persons under age seventeen who are brought to the courts as in need of care, protection and control.

Most crimes are 'petty offences' such as driving offences. In 1974, about 1.2 million motoring offences and almost half-a-million other non-indictable offences were dealt with in magistrates' courts. About 98 per cent of criminal cases are dealt with in the courts so far described in this Table.
   Some of the cases brought before the courts will be dismissed, for example for lack of evidence, and no sentence will be passed.

Part 2

C   *Crown Court*
Under the 1971 Courts Act, the Crown Court replaces the old system which consisted of courts called quarter sessions and courts called assize courts. Crown courts have a number of full-time and some part-time judges who preside at the courts. More serious cases are passed from the magistrates' courts to these courts; the maximum sentences which can be passed in these courts are longer than those that can be passed in the magistrates' courts.

D   *The Central Criminal Court*
This is now a crown court; it is the special criminal court of London which is held at 'The Old Bailey'.

* These courts also deal with some civil cases.

account, 'there is virtually nothing which can be presented as a common feature [in the court system] without . . . reference to exceptions.' The two systems of courts which exist in England and Wales for dealing with civil and criminal cases are summarised in Tables 10.1 and 10.2.

The individual and the judicial system

There are ways in which we hope to look after the rights of the individual and to make sure that in the eyes of the judicial system he remains innocent until proved guilty. For example, in both the civil court system and the criminal court system the individual has a chance to appeal against the verdict of the court. Some of the courts outlined in Table 10.2, such as crown courts, hear appeals, but these may 'also be taken to specialised higher courts such as the Court of Appeal and the House of Lords.

Although there are such safeguards built into the court system, the time and money involved in taking a case through the courts of appeal deters many people from appealing against the decision of a lower court. Also, the individual does not always know enough about the ways in which his rights are safeguarded to make use of them. For example, many people do not know or make use of their right to apply for legal aid although the availability of legal aid is publicised in all police stations and Citizens' Advice Bureaux. Since the Legal Aid and Advice Act of 1949, people who cannot afford to pay the costs of a solicitor and counsel to defend them in court may apply to the individual court for legal aid to help them with these costs. The Legal Advice and Assistance Act, 1972, and the Legal Aid Act, 1974, make it possible for a person whose means are below a certain amount to receive assistance to a certain value from a solicitor. This depends, of course, on the individual knowing his right to apply for legal aid, and the whereabouts of a solicitor. Brian Abel-Smith, Michael Zander and Rosalind Brooke, in their study of legal problems in three London Boroughs (*Legal Problems and the Citizen*, Heinemann, 1973), found seventy-eight per cent of social class 1 and sixty-five per cent of social class 2 knew that it is possible to get free or cheap advice in a solicitor's office. However, only 54 per cent of social classes 4 and 5 knew this. Similar differences existed between the social classes in their knowledge of the whereabouts of a solicitor. Between 1974 and 1975 the number of people receiving legal advice, and assistance under £25 increased by 82 per cent compared with 27 per cent between 1975 and 1976. This increase may reflect rising costs of legal services rather than any increase in the scope of legal advice and assistance. Matrimonial and other family matters take the highest share of legal advice and assistance (57 per cent in 1975–6). The decision to give legal aid rests with the individual court and the Home Office points out that over eighty per cent of applications for legal aid for summary trial in magistrates' courts are granted. However, this figure does not take into account regional differences in the granting of legal aid or the fact that this percentage represents only a few of the people who come before the courts. For example, in only about three per cent of all cases tried summarily by the magistrates is the accused represented by a lawyer under the legal aid scheme. In *Social Needs and Legal Action* (Martin Robertson, 1973) Pauline Morris, Richard White and Philip Lewis suggest that there is a difference in the way in which the necessity for legal aid is seen by the public and by the legal profession. For example, a lawyer will put a client's case in the best possible light *from the court's point of view*, and this switch in emphasis is not often considered by the public in their decision to apply for legal aid. Lawyers are concerned with 'presenting' a case. In the course of the legal processes a dispute may be altered out of all recognition to the client, and the use of a lawyer essential. Morris, White and Lewis see this as part of the mystification process which preserves the professional expertise of the legal profession. They point out also that persons who hire lawyers are more likely to be successful in their claims that those who do not. Inflation in recent years has now led to a situation where only the very poor are entitled to legal aid.

There are other problems facing the person who attends a court. Even when his case has been dismissed or he has been shown to be innocent, public opinion is such that, very often, the fact that he has been to court is enough to make him seem guilty in the eyes of the general public.

Sentencing

In determining the guilt of individuals and in passing sentence, some of the following information may be used by the bench:

1 police reports on the accused
2 reports of the Probation Service
3 medical reports
4 the case of the prosecution
5 the case of the defence.

These reports often reflect the ideas which each group holds about the background of an offender. We have seen already that the judgement of the police is sometimes biased against some groups in society and this affects the material which the police present to the bench. The bench itself is influenced in its decision by police reports.

The people who sit on the bench themselves, like anyone else, have views which influence their judgement. The bench is sometimes criticised for ignoring new schemes and ideas that develop about the treatment of offenders, for example, in prisons, and sentencing people to punishments which are no longer thought suitable for offenders. In Holland, part of the compulsory training of judges at all levels in the system is in penal reform.

1   The range of sentences available under the law.

2   The nature and gravity of the particular offence of which the offender has been found guilty.

3   The character and past record of the offender.

4   The present circumstances of the offender, including, for example, whether or not he is employed and what his home circumstances are.

5   The prevalence of such offences as those of which the offender has been convicted.

6   The range of penalties which it is usual to impose on offenders for similar offences.

7   The recommendations of probation officers.

Table 10.3   Factors taken into account when passing sentence
(Source: Social Trends, 1976, CSO)

In 1967, the Criminal Justice Act provided for a new type of sentence, the suspended sentence. Under this scheme a person does not go to prison: his sentence is suspended, but, if he commits another offence before his suspended sentence is up, he will have the length of this sentence taken into account in any subsequent sentence which is passed on him as a result of his second offence. The effects of this Act have now had some time in which to show. In 1972 the Criminal Justice Act made some alterations in the system of suspended sentences. The old provision that, in certain cases, courts must give suspended sentences, has been removed. Under the 1972 Act, the maximum period of suspension has been lowered from 'from one to three years' to 'from one to two years with a period of supervision'. Another important part of the Act affects the sentencing of offenders by stating that, in most cases, the court shall not pass a sentence of imprisonment on a person aged twenty-one years old and over who has not been sentenced to prison before, unless it states its reason for doing so and has ensured that the offender is legally represented or has refused to be represented. Courts are required to obtain and consider information about an offender before reaching any decision to pass a sentence of imprisonment. Table 10.3 shows some of the factors which a court typically takes into account when passing sentence.

This Act reflects the hope of most people concerned with penal reform today that, as far as possible, persons convicted of having committed petty offences will be kept out of our over-crowded prisons.

33.4 The penal system

The penal system is made up of the many different types of institutions which exist to carry out sentences requiring an individual to be kept in detention or under supervision. Despite this *custodial function*, not all institutions are prisons. Young offenders cannot be sentenced to prison and there are other types of institution which are designed for the young offender.

The organisation of these institutions has been changing recently as a result of two Acts, the Children and Young Persons Act (1969) and the Criminal Justice Act (1972). Children under ten years old can be taken into the care of local authorities, and children between the ages of ten and sixteen also can be placed in the care of local authorities, although this does not rule out the possibility of criminal prosecution of the young person in some circumstances. This Act also required local authorities to establish Community Homes for young people in care. The intention here is to keep young people out of custodial institutions, and, by replacing the old system of approved schools and remand homes, emphasising the therapeutic nature of reform rather than reform through hard labour. In May 1976, a Government white paper, reporting on the effectiveness of the Act, noted that children were still being sent to institutions in the prison service such as borstals and detention centres. This practice has continued and grown, despite the lack of evidence that young offenders benefit from such experiences. This is, however, partly to do with lack of appropriate facilities.

The treatment of young offenders is also affected by the Criminal Justice Act, 1972 which installed a system of community service for offenders. Anyone aged seventeen or over found guilty of an offence which is normally punishable by imprisonment may receive a community service order in place of a sentence. This means working in the community for between forty and 240 hours, in some activity that is designed to help people in the community. At present, this is an experimental scheme.

Borstals continue to be part of the system of institutions for young people. These are for persons between fifteen and twenty-one years old who have committed a serious offence. In borstals young persons receive education and training in skills for various trades.

Adult offenders

An adult who is sentenced to a period of imprisonment will be sent to one or more of the sixty or so prisons in England and Wales. These are of two main types, local prisons and central prisons, both categories including some open prisons where prisoners are not confined to cell blocks behind prison walls.

There are several different types of local prisons, but the largest group consists of general local prisons. These receive prisoners from court, most of whom will remain there for the length of their sentence. Central prisons are for prisoners serving longer sentences and some of these have

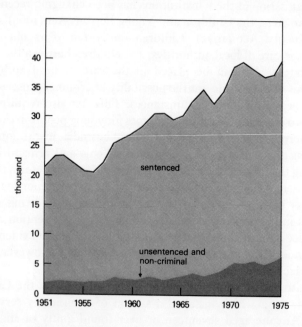

Figure 10.2 *Average population in prisons, borstals and detention centres, 1951–75*
(*Source: New Society*, 29 July 1976)

special security blocks. In mid-1978 the prison population was about 41 000, reflecting a general increase in numbers in recent years. The percentage increase in women prisoners has been greater than for men, but women in prison only constitute four persons for every 100 000 of the population, compared with 167 for men. At present almost all prisons are overcrowded, the general local prisons having taken the brunt of the increase in prison population. In addition to sentenced prisoners, general local prisons house prisoners who are on remand and awaiting trial or sentence and this adds to the overcrowding and confusion. Today, some ten per cent of the prison population consists of unsentenced persons on remand.

From Figure 10.2 it can be seen that recent increases in the prison population have included increases also in the numbers of unsentenced and short-term prisoners.

As a result of the Government White Paper *People in Prisons* (1969) there were plans for new prisons. Economic cutbacks have affected these plans. However, the provisions of the 1972 Criminal Justice Act may eventually improve prison conditions by reducing the numbers of people sentenced to a term of imprisonment. A growing problem in recent times has been the ever-increasing number of prisoners serving life sentences (since the abolition of the death penalty) for crimes of terrorism and murder.

What is it like in prison?

'Prisons are becoming more like rest homes.' So said Mr Duncan Sandys, MP, on 26 September 1967. We have seen that prisons are overcrowded; how does this affect the lives of the prisoners? Are prisons 'more like rest homes?'

Many of the prisons in use today were built in the nineteenth century. Pentonville prison in London was a model prison of its day, and many of the older prisons are modelled on it. Cells in Pentonville are thirteen feet by ten feet by seven feet and, today, house three people. An ex-prisoner from Chelmsford prison describes what it is like to be in a cell:

'. . . when you first go in you're in this sort of dog kennel, because it's no bigger than that, with one bunk on top of the other, and the third bed on the floor. You get three chamber pots, three wash bowls, three tables, three chairs, three washstands, and you're normally there from four in the evening to seven o'clock the next morning. You've got to be very easy going, very passive—it's easy to get into fights.' (Frank Norman, *Lock 'Em Up and Count 'Em*, Charles Knight & Co, 1970)

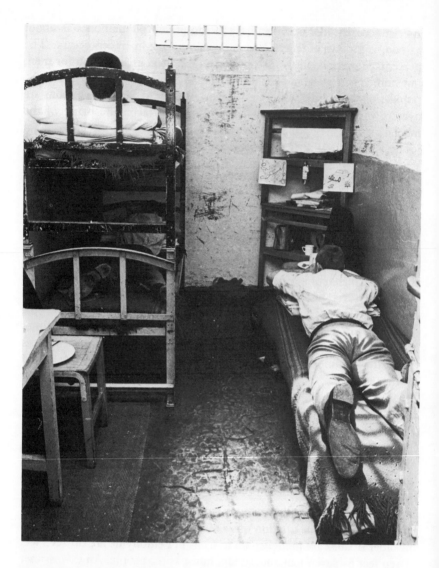

A cell thirteen feet by ten feet by seven feet for three people

At present (1980) 15 000 prisoners sleep two or three to a cell. Under
conditions of old buildings, overcrowding and understaffing it is hard for
prisons to carry out any programme of treatment by which the prisoner is
encouraged to reform. As for long-term prisoners, such as the increasing
number of those serving life sentences, Stan Cohen (*New Society*, 14

November 1974) suggests that for them prisons are little more than human warehouses, places where people are stored until society can think of something else to do with them.

There are, however, two new prisons in England which have enough staff and resources to come closer to the idea of a treatment-centred prison. These are Grendon Underwood, a small psychiatric prison hospital in Buckinghamshire, and Coldingley, a prison in Surrey, which sets out to carry on industrial work under the same conditions as the outside world. In 1975, Cornton Vale, a women's prison in Scotland, was established along treatment-centred lines.

How effective is the penal system?

People who habitually break the criminal law are referred to as *recidivists*. The number of recidivists is usually taken as a guide to the success of the penal system in reducing the level of criminal activity in society. By 1971 of those adult male prisoners discharged in 1968 for sentences of four or more years, as many as 36 per cent had been reconvicted and 23 per cent sent back to prison. By 1973, of a sample of adult male prisoners discharged in 1971 for sentences of between four to ten years, 39 per cent had been reconvicted. Figures are also high for young offenders. At the present time, these figures show no sign of reducing. However, the figures must be looked at with caution, for they cannot be taken too literally as an indication of the success or failure of the penal system. For example, of the people who are not reconvicted we can never know whether this is because the penal system has been successful in reforming them, or because they may have died, or may still be involved in breaking the law but because of their time spent in prison now know how not to get caught. It is not yet possible to assess how the 1972 Criminal Justice Act will affect the numbers of recidivists. It may be that by keeping some offenders out of prison, and therefore free from exposure to a criminal subculture, recidivism will be lowered.

The problem of recidivism is also affected by the way the public thinks about prisoners. The Home Office Report *The Effectiveness of Sentencing* (1976) suggests that retribution is still seen as the courts' main function in the public mind. Prison is seen as the means by which retribution is carried out, there is a stigma attached to a person who has been to prison, which sometimes makes it hard for him to get a job and to set up a life for himself outside. This becomes even more of a problem in times of high unemployment. The Rehabilitation of Offenders Act (1974) aims to reinstate discharged prisoners in the eyes of the community by making it an offence to make unauthorised disclosures of previous convictions once a person has completed a rehabilitation period. This means that ex-prisoners do not necessarily have to give information of previous convictions when applying for some jobs. It is considered that this will make it easier for ex-prisoners to find work and participate in the community.

Sometimes, during his period 'inside', a prisoner will have lost contact with his family and this makes life outside all the more difficult. Greater efforts to keep family members in touch and better after-care might help the prisoner in his move from prison life to the outside world, but funds are just as short in these areas of the prison service as in others. A variety of voluntary prisoner-initiated organisations, such as NACRO, PROP, RAP, Prisoners' Human Rights Committee, Prisoners' Families and Friends Association, have sprung up in recent years to safeguard the welfare of the prisoner both in prison and in his search for work and somewhere to live on leaving prison.

In 1967, the Criminal Justice Act introduced the parole system so that a prisoner can now be released on licence after serving one-third of his sentence or one year, whichever is longer. Parole is not the same as remission for good conduct. Parole works in addition to this and allows prisoners to be free, but supervised. A prisoner seeking parole will first be considered by the Local Review Committee of the prison, then, if he is not rejected, papers about the prisoner are passed on to the Parole Unit of the Home Office. The decision to release a prisoner on parole depends on the Parole Board, appointed by the Home Secretary. Parole is by no means automatic, and once the paroled prisoner is out he is given a licence which stipulates he must report regularly and it is expected that he will make every effort to get regular employment. The Parole Board is free to revoke parole if the formal conditions are not adhered to by the paroled prisoner. Although the parole system takes the prisoner out of the prison environment it is not yet certain whether parole has any direct advantages for the reform of the prisoner. According to West and Hunt (*The Future of Parole*, D. J. West and Lord Hunt, Duckworth, 1972) the institution of the parole system has the advantage of bringing the issue into the limelight, stimulating interest in the needs of prisoners. Improved selection procedures and more streamlined handling of information on prisoners may have led to the phenomenon of an increase in the percentage of prisoners allowing themselves to be considered for parole. The parole system does help to lower the number of people who are in prison and this, as we have seen, could have an effect on the success of prisons as reforming institutions.

In estimating the effectiveness of the penal system in the political context of the wider society, the present state of affairs could be summarised in this reflective graffiti written on the wall in Pentonville and noticed by the criminologists Terence and Pauline Morris (in *Pentonville*, Routledge & Kegan Paul, 1963): 'As long as there are prisons men will exist to fill them. It is regrettable.'

Terms used in this chapter

social order	belief systems	formal control
social control	rites de passage	retributive
norm	sect	reformative
mores	summary jurisdiction	custodial function
folkways	Ecumenicalism	recidivists
beliefs		

Further reading

M. Argyle & B. Beit-Hallahmi, *The Social Psychology of Religion* (Routledge & Kegan Paul, 1975).
M. Banton, *Police-Community Relations* (Collier, 1973)
J. Brothers, *Religious Institutions* (Longman, 1969)
M. Hill, *A Sociology of Religion* (Heinemann, 1973)
M. Jones, *Crime in a Changing Society* (Penguin, 1967)
T. Luckman, *The Invisible Religion* (Macmillan, 1967)
D. A. Martin, *The Religious and the Secular* (Routledge & Kegan Paul, 1969)
J. B. Mays, *Crime and its Treatment* (Longman, 1970)
T. & P. Morris, *Pentonville* (Routledge & Kegan Paul, 1963)
R. Robertson (ed.), *Sociology of Religion* (Penguin, 1969)

Questions from GCE 'O' Level Sociology Examination Papers

1   What is meant by 'social control'? Describe some of the ways by which social control is achieved. (AEB, November 1974)
2   What are the social functions of religion? (AEB, June 1973)
3   Why are sociologists interested in religion? What kinds of studies of religion do sociologists make? (AEB, June 1972)
4   Church attendance figures are sometimes used as indicators of the strength of religious belief. Do you consider it acceptable to use the figures in this way? (AEB, November 1974)
5   'Despite declining church attendance, religious influence in society remains significant.' Discuss. (AEB, June 1976)

6   Church of England
Persons enrolled per 1000 population of appropriate age in England

Date	No. on roll in thousands	Enrolment rate per 1000 population
1930	3693	147
1940	3423	120
1950	2959	96
1960	2862	89
1964	2692	81

Do the figures in the above table tell us anything about
a   a decline in religious belief?
b   a decline in religious influence in England over the last forty years? (AEB, June 1971)

7   What means exist in this country for the enforcement of law? (AEB, June 1968)

8   What factors within society help to maintain law and order? Discuss some of the proposals which have been made in recent years to promote law and order in this country. (AEB, June 1968)

9   What forces, other than law, influence social behaviour? (AEB, June 1968)

10   'Innocent until proved guilty.' This is generally regarded as one of the ways in which the individual is safeguarded by the English legal system. Describe some of the ways in which an individual's rights are protected. How satisfactory are the safeguards:
a   from the point of view of the general public?
b   from the point of view of the police? (AEB, November 1970)

11   'We all know something about criminal law: the law forbidding theft, fraud, murder. . . .' Why do most people obey these laws? What machinery exists to ensure that these laws are upheld? (AEB, June 1969)

12   'Conformity to norms and values within any society is achieved in general by social control.' Explain how this applies in modern Britain. (AEB, June 1977)

13   'The influence of the established church in Britain has declined.' Discuss. (AEB, June 1977)

14   Do increases in criminal statistics always mean increased social disorder? (AEB, June 1979)

11 Social Problems
Unit 34 Deviancy and Crime

A social problem is a condition in society which is judged to be undesirable and in need of reform or elimination by influential groups in society. Conditions such as poverty, unemployment, crime, delinquency and drug-taking are referred to as social problems although not everyone necessarily agrees that all these conditions should be viewed in this way. For example, the person who smokes marijuana may not agree that his behaviour constitutes a social problem; still less would other drug-takers, such as cigarette smokers or beer drinkers, see their behaviour in this light or expect to be categorised in this way.

In society, some voices are heard louder than others; groups who are powerful and influential make decisions about which conditions in society are social problems and should be remedied, and we usually become accustomed to looking at these conditions in this way. The behaviour which is viewed as a problem is usually recorded in official statistics. These are scrutinised for trends showing an increase or decrease in social problems. Official statistics show that many social problems, such as crime or suicide, occur more often in urban areas. However, this does not mean urban life necessarily causes social problems. For example, abortion, while considered less of a problem since its legalisation (in 1967), occurs more often in towns. However, this is because low-cost legal abortion services exist in towns and many women move to urban areas to have their abortion.

34.1 Deviancy

Abnormality has always interested and fascinated people. Behaviour which is out-of-the-ordinary arouses the curiosity of people far more readily than normal, everyday behaviour. The mass media have recognised this fascination very profitably for years.

The person who ignores or breaks the rules of a social group or of society is called a *deviant* by others in society. If the social rules are not considered to be very important, as in the case of fashions, then the people who break the rules are merely eccentrics. If the rule is a more important norm or a law, then the people who persistently break these rules are likely to be penalised and their behaviour may be seen as a social problem by many in society.

There are several important points to be remembered when we think about deviancy and deviants.

1   There is nothing about an action that, in itself, makes it deviant. What is thought of as deviancy is a result of the ideas we have in society, about what actions are right and appropriate. For example, a pupil who shouts and cheers may be considered a model of perfection at the school football match but the same behaviour will be considered inappropriate in school assembly. The action, however, is the same in both cases.

2   Behaviour which is looked on as being deviant in one society may not be seen in that way in another. For example, in our society, drinking alcohol is considered to be a pleasant way to pass the time with friends. In Moslem society, this is strictly forbidden. The deviant, in fact, would be the drinker rather than the teetotaller.

3   Ideas about what is deviant change over the years as the norms and values of society change. For example, in the early twentieth century a woman who

No daughter of mine is going to be seen with a shambles like you, mate . . .!

smoked in public was looked upon as being something of a 'tramp'. Smoking was not considered appropriate for a woman.

4   When we label some people in our society deviant we ought also to look at how they have come to be put in this position. In other words, whose rules have they broken? For example, are these rules drawn up and enforced mainly by powerful middle-class groups in society? If so, these may not be the norms with which every group in society agrees.

5   Having called some actions deviant and the people who commit them deviants, we react to these people as being different from ourselves. We set the deviant apart from us, and get fixed ideas into our head about how he thinks, what he does or how he dresses. The mass media help to keep these impressions alive and we build up a kind of fixed picture of, for example, what an alcoholic is like. These fixed pictures are called *stereotypes* and they mould our ideas about deviants in society. We also have stereotypes with which to view every type of behaviour in society from that of policemen to that of publishers. The attitudes that people hold about the deviant do not go unnoticed by the deviant himself. When this labelling process has the effect of preventing the ex-prisoner, the homosexual, or the unmarried mother from getting a job and somewhere to live, these individuals begin to think of themselves as being fundamentally different from other people. The results can be far-reaching, forcing the person into the stereotyped role society has given him.

6   To try and remedy social problems, we often try to find explanations for why a person has wandered away from what we call normal behaviour. For example, we may say an alcoholic can't cope with the problems of his life and therefore he turns to drink. But the alcoholic himself may explain his behaviour in a very different way. We often forget that people do things for reasons which seem sensible to them, although other people would not always see the sense in what they do.

'Tell me about those tax loopholes you keep dreaming about.'

7   Not all forms of deviancy are equally condemned. For example, it is usually considered wrong for a person to steal money from a friend; however, where a person steals from his workplace or avoids paying income tax, this deviant behaviour may be tolerated and encouraged. The latter are examples of illegal deviant behaviour which many people in society today do not regard with disapproval.

34.2   Crime and juvenile delinquency

Crime is behaviour which breaks the criminal law. Delinquency is a term which describes law-breaking whether this committed by an adult or a young person. Juvenile delinquency in Britain is considered as any violation of the law by someone less than seventeen years old.

We hear a lot about crime and delinquency nowadays and the press ensure that these problems are kept alive in the public's mind. It is said that crime is increasing at present. What are the facts? The information that we have about crime comes from the statistics published by the Home Office in their *Criminal Statistics for England and Wales*. These are a record of crimes known to the police and of convictions.

Non-indictable offences

Out of the total number of non-indictable offences, traffic offences are by far the largest single group. In 1974, there were about 1.2 million persons found guilty of traffic offences, which represented about three-quarters of the total non-indictable offences.

Indictable offences

In the previous chapter, Figure 10.2 showed the numbers of persons found guilty of indictable offences, in thousands, from 1951 to 1975. The graphs show a steady increase in the numbers of persons found guilty of indictable offences, and in particular a sharp increase in the numbers of convictions for theft in recent years. The average daily prison population in 1978 was 40 000 males and 1400 females.

Criminal statistics

Criminal statistics are notoriously misleading and it is a good idea to see why this is so before jumping to the conclusion that we have an enormous crime wave. Crime has increased, but the statistics need interpretation.

For example, the statistics only record crimes known to the police and the numbers of persons found guilty. The police may not be equally interested in all groups of the population as suspects: on the whole middle-class law-breakers are less likely to be detected and therefore do not appear so often in criminal statistics as they ought. Also changes in methods of detection can affect the numbers of cases known to and cleared up by the police.

Criminal statistics therefore present only a partial picture of the extent of crime in society and their fluctuations over a short period are not necessarily a good guide as to whether crime is increasing or decreasing. In the same way we must be careful about theorising on what is criminal behaviour. We have only a little information about some people who are found guilty of breaking the law, and it would be misleading to think that this holds good for all law-breakers.

What do we know about juvenile delinquency?

Today, about four out of ten persons convicted of burglary and a quarter of persons convicted of theft were juveniles (persons under seventeen years old). The most common juvenile offence is theft. The overwhelm-

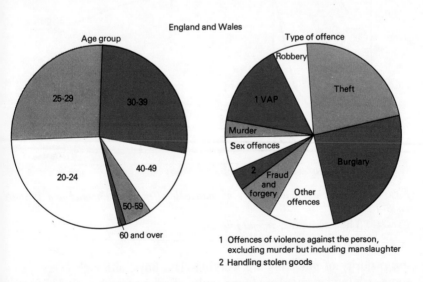

Figure 11.1 *Adult male sentenced prison population, England and Wales, June 1975*
(Source: Home Office)

Crime and juvenile delinquency

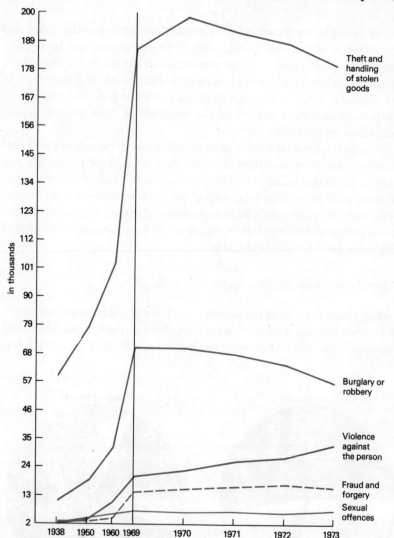

Figure 11.2 *Persons found guilty of indictable offences in England and Wales 1938–1973*
(*Source:* The Economist, *annual release*)

ing majority of offenders are working-class boys, although every year some girls (and women) are found guilty of offences such as shop-lifting. In the late 1960s the peak age for juvenile crime was in the fourteen-to-fifteen age group. It has been suggested that this may be because working-class adolescents experience a great deal of frustration in being at school rather than out in the world and feel this most keenly in the year before they are due to leave.

Explanations of crime and delinquency

The recorded crime rate for adolescents and young people is much higher than for other age groups in the population. If we are going to explain crime, then, we have to account for its being more prevalent among young working-class males than other groups in society. However, it must be remembered that in trying to explain crime by reference to the pattern of criminal behaviour recorded in our criminal statistics, we can only put forward an explanation which applies to people who are recorded in those statistics. These explanations will not hold good for the offender who avoids getting caught or for those wrongfully convicted.

Over the years, many theories have been suggested to explain why people become criminals. These have ranged from the idea that criminals have certain characteristic physical features, to the suggestion that family background accounts for criminal behaviour. It is likely that there is no one clear and simple explanation of criminal behaviour, particularly when we bear in mind the only reason these people are categorised together is due to the fact that they have broken the law. The criminologist D. M. Downes, in his book *The Delinquent Solution* (Routledge & Kegan Paul, 1966) suggests that, from his study of delinquents in Poplar and Stepney, working-class areas in the East End of London, there are social factors which account for the high rate of delinquency in working-class areas. The boy from a working-class home is rejected by the middle-class school system early on in his school career; he is no good at school work and therefore he is termed a failure. This is a humiliating experience and leaves him uninterested in school. Because of his lack of success at school he is bound to take an unskilled or semi-skilled job when he leaves school and this is equally boring and monotonous. (With changing technology, such as automation, these jobs may become scarcer.) Also he has failed in the eyes of society to get a good job and he is, once again, a failure. Under these circumstances his leisure time becomes his opportunity to find satisfaction and success. But youth clubs and other youth organisations are run according to middle-class norms and values and do not hold any attraction for him. Downes says that working-class youths' 'aversion to the present Youth Service sends them on the town'. In this situation, the youths, out for excitement and something to give them a sense of satisfaction and success, are likely to end up committing delinquent acts. After marriage, at an early age, the working-class youth will 'settle down'. This is reflected in a lowering rate of convictions for groups from the early twenties. Downes is not optimistic about the future of working-class youths and adolescents: 'The streets of our urban slums are slowly filling with young men who have no prospect of finding manhood through work: who are coming of age in a society which neither wants them nor needs them.' Recently, sociologists have noted how the social organisation of the school may encourage delinquency. For example, Hargreaves in *Social Relations in a Secondary School* (Routledge & Kegan Paul, 1967), found that streaming had the effect of sharply segregating pupils from one another and encouraging teachers to categorise pupils according to their stream. By the third and fourth year at school, a 'delinquescent' subculture had emerged among lower stream pupils. This emphasised anti-school values and pushed boys towards delinquent behaviour.

Some sociologists have suggested that traditional theories overlook one or two things. For example, in society we react in certain ways to someone who has been convicted of an offence. It is often difficult for the ex-convict, or the boy who has been in trouble, to get a job. By setting people apart in this way, we contribute to their problems and put them into situations where they are more likely to continue committing criminal offences. Also, the fact that crime is seen as largely confined to working-class youth may tell us that the laws in society are made and enforced by middle-class groups rather than anything specifically about the criminal.

Unit 35 Drug-taking

35.1 What are drugs?

If we wanted to stop the pain of toothache we might go to a chemist's shop and buy some aspirin. If we were suffering from a more severe pain it is likely that we would go to the doctor and he would give us a prescription to take to the dispensing department of the chemist's shop. Here the pharmacist would give us the drug which the doctor had prescribed for our condition. Drugs are substances usually used in medicine, for example to reduce the level of pain. However, some substances which are also called drugs, such as cannabis, are not usually used in medicine. When we think of drugs as a social problem we are not concerned with their use, under careful supervision, for healing the sick. The social problem is the compulsive use of drugs by people, not because they are ill but because they want to experience the effects which the drug can produce, such as a sense of happiness and well-being. There are basic terms which are used when looking at drug-taking and before going any further we should look at these.

Drug addiction

Some drugs, after prolonged use, can have the effect of causing a person's body to become dependent on the drug. At this point the person has become addicted. For example, the prolonged use of heroin results in a person becoming physically addicted and developing a compulsive need to take the drug.

Drug habituation

There are other drugs which do not cause physical addiction. Instead, a person may become dependent on the drug because he develops a state of mind where he wants to continue using the drug, because it gives some satisfaction and pleasure. This is called drug habituation. Cannabis is usually associated with this.

Drug dependency

The terms addiction and habituation have often proved to be difficult to apply. This is because there are so many ways in which individual people are affected by various drugs that there is not always a hard and fast division between drug addiction and drug habituation. In 1965, a World Health Organisation Expert Committee on Addiction-Producing Drugs decided that it was better to use the term drug dependency as this would include all the variations in the effects of drug-taking. This expression is generally used today, but the terms 'drug addiction' and 'drug habituation' continue to crop up.

Table 11.1 shows the main types of drugs, with examples of each kind, their broadest effects and the type of dependence which may develop amongst people using the drug. The information in the table must not be taken as being a hard and fast rule that anybody taking a particular drug will end up addicted. Jock Young in *The Drugtakers* (MacGibbon & Kee, 1971) has pointed out that people come to take drugs and learn about them in all manner of circumstances. These personal backgrounds and the ideas that people in society have about drug-taking will make a lot of difference to the way a particular drug affects an individual.

35.2   Drug-taking in Britain

Drug-taking in Britain is no new thing: alcohol has been drunk in large quantities and enjoyed for many generations and it has been estimated that seventy-five per cent of men and fifty-eight per cent of women regularly smoke tobacco. In 1978 people in Britain spent £4000 million on tobacco; in 1969 it was about the same as the total amount spent annually on new cars, furniture, televisions and refrigerators, combined (N. Tomalin: 'Cigarettes; the Secrets of the Trade', *Sunday Times*, 8 June 1969). Also, it has been pointed out that there are about 90 000–100 000 deaths per year attributable to tobacco, although in 1975 deaths from lung cancer and other diseases associated with smoking decreased slightly for the first time. Growing awareness of the dangers of smoking and the medical profession, ASH (Association for Smoking and Health), and the government's campaign against cigarette smoking may have contributed to this decline.

We hear a lot about the drug scene from newspapers, magazines and television and this usually concerns the use of drugs such as heroin and cannabis. It is often overlooked that in Britain there are large numbers of people who are dependent on other drugs such as barbiturates, and these are not the depraved young people that the press tells us about. For example, about seven per cent of all National Health Prescriptions are for barbiturates and many of the people who depend on them are women in the forty-five to sixty-four age group. Table 11.1 summarises some kinds of drug-taking; we will concentrate on cannabis and heroin, while bearing in mind that this is not the entire picture of drug-taking in Britain today.

Cannabis

People using cannabis usually smoke it in a form of cigarette mixed with tobacco known as a joint. Smoking marijuana normally takes place when people are in groups: it is a habit which gives more satisfaction to the individual when he uses the drug in the company of other people. Sometimes the joint will be passed around between members of the group so that it can be shared by everyone. Jock Young considered the way of life of groups of young people, living in Notting Hill, London, who smoked marijuana regularly. ('The Role of the Police as Amplifiers of Deviancy, Negotiators of Reality and Translators of Fantasy' in *Images of Deviance* ed. Stanley Cohen, Penguin Books, 1971.) He noticed that smoking marijuana is not usually the sole purpose of the group meeting together. Pleasure from many other sources, such as listening to music,

Some important categories	Example	Nickname	Effects	Dependence
sedatives	barbiturates	'downers' 'sleepers' 'mandies'	Relaxes the individual; removes inhibitions	Can be 'state of mind' type, although sometimes also physical
stimulants	amphetamines	'spansules' 'bombers' 'B' 'dubes' 'dex'	Excites the individual; he gets very 'worked up' and full of nervous energy	Can be 'state of mind' type
analgesics (pain killers)	heroin	'H' 'smack'	A state of sleepy well-being immediately after a dose (a 'fix')	After a while severe physical type. Compulsive need to take the drug
drugs which heighten the awareness	cannabis (marijuana; hashish; hash)	'grass' 'pot' 'dope' 'weed'	Increases the individual's 'sensitivity' and 'awareness' for example, to music	It is thought dependence does not arise in taking the drug. The individual merely prefers to continue to use it

Table 11.1 A summary of drug-taking

painting, talking, is heightened by the use of marijuana, and therefore the drug is part of the whole way of life of people who are more interested in these things than in joining the rat race to compete for a good job.

According to the research carried out by the Government Advisory Committee on Drug Dependence, 1968 (the Wootton Committee Report) an estimated 30 000 to 300 000 people in Britain have used marijuana. However, this figure has been criticised as being far too conservative an estimate. The report said that as far as we know at present cannabis is not a drug which leads to addiction, but the Committee was concerned that smoking marijuana might lead the drug-user on to taking more harmful drugs, such as heroin. Jock Young thinks that this happens in some cases not because of the drug itself but because of the way people react to deviants in our society. For instance, selling or being in possession of marijuana is illegal and this means the groups who smoke marijuana run the risk of arrest. This results in the marijuana smoker thinking of himself as different and in an atmosphere where people see themselves as deviants the use of stronger drugs may creep in. On the whole, though, the pleasure-seeking way of life of the cannabis user is so different from the obsessive world of the junkie that the cannabis user is not automatically attracted to trying something stronger.

Heroin

Heroin can be taken into the body in a number of ways, such as by tablet, or by injecting under the skin ('skin popping'), or into a main vein ('main lining'). The slang term for a person who becomes addicted to heroin is a junkie. In 1974 there were just under 2000 registered addicts in Britain, including known heroin and methadone addicts. However, a total of 3270 addicts had registered with the authorities at some point during the year. In recent years there has been a slight decrease in the proportion of registered addicts that are under twenty-one (38 per cent in 1966 compared to 14 per cent in 1974). The age group most prone to addiction continues to be the mid-twenties. A person using heroin does not become addicted immediately, but gradually he needs more doses to achieve the same effect and his body eventually becomes addicted to the drug. When this happens, the individual will be totally preoccupied with where his next dose ('fix') is coming from. As soon as the effects of one dose have worn off he must start thinking about the next one. If he cannot get another dose, very severe pains and complications set up in his body. Severe addiction can lead to death. This may not result directly from his addiction but be caused by the addict's neglect of himself, for instance

Young drug addicts, discussing some of their problems at a special clinic

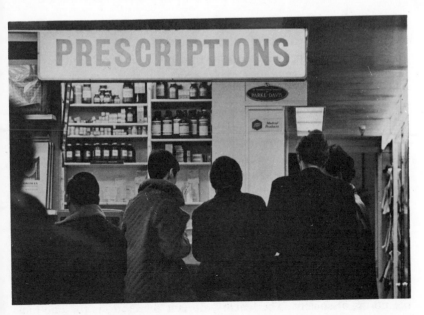

Young people at a drugs counter

through lack of hygiene while giving himself an injection.

Since 1968 the heroin addict has been able to get his supplies through government-organised treatment centres. Not all addicts obtain their supplies in this way and illegal supplies are still available. It is thought that the legal prescription of heroin to addicts through treatment centres has helped to prevent the development of widespread organised crime in this country. In the USA, by contrast, there is no parallel system and the heroin addict steals and robs to get money to buy heroin supplies through the channels of organised crime. Today, addicts are mainly people who have become 'hooked' on the drug as a result of drug-abuse rather than, as was once the case, as a result of medical treatment with the drug. There are members of the medical profession who are addicts; however, not much is known about these people, perhaps because this matter can be hushed up or dealt with within the medical profession itself.

It is often suggested that one of the best reasons for making the selling and possession of cannabis illegal is that this prevents people taking cannabis and beginning a career of drug-taking, possibly ending up as heroin addicts. However, although many heroin addicts have taken cannabis, not all cannabis smokers automatically go on to try heroin.

Explanation of drug-taking in Britain and the control of its use

Drug-taking is often very broadly explained by reference to the strains and stresses of a modern industrialised society. However, drug-taking is not a new problem in society and since not everyone turns to illegal drug-taking this is not a very good explanation. But there are other ways in which people legally relieve their frustrations, for example by taking alcohol and smoking tobacco. The people who drink in moderation or smoke tobacco are not looked on by society in the same way as the people who use illegal drugs. Some portions of the mass media paint a picture of the illegal drug-taker as a depraved or weak individual unable to stand up to the realities of life. Some sociologists think that this picture and the public's response to the drug-taker contribute to changing him into the person the public thinks he is. Philip Bean goes a little further than this and, in his book *The Social Control of Drugs* (Martin Robertson, 1974), he develops Gusfield's idea that the severity of public response is affected by what is taken to be the deviant's attitude. For example, the 'repentant' deviant, the 'cynical' deviant and the 'sick person' deviant are all considered less of a problem than the 'enemy' deviant, who flatly rejects the norms of society. The 'enemy' deviant therefore, is the one most severely penalised. Bean suggests that illegal drug-takers have shifted in the public mind from being the 'repentant' deviants of the 1930s to being the 'enemy' deviants of the 1960s.

The control of drug-taking presents many problems. Cannabis is illegal at present although many people think that there is no reason why its use should not be legalised. The Misuse of Drugs Act, 1972, introduced penalties which are different for the illegal possession and for the illegal selling of drugs. Illegal possession now merits a lower penalty than the selling of drugs. It is too early to know if this is substantially affecting the abuse of drugs in our society; it might have the effect of making the illegal selling of drugs become the concern of big well-run organisations that are successful in avoiding detection.

In 1974, the number of persons stopped and searched for drugs under the 1972 Act, was 14 831, of whom 4115 were found to be in illegal possession of drugs controlled by the Act. The numbers of persons proceeded against on drug offences increased from 9673 (1970) to 15 019 (1973). Cannabis convictions rose from 11 941 (1972) to 13 118 (1973), while opium convictions more than doubled in this time.

Smoking tobacco and drinking alcohol are commonplace among adults

35.3   Alcoholism

Alcohol

It is no accident that, after looking at particular examples of drug-taking in society, we have turned to consider alcoholism because alcohol, too, is a drug. It is a sedative type of drug and therefore in the same category as barbiturates (see Table 11.1).

Alcohol relaxes people and relieves their tensions and anxieties. In 1954 and 1955 the World Health Organisation Expert Committee on Addiction-Producing Drugs concluded that alcohol was a drug which is somewhere between those drugs, such as heroin, which, in time, almost always lead to addiction, and drugs, such as cannabis, where there is a desire to carry on using the drug, but nothing more. In other words, alcohol can sometimes lead to physical addiction but it need not always have this effect. Jock Young in *The Drugtakers* says that the way to understand the varying effects which a drug produces is to look at the circumstances in which the drug is taken. For example, in drinking alcohol a person might *want* to reach the point where he had lost control over his drinking and this could be the difference between one person becoming an alcoholic while another does not.

As some of us never touch a drop there must be some of us getting a double ration.

'Have a drink?'

According to one inquiry, forty-seven per cent of British people over sixteen years old drink regularly at least once a week, and 11.5 per cent drink every day (Hulton Readership Survey). Drinking alcohol is a social habit which, in moderation, is encouraged in our society; it is also a very lucrative and time-honoured business. It is estimated that in recent years £30 million annually is spent in promoting drink.

In our society there are norms about drinking. For example, we have unwritten rules to the effect that a person should know when to stop drinking. It is acceptable to drink in moderation, but to drink regularly to the point of being completely drunk is not acceptable. Amongst men, drinking is often taken as a sign of being manly. During 1980 the average expenditure on alcohol, per head of all adults over 18, was more than £200.

Who are alcoholics?

Because alcoholism is very often seen as being a sign of weakness and inability to stand up to life, people go to some lengths to try to conceal their dependence on alcohol. The social stigma attached to alcoholism affects the life of the individual in many ways, isolating him from other people in society. At work, if a man is discovered to be an alcoholic he may be sacked immediately. The information that we have about alcoholics is therefore very limited. According to the Office of Health Economics, there are in the region of 200 000 to 400 000 alcoholics in Britain (*Alcohol Abuse*, Office of Health Economics, 1970). In the four years between 1970 and 1974 the number of people admitted to hospital and treatment units for alcoholism increased by 54 per cent in England and Wales. Scotland has the highest proportion of known alcoholics in Europe, and it is seven times greater than that in England and Wales.

We know something about a proportion of these alcoholics, because some of them are treated through charitable organisations and others may receive treatment in National Health hospitals.

It has been estimated that there is one woman dependent on alcohol to every three men who are so dependent (M. M. Glatt, 'Alcoholism and Drug Dependence under One Umbrella?', *World Dialogue on Drug Dependence*, ed. E. D. Whitney, Beacon Press, 1970). The person who is dependent on alcohol is often middle-aged and male, but there has recently been an increase in the number of young people requiring treatment. The National Council on Alcoholism noted that a quarter of the new cases referred to their regional centres in 1974 were people under age 29 (National Council on Alcoholism, 12th Annual Report, 1974). There are some alcoholics amongst publicans; this may be because they have more opportunity to drink to excess.

Alcoholism as a social problem

One of the reasons why alcoholism is considered to be a social problem is that it costs the country money. For example, the Medical Council on Alcoholism estimates that alcoholism costs industry as much as £500 million a year as a result of employees who are dependent on alcohol absenting themselves from work. There are other reasons which cause alcoholism to be considered as a social, rather than an individual, problem: for example, prisons would be less overcrowded if it were possible to eliminate the problem of the drunkard who is arrested and ends up in gaol because he is unable to pay a fine. Drunken driving threatens the life not only of the person who has been drinking but also the lives of other people on the road at the same time, so this too is a cause of concern to society. People are also concerned about alcoholism as a social problem because it affects the lives and happiness of individuals and their families, often because of the social stigma which is attached to alcoholism in our society.

Despite the fact that alcoholism is a serious problem, it does not receive as much attention, for example from the media, as other forms of drug-abuse. The fact that drinking is a time-honoured social custom tends to overshadow the social problem of alcoholism.

Explanations

It is misleading to try and look for one way of explaining alcohol dependency. The range of backgrounds of people who are known to be alcohol dependants and the number of different circumstances in which they come to be dependent make it impossible even to talk of alcoholism as a single problem. It would be better, in fact, to talk of alcoholisms.

Some sociologists suggest that a person who does not know the norms which surround restrained drinking in the company of other people is more likely to become a compulsive drinker than someone who knows the rules of drinking socially.

However, we have at present no very satisfactory ideas explaining alcoholism. The only thing we do know about it is the way in which people tend to react to someone who has passed beyond the level of drinking which we look on as being acceptable. The stigma attached to someone in this condition is likely to have the effect of pushing the excessive drinker still further into the state of being dependent on alcohol.

How can we prevent alcoholism?

Not knowing very much about the real sources of the problem we can only attempt to deal with the symptoms; that is, try to get a person off his dependence on alcohol. The work of organisations such as Alcoholics Anonymous helps in this way, and, as a result of the two Criminal Justice Acts (1967 and 1972), the Government is taking steps to deal with the problem of the habitual drunken offender and to remove him from the prison to specially-staffed treatment centres. About 100 000 cases of drunkenness come before the court annually (in Scotland the figure is five times as high).

Of course, one of the most important ways in which the problem can be tackled is by trying to change people's ideas about the alcoholic and to reduce the social stigma which surrounds alcoholism.

Unit 36 Some Other Social Problems

36.1 Illegitimacy

Illegitimacy is a term which is used to describe the conception and birth of children to couples who are not married to one another. This is often seen as deviant behaviour because sexual intercourse outside marriage appears to threaten the place of marriage, which in our society is seen as providing a firm relationship within which children can be cared for on a long-term basis. Were sexual intercourse entirely unregulated, the child-rearing functions of the family would be difficult to carry out.

In the period 1870–2 recorded illegitimate births were 5.6 per cent of all live births in England and Wales. It must be remembered, however, that a large number of illegitimate births were not recorded in the nineteenth century, because of the social stigma associated to illegitimacy. The proportion of illegitimate to all live births had declined to 3.9 per cent in the period 1900–02 and since that time there has been an increase in the proportion of illegitimate births, until by 1980 this proportion was almost 10 per cent.

Illegitimacy and the permissive society

The recent steep increase in illegitimate births is seen by many people as confirming their suspicions that an increasingly permissive society has brought about a detached and cynical attitude towards sex amongst young people and that promiscuity is widespread. According to a report for the Office of Population Censuses and Surveys in 1977 three-quarters of all illegitimacies are born to mothers of manual working-class backgrounds. Statistics on the numbers of illegitimate births do not necessarily give us a clear-cut guide as to whether people are observing the sexual mores of society. For instance, many children conceived outside marriage may have been legitimised because the parents later got married. However, there has been a decline in the number of births legitimised in this way. This may tell us something about the way people are thinking about illegitimacy today; perhaps we are more prepared to accept the fact that a couple or a mother on her own can bring up her child without being married. The majority of unmarried mothers today want to keep their baby. This has been made possible by the change which has taken place since the nineteenth century in the woman's role, making her able to be independent of men and to earn her own living. The extension of the child interim benefit scheme to provide an allowance for the first child in a one-parent family, which began in April 1977, was the first official recognition of the financial problems faced by all types of one-parent families. Nevertheless the problems are still great, as is shown in this extract.

Dear Sir or Madam,
  . . . I'm an unmarried mother with a child of three who is getting on for four. I'm in my mother's house which is overcrowded. It's a council house and I'm to get out . . . I just don't want to be chucked out into the street as I have nowhere to stay so could you help me? What do other girls do when they are in a position like me?
(From *Case Histories*, a selection of letters, etc. from the National Council for the Unmarried Mother and Her Child, 225 Kentish Town Road, London NW5 2LX)

The unmarried father, has, of course, also broken one of the norms of society, but there is a dual standard which exists with regard to sexual relationships, and the same social stigma is not attached to an unmarried father as to an unmarried mother.

36.2   Abortion

Abortion is the ending of a woman's pregnancy by preventing the further development of the foetus. This is achieved by many different techniques and the practice itself is very old. It has been used in many parts of the world for centuries and at the present time Hungary, Poland, Czechoslovakia and Japan are among the countries where legal abortion is widely performed.

Abortion in Britain

Before the Abortion Act of 1967 legal abortion was not possible in this country. It has always been possible to obtain abortion illegally, however. The 1967 Act made it possible for people in particular circumstances to obtain an abortion legally. These are where continuing pregnancy

1   risks the life of the pregnant woman, or
2   might cause her injury, physically or mentally, or
3   might injure the physical or mental health of any of the children already in her family.

Since this time there has been one attempt to modify the existing Abortion Law and, in 1974, the Lane Committee issued recommendations for better regional distribution of abortion facilities. There is still a great deal of controversy surrounding the central issue of the Act: that is, the individual's right to abortion, and it is likely that the law will soon have to be changed. However, it is difficult to know what form these changes will take and whether they will favour abortion 'on demand' or the point of view of the anti-abortionists.

The National Health Service is under no obligation to carry out abortions and doctors and nurses are free to refuse to perform abortions if they think that such an act is morally wrong. Death from abortion has lowered since the introduction of the Act. For example, only eleven mothers died from abortion in 1974 compared to thirty-five in 1969. During this time new techniques, such as vacuum extraction, have improved the safety of abortion. The National Health Service continues to be overloaded and the number of cases it has dealt with has decreased in recent years. In 1969, 60 per cent of abortions were obtained through the National Health Service; in 1978, this figure had dropped to 49 per cent. One half of legal abortions are performed through alternative agencies such as the British Pregnancy Advisory Service and the Pregnancy Advisory Service.

The difficulties of obtaining an abortion are not always appreciated:

> ... [I am now] three-and-a-half months pregnant. My doctor did all he could for me and tried to get my pregnancy terminated at our local hospital but without success.
>
> I have been up to London to see if I could get an abortion but that was unsuccessful ...
>
> (Taken from a letter sent to the National Council for the Unmarried Mother and Her Child. The writer was separated from her husband and had two children.)

Many cases do not come within the terms of the Act and, even when they do, it is not certain that the local hospital will be able to help. Under these circumstances, illegal abortions continue to be performed. It has been estimated by François Lafitte in his article 'Abortion in Britain Today' (*New Society*, 14 December 1972) that there are probably 'several thousands' of cases of successful illegal abortions per year in Britain.

Abortion, whether legal or illegal, is often pointed to as evidence that young single people are increasingly promiscuous in their relationships with one another. In this sense, abortion is seen as a social problem because it appears to be the result of behaviour which breaks the sexual mores of society and takes parenthood irresponsibly. Newspaper reports which describe hundreds of young people flocking to clinics and hospitals to have abortions help to keep this picture alive.

Who has an abortion and why?

In 1979 there were 147 451 legal abortions of which 120 611 related to England and Wales residents compared with 127 904 in 1976. The highest year was 1973 when 167 149 abortions were reported. Figures for women who are ordinarily resident in this country declined less than those for women who came here temporarily from other countries. This decline is reflected in all age groups except girls under sixteen. However, before rushing to the conclusion that there is increasing promiscuity among young people, these statistics should be evaluated. Between 1974 and 1975 there was an increase of 9 per cent in the number of legal abortions in this age group. Some of this increase can be accounted for by an increase in the proportion of the population in these ages; however, even taking this into account there remains a real increase in the number of recorded abortions (three-and-a-half-thousand abortions were given to girls under sixteen years in 1977). Against this, it must be remembered that the figures may also be reflecting a corresponding decline in illegal abortions in this time.

also be reflecting a corresponding decline in illegal abortions in this time.

About half of all legal abortions are to single women. In 1978 there was a significant increase in abortions, most noticeably by women aged 20–34 years.

The surprising feature of the legalisation of abortion has been the extent of the demand from married women, many of whom already have several children. As for unmarried women, according to one study, far from being cynical and callous individuals as newspaper reports suggest, the young unmarried women who have abortions have them as a 'result of sexual inexperience, ignorance, an idealistic set of sexual morals, and a romantic vision of sex and human relationships'. (*Abortion and Contraception—A Study of Patients' Attitudes*, T. M. Williams and K. Hindell, PEP Report No. 536, 1972.)

36.3   Suicide

Suicide is death resulting from a deliberate act of self-destruction. In 1976, there were 3693 recorded suicides (2329 males and 1484 females) in Britain. This figure represents about 0.67 per cent of all deaths. The number of recorded suicides has dropped since the early 1960s when the figures were well above 5000 suicides per year. Sex differences in suicide rates persist: in 1901 there were three male suicides for every one female suicide, today there are roughly two male suicides for every one female suicide. However, as with any statistics, these figures should be viewed with caution.

Attempted suicide

Sometimes a person does not succeed in taking his own life. When this happens it is called attempted suicide. Often there are circumstances which makes the person's act appear a little different from a suicide attempt which has been successful. For example, a woman may turn on the gas at a time when she knows her husband normally returns from work. It would seem as though she had intended her husband to find her before the gas had its effect. Attempted suicide is often seen as being a way in which people draw attention to their conflicts and problems, without any real intention of committing suicide.

The official record of suicides

Before the 1961 Suicide Act, suicide was considered a criminal offence and people who had survived a suicide attempt could be prosecuted. This is not the case today. Before a death can be categorised as a suicide it has to be considered by a coroner and an inquest held. It is up to the coroner to establish that a person *intended* to take his own life as this is the official difference between suicide and other categories of death, such as accidental death.

Explanations of suicide

There are many problems which surround attempts to explain the conditions which give rise to suicide in society. For example, we have only a very limited amount of information to go on: a person only becomes part of our information when he has committed suicide and, of course, at that point it is too late to ask him any questions about the circumstances that led him to take his own life.

The statistics which we have give us information about the suicide rate in society, but as with all statistics, they must be used with caution. There may be circumstances where a death which is a suicide goes unrecorded. For instance, suicide may be covered up by a family for insurance purposes: or, because many Christians see committing suicide as a sin, a family may go to some lengths to ensure that the suicide of a member is officially recorded in some other way, for example, as accidental death. Also, in areas where deaths often happen through accidents, suicides may be mistakenly recorded as accidental death. For example, a person may drown in a dangerous river or canal, and this may be usual enough, locally, for a suicide to go undetected.

Sociologists do not try to explain suicide in terms of the individual's personality. Instead they look for an explanation in the ways in which we live our lives in society. A sociologist might ask: 'Are there particular pressures that some people have to face in society today that lead them to take their own life?'

Using statistics on suicide, sociologists have put forward theories which show how suicide can be associated with social factors. One of the most significant early studies to approach suicide in this way is that of Émile Durkheim. He claimed to have shown that the suicide rates were associated with the quality and degree of integration of the individual in social groups. For example, in some cases, the individual's sense of personal responsibility for his actions is so intense that, where there is a corresponding lack of support from the social group, the individual may feel the burden of responsibility so keenly that suicide results. Durkheim called suicide associated with such social circumstances, *egoistic suicide*.

By contrast, *altruistic suicide* results from a high level of individual integration and commitment to the social group so that, under some circumstances, the individual will take his own life because of his close identification with the needs and demands of the group. Durkheim distinguished a third set of conditions associated with suicide, in this case termed *anomic suicide*. Anomic suicide occurs when the individual experiences a period of social or personal disorganisation. This may occur, for example, when a period of economic crisis disturbs the pattern of the individual's life; the pressures and uncertainties accompanying such circumstances may lead a person to commit suicide. Although Durkheim's study, *Le Suicide*, 1897, is still regarded by many as a classic investigation, it contains a serious flaw. Roman Catholic countries had a much lower suicide rate, but as a person who committed suicide was damned and could not be buried in consecrated ground it is very likely that genuine cases of Catholic suicide would be recorded as 'accidental' deaths and hushed up by the authorities for the sake of relatives.

Some of the factors which, it has been suggested, are associated with suicide are:

1   being male
2   increasing age
3   having a history of a broken home in childhood
4   being widowed, single or divorced
5   being childless
6   living in big towns
7   having a high standard of living
8   having a history of mental disorder or physical illness
9   economic crisis
10   high density of population.

Heavy drinking of alcohol is also frequently associated with suicide, although it would be difficult to determine whether this is any way a cause of suicide, since both actions may derive from a third factor such as loss of job.

Although one or more of these factors may be likely to appear in the background of a person who has committed suicide, it is important to remember that, despite this, we cannot say with certainty that a broken home or any other specific factor was the *cause* of a person committing suicide.

Research results of this sort very often seem to do no more than confirm the impression of the man in the street that a person who is isolated and therefore unhappy is more likely to commit suicide than a person who is totally wrapped up in a full and happy life. The voice of the expert gives a little more authority to these ideas and they are readily taken up and used by the mass media and so become part of everyday ideas about suicide.

Mr S was a thirty-year-old married man with two children; he gambled, ran into financial trouble, and couldn't sleep. Instead of finding out why, his doctor gave him a prescription for sleeping tablets.

In this newspaper account, the doctor who is describing what happened in this case is quite certain that a background of gambling leading to financial trouble will, given the opportunity of a bottle of pills, make the man commit suicide.

Some sociologists have suggested that, in trying to explain suicide, we should look into some of the ideas that we have about suicide in our society, rather than concentrate on using official statistics. After all, suicide cannot be precisely recognised in the same way as, for example, a birth; the coroner has to decide if a suicide has occurred. The way in which he reaches his decision will tell us something about the ideas that are commonly held in society about the circumstances under which suicide occurs. For example, he will be more likely to suspect a suicide

	1964	1965	1966	1967	1968	1969	1970
Population in millions	47.40	47.76	48.08	48.39	48.67	48.83	48.94
No. of suicides	5566	5161	4994	4711	4584	4370	3939
Suicide rate per 100 000	11.70	10.80	10.40	9.70	9.40	8.90	8.00
Samaritan branches	56	68	75	86	92	95	115
No. of new clients	12 355	16 422	20 875	31 780	42 241	51 412	68 531
No. of volunteers	nr	6537	7116	7688	11 204	8910	12 832

nr   not recorded

Table 11.2   The Samaritans and suicides in England and Wales
(Source: *New Society*, 15 March 1973, table compiled by Richard Fox)

has taken place where a person has died from gas poisoning in front of a gas oven than if she had died in a road accident, because we do not usually think of suicide taking place in the latter way. Coroners often look for evidence of suicide in the circumstances of a death. If, for instance, a person went to a great deal of trouble to make sure that his attempt would succeed, then the coroner is likely to decide that the death was a suicide. In other words, the coroner adds to the ideas in society about what are the circumstances which make a death into a suicide.

The ideas we have about what pressures drive a person to suicide will also cause some people to be more likely to commit suicide than others. For example, a young man who is a student knows that sometimes students commit suicide. If he finds that there are pressures which are making life unbearable he may see suicide as an appropriate way to solve his personal problems. It is not possible to ascertain the effect that the Samaritan movement has had upon the recorded rate, but there is evidence to show significant reductions in suicides in towns having branches of the Samaritans when compared with matched towns without such branches. Table 11.2 indicates a decline in the suicide rate from the early 1960s; however, in the past few years after the drop in 1976 to 3693 the numbers of suicides have increased slightly. There has been a much more pronounced increase in the number of 'para-suicide' cases (attempted suicides) admitted to hospitals. The Samaritan organisation observes that many of the calls they receive now are from people in economic stress, and see this as a symptom of the effects of the New Depression of the 1970s.

Unit 37 Minority Groups and Social Integration

37.1 Minority groups

A minority group is any group in society which, by virtue of some particular characteristics, such as having a different culture or religion, or being racially separate, is sometimes placed at a disadvantage in society. This is often because the group is treated as different by other people in society and, because of this, denied the opportunities which are open to others. The term is sometimes used to apply to categories of people, even though they may be neither minorities nor groups. For example, women have been called a minority group because they are discriminated against in a male-orientated society. On the other hand, some groups which are a minority, but which are privileged, such as royalty, are not termed minority groups.

Ethnic groups

Many minority groups are also ethnic or racial groups. An ethnic group is a sub-group of the larger society, having a distinct cultural tradition and a sense of common identity. For example, ethnic groups in Britain include: Chinese, Jews, Indians, Irish, Maltese, West Indians. Ethnic groups may also be racial groups, but the two types of groups are not necessarily identical and should not be confused. (Racial groups are considered later on in this chapter.)

Many minority group members came to Britain in search of work, a home or freedom from persecution. In the nineteenth and twentieth centuries, many Jews, fleeing from persecution in Europe, were amongst the immigrant groups who came to live in this country. In the 1940s Britain was host to about 30 000 Poles who came to this country as a result of events in their own country during World War II and many of these later settled and remained in Britain. In 1956, Britain absorbed 30 000 Hungarians in the wake of the Russian invasion of Hungary, about the same number as the British Asians who came to live in Britain as a result of the Africanisation policy in Uganda in 1972. Many of the groups and individuals who have come to this country in the past from other countries, for all manner of reasons, now pass unnoticed in the population of Britain. Other groups preserve their special way of life because this is important to them and maintains a long tradition. This is true, for instance, of Orthodox Jews, for whom their distinctive life-style serves to link members of this ethnic group across the world. Other groups are in the position of wanting to preserve their cultural heritage, but not wishing this to exclude them from full participation in society on an equal footing with other members of society.

Immigrants

As we have seen already in Chapter 5, in the past many people have come from different parts of the world to live in Britain. Today, also, many people come from other parts of the world, such as Europe and countries in the Commonwealth to make Britain their home. The terms New Commonwealth, and Old Commonwealth are sometimes used about Commonwealth countries. New Commonwealth countries are those which were formerly part of the British Empire but have achieved independence and joined the Commonwealth since 1945; Old Commonwealth countries are countries such as Australia, Canada and New Zealand, which have been self-governing Dominions for many years. Among the people from both the Old and the New Commonwealth

Immigrants from the New Commonwealth have added to our skilled and professional labour force. This Asian woman is teaching a withdrawal group.

countries who have come to Britain in recent years are groups from Asia and the West Indies. We hear a lot about coloured Commonwealth immigrants in our society but we do not often realise how many people there are from other places also living in Britain.

Asian immigrants

Asian immigrants first began coming to this country in significant numbers in the 1950s. Some Commonwealth Asian immigrants come from India and Pakistan, but others come from Kenya and Uganda. For example, in 1967–8 Kenya began a policy of Africanisation and many Asians living in Kenya, holding British passports (and therefore freely entitled to enter this country) left Kenya and came to live in Britain. In the middle of this crisis, the Government passed the Commonwealth Immigrants Act (1968) which limited the numbers who could enter to those possessing employment vouchers and their dependants, After that date 1500 vouchers per year were issued. Events in Uganda in 1972 forced several thousand British and other Asians to make Britain their home. The Ugandan and Kenyan Asians came to this country under emergency circumstances and had to leave behind skilled and professional jobs and high standards of living.

West Indian immigrants

West Indians first began to come to this country in the 1950s and, together with Asian immigrants, have helped to meet Britain's demand for labour. Both groups stood to improve their standard of living. For example in 1969 the average income per head for people in Jamaica was £223, and for people living in India it was £37 in 1970, whereas the figure was £833 for England in 1970. The majority of West Indian immigrants are from Jamaica. It is often not realised how different the West Indian islands are from one another and what great distances separate the islands.

Immigration and legislation

Immigration has become a controversial issue in recent years and there is a wealth of information, some reliable and some not so reliable, which has been put out by various official bodies and individuals on the subject. The controversy hinges around the number of immigrants who come to this country from the New Commonwealth. For instance, many people see

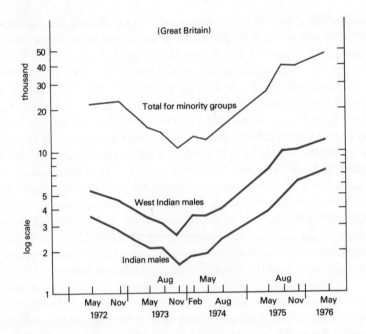

Figure 11.3   *Unemployment among minority groups*
(Source: New Society *9 September 1976)*

Asian and West Indian immigrants taking up jobs that, they say, white people need. Arguments of this sort overlook the fact that the areas with the highest unemployment rate, such as Scotland and Wales, are areas where there are very few coloured Commonwealth immigrants. Similarly, an article in *New Society*, 9 September 1976, reveals unemployment to be disproportionately higher among minority workers and youths in the recent recession. Immigrants from the New Commonwealth countries have increasingly been adding to our skilled and professional labour force. In the case of medicine, for instance, many Asians are included amongst the overseas doctors who made up 56 per cent of the total registrars employed by the National Health Service in 1973. On the whole though, immigrants from the New Commonwealth are taking jobs, such as driving buses and working in factories, that many other people would prefer not to do. This has led some sociologists to see coloured immigrant workers as a new, exploited, underclass in the British class system.

It has been suggested that if too many people were admitted from New

Commonwealth countries our social services and educational facilities
would come under strain, particularly as immigrants from these
countries have a higher birth rate than native Britons. Asians and West
Indians come to this country from areas where it is customary to have
larger families and they are usually young and therefore produce
children; as they become older, three generations will be represented and
therefore there will be fewer children born per thousand of the New
Commonwealth immigrants, in addition to which immigrants may well
have adopted the idea of having smaller families. In the 1971 census it
was found that the average household size of New Commonwealth
immigrants was 4.04 persons compared with 2.87 for the population as a
whole. This reflects the preference of many immigrant families,
especially Asian families, to preserve the tradition of caring for three
generations of family members under one roof. New Commonwealth
households make up about two per cent of all households, but the people
in them constitute over three per cent of the total population.

The Commonwealth Immigrants Act of 1962 set up a system of work
vouchers for immigrants coming to this country, which had the effect of
lowering the numbers of people, particularly unskilled people, coming
into Britain. Since that time there has been a Government White Paper
(1965) and a Commonwealth Immigrants Act (1968), which also imposed
various standards for controlling and limiting the number of immigrants

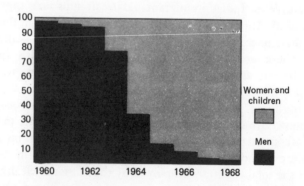

Figure 11.4   *Pakistani immigration figures – percentage of working men to women
and children*
*(Source: Compiled from the Home Office statistics for immigration by Clifford Hill
in his book* Immigration and Integration *Pergamon Press, 1970)*

per year entering the country from the New Commonwealth. The result of this legislation has been that almost the only people who now enter Britain from these countries (apart from emergency groups such as the Ugandan Asians) are the wives and families of immigrants already in Britain. Figure 11.4 shows the changes which have taken place in the case of immigrants from Pakistan. Currently, the main legislation is the Immigration Act of 1971 and the supplementary legislation set out in various subsequent Statements of Immigration Rules. The Act introduced the terms *patrial* and *non-patrial* which, in future, will be used to find out a person's right of entry into this country. Broadly, patrials have recent ancestors who were closely associated by birth with Britain.

Non-patrials do not have this background and therefore will be admitted to this country only if they are allowed a work permit. This will be for a particular job and normally given at first for a fixed period of twelve months. Some dependants will also be admitted. Under this Act non-patrials may apply for citizenship under certain conditions, and provision is made for deportation in some circumstances. Non-patrials already in Britain are not included under the terms of the Act. The main effects of this Act will be to make it even more difficult for members of the New Commonwealth to enter this country, because they are mostly non-patrials, and to cause some anxiety to existing residents who feel that, as non-patrials, their position is insecure. The recent departure of Pakistan from the Commonwealth made the position of immigrants from Pakistan temporarily insecure. However, the 1973 Pakistan Act re-instated the rights of Pakistan immigrants in this country on a footing with other New Commonwealth groups. Despite formal rights, citizenship, entrance of dependants and other matters of importance to immigrant families in this country are not automatically ensured by residence here. The decisions of the Home Office on these matters can sometimes appear unjust, and advisory bodies, such as the Joint Council for the Welfare of Immigrants, have sprung up to supplement the Government's independent advisory agency (the United Kingdom Immigrants' Advice Service) to help immigrants appeal decisions.

37.2 Race relations

Race and racial groups

We hear a lot at present about *race relations* in society. What is it all about? First, we must look at the terms *race* and *racial group*. Race is a classification for grouping together people in society who have the same characteristic physical features, such as shape of eyes, head, skin colour or eye colour. If people have a certain set of characteristics, then we say they belong to a certain race. Any other ideas that we might have about the characteristics of racial groups, for example that all black people have a good sense of rhythm, derive from the stereotypes of racial groups that we build up in society. Tensions between racial groups spring up where these stereotypes affect human relationships. *Race* and *nationality* are not to be confused: race depends on physical characteristics, nationality on the person being a citizen of a certain nation, such as France or the USA. The nation itself exists because of political boundaries which separate one area of land, or nation from another.

Prejudice

Prejudice is a favourable or unfavourable attitude directed towards members of a social group to which one generally does not belong. These attitudes rest on oversimplified and overgeneralised beliefs about the social characteristics of members of certain groups. For example, prejudice may be directed towards an individual because he is a member of a particular religious, ethnic or racial group. This is because ideas about the individual derive from preconceived beliefs about the social characteristics of all members of this group. In other words, prejudiced attitudes depend on the use of social stereotypes. We can see then that prejudice, whether favourable or unfavourable, has no reliable basis and is a misleading way in which to view individuals and groups in society.

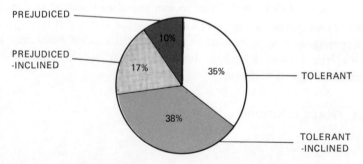

Figure 11.5   *Incidence of prejudice among respondents in the survey* (*Source:* Colour and Citizenship, A Report on British Race Relations, *E. J. B. Rose* et al. *for the Institute of Race Relations, Oxford University Press, 1969*)

Racial prejudice

Racial prejudice is where these unreflective attitudes are adopted towards members of a group who possess particular racial characteristics. Where there is intolerance between members of different racial groups, the basis of this conflict often lies with the prejudices which each group holds about the other.

The question of the extent of racial prejudice in Britain was the subject of a sample survey carried out in 1966–7 in five London boroughs having a high proportion of New Commonwealth residents. Some broad results of the survey are summarised in Figure 11.4.

From the chart we can see that a majority of people were recorded as tolerant or tolerant-inclined in their attitudes towards members of other racial groups. The results of this and other research by the Institute of Race Relations led the social scientists involved to be optimistic about the future of race relations in Britain, although others have been critical of these conclusions. According to Alan Marsh, at the Social Science Research Council Survey Unit (1976), there has been some increase in the extent of racial intolerance in Britain since the 1960s. He finds this concentrated in working–class youth and older people over sixty-five with elementary level education. These findings must not be interpreted as indicating everyone in these social groups has become more racially intolerant over the last ten years or so. Also, the findings themselves appear inconclusive as other researchers have found more subtle influences at work. For example, in 1976, Alan Little and David Kohler of the Community Relations Commission found that, although 58 per cent of their nationally representative sample thought that race relations were deteriorating in the country as a whole, 53 per cent thought that relations were 'very good' or 'good' in the area in which they lived. Little and Kohler found that people appeared to have more favourable attitudes to coloured immigrants born in this country than towards immigrants living in Britain. This may indicate greater acceptance of immigrants in the long term, particularly as groups get to know each other at school and at work. The survey also showed that race relations are not considered by local residents to be among the most serious problems facing them in their local area. It ranked fifteenth in the problems most prominent in people's minds. Little and Kohler point out that the mass media appear to have a big effect in influencing people's opinions about race relations outside the area they don't know about. Inflammatory headlines make people think there is a general deterioration in race relations across the nation.

Discrimination

Discrimination is where one group of individuals is treated differently from others, the root of this action lying with the prejudiced attitudes of one group towards another. Discrimination may be to the advantage of the group treated differently, of course, but usually we think of the term being applied to a group in society which is treated less favourably than the rest of the population because of mode of life, sex, or racial characteristics.

Racial discrimination

If there is widespread injustice towards people in society because of their race, and in particular because of the colour of their skin, we should all be concerned because there are no reasonable grounds for behaving in this way: a man has no control over his skin colour any more than he has control over how tall he is. Several surveys have tried to find out the nature and extent of racial discrimination in Britain and almost all of them point to employment and housing as being some of the ways in which coloured Commonwealth immigrants experience discrimination. For example, a PEP study in 1973/4 found that there were conspicuous differences in employers' responses to job applicants depending on whether the applicant was white or coloured. At work there is always the possibility that the immigrant worker will receive the worst jobs. In a study of fourteen plants, David Smith (*Racial Discrimination in Employment*, PEP, June 1974) found that active discrimination was less of a problem than the inertia of management and unions to safeguard the rights of minority employees. Although white workers sometimes objected initially to the hiring of minority group members this seldom extended to outright resistance. Tolerance and acceptance of immigrant workers as individuals was much more common, and very few cases of industrial action were directly related to racial issues.

Housing is another area in which New Commonwealth immigrants experience difficulties. Contrary to popular belief many immigrants, particularly Asians, own their own home. However, the property owned is often older and of poorer quality because of the weak position of immigrants in the housing market. Sheila Allen, in *New Minorities, Old Conflicts* (Random House, 1971), points out that this has been the common experience of earlier immigrants to this country. For example, in Bradford, the concentration of new immigrants follows the pattern of Irish settlement in the mid-nineteenth century. Urban problems associated with immigrant housing in city centres are therefore not confined to this century, and are more a reflection of the property available to immigrants than of immigrant characteristics. Fewer live in private rented or council housing. In *Racial Minorities and Public Housing* (David J. Smith and Anne Whalley, PEP, September 1975), the housing policies of ten local authorities were examined, and, although there was little evidence of deliberate racial discrimination in housing policies, the priority systems used for the allocation of housing had the effect of placing immigrant families in the poorest standard public housing. Because of language problems many families were unable to explain their problems to officials. In general, immigrants are reluctant to apply for public housing and, according to Dilip Hiro, this is a reflection of immigrants' 'Awareness, and acceptance, of widespread discrimination' against them in housing (*Black British, White British*, Eyre & Spottiswoode, 1971). Problems such as these, combined with the general housing shortage, confine the Commonwealth immigrant to living in certain areas in the towns and cities where he can get accommodation. This is usually old, decaying property and, mistakenly, this is often taken to show that Asian and West Indian families do not know how to look after a home.

Difference in culture

People are inclined to forget that most New Commonwealth immigrants come from countries with a very different way of life, often having a different language and religion from ourselves and from other immigrant groups. The majority of Pakistanis are Muslim whereas most Indian immigrants are either Hindu or are members of the Sikh religion.

Problems may arise from the fact that families in New Commonwealth countries are often larger than in our own society and their members are used to having relatives living close at hand. This customary dependence on the extended family can raise problems for the married woman living over here, as is shown in this extract, where John Rex and Robert Moore in *Race, Community and Conflict* (Oxford University Press, 1967) describe the life of 'Mrs K' (from Pakistan):

[Mr K] kept his wife in strict Purdah and she has not been out of the house for two-and-a-half years. Having no female kin to help her with the housework and the children she found her pregnancy very difficult and she always misses her own family. She has no visitors, no women to chat with. Mrs K. would prefer to be back in Pakistan.

Also, sometimes there is tension in a family as the children grow up and take on the ways of the society in which they live. Amongst Asian families in particular, the preservation of traditional cultural values is very important and the adoption of youth culture values, particularly by the girls, may create stresses in the family. In their study *Between Two Cultures* (1976), the Community Relations Commission found that Asian girls often experienced a sense of frustration at not being allowed what they considered to be the greater freedom of English adolescents in their dress and social relationships with boys. Despite these difficulties, the family unit, extended or nuclear, continues to have a central importance for all generations. Some of the traditions of family life, such as arranged marriages, are becoming less popular. For example, the Community Relations Commission found that 57 per cent of parents and 67 per cent of young people foresee the breakdown of the system of arranged marriages. However, this does not mean to say that family life is valued any the less. Religion continues to be an important part of life, but the Commission found that many parents were worried by the scarcity of religious facilities and the absence of appropriate religious teaching in schools. The Commission found that this problem, while general to all Asian groups, is particularly acute for Hindus living in this country. A survey conducted for the BBC in 1977 showed that within twenty years West Indian families had fallen to the same average size as those of the rest of Britain, and families of Indian origin also showed a marked decrease in size over the same period.

Legislation

Since 1965, there have been attempts to outlaw discrimination against anyone, whatever his skin colour, nationality or cultural background. These have gradually been extended by various legislation (the Race Relations Act of 1965 and the Extension of the 1968 Race Relations Act in 1972) to cover almost every aspect of life. For example, it is now illegal for an employer to refuse to employ a person on the ground of 'colour, race or ethnic or national origins'.

The 1976 Race Relations Act is the most recent race relations legislation in Britain. It makes discrimination on the grounds of colour, race, nationality or ethnic or national origins illegal. This applies whether discrimination is direct or indirect, that is, where it is the unintended outcome of an act. The Act is effective in a number of different areas. For example, employment, education, the provision of goods and services (such as access to public places, hotels, banking and finance, transportation, entertainment, professional services, housing and access to clubs). Because strict equality of treatment would end in more inequality than equality, the Act makes some exceptions, and also provides for 'positive discrimination' in some circumstances. For example, an employer who needs to employ members of a particular race, such as a Chinese restaurant owner, will be allowed to do so. Where services exist to benefit racial or ethnic minorities, such as training, or English language classes, the Act provides for the continuation of such 'positive discrimination'. A further important provision of the Act is that it now becomes a criminal offence to publish and distribute inflammatory material which might lead to racial hatred. The Act also set up the Commission of Racial Equality. Amongst its duties, this is concerned with promoting equality of opportunity, eliminating racial discrimination and maintaining good relations between different racial groups.

Terms used in this chapter

social problem	drug dependency	patrial
delinquency	minority groups	race relations
juvenile delinquency	drug habituation	racial discrimination
deviance	egoistic suicide	ethnic group
stereotype	altruistic suicide	racial group

Further reading

S. Allen, *New Minorities, Old Conflicts* (Random House, 1971)

M. Banton, *Racial Minorities* (Fontana, 1972)

H. S. Becker, *Outsiders: Studies in the Sociology of Deviance* (Free Press, 1963)

Community Relations Commission, *Between Two Cultures* (1976)

W. W. Daniel, *Racial Discrimination in England* (Penguin, 1969)

N. Deakin, *Colour, Citizenship and British Society* (Panther, 1969)

P. Evans, *The Attitudes of Young Immigrants* (Runnymede Trust, 1972)

D. Hiro, *Black British, White British* (Eyre & Spottiswoode, 1971)

E. Krausz, *Ethnic Minorities in Britain* (Paladin, 1972)

J. B. Mays (ed.), *Juvenile Delinquency, the Family and the Social Group* (Longman, 1972)

V. Saifullah-Khan, 'Purdah in the British Situation' in D. L. Barker & S. Allen (eds), *Dependence and Exploitation in Work and Marriage* (Longman, 1976)

G. Wansall & M. Berling, *Caught in the Act* (Penguin, 1974)

D. J. West, *The Young Offender* (Penguin, 1967)

Questions from GCE 'O' Level Sociology Examination Papers

1   What do you understand by deviance? Give some examples of deviant behaviour, including at least one example of behaviour which is deviant and illegal, and at least one example of behaviour which is deviant but not in itself illegal. (AEB, November 1971)

2   Why is the crime rate for adolescents much higher than for any other age group? (Oxford Local Examinations, 1970)

3   Why is juvenile delinquency more common amongst the working class than amongst the middle class? (Oxford Local Examinations, 1972)

4   Account for the difference between male and female rates of juvenile delinquency. (Oxford Local Examinations, 1973)

5   Outline the major reasons which have been suggested for the continuing rise in juvenile delinquency in Britain. (Oxford Local Examinations, 1974)

6   What, if any, is the connection between social class position and criminal behaviour? (Oxford Local Examinations, 1975)

7   'All crime is deviant but all deviance is not necessarily criminal.'
a   What is deviance?
b   Explain what is meant by the above statement, giving examples where appropriate. (AEB, November 1974)

8   Is there a race problem in Britain? (Oxford Local Examinations, 1972)

9   What are the most important problems facing immigrant groups in Britain? (Oxford Local Examinations, 1973)

10   What are the causes and consequences of colour prejudice? Reference should be made to the United Kingdom and at least one other country. (AEB, June 1969)

11   Outline the major changes which have taken place in the pattern of migration into and out of Britain since 1945. (Oxford Local Examinations, 1974)

12   What sociological evidence is there that racial prejudice and racial discrimination exist in Britain? (Oxford Local Examinations, 1975)

13   Many immigrant groups settle in parts of cities which have the poorest material resources. How far does this explain why immigrants are often associated with 'social problems'? (AEB, November 1976)

14   Urban living and rural living are different mainly because of contrasts in the social environment rather than the physical environment. What are the major differences between these social environments? (AEB, June 1978)

12 The Individual and Society

Unit 38 What Makes the Individual?

38.1 Intelligence and personality

We have seen how society is shaped on the small scale and the large scale: the way in which our lives may be influenced by economic forces, by government decisions, or by changes in population; how the individual is moulded by the family, peer group, school and work. A human being undergoes a multitude of experiences which cause attitudes and opinions to be formed. Class position in society has a strong influence in determining behaviour and performance. Physical characteristics and environmental surroundings together play their part in making the individual what he or she is as a person. But how far is our personality predetermined by inherited characteristics, and how far do our experiences in life influence character and achievement?

There is some argument among geneticists and psychologists about the degree to which *inherited characteristics* cause an individual's behaviour, and how far *environmental experience* makes us behave in a certain way. In Victorian times it was believed almost all behaviour patterns were inherited; humans could be classified and stereotyped. An imperial myth was that Britons possessed innate (or inborn) qualities of leadership and determination, and that the coloured peoples of the British Empire needed British leadership and rule as they were incapable of governing themselves. Among the lower strata of society criminal behaviour was thought to be inherent and criminal types could be recognised by their facial features. One Victorian criminologist thought that he could obtain a picture of the typical criminal by superimposing all the photographs from the police 'Rogues' Gallery' upon one another: the end result was a rather benign elderly gentleman. If intelligence is used as a guide (and there is much controversy as to what intelligence actually is) in determining how much of our personality is inherited, and how much is gained from environmental factors, the proportion of sixty per cent inheritance to forty per cent experience is most widely accepted by geneticists and psychologists. One method of calculating this proportion is to look at the case histories of identical twins, usually orphaned, who have been brought up in different family circumstances from an early age. The comparative results of IQ tests and the kinds of occupation that they enter provide the measure that social scientists will require; a twin that has been brought up in a middle-class situation is more likely to do better in a verbal intelligence test than a brother or sister brought up in a working-class environment.

Just as we cannot choose our genetic make-up, we have no choice of the family circumstances that we are born into. The different rates of social mobility and *attainment* indicate how important the family is as a determining factor of the individual's eventual position in society. Not only is class background important, but even family size has an effect: verbal intelligence tests have shown that children from large families perform less well than those from smaller families (John Nisbet, 'Family Environment and Intelligence', *Eugenics Review XLV*, 1953). Of course, working-class families tend to be larger than middle-class families and this is likely to be a decisive factor in determining a lower verbal ability among working-class children. The youngest son may marry the princess in the fairy stories, but sociological evidence shows that the eldest child is more likely than the youngest to perform well in school and likely to obtain better employment after school. The contact between parent and child is of considerable importance and it may be argued that in large families the parents' attention has to be divided between too many children, or that most attention is given to the first-born child. Studies of very bright children in Britain and the USA have destroyed the myth of the 'weedy intellectual'; the exceptionally gifted in intelligence are usually found to be healthier, taller and stronger than average, while the least intelligent are often weaker and smaller than average. Once again, class differences may account for middle-class physical superiority (due to better feeding and environmental factors) being linked to higher intelligence performance.

38.2   Class, education and the individual

Half of what we learn for life is learnt before the age of five years. Children who were fortunate enough to go to nursery school usually do better in the primary and secondary school than those who did not receive any *pre-schooling*. Pre-schooling and the kind of education that a child experiences have a significant impact upon behaviour and attainment. Class underlies almost everything that we experience, and different class situations during our earliest and school years affect the social structure of Britain. The average working-class child comes from a larger family than the average middle-class child; more middle-class than working-class children attend nursery and pre-school playgroups. We have seen in Chapter 4 how linguistic ability is related to class, and how this provides middle-class children with an advantage over working-class children. The middle-class advantage is continued at school until the statutory leaving age is reached, when more middle-class pupils stay on past the age of sixteen years. Middle-class parents tend to take more interest in their children's education: for example, they are likely to provide them with better facilities for homework; and maybe they are more prepared and able to help with the homework. Children from the Registrar General's Class 5 have been found six times more likely to be poor readers at the age of seven than children from Social Class 1 backgrounds. A child from Social Class 5 is fifteen times more likely to be a non-reader at the age of seven years than a child from Social Class 1, according to a study made of 17,000 babies born in March 1958 who have had their development traced regularly every four years (Butler, Davies and Goldstein, *From Birth to Seven*, Longman, 1972). The class gap is hard to close after children have entered school despite the structural changes in education designed to compensate for the disadvantages, such as more money for schools in deprived areas, and possibly the introduction of comprehensive education. Social mobility in a society where there was complete equality of opportunity would rest largely upon educational attainment. Theoretically our educational system does provide an equality of opportunity, but the middle-class head-start is maintained throughout the school years.

Ralph Turner's sponsored mobility demonstrates the greater educational advantage enjoyed by the middle class and ensures that the contest factors of ability and effort become sponsored by the extra impetus given to middle-class children from their earliest years. It is not surprising, therefore, that a middle-class student is more than six times as likely to receive the benefits of a higher education than the working-class student.

38.3 Work, welfare and the individual

Having established that middle-class school-leavers are more likely to enter middle-class occupations, what are the effects of work upon the life and welfare of the individual? After all, the greatest proportion of our lives is not spent at school or in retirement, but at work of some kind.

The average working week in Britain, including overtime, is forty-four hours, which means that the working day is divided between one-third sleeping, one-third working, and one-third travelling, eating and relaxing. Because so many of our waking hours are spent at work, the work situation must affect the individual significantly. In 1847, Marx wrote in *The Communist Manifesto*:

Owing to the extensive use of machinery and to the division of labour, the work of the proletarian has lost all individual character, and, consequently, all charm for the workman. He becomes an appendage of the machine, and it is only the most simple, most monotonous, and most easily acquired knack that is required of him.

There are few really oppressive work situations now to be found in Britain; nevertheless most work performed is of a routine kind, and the number of people engaged in creative work or decision-making is comparatively small. We are an industrialised nation, and many people do work in manual, routine jobs on the production line in factories. Because this work is often boring it is necessary for them to have sufficient time for leisure and recreation. It has been argued that industrial unrest is not so much due to an economic need for higher wages, which may be the pretext for strike action, but rather a deeper dissatisfaction with the work situation. Routine clerical work too can be stultifying, and work studies have shown that greater efficiency can be achieved by varying the tasks performed in offices. For example, if, instead of being assigned a particular aspect of the clerical process with limited responsibility, people are allowed to see a matter through thus having more variation of occupation and accepting greater responsibility, productivity increases. The kind of job that we do may well indicate the kind of person that we are, but also our attitudes and opinions may be modified and reinforced by our experience in the work situation and our contact with others at work.

To have allowed a national holiday on the Queen's Silver Wedding Anniversary in November 1972 to all, instead of to school children only, would have meant a greater number of working hours lost than the total number of hours lost through strike action in the same year. Our Common Market partners have more paid public holidays than we enjoy in Britain, yet economic growth is higher in Europe than in Britain. This does not necessarily mean that there is a direct connection between the holidays enjoyed and economic production—there are too many other variables, but arguments may be advanced for more public holidays in Britain. Few would deny that Members of Parliament are extremely hard-working, but the Parliamentary session lasts for only 160 or so days a year.

This century has seen the development and expansion of welfare services. A welfare state is one which attempts to ensure reasonably high material living standards for all. The basis of our Welfare State was laid down in the Beveridge Report of 1942. It was conceived in a spirit of war-time political consensus but in recent years many aspects of the Welfare State have received severe criticism from both the political Left and the Right. The Left argue that welfare provisions do not go far enough or that they benefit the wrong groups; the Right consider that there are too many parasites living off the benefits of the State. Theoretically Social Security acts as a safety net which catches those who are unfortunate enough to be without the minimum of economic resources; but though the majority of those who take advantage of social security provisions are legally and morally entitled to their benefits, a small minority undoubtedly abuse the system, and equally a minority miss the net altogether, such as the elderly lady who died of cold and hunger in January 1973 after eating cardboard. A measure of protection is afforded to the individual through the Welfare State, but it will be a good measure of our social progress when the Welfare State becomes unnecessary: we have not yet reached that time by a long way.

Unit 39 Society Today

39.1 How society is shaped

We have seen some of the conditions and constraints that will limit the individual's freedom of choice and action and how behaviour may be conditioned in many ways. As a condition, freedom is hard to define; it is much easier to see the things which limit freedom of action than to list the things that we are free to do. The forces which shape society are those which limit choice and freedom of behaviour. Economic forces may affect the choice of occupation open to someone, the amount of money that may be earned, what they may buy and what they may sell. Political forces may control economic forces to some degree; at the same time economic forces may condition political forces. The question is, how important are these invisible forces in shaping society, or how far can the individual change or re-direct those forces?

A political leader may be able to directly change the course of history

Hitler addresses the Hitler Youth at a rally in Nuremberg

by profoundly altering matters of State which would have taken a different course had it not been for his direct intervention: the more powerful the leader is, the less responsible he is to other members of his government and the more dramatic can be the effect of such intervention upon events. Examples of individuals who shaped society are Stalin and Hitler who were able to impose their will upon whole nations: their personal feelings and prejudices led to dramatic political, social and economic upheaval in Europe. Fortunately there are few men such as Hitler or Stalin to wield such enormous power. Yet if Hitler or Stalin had not been born, would matters have been very much different? Were the invisible forces of history such in Germany in the 1930s that an extreme right-wing dictator would have emerged anyway, offering a solution to the social and economic problems of the Weimar republic?

Some social theorists maintain that events in history are cyclical, that history tends to repeat itself (of course not exactly) over a period of time. An example of this theory would be to say that war inevitably breaks out in Europe every generation. Two opposing theories of history are: that history, or the conditions in society, are largely *predetermined*; or alternatively that *chance* really governs what will happen. Between these views is a middle view that to a greater or lesser degree the invisible forces of history and social conditions do exist, but certain people or events are able to alter the pattern of things to a greater or lesser degree.

Revolutions and wars are times of great social change. Technological progress has been one of the few benefits of war (eg the development of aviation during the First and Second World Wars) and this has been accompanied by social change. Are revolutions and wars made by individuals, or by the populations that participate in them and who act together (in T. S. Eliot's words) as 'vast impersonal forces'? If we accept the view that history is a mixture of predetermination and chance, we must look a little more closely at these vast impersonal forces for they are composed of individuals who possess a common cause born out of a common experience which the leadership must recognise if it is to direct them with any degree of success. Carlyle may have been responsible for the statement that 'history is the biography of great men', but in his *History of the French Revolution* he wrote:

Hunger and nakedness and righteous oppression lying heavy on twenty-five million hearts: this, not the wounded vanities or contradicted philosophies of philosophical advocates, rich shopkeepers, rural noblesse, was the prime mover of the French Revolution; as the like will be in all such revolutions in all countries.

A 'which comes first, the chicken or the egg?' type of question confronts us: does the individual make society, or society make the individual? The answer, like that of the chicken and the egg, is that really they are inseparable. Society shapes the individual, but the individual helps change society. When a dictator or small group of people significantly alter the shape of society they still require thousands of others to execute their wishes. Very few historians or social scientists would be bold enough to ascribe a relative importance to such factors as social, economic or political forces in shaping historical events; yet any serious attempt to understand what happened in history, or what is happening in society, must require the apportioning of some weight to both the invisible forces and individual factors that are at work.

39.2 The future of society

We all have different visions of what will happen in the future, but no one can be certain about his predictions, least of all a social scientist. Certain trends are discernible and it is upon these that we may base our conclusions.

Before considering the future of society, we must consider the proposition that mankind *will have* a future. Various prophets of doom maintain that there is a high risk of international thermo-nuclear war, either by accident or design, and that none would survive. Current NATO strategy is mainly based on the assumption that a war with the Soviet Union and her allies would be a 'conventional' one only employing small-scale nuclear weapons at worst, since a total nuclear war would ensure mutual self-destruction. Yet how quickly might such a war escalate from the smaller 'tactical' nuclear weapons that NATO is ready to employ in the event of a Soviet attack, to a full-scale nuclear holocaust? It is argued that we have already been close to nuclear war on several occasions, such as the Cuban Missile Crisis of 1962, and because of our political and geographical position in Europe Britain would be directly involved in any war between East and West. No matter how optimistic some might be about our chances of survival in a nuclear war, there is already more than the equivalent explosive power of a ton of TNT for every man, woman and child on this planet in the stockpiles of nuclear weapons held by the great powers. A dozen hydrogen bombs on Britain would be more than sufficient to exterminate our entire population. Another world war using nuclear weapons would leave our planet as a lifeless radioactive sphere spinning in space for eternity. The world's economic progress is hindered by military spending, which on a global scale totals some £300 000 million a year (1980).

	£ million
United States	737
USSR	688
United Kingdom	209
France	199
West Germany	49

Table 12.1 Value of major arms exports to the Third World in 1975 (figures at 1973 prices)
(Source: *SIPRI Yearbook*, 1976)

Yet, as a former director of the World Health Organisation has pointed out, diseases such as leprosy, malaria, trachoma and yaws might be finally eradicated (as smallpox has been) if the advanced countries diverted £1000 million—the cost of just one aircraft carrier—to the fight on these diseases. Military expenditure means the spending of vast sums of money on things which do not improve living standards. Not only does it contribute to international inflation, which hurts underdeveloped countries most, but it adds fuel to the risk of international war in an arms race. (The above facts and figures are taken from an article by C. Gordon Tether, 'Butter Before Guns' in the *Observer*, 10 April 1977.)

Some economists estimate that the world's natural resources are diminishing so rapidly that even if all national populations were to stabilise themselves (and there is little chance of this in many of the underdeveloped countries) there would not be enough resources to provide an adequate standard of living for everyone within the next two centuries. Linked to the problem of diminishing resources are the problems of *ecology* and the environment. Man's exploitation of the earth has meant that many parts of the world are faced with pollution problems. On his journey across the Atlantic on the raft *Ra*, Thor Heyerdahl found a disturbing amount of oil pollution and other evidence of indestructible garbage floating on the high seas. The problem of *pollution* in our cities is a familiar one, but recently scientists have found high levels of the poison DDT in the bodies of penguins in the Antarctic, thousands of miles from continents where the DDT could have been sprayed. Fortunately there is a growing consciousness of the problems of pollution, together with a recognition of diminishing resources, but international action can be the only solution and this is as yet in its earliest stage, since the first international conference on these problems was held in Stockholm in 1972.

Not all scientists and social scientists agree upon the extent of the world's resources, or the future size of population and its needs. How far mankind will be able to overcome these problems is likewise a matter of dispute. The projections range from the optimistic to the pessimistic, yet there is a measure of agreement that something *has* to be done in the field of conservation. Such things as scientific and technological discovery, the use of different materials, the re-use and *re-cycling* of resources and the education of people to these problems may mean that we shall obtain a cleaner planet and preserve our resources in the future.

In previous chapters we have examined some of the changes that are taking place in the institutions of society: for example how the family is no longer so dependent upon the extended family system; how education has expanded; or how the population of Britain appears to be stabilising. Although we have not found complete solutions to the various problems of society such as poverty, homelessness or the growth of crime, at least it can be said that in most respects Britain is a better place to live in for the average citizen than it was a generation or more ago.

Social change is occurring more rapidly than ever before. Possibly we are sacrificing such things as *community spirit* and the better aspects of traditional life-styles in exchange for material progress, and the modern concentration upon economic growth of all kinds may well have contributed to many of the social problems and difficulties that have been described. The study of sociology should make us aware of the many changes that are taking place within society, and perhaps able to point out some of the least desirable aspects of change. The growing recognition of sociology as a subject and the validity of the findings of sociological research have meant that governments, politicians and planners do not embark upon schemes (although there have been some highly-publicised exceptions) without weighing up the cost in human terms.

We have seen how sociology is linked to the other disciplines of social science from our study of the subject. Changes in sociology are linked to changes in the other disciplines: economic change must mean social change; political change may cause both economic and social changes. At the same time it would be impossible to calculate how much freedom of choice is open to those who exercise the greatest immediate power in society, the politicians, since there are so many variables of human behaviour found within the individuals who collectively make up society. We can only say that in the last quarter of the twentieth century society will probably undergo its greatest transformation, greater even than the change that occurred at the end of World War I in the first quarter of the century. As sociologists and students of sociology we should seek not only to understand these changes but also to ensure that they are what is best for society and mankind. Einstein once said, 'Imagination is more important than knowledge.' We must add our knowledge to an imagination about the future.

Terms used in this chapter

genetic factors
attainment
arms race
routine
pre-schooling

invisible forces
predetermination
ecology
re-cycling
pollution

Questions from GCE 'O' Level Sociology Examination Papers

1   What forces other than school and family control the social behaviour of the individual? (AEB, November 1969)

2   In what ways has your study of sociology affected the way you see the world? (AEB, Specimen Paper for New Syllabus, 1972)

3   Some of the rules and customs which we regard as important in this country are also accepted elsewhere; others are not. Explain this. (AEB, June 1970)

4   'The content of moral prohibitions varies wildly not only as between one society and another but even within the same society as between one social class and another or between one historical period and another.' Discuss.

Explain the difficulties that an individual might face in going to live in a society very different from his own. (AEB, November 1970)

5   Select any two of the following groups *a* to *d* and by giving examples or by any other method show clearly that you understand the difference between the pair of terms in each of the selected groups.

a   deviant and delinquent
b   an extended family and a nuclear family
c   ability and achievement
d   comprehensive school and secondary modern school.
(AEB, November 1972)

6   Choose two of the following terms, state briefly what they mean, and show how they helped you to understand some aspect of society:

norm   socialisation
social class   attitude
stereotype   peer group
(AEB, Specimen Paper for New Syllabus, 1972)

7   Take any two technical terms you have encountered in your study of sociology (eg social class, stereotype, bureaucracy, social institutions, socialisation, role, status etc.) and show how they have helped you to understand your own society. (AEB, June 1971)

8   Select two of the following groups *a* to *d* and by giving example or by any other method show clearly that you understand the difference between the pair of terms within each of the selected groups.

a   automation and industrialisation
b   an urban area and urbanisation
c   migration and mobility
d   a pressure group and a political party.
(AEB, June 1972)

9   The following statement is a comment on the roles of men and women in society: 'How else could matters be arranged? As a matter of fact, matters can be, and are, arranged very differently in other parts of the world. Our concept of what is 'natural" to men and "natural" to women . . . is culture bound. What we think of as "natural" is simply what we are used to.'

(*Understanding Society*, Open University)

What is the value of the term 'socialisation' in explaining the above passage? (AEB, November 1974)

10 Can you suggest any sociological reasons why today our society is faced with the problems of:

a   juvenile delinquency
b   the care of the aged?
(AEB, November 1969)

11 Select two of the following groups a to d and show clearly that you understand the difference between the pair of terms within each of the selected groups.

a   nuclear family and extended family
b   class and caste
c   social group and a collection of people
d   education and socialisation.
(AEB, November 1970)

12 Show clearly, in any way you choose, that you understand the difference between three of the following *pairs* of words:

a   ascribed role and achieved role
b   race and nationality
c   culture and society
d   laws and norms
e   mores and folkways
f   class and status
g   sociology and anthropology.
(AEB, June 1970)

13 Briefly explain what is meant by *three* of the following terms:

a   peer group
b   automation
c   social mobility
d   urbanisation
e   bureaucracy

14 The following statements are incorrect or misleading. Select *three* of them and briefly explain why you think each is *misleading or incorrect*.

a   All pressure groups rely on strike action to achieve their aims.
b   The extended family is simply a family with many children.
c   Bureaucracy is just 'red tape'.
d   Comprehensive schools are grammar schools containing pupils of both sexes.
e   Automation involves machines being used by men to make their work easier. (AEB, November, 1975)

15 Explain clearly but briefly what you understand by three of the following terms:

bureaucracy	stratification
social control	deviance
socialisation	attitude
segregation	stereotype (AEB, June 1970)

16 In what ways has studying sociology helped you to understand the family in Britain today? (AEB, November 1974)

17 Select *two* of the following groups *a* to *e* and show clearly that you understand the difference between the pair of terms in each of the selected groups.

a   role and status
b   socialisation and education
c   capitalism and communism
d   proletariat and bourgeoisie
e   control group and experimental group.
(AEB, November 1974)

18 'Many children are already failures by the age of five—and some are simply born failures... For even at that tender age a large percentage of our children have already failed in the accepted sense of the word. Many of our children are born to fail.' (A primary school headmistress, as reported in *The Sun* on 7 June 1977.) In what ways do the findings of sociologists support or reject this view? (AEB Specimen Paper, 1980)

Glossary

Achieved status *see* Status, achieved

Age grouping the division of the population of a society into groups according to their chronological age. These groups usually span five-year intervals, such as 15–19, 20–24, 25–29 inclusive. Age grouping has many uses; for example as an aid in predicting future proportions of young people entering the labour market. It can also indicate the proportion of the population in the dependant age groups (those under sixteen and over sixty-five), which must be supported by the working population.

Alienation a feeling of being powerless and unable to control one's own destiny, together with a sense of meaninglessness, the norms and values of others having no apparent relevance to one's situation. Karl Marx and many social scientists since then have used the term to describe the estrangement experienced by the worker in capitalist society, who receives neither satisfaction from his work nor the full product of his labour.

Anomie the term first used by the French sociologist, Émile Durkheim, to apply to the situation induced by the breakdown or confusion of social norms and values. Durkheim identified anomic suicide as the suicide resulting from the individual not being properly integrated into the values of society. Such circumstances occur where individual fortunes change very suddenly or society itself undergoes rapid social change.

Anthropology a social science concerned with the comparative study of societies, and with the biological development and adaptation of man to his environment. There are several different branches of anthropology, such as cultural anthropology and physical anthropology. In general, cultural anthropologists study non-literate and traditional societies. Some of the methods used by cultural anthropologists, such as participant observation, are increasingly being used by sociologists to examine aspects of modern industrialised societies.

Anticipatory socialisation *see* Socialisation

Aristocracy a hereditary upper class. This may also be the governing class of a society. *See also* Nobility; Élite.

Ascribed status *see* Status, ascribed

Automation the 'name given to industrial processes which use machinery and computers not only to make goods but also to control, by "feed-back" mechanisms, the rate of production, the input of raw materials and the co-ordination of separate processes. In automated factories less manpower is needed, but workers have to understand the whole process and their responsibility is much greater.' (AEB O-Level Sociology, June 1973). *See also* Mechanisation.

Bias the introduction of distortion into research with the result that accurate results are unobtainable. All scientists take steps to eliminate bias but it can arise inadvertently. In sociology, biased results arise from oversights such as including leading questions in questionnaires and careless sampling procedures leading to unrepresentative samples. *See also* Objectivity; Questionnaire; Sample.

Bilineal *see* Descent

Birth rate (crude) number of births per 1000 of the population in a specified period, usually a year. The term 'crude birth rate' is often simplified to 'birth rate'. The birth rate in Britain in 1976 was 11.9. *See also* Fecundity; Fertility.

Bourgeoisie a late medieval term, originating from French and referring to the French middle classes, distinguishing them from the peasant class and from the upper-class gentility. Karl Marx used the term more generally to apply to the owners of the means of production in a capitalist society, contrasting them with the propertyless proletariate. He also distinguished the shopkeeping class, the petty bourgeoisie, from the industrial bourgeoisie. *See also* Proletariat; Social class.

Bureaucracy characteristic qualities of large-scale formal organisations. According to the sociologist, Max Weber, if one could isolate the essential features of any bureaucracy they would comprise the following:

  a hierarchy of positions linked to one another by a chain of command coming from the top
  a differentiated form of organisation where there is specialisation of tasks, individuals becoming experts
  a career structure where advancement occurs on the basis of seniority

or merit, the latter assessed objectively on the basis of tests

a system of administration where use is made of written documents

a system of formally instituted rules and regulations which are unambiguous and observed by everyone, without exceptions being made for particular individuals (the boss's son, for example), or special circumstances.

As these characteristics are components in an abstract idea of what a bureaucracy is like, it is not surprising that sociologists have noticed actual bureaucracies are not as smooth-running or impartial as Weber's formulation suggests.

Although the term 'bureaucracy' has come to be used pejoratively in everyday speech, in connection with 'red tape' etc., the sociologist uses the concept analytically and therefore implies no judgement of bureaucracies. Bureaucracy is the characteristic form of organisation of many formal organisations today, such as government departments, industrial corporations, schools, hospitals and military establishments. *See also* Formal organisation.

Capital forms of wealth which are not used immediately for consumption but can be used instead to generate more wealth; for example, money and industrial plants constitute capital.

Capitalism a type of economic system. It is based on the principle of private individuals possessing, accumulating and investing capital for profit. In a capitalist economy the means of production are privately-owned. The capitalist system operates on the basis of free competition, the prices of goods, services and wage rates being determined by the balance between supply and demand, operating in an unrestricted, competitive market. In a capitalist economy, the worker is obliged to sell his labour in return for wages.

This description of capitalism must be understood as being largely theoretical. The countries which are thought of today as being capitalist societies, for example the USA, deviate from this pattern through their monopolies and labour unions, and through Government intervention affecting the unrestricted operation of free competition. Countries such as Britain, where some business is privately-run and some is State-owned, have what is called a mixed economy. *See also* Communism.

Case-study method a method of studying aspects of society by intensively examining individual instances of the condition of interest. For example, a sociologist interested in juvenile delinquency may intensively study the structure of a particular gang. The social unit examined can also be individuals, factories, schools, communities. By drawing on a number of case studies, the sociologist aims to build up a general account of a social phenomenon.

Caste a type of social stratification system, where position at birth determines all other aspects of the individual's later life. The classical Hindu system in India is an example of a caste system. In theory, all Hindus belong to one of the following (ranked from high to lowest caste): the Brahmins (priests); the Kshatriyas (warriors); the Vaishyas (traders); or the Sudras (servants and slaves). Outside these castes are the 'outcastes', persons who, because of Hindu religious beliefs, are considered polluted because they work at activities such as tanning. Position in society is ascribed, and marriage occurs within the same caste (endogamy). A caste system is a closed stratification system; that is, it does not permit social mobility between social strata. In other words, individuals cannot move into a different social stratum as a result of their own efforts. *See also* Social stratification; Social mobility; Social class; Estate; Status, achieved; Status, ascribed.

Class *see* Social class

Cohort this term is frequently used in demography and applies to a group of people having a common characteristic. For example, persons married in 1977 are the 1977 marriage cohort; persons born in 1977 are the 1977 birth cohort. It is often helpful to relate events, such as marriage, to a particular birth cohort. In this way, it is possible to see with each successive birth cohort whether the timing of such events as marriage occurs at an earlier or later age. Cross-sectional figures, that is, figures on all marriages occurring in a particular year, do not readily reveal such trends. *See also* Cross-sectional study; Longitudinal study.

Communism a form of economic and social organisation where all property is communally held, that is, owned by everyone. Few such communities have existed in the past or in the present. It is held that the early Christians and some present-day religious sects, such as the Hutterites of North America, are examples of communist communities. The so-called communist countries, such as the USSR, are socialist societies where property is State-owned and State-distributed. (USSR stands for the Union of Soviet Socialist Republics.) In theory, such societies anticipate the gradual disappearance of the State and, with the emergence of a fully classless society, the establishment of communism. *See also* Capitalism.

Community generally, a limited geographical area where inhabitants have a sense of belonging to the locality, identifying with, and participating in its social and economic activities. At one time the term was used to apply to a social group where members are socially and economically interdependent. The geographical mobility of the population in a modern industrialised society and the society-wide interdependence of its members have made such groups less frequent in present-day society. However the term can be used in this sense to apply to traditional societies. A community has contact between its members, and is therefore different from an association, where people are linked in more impersonal relationships in order to carry on specific activities. For example, there are educational associations (e.g. the Workers' Educational Association), welfare associations (e.g. the NSPCC), sports and athletics associations (e.g. the FA) and human rights associations (e.g. the National Council for Civil Liberties).

Conjugal family *see* Family, nuclear

Conjugal role *see* Role

Consanguine family *see* Family, extended

Contest mobility a term used by the American sociologist, Ralph Turner, to describe a pattern of social mobility which relies on individuals competing with one another to get ahead as in a race. It is argued that the American educational system is an example of a contest mobility system in which individuals can continue to compete for advancement until almost the end of their educational career. At that point, the winners will be objectively selected to go on to the next stage, but even then, the losers are free to find alternative ways of getting to the same point as do the winners. *See also* Sponsored mobility; Social mobility.

Control group the group of people who provide the standard of comparison for an experimental group in a social experiment. A control group provides this standard because its members are as nearly alike as possible to members of the experimental group. They are not, however, exposed to the independent variable of interest. Consequently, where there are differences in the two groups (only one having experienced the experimental variable), then the researcher can be fairly sure it is the effect of this variable accounting for the differences between the two groups, since everything else has been controlled. *See also* Experimental group; Hypothesis; Scientific method.

Conurbation an extensive area of dense urban development including a number of administratively distinct towns.

Correlation a measure of the association between variables. It indicates to what extent a change in one variable is accompanied by a change in another. For example, height and weight are two variables. We expect a child's weight to increase as he grows taller. In other words, a change in height is accompanied by a change in weight. In this instance, both increase. This is called a positive association. Were the reverse true, weight decreasing with height, we would have a negative association. The nature of the association between variables is expressed in the correlation: 1, for perfect association, which is shown as either $+1$, where association is positive, or -1, where association is negative. However, either positive or negative perfect association is unusual, particularly in social phenomena. Rarely is a change in one variable accompanied by just the same amount of change in another. Hence correlations are more usually under 1, for example, -0.5, $+0.88$, approaching a perfect correlation but still some way from it. *See also* Variable.

Crime behaviour which violates the criminal law. *See also* Deviancy; Juvenile delinquency.

Cross-sectional study the simultaneous comparison of two or more groups. For example, where first, third and sixth form pupils are tested to see whether they are influenced by the mass media in their opinions on race relations. If results show that sixth formers are least influenced, this might be interpreted as showing education makes people more objective and self-reliant in their opinions. However, this interpretation illustrates the problems with such studies. Other factors, outside school, could be responsible for the result, as could differences in the children themselves or the fact that maturity itself could have produced the sixth formers' independent judgement. Although more time-consuming, a better research design is to follow the same group of children through their school life, recording their attitudes at first, third and sixth form. *See also* Longitudinal study; Cohort.

Culture the range of socially-acquired characteristics which are transmitted from one generation to the next; for example, language, values, beliefs, customs, knowledge and skills are components of the culture of a society. These are learnt by members of society who pass them on to the next generation through the process of socialisation. *See also* Socialisation; Internalisation.

Death rate (crude) the number of deaths per 1000 of the population, occurring within a specific period, usually one year. The crude death rate is often called simply, the death rate. Adjusting for the age distribution of the population, the death rate in Britain in 1976 was 11.8. *See also* Infant mortality rate.

Deferential voter the working-class Tory voter. Although this action would appear to be a vote against working-class interests, he votes Conservative because he believes the upper classes are the rightful leaders of society and that the Conservative party best supports this state of affairs.

Delinquency *see* Juvenile delinquency

Democratic government *see* Government, democratic

Demography the study of the size, structure and growth of human populations.

Dependent age groups *see* Age grouping

Descent the reckoning of relationships of living members of the family group to family ancestors. The method of reckoning descent usually has implications for the inheritance of property. For example, in patrilineal descent, inheritance will be passed through the male line. In matrilineal descent, it will be passed through the female line. Bilineal descent reckons descent through both the male and the female lines, both sides of the family having equal importance and inheritance passing through both male and female lines.

Deviancy non-conformity to social norms. Where these are strongly upheld, deviancy is considered serious and is formally punishable by the agencies of social control. In modern society, there are innumerable groups, some more powerful than others and therefore more able to make others conform to their norms. At any time, a person who conforms to the norms of one group may be considered a deviant by members of another group.

Discrimination differentiation between people on the grounds of some criteria, which may be relevant, but frequently are not. For example, people are differntiated on the grounds of measured intelligence. The term does not automatically mean unjustly depriving the deserving of their rights, but it has come to be used increasingly in this sense. The United Nations describes discrimination as: 'any conduct based on a distinction made on the grounds of natural or social categories, which have no relation either to individual capacities or merits, or to the concrete behaviour of the individual person'. (*The Main Types and Causes of Discrimination*, UN Commission on Human Rights.) Since 1975 it has been illegal in Britain to discriminate against individuals on the grounds of sex or marital status (Sex Discrimination Act, 1975). Also the 1976 Race Relations Act stipulates that it is illegal to discriminate against individuals on the grounds of colour, race, nationality, ethnic or national origins. *See also* Racial discrimination.

Distribution *see* Geographical distribution

Division of labour the specialisation of occupational roles and tasks within a society. In a traditional society tasks are principally differentiated by age and sex. There is greater differentiation in modern industrialised society and tasks are principally allocated on the basis of other criteria, such as educational qualifications. However, for no good reason, there persists a division of labour along sex-related lines in our present society.

Education the formal transmission of culture from one generation to the next. In a modern industrialised society, components of culture, such as technical knowledge, change very rapidly. Consequently, education passes on new knowledge, unknown to an earlier generation, and itself contributes to the development of new knowledge. Although culture is formally transmitted through lessons and lectures other forms of learning also take place in schools and colleges. For example, children learn co-operation informally through the games they play in the school playground. Both the formal and informal aspects of learning are part of the wider process of socialisation.

In Britain, formal education is divided into a number of levels. Pre-school groups such as nursery schools exist in some areas, but for most children the infant school is their first experience of learning outside the home environment. After leaving the infant level the child continues in the primary school until he is about eleven when he transfers to the secondary school. Until the mid-1960s the secondary educational system comprised the tri-partite system, that is, the technical school, the secondary modern school and the grammar school. When the tri-partite system was begun in 1944 it was officially expected that these three types of schools would have parity of esteem, that is, be seen as offering equally important forms of education. Since the mid-1960s comprehensive schools have been gradually introduced. Outside this State system of primary and secondary education there exists the private education system. In some ways it is organised similarly to the State system of education, particularly at the primary level. *See also* Socialisation.

Élite a minority of persons occupying the most influential and prestigious positions in society. An élite group may be a political, business, scientific, artistic, or religious élite. The members of an élite generally know and co-operate with one another. The élite may be a hereditary élite, in which case, from one generation to the next, members of the same families come to occupy positions of power and influence. The cohesive nature of the ruling élite has been noted by the American sociologist, C. Wright Mills, amongst others. British research has indicated the self-perpetuating nature of élites in our society, where, generation after generation powerful positions in government, law, the military, business and finance are occupied by members of the same families. Members of élite groups in Britain have generally been educated at public or prominent independent schools and many also at Oxbridge colleges. *See also* Aristocracy; Nobility.

Embourgeoisement the idea that, with increased affluence, the working class are becoming middle-class. The proposition was tested by J. H. Goldthorpe and D. Lockwood in the 1960s, who found little evidence to support the idea that the working class were relating to or being accepted into the middle class. They suggested that, instead, a new type of working class was emerging, the privatised working class. *See also* Privatised worker.

Emigration the permanent or semi-permanent movement of in-dividuals or groups from their home country to another country where they intend to take up residence. *See also* Immigration; Migration.

Empirical based on observation or experimentation. For example, in sociology, it is an empirical fact that working-class children do less well on measured achievement tests than do middle-class children.

Estate a stratification system where social strata are differentiated according to particular sets of rights and duties, reinforced by the law. An estate system is not as closed to social mobility as a caste system, since it permits some movement of individuals within estates (each estate includes different occupations and socio-economic levels). However, an estate system does not permit as much social mobility as a class system. Feudal society was based on an estate system. In medieval England, the estate system broadly comprised the King, Lords and Commons as the main estate divisions with a less clearly defined division into Clergy,

Nobility and Commons. *See also* Social stratification; Caste; Nobility; Social class; Social mobility.

Ethnic group a social group where members share a sense of identity in a common cultural heritage. An ethnic group is usually also a minority group, existing as a subgroup of the larger society. It is possible for an ethnic group and a racial group to overlap but this is not necessarily the case. *See also* Minority group; Social group; Race.

Expectation of life the average biological age span of a human being under conditions where death does not occur prematurely due to injury, accident or unusual events such as plagues or natural disasters. In modern western societies life expectancy is higher for women than for men. In 1977 in Britain, expectation of life at birth was 69 for men and 76 for women. It has been suggested that this is due to the difference in culturally induced life styles between men and women, and, in particular, to smoking.

Experimental group the group of persons who are exposed to the experimental variable of interest (an independent variable) in the course of a social experiment. In this way, the experimental group contrasts with the control group, which provides the standard by which the researcher evaluates his results and judges the correctness of his hypothesis. *See also* Control group; Hypothesis; Scientific method.

Family a socially recognised kinship unit, comprising persons who are bound together in relationships such as wife, husband, mother, father, grandparent, grandchild, son and daughter. At its broadest level, the family comprises the three or more generations of relatives who are the extended family. At the other end of the spectrum, the self-contained unit may comprise father, mother and child, and in this case is called the nuclear family. It is claimed that the family performs certain social functions, such as the bearing, rearing and socialisation of children and, in some societies, the provision of the basic social and economic needs of life, such as food and shelter. *See also* Family, extended; Family, nuclear.

Family, extended (consanguine) a type of family organisation, also called the consanguine family, where primary emphasis is on the blood relationship between all members of the three (or more) generation group, rather than on the core nuclear family. The extended family comprises a mutually supportive network of social and economic relationships, providing members with such things as food, shelter, protection, and health care and supported by a system of rights and duties between members. *See also* Family; Family, nuclear.

Family, nuclear (conjugal) a type of family organisation, also called the conjugal family, which is the basic family unit comprised of father, mother and offspring. In a modern industrial society this family unit usually lives separately from the wider extended family, and is able to be economically independent of it. The family of orientation is the nuclear family into which an individual is born; the family of procreation is the family formed with the individual's own marriage and the bearing of children. *See also* Family; Family, extended.

Fecundity the maximum physiological capacity of women of childbearing age to bear children. Despite its seeming fixity, this biological capacity varies across different societies according to such things as diet and typical health of the mother. *See also* Fertility.

Fertility the number of births in a population. Fertility differs from fecundity since no population ever reaches its maximum possible number of births. Naturally, fertility is influenced by the same factors that influence fecundity, but also by some additional ones. For example, it is influenced by demographic factors, such as the age at which marriage occurs; by social factors, such as attitudes towards the use of contraception; by economic factors, such as the postponement of having children until they can be adequately provided for; by psychological factors, such as a preference for a particular type of contraceptive, which may be more, or less, effective than other types. Fertility is measured in terms of fertility rates, one of the commonest being the general fertility rate. This is the number of births per 1000 women of childbearing age, (women aged between 15–44, or 15–49) occurring during a specified period, usually a year. *See also* Fecundity; Birth rate.

Floating voter the voter who has no fixed allegiance to one or another political party and may cast his vote differently from one election to the next.

Folkways a social norm, or standard of behaviour which is generally observed in society but which is not considered to be morally obligatory. People conform to folkways, such as wearing a tie, without attaching very much importance to it. Consequently, ignoring a folkway seldom invokes serious punishment.

Formal organisation a highly organised social group, formally arranged to efficiently achieve particular goals and objectives. For example, a school is a formal organisation, its goal the education of the pupils. Other formal organisations include hospitals, industrial corporations, colleges, government agencies. *See also* Bureaucracy.

Functions *see* Social functions

Genetic factors factors which are responsible for the inherited characteristics of the individual. These genetic factors are often contrasted with environmental factors—those features of the environment to which the individual has been exposed and which influence what he has learnt in society. *See also* Heredity.

Geographical distribution the dispersion of a population over a particular geographical area. Usually this is examined in the context of a population distributed across a particular administrative or political area, such as a county or a nation. Geographical distribution should not be confused with demographic distribution. This applies to the distribution of the population according to some demographic criterion such as age, sex, or marital status.

Government, democratic form of government which rests on the principle of government by the people. A democratic government depends on participation of the population in the political process. In this way, the government rules with the consent of the population, reflecting popular will in political decisions. The ideal of all eligible members of society participating in government has seldom been realised. In ancient Athens there was a system of direct democracy whereby citizens themselves legislated (voted on laws). However, this is too unwieldy in modern, highly populated and highly specialised societies. Instead, in countries such as Britain, there is a representative democracy, where, through free elections and a secret ballot, representatives of the people are elected to sit in Parliament. In Britain, MPs sit in the House of Commons. In a democracy, government expresses majority will, but, in keeping with the spirit of democracy, steps are taken to protect minority rights. Democratic principles need not be confined to central government. In democratically-based societies they are applied also at the level of local government, national associations, community organisations, and informal groups. *See also* Government, totalitarian.

Government, totalitarian a form of government where the central State Government has absolute power over the rest of the population. No dissenting or opposing political parties are permitted in this form of government. The mass of the people have few, if any, rights against the government which controls and regulates the basic essentials of life, such as the production of goods and services, employment, education and housing. The absolute authority of totalitarian governments permits them to perpetuate themselves in power without regard to the will of the people. *See also* Government, democratic.

Group *see* Social group

Hereditary élite *see* Élite

Heredity the passing on of characteristics, such as particular physiological features, from parents to their children through the genes of the parents. Hereditary characteristics are often contrasted with learned characteristics, such as language, which are environmentally derived and acquired in the course of socialisation. *See also* Genetic factors.

Hierarchy a system of ranking individuals or groups into a continuous series of superior and subordinate positions. *See also* Bureaucracy.

Hypothesis a speculative statement asserting a relationship between two or more variables. The statement is drawn from existing theory and from the results of existing empirical research. In sociology, a hypothesis must refer to social factors which are measurable and relationships which can be investigated using scientific procedures. For example, the sociologist cannot test the proposition: 'God is dead'. *See also* Variable; Experimental group; Control group; Scientific method.

Immigration the arrival in a country of persons who have left their former country of residence and who wish to make the new country their permanent or semi-permanent home. *See also* Emigration.

Industrialisation the process whereby craft technology is replaced by machine technology and home production of goods is replaced by factory production. In western Europe, these fundamental changes brought far-reaching social and economic changes, such as the growth of cities, the growth of an urban working class, forced to sell its labour in return for wages, and the decline in importance of the extended family as an economic unit. *See also* Urbanisation.

Infant mortality rate the number of deaths occurring to infants under one year old per 1000 live births, in a specified period (usually one calendar year), in a particular population. The infant mortality rate is often used as an index of the general level of health and medical sophistication in a country. In 1975, the infant mortality rate was 16 per 1000 in England and Wales. *See also* Death rate.

Institution *see* Social institution

Interest group a social group formally organised to achieve certain goals important to its members. A protective interest group aims to safeguard the rights of individuals who might otherwise be unprotected. The activities of groups such as the National Council for Civil Liberties are protective in character. A promotional interest group sets out to advance a certain state of affairs, which can be, for example, economic, religious, educational, political or recreational. For example, the Ramblers' Association organises campaigns to preserve the open countryside and footpaths for recreation. *See also* Pressure group.

Internalisation the process whereby the values of others are assimilated by the individual, finally becoming part of his own make-up. Internalisation is particularly crucial in primary socialisation where the child internalises the values of significant adults, such as his parents, and develops a conscience.

Interview a method of scientific inquiry where an interviewer conducts a conversation with an informant for the purposes of collecting information about a particular social issue. An interview can be unstructured, that is, the informant is generally unrestricted in what he talks about, or it can be structured. In that case, the interviewer has a prearranged set of questions, often on an interview schedule, which he would like answered. An interviewer is careful to remain objective in the course of an interview. Adopting this stance guards against introducing bias into the research.

Juvenile delinquency law-breaking by individuals below the legal age of adult responsibility. In our society, this is persons under 17 years old. The lower age limit of delinquency is determined by the 'age of criminal responsibility'. This is now 10 years old, having been raised from 8 in 1964. *See also* Crime; Deviancy.

Kibbutz (pl. Kibbutzim) an Israeli collective community. The basic organising principle of the kibbutz is the collective ownership of property and communal participation in the activities of the group. In about the last twenty-five years kibbutzim have been gradually changing. Today it is more common to find women involved in the tasks which are traditionally considered to be feminine activities. Earlier, all tasks were shared, irrespective of sex. Also, the communal upbringing of the children of the kibbutz is now less separated from the family group.

Life expectancy *see* Expectation of life

Longitudinal study a method of study which follows individuals or a group of people over a delimited time period. The record of individuals' progress can be kept continuously, in the way in which a diary is kept, or periodically examined in the course of the time period. In Britain, a longitudinal study is being conducted by Dr J. W. B. Douglas and his colleagues, following the life experiences of a cohort of persons born during one week in March 1946. Although generally more costly and certainly more time-consuming than a cross-sectional study, a longitudinal study has many advantages over the latter, particularly when the researcher wants to examine changes over time such as the effect of school on children's attitudes. Here, she can be more certain of unambiguous results if the same group of children are followed through their school career. *See also* Cross-sectional study; Cohort.

Marriage a social institution in which the marriage partners are bound together in a set of mutual rights and obligations, often sanctioned by law.

Marriage, arranged where the bringing together of the marriage partners is organised by someone other than the individuals themselves. For example in Islamic marriages the marriage partners are often selected by the parents of the two individuals concerned.

Marriage, monogamous a marriage where one man is married to one woman.

Marriage, polygamous marriage involving more than one spouse simultaneously. Such a marriage may be polygynous, that is where a husband has more than one wife at the same time, or it can be polyandry, where the wife has more than one husband.

Mass media means of communicating with large numbers of people, without requiring personal contact. Examples of mass media include TV, radio, newspapers, magazines, comics, books and films.

Mechanisation the replacement of craft technology, which depends on human skill and ingenuity in using tools, by machine technology. *See also* Automation.

Migration the permanent or semi-permanent movement of persons from one place or residence to another. This is usually measured in terms of movement across administrative boundaries, such as national borders or county lines. A migratory flow involves the substantial movement of population from one area to another. The overall balance between out-migration and in-migration in an administrative area produces either a gain or a loss to the size of the total area population. This balance is called net migration and, where it is measured annually, annual net migration. *See also* Emigration; Immigration.

Minority group a social group differentiated from the wider society by members' possession of special characteristics, such as shared ethnic, racial or religious characteristics. Very often members share common sentiments, based on the possession of common characteristics, but this need not always follow. A minority group is often, although not always, at a disadvantage in some way in society, being discriminated against by other groups in society. In practice, the term is often applied to categorise persons having real or imagined characteristics, whether or not they constitute a social group or are a minority in society. For example, women are sometimes referred to as a minority group. *See also* Social group.

Mobility *see* Social mobility

Models *see* Role learning

Mortality *see* Death rate

Net migration *see* Migration

Nobility persons having exalted positions in the upper strata of society by virtue of their inherited or acquired rank. The origins of nobility lie in the estate stratification system. In France, descendants of the original nobility were *noblesse de l'épée* owing their position of privilege to their warrior background. Later, persons were appointed to the nobility in recognition of their service, a *noblesse de robe*, and thus it became possible for position to be acquired as well as inherited. Nobility themselves are ranked. For example, in Europe, a duke was a military leader and therefore ranked higher than a count, who was an administrative official. *See also* Aristocracy; Élite; Estate.

Norm, social norm a standard or rule governing expected behaviour, held in common by members of a social group. A norm can be an informal standard or embodied more formally in rules and laws. [Note: a social norm is not the same as a statistical norm.]

Nuclear family *see* Family, nuclear

Nursery school *see* Education

Objectivity the stance adopted in scientific research which aims to safeguard against the introduction of bias. Objectivity aims to eliminate the effect of personal factors, such as pre-conceived ideas, in distorting any aspect of a research study. *See also* Bias.

Observation *see* Participant observation

Occupational group persons categorised as a social group by virtue of their having the same or broadly similar occupations. Occupational classes are frequently used as the criteria for social classes. For example, the Registrar General lists five occupational groups and uses these as the basis for identifying five distinct social classes in Britain today. *See also* Social class; Social stratification.

Opinion poll a systematic survey of the opinions and attitudes held by a sample of the population or a social group, on a particular issue or issues. Social scientists use opinion polls in order to estimate voting behaviour. For example, a public opinion poll is taken prior to the General Election to get an idea of the likely result. Where it is carefully designed and voting attitudes do not drastically change, an opinion poll can often turn out to be a good predictor.

Participant observation a method of scientific inquiry where the researcher becomes a member of the group he is interested in studying and uses this vantage point to get a better understanding of its activities. Used particularly in social anthropology, the method has also been used extensively by sociologists to study, for example, deviant groups. The method is sometimes criticised because of the difficulty of maintaining objectivity and therefore the high risks of introducing bias into the research.

Patrilineal descent *see* Descent

Peer group a primary social group where members are on a relatively equal footing due to the fact that they share some feature in common, such as similar ages or work-experiences. For example, children's play groups are usually peer groups; a group of friends at work or at college also constitute peer groups. *See also* Social group.

Pilot survey *see* Social survey

Polygamy, polygyny, polyandry: *see* Marriage, polygamous

Population increase the growth in size of a total population, over a specified time-period, usually a year. Population increase can be considered purely in terms of increase due to the excess of births over deaths. This is natural increase and is usually expressed in a rate, the rate of natural increase, over a year. However, a more generally useful measure is the annual growth rate. In addition to the excess of births over deaths, this measure takes into account the effect of net migration. Only where there is no migration into or out of a country will the rate of natural increase be the same as the growth rate. *See also* Birth rate; Death rate; Migration; Emigration; Immigration.

Poverty a level of subsistence which is less than minimally adequate. Although there have been numerous attempts to measure poverty, for example, by trying to estimate a poverty line, the relative nature of poverty makes it difficult to measure precisely. A standard presently used for the poverty line is based on the National Assistance, or Supplementary Benefits scale. It has been suggested that there is a culture of poverty, which virtually imprisons people in the same ways of life, leading to poverty generation after generation. *See also* Culture.

Pre-coded questionnaire *see* Questionnaire, pre-coded

Pre-school groups *see* Education

Pressure group a social group concerned with influencing government or legislative bodies in order to forward members' interests or the interests of a larger social group which it claims to represent. *See also* Interest group; Social group.

Primary education *see* Education

Primary group *see* Social group

Primary socialisation *see* Socialisation

Privatised worker the worker who, according to J. H. Goldthorpe and D. Lockwood, typifies the new, privatised, working class in modern Britain. The privatised working class, while continuing to vote Labour, has become sufficiently affluent to have a life style different from that of the traditional working class. Living on a new housing estate, geographically separated from the extended family, the privatised worker and his family spend their time, money and attention on home-centred activities and their children. Despite these changes, the privatised worker remains fundamentally working-class, neither identifying with or being drawn into the middle class. *See also* Embourgeoisement.

Proletariate originally referring to the lowest social class in Ancient Rome, it was used also by Karl Marx, to apply to the propertyless class of workers in a capitalist society, who are obliged to sell their labour in return for wages. According to Marx, the divisiveness of the capitalist economic system would inevitably lead to confrontation between the proletariat and the bourgeoisie (the capitalist class owning the means of production), resulting in triumph for the proletariat. *See also* Bourgeoisie; Capitalism; Social class.

Questionnaire a list of carefully-prepared questions. The questionnaire may be sent either to respondents through the post (a mail questionnaire) or used with informants in the course of an interview (an interview schedule). Bias is avoided by eliminating such things as leading questions from the questionnaire. *See also* Questionnaire; Interview schedule; Questionnaire, mail; Questionnaire, pre-coded.

Questionnaire, interview schedule a questionnaire specially designed so that it can be used by an interviewer in the course of an interview with an informant. Special formats are used in interview schedules, making it easy for the interviewer to keep his place in the questioning without breaking the continuity of the interview. Also, an interview schedule contains directions for the interviewer on how to lead into particular questions in the course of the interview. Conducting interviews without introducing bias is hard, and for this reason researchers usually prefer to use trained interviewers. Training teaches the interviewer to be objective and teaches him how to obtain valid answers without letting personal feelings intrude into the interview. *See also* Questionnaire; Questionnaire, mail; Questionnaire, pre-coded; Bias; Objectivity.

Questionnaire, mail a questionnaire sent through the post, designed to be completed by the respondent. Such a questionnaire needs to be clearly and unambiguously worded, so that there can be no different interpretations put on questions by respondents or misunderstanding of what is required. By taking these precautions, bias is avoided. Non-response is the greatest problem with this method of scientific inquiry. Including a stamped addressed envelope for the completed questionnaire often induces a higher response rate. *See also* Questionnaire; Questionnaire, interview; Questionnaire, pre-coded; Bias; Objectivity.

Questionnaire, pre-coded a questionnaire where a range of alternative answers to the questions (such as 'yes', 'no', 'don't know'; or 'agree', 'disagree', 'don't know') are set in advance of the questionnaire being given to respondents. Each possible answer to these close-ended questions is allocated an individual score, such as 'yes' scoring 1; 'no' scoring 2, and 'don't know' scoring 0. This pre-coding of questions helps speed up the collection of respondents' answers and analysis of results. In a preliminary inquiry, the researcher is interested in learning all about respondents' views and therefore may use open-ended questions, which cannot be pre-coded. *See also* Questionnaire; Questionnaire, mail; Questionnaire, interview schedule.

Race persons having in common inherited physical features such as shape of head, eyes, nose, lips and hair colour. There is no necessary association between inherited physical characteristics and mental traits or cultural life-styles. The major racial groups are Australoid, Caucasoid, Mongoloid and Negroid. However, there are no clear-cut boundaries between racial groups, and inherited characteristics such as particular skin colour overlap across different racial categories.

Racial discrimination the unjust imposition of restrictions and deprivations on members of a particular racial group. *See also* Discrimination; Racial prejudice.

Racial prejudice generally the holding of hostile and unfavourable attitudes towards members of a particular racial group. The term is often applied more broadly to members of particular ethnic groups. *See also* Racial discrimination; Discrimination; Ethnic group.

Rate of growth *see* Population increase

Rites de passage the ceremonies which mark socially significant transitions in the individual's life, such as birth, puberty, marriage and death.

Role, social role a pattern of expected behaviour associated with a particular social status. For example, in some societies the ascribed status of 'old man' is associated with great wisdom and therefore it is expected that he will make wise and authoritative decisions on behalf of his family and his society. The achieved status of 'nurse' is associated with behaviour expected to be kind and considerate in dealing with sick patients. In any society certain expected behaviour goes with being either male or female. Such sex roles are culturally determined and differ from society to society.

Role learning the acquisition of expected ways of behaving associated with a particular social status. For example, the individual learns the behaviour which is culturally expected from members of each sex and in this way learns a sex role. Role learning occurs as part of socialisation. In infancy the child imitates the behaviour of important figures in his world, such as his parents. They become his role models and he models his behaviour on them, internalising their ideas about right and wrong. Role learning occurs also in children's play where, through anticipatory socialisation, adult roles such as wife, mother, teacher, bus driver, are rehearsed. Role learning continues through life as individuals occupy new statuses deriving from changes in the life cycle and changes in occupation. *See also* Socialisation; Internalisation; Role; Status.

Sample a number of cases selected from the population of interest, having characteristics representative of that population. Where the term population is used in reference to sampling, it can refer to the total population of the society, or to a subgroup of society. For example, for the purposes of taking a sample, farmers, women in industry, inhabitants of town X, schoolchildren at school Y, prisoners, could each constitute a separate population from which the sample could be drawn. *See also* Sample, random; Sample, stratified; Sampling frame.

Sample, random a sample selected on the basis of chance where each member of the population has the same, known chance of being included in the sample. For example, suppose the sociologist wants a 10 per cent sample of school children from a school of 1000 children. The 1000 are the population, the list of names of all the children in the school, the sampling frame. First, the sociologist transfers each name to a separate card then places the cards in a box. After the box has been shaken so that all the cards have been thoroughly mixed, the first hundred names to be drawn are the random sample. The general method of random sampling is used by social scientists to avoid a biased sample. In reality, more sophisticated procedures are used than drawing names out of a box, but the principle remains the same. *See also* Sample; Sample, stratified; Sampling frame.

Sample stratified a sample drawn from a population which has been stratified into divisions according to certain criteria. For example, a population can be stratified using stratification factors such as sex, age, marital status, ethnicity, religious affiliation, type of school, type of industry. The factor selected depends on the purpose of the survey. For example, a survey into religious participation in Britain might stratify by type of religious organisation to make sure that even the smallest sect is represented in the final sample, randomly selected from the different categories of religious bodies. *See also* Sample; Sample, random; Sampling frame.

Sampling frame a list or file of all the units in the population of interest, from which the sample is drawn. For the sample to be unbiased, the sampling frame must be up-to-date and complete, not including the names of people who have died or moved away. A representative sample of the general population cannot be achieved using a telephone directory as a sampling frame. This only lists people with telephones and they are likely to differ from persons without telephones, for example, by being richer. In Britain, the register of electors is often used as a sampling frame. Compiled every October and published the following February, there are periods in the year when it is seriously out of date. *See also* Bias; Sample; Sample, random; Sample, stratified.

Scientific method the building of a body of scientific knowledge from theory and from the results of accumulated research, relying on the use of standard systematic procedures. These procedures are: (1) identifying a problem; (2) selecting appropriate methods to study the problem; (3) collecting relevant data; (4) analysing the data; (5) interpreting the data; (6) reporting findings and conclusions. At every stage the researcher will take precautions to ensure that his research is unbiased and objective. *See also* Bias; Objectivity; Variable; Experimental group; Control group.

Secondary education *see* Education

Secondary group *see* Social group

Secondary socialisation *see* Socialisation

Secularisation the process whereby religious values and institutions acquire diminished importance in society. Sacred values are replaced by secular values.

Sex roles *see* Role; Role learning

Sibling a brother or a sister.

Social class persons sharing similar socio-economic characteristics which differentiate them from individuals in other categories. The social differences bind together persons sharing like characteristics into social strata in a stratification system. Criteria underlying social class differences include: different levels of wealth, prestige, power, education, life styles, attitudes, values and social perspectives. Without a doubt, economic factors are centrally important to class distinctions, and occupational groups are frequently used as the basis by which social classes are identified. For example, the Registrar General uses a five-point scale of social classes based on occupational groupings. In contrast, subjective social class is that social class to which the individual assigns himself. Karl Marx identified the major social classes in capitalist society as the proletariat and the bourgeoisie, differing in their relation to the means of production. Max Weber identified status groups as aggregates of people sharing the same life-chances. A class stratification system permits social mobility between social strata because it is primarily based on achieved status. *See also* Social stratification; Status, achieved; Status, ascribed; Social mobility; Proletariat; Bourgeoisie; Estate; Class.

Social control cultural or social restraints on personal action. Social controls can be positive (rewarding) or negative (punishing). Informal social controls include praise, rebukes, ostracism and sarcasm. Formal social controls are concerned with enforcing important social norms, such as mores and laws, and therefore involve more severe restraints, such as fines, imprisonment and banishment. Social control is also personally enforced by the individual's conscience. *See also* Social order; Norms; Socialisation; Internalisation.

Social functions the consequences which particular social phenomena have for the preservation of the wider society. For example, it is claimed that the family performs a number of social functions, including reproduction and the socialisation of children. These things need to be carried on if society is to continue; so by performing these social functions the family helps to preserve and maintain society.

Social group a collection of persons, having common goals and norms, who experience some feeling of shared identity and unity. Groups vary in size and level of personal contact. Primary groups, such as the immediate family, workmates or school friends are all small, face-to-face groups, permitting close and informal relationships. In contrast, secondary groups, such as trade unions, are large and impersonal, members being linked to the national membership through meetings and letters. Important social groups include: peer groups, occupational groups, ethnic groups, minority groups, interest groups, pressure groups. There are Glossary entries on each of these.

Social institution a practised way of carrying on some activity in society. Examples of social institutions include: family, marriage, holidays. Social institutions are supported by social norms.

Social mobility the upward or downward movement of individuals or groups from one social stratum to another in a stratification system. Mobility is virtually impossible in a caste system, somewhat more possible in an estate system and most possible of all in a class stratification system, where social position is mainly based on achieved status. In addition to applying to individuals, social mobility can be inter-generational. That is, mobility occurring in one family, from one generation to the next. *See also* Social stratification; Caste; Estate; Social class; Status, achieved; Status, ascribed.

Social order social cohesion. This is maintained by the relatively stable interlocking of all the components of society. *See also* Social control; Norms.

Social problem any situation judged undesirable by sections of the population or by influential groups in society. *See also* Social control.

Social role *see* Role

Social status *see* Status

Social strata (sing. Social stratum): *see* Social stratification

Social stratification social differentiation where individuals or groups are ranked in a hierarchy of social strata on the basis of criteria such as achieved occupation, position inherited at birth, possession of land or property. Caste and estate stratification systems are closed stratification systems permitting little or no social mobility. Social class stratification systems are open stratification systems, and social mobility is based on achieved rather than ascribed status. *See also* Social mobility; Caste; Estate; Social class; Status, achieved; Status, ascribed.

Social structure the basic organisation of society, a social group, or a social system, comprising a relatively stable set of relationships. *See also* Social system.

Social survey a systematic gathering of information, collected to study a particular social issue, such as poverty. Important early social surveys include: Charles Booth's survey of London's population *Life and Labour of the People* (1897), and Seebohm Rowntree's study of measured poverty in York, *Poverty; A Study of Town Life* (1899). A pilot survey is a miniaturised version of the intended final survey. Using fewer people than the final sample, it aims to discover what unforeseen problems and hitches may arise if the existing form of the survey is used in the final study. *See also* Questionnaire; Questionnaire, interview schedule; Questionnaire, mail; Questionnaire, pre-coded; Interview; Sample; Sample, random; Sample, stratified; Sampling frame; Bias; Objectivity; Scientific method.

Social system a skein of statuses and roles which are linked to one another because of being broadly concerned with the same social activities. For example, the family and kinship system is made up of interdependent statuses and roles, such as husband-wife, parent-child, grandparent-child, which have to do with the raising and socialisation of children and the mutual support and affection of group members. Other examples are the religious system, the political system and the economic system. Social systems also occur in a smaller way where two or more individuals are bound up together in some common social activity. *See also* Social structure.

Socialisation the life-long process whereby an individual acquires the culture of his society. The critical phase of socialisation is primary socialisation. That is, socialisation occurring in the early years of life when, among other things, language is learnt and conscience formation takes place through the process of internalisation. In anticipatory socialisation, the child explores through play adult roles such as mother, wife, doctor, patient. Secondary socialisation is the socialisation which occurs after the formative years and carries on through life through contact with school friends, workmates, leisure-time companions. Formal socialisation into the knowledge and skills of modern society takes place in schools and colleges. Thus education can be seen as part of the wider socialisation process. *See also* Internalisation; Role; Role learning; Culture; Education.

Sponsored mobility a term introduced by the American sociologist, Ralph Turner, to describe a form of social mobility, where only selected individuals are allowed to get ahead through the educational system to reach the upper stratum of society. He considers the English educational system supports sponsored mobility and contrasts this with the US system of contest mobility. *See also* Contest mobility; Status, achieved; Social mobility.

Status, achieved a social position attained by personal effort. For example, by his or her own efforts a person can become a bank clerk, an economist, an MP or Prime Minister—but not the monarch! This is because this is an ascribed status, not depending on personal effort. Theoretically, achieved status is the main way in which positions are filled in a class stratification system. However, research shows there are many barriers in society which continue to prevent Britain from being a truly open society. *See also* Status, social; Status, ascribed; Role; Role learning; Social stratification; Caste; Estate; Social class; Social mobility.

Status, ascribed a social status that is based on inherited position in society or on an unalterable attribute such as age, sex, or race. Such positions as girl, old man, Brahmin or aristocrat are ascribed statuses. Although found in every stratification system, ascribed status is particularly important in deciding the position and life-chances of persons in a caste or estate stratification system. *See also* Status, social; Status, achieved; Role; Role learning; Social stratification; Caste; Estate; Social class; Social mobility.

Status, social a position in the social structure of society or of a social group. A status carries with it the idea that whoever fills that position will behave in certain expected ways. For example, the status 'doctor' carries with it the role of diagnosing illnesses and prescribing cures. *See also* Status, achieved; Status, ascribed; Role; Role learning.

Stereotype a set of biased and oversimplified ideas about the characteristics of members of a particular social group. For example, a common sexual stereotype is to depict women as less capable than men.

Totalitarianism *see* Government, totalitarian

Urbanisation the process whereby a greater proportion of the population comes to live in towns and conurbations than in rural areas, and a greater proportion is employed in industrial rather than agricultural activities. In Britain, widespread urbanisation accompanied industrialisation, beginning in the eighteenth century. Today, rapid urbanisation is occurring in the less developed countries. In many cases, this is taking place without extensive industrialisation, and is resulting in unemployment, poverty and overcrowding. The rate of urbanisation in less developed countries exceeds anything experienced in western Europe at the time of most rapid urbanisation in these countries. *See also* Industrialisation; Conurbation.

Variable any characteristic of an individual or a group which has the property of varying by different amounts. For example, income is a social variable, since it varies by different amounts and can be ranked along a scale from high to low. Other examples are: number of siblings, number of GCEs or CSEs, years of schooling, weeks of holiday. Note that all these variables can be easily counted (quantified). In contrast, qualitative variables, such as ethnicity, attitudes towards abortion or religious affiliation, can only be ranged into parallel categories, such as Protestant, Catholic, Non-Conformist, Jew. Variables are central to the scientific study of society. To find out how society works, the sociologist puts forward hypotheses about what factors underly particular behaviour. In a hypothesis, the variable claimed to be influencing behaviour is called the independent variable, the behaviour which is affected, the dependent variable. For example, the independent variable, social class differences, affects the dependent variable, children's performance in school achievement tests. In this case, research has confirmed the original hypothesis, but we still need to know a good deal more about how this relationship between the independent and the dependent variable really works. For this, research needs to examine a host of other hypotheses with more explicit independent variables. *See also* Hypothesis; Scientific method.

White-collar worker employee engaged in non-manual, non-professional occupations, such as book-keeping, secretarial, clerical and sales work, and technical work of various types. The growth of white-collar trade unionism has been interpreted as an employee's response to a loss of prestige and sense of anonymity with the proliferation of these occupations, and also as a readiness to resort to industrial action previously more distinctively associated with working class occupations.

Youth culture the beliefs, attitudes, values, activities and pastimes which, it is held, generally predominate among teenagers and young people, segregating their culture to some extent from that of the wider society. However, much of the distinctiveness of youth culture is commercially induced. *See also* Culture.

Index of authors and published works

B. Abel-Smith & P. Townsend, *The Poor and the Poorest*, 232

B. Abel-Smith, M. Zander & R. Brooke, *Legal Problems and the Citizen*, 320

M. Abrams, *Teenager Consumer Spending*, 140

M. Abrams, *Class Distinction in Britain*, 209

M. Abrams & R. Rose, *Must Labour Lose?*, 37, 38

S. Allen, *New Minorities, Old Conflicts*, 366

L. Bagrit, *Automation*, 276

F. G. Bailey, *Tribe, Caste and Nation*, 32

L. Bailyn, *Mass Media and Children*, 187

J. A. Banks, *Prosperity and Parenthood*, 71

D. L. Barker & S. Allen (eds), *Dependence and Exploitation in Work and Marriage*, 80, 82

P. Bean, *The Social Control of Drugs*, 344

C. Bell. *Middle-Class Families*, 67

C. Benn & R. Simon, *Halfway There*, 131

N. Bennett, *Teaching Styles and Pupil Progress*, 132

B. Bernstein, *see* Halsey, Floud & Anderson

Lord Beveridge, *Full Employment in a Free Society*, 261

T. Blackstone, *Education and Day-Care for Young Children in Need*, 81

R. Blauner, *Alienation and Freedom: the Manual Worker in Industry*, 274

J. Blondel, *Voters, Parties and Leaders*, 204, 213

C. Booth, *Life and Labour of the London Poor*, 227

D. Boyd, *Elites and their Education*, 133, 134

A. Boyle, *Only the Wind Will Listen: Reith of the BBC*, 182

A. Briggs, *1700–1815 How They Lived*, 67

L. Broom & P. Selznick, *Sociology*, 48

R. Brown, *see* Barker & Allen

J. Burnham, *The Managerial Revolution*, 44

N. Butler, R. Davie & H. Goldstein, *From Birth to Seven*, 125, 128, 373

T. Carlyle, *History of the French Revolution*, 377

H. Carter & P. C. Glick, *Marriage and Divorce: A Social and Economic Study*, 94

N. Dennis, S. Henriques & C. Slaughter, *Coal is Our Life*, 285

J. Dominian, *Marital Breakdown*, 100

J. W. B. Douglas, *The Home and the School*, 110, 111, 113, 118, 126, 131

D. M. Downes, *The Delinquent Solution*, 337

E. Durkheim, *Le Suicide*, 355

J. Eyden, *The Welfare Society*, 233

H. J. Eysenck, *The Inequality of Man*, 124

H. J. Eysenck, *Sense and Nonsense in Psychology*, 215

B. Fay, *Social Theory and Political Practice*, 11

S. E. Finer, *Anonymous Empire: A Study of the Lobby in Great Britain*, 216

R. Firth, J. Hubert & A. Forge, *Families and Their Relatives*, 66

R. Fletcher, *The Family and Marriage in Britain*, 101

M. P. Fogarty, *et al.*, *Women in Top Jobs*, 79

K. Fogelman (ed), *Britain's Sixteen-year-olds*, 129

H. Ford, *My Life and Work*, 271

J. K. Galbraith, *The Affluent Society*, 255

J. K. Galbraith, *The New Industrial State*, 275

H. Gavron, *The Captive Wife*, 64, 66, 91

M. M. Glatt, *see* Whitney

A. Glucksmann, *Violence on the Screen*, 186

J. H. Goldthorpe, D. Lockwood, *et al.*, *The Affluent Worker in the Class Structure*, 40

J. H. Goldthorpe, D. Lockwood, *et al.*, *The Affluent Worker*, 63, 274

W. Goode, *After Divorce*, 95

C. L. Graves, *Mr. Punch's History of Modern England*, 73

J. Halloran, *Television and Delinquency*, 187

A. H. Halsey, J. Floud & A. Anderson (eds), *Education, Economy and Society*, 118, 119

D. H. Hargreaves, *Social Relations in a Secondary School*, 338

H. Himmelweit, *Television and the Child*, 188

D. Hiro, *Black British, White British*, 367

R. Hoggart, *The Uses of Literacy*, 126

R. Holman, *Socially Deprived Families in Britain*, 230

J. H. Hutton, *Caste in India: Its Nature, Function and Origins*, 31

B. Jackson, *Streaming: an Education System in Miniature*, 131

B. Jackson & D. Marsden, *Education and the Working Class*, 113, 118

P. Jephcott, N. Seear & J. Smith, *Married Women Working*, 81

R. King, *Education*, 129

J. Klein, *Samples from English Culture*, 61

J. Lambert, *Crime, Police and Race Relations*, 316

O. R. McGregor, *Divorce in England*, 90, 93, 98, 99

A. MacIntyre, *Secularization and Moral Change*, 309

R. MacIver & C. H. Page, *Society*, 59

P. Marris, *The Experience of Higher Education*, 128

D. Martin, *The Religious and the Secular*, 302, 304

K. Marx & F. Engels, *Selected Works*, 275

K. Marx & F. Engels, *The Communist Manifesto*, 28, 374

H. Mayhew, *London Labour and the London Poor*, 18

J. S. Mill, *The Subjection of Women*, 75

C. W. Mills, *The Power Elite*, 44

P. Morris, R. White & P. Lewis, *Social Needs and Legal Action*, 321

T. & P. Morris, *Pentonville*, 329

C. A. Moser, *Survey Methods in Social Investigation*, 17

J. & E. Newson, *Four Years Old in an Urban Community*, 74

F. Norman, *Lock 'Em Up and Count 'Em*, 325

G. Orwell, *Nineteen Eighty-Four*, 189

S. R. Parker, *The Sociology of Industry*, 262, 285

S. Pollard & D. W. Crossley, *The Wealth of Britain*, 268

J. Prebble, *The Highland Clearances*, 158

W. Radcliffe, *see* Briggs

R. & R. Rapoport, *Dual Career Families, Re-examined*, 88, 89

J. Raynor, *The Middle Class*, 44

I. Reid, *Social Class Differences in Britain*, 41

J. C. W. Reith, *Into The Wind*, 182

J. C. W. Reith, *Wearing Spurs*, 182

J. Rex & R. Moore, *Race, Community and Conflict*, 367

E. J. B. Rose *et al.*, *Colour and Citizenship, A Report on British Race Relations*, 364

B. Rosen, *The Achievement Syndrome*, 126

C. Rosser & C. Harris, *The Family and Social Change*, 49

B. S. Rowntree, *Poverty: A Study of Town Life*, 18

B. N. Seear, *Re-entry of Women to the Labour Market after an Interruption of Employment*, 83

G. Shanas, P. Townsend & J. D. Wedderburn, *Old People in Three Industrial Societies*, 62

N. J. Smesler, *The Sociology of Economic Life*, 272

S. Smiles, *Self-Help*, 225

A. Smith, *The Wealth of Nations*, 270

D. Smith, *Racial Discrimination in Employment*, 366

D. J. Smith & A. Whalley, *Racial Minorities and Public Housing*, 367

D. Stevenson, *Fifty Million Volunteers*, 141

H. Taine, *Notes on England*, 304

R. H. Tawney, *Religion and the Rise of Capitalism*, 27

R. M. Titmuss, *Essays on the Welfare State*, 41

R. M. Titmuss, *Income Distribution and Social Change*, 269

R. M. Titmuss, *Problems of Social Policy*, 83

A. Touraine, *An Historical Theory in the Evolution of Industrial Skills*, 275

P. Townsend, *The Family Life of Old People*, 14

J. Tunstall, *The Fishermen*, 284

T. Veblen, *Theory of the Leisure Class*, 288

M. Weber, *Class, Status and Power*, 43

D. J. West & Lord Hunt, *The Future of Parole*, 328

E. D. Whitney (ed), *World Dialogue on Drug Dependence*, 347

H. L. Wilensky, *The Uneven Distribution of Leisure : The Impact of Growth on Free Time*, 284

T. M. Williams & K. Hindell, *Abortion and Contraception—A Study of Patients' Attitudes*, 353

P. Willmott & M. Young, *Family and Class in a London Suburb*, 65

B. Wilson, *Religion in Secular Society*, 309, 311, 312

J. Young, *The Drugtakers*, 339, 346

J. Young, *Images of Deviance*, 340

M. Young & P. Willmott, *Family and Kinship in East London*, 60, 62

M. Young & P. Willmott, *The Symmetrical Family*, 63, 70, 72, 75, 88, 101

F. Zweig, *The Worker in an Affluent Society*, 39

Other publications

Alcohol Abuse (Office of Health Economics, 1970), 347

American Sociological Review (R. Turner), 34

Automation (HMSO), 276

Between Two Cultures (Community Relations Commission), 368

Britain (HMSO), 258

British Journal of Industrial Relations (R. K. Brown, J. M. Kirby & K. F. Taylor), 82

British Journal of Sociology (C. Gibson), 100

Case Histories (National Council for the Unmarried Mother and Her Child), 350

Church Information Office:

    Baptist Handbook, 306

    Church of England Year Book, 306

    Congregational Year Book, 306

    Minutes of the Methodist Conference, 306

Classification of Occupations (1970) (HMSO), 282

Comprehensive Education (D. Marsden), 115

Concise Oxford Dictionary, 285

Criminal Statistics for England and Wales (Home Office), 334

Crowther Report (HMSO), 111

Employment Policy (HMSO), 261

Eugenics Review XLV (J. Nisbet), 372

Guardian (A. Hartley), 139

Inland Revenue Statistics (HMSO), 268

Manchester Guardian (C. P. Scott), 191

News of the World, 177
New Society, 127, 223, 232, 325, 356, 361
New Society (S. Cohen), 326
New Society (S. Ginsberg), 80
New Society (F. Lafitte), 352
New Society (A. Piepe & A. Box), 184
New Society (J. West), 82
Observer (C. G. Tether), 379
Papers of the Royal Commission on Population, 71
Political and Economic Planning, 80
Population Trends, 98
Public Schools Commission, First Report (HMSO), 133
Putting Asunder (Church of England), 97, 311
Research on Poverty, 1968 (Social Science Research Council), 231
Royal Commission on the Distribution of Income and Wealth (HMSO), 267
Social Mobility in Britain, 34, 37
Social Trends, 71, 165, 168, 180, 323
Sociology (R. Robertson), 302
The Effectiveness of Sentencing (1976) (Home Office Report), 327
The Newspaper Press Directory (1971), 179
The Social Science Teacher (I. Morgan), 267
The Sunday Times (D. E. Butler), 212
The Sunday Times (N. Tomalin), 340
The Times, 241
The Times Educational Supplement (V. R. Rogers and J. Barron), 133
UN Demographic Year Book, 91, 155
Wootton Committee Report (Government Advisory Committee on Drug Dependence, 1968), 342
Voluntary Worker in the Social Services (NCSS), 248

General Index

abortion 101, 311, 331, 351–3
Abortion Act (1967) 311, 351, 352
Abrams, Dr Mark 286
abstainers, negative and positive 202–6
Acts of Parliament, introduction of 198
  for individual Acts, *see* under their titles, *e.g.*
Administration of Justice Act 318
adoption 49, 235
adult education 139
adultery 313
adult offenders, punishment of 324–9
advertising 189, 190, 263
  and full employment 263
  expenditure 190
  industry 179
age distribution of population UK 162–4
age grouping 384
agricultural population, recession and
  emigration 158
alcohol
  and suicide 355
  drunken driving 348
Alcoholics Anonymous 248, 349
alcoholism 346–9
  cost to industry 348
  treatment centres 347, 349
alienation 272–4, 384
Amalgamated Society of Engineers 32
Annan Committee 186, 188
Annan, Lord 137
anomie 384
anthropology 6, 384
approved schools 323
Arkwright, Richard 270
armament, expenditure on 378
Aryans 30
Arusha 53
ascribed social status 54
Asian doctors, as UK immigrants 159
Asian immigrants 360
attainment, pre-schooling and 117–22
Australia

compulsory voting 202
emigrants to 158
immigrants from 158
industrial relations 281
automation 274–7, 337, 385
  effect of 164
  social consequences 276
Automobile Association 216

Balfour's Act (1902) 107
banding 131
baptism 306
Baptists 247, 305, 306, 307
bargaining in industry 279–81
Barnardo, Dr Thomas 228
behaviour
  abnormal 331
  criminal 371
  in society 39
  patterns 3, 7, 48, 371
  pre-schooling and 372, 373
beliefs 298–300
  systems 299, 300
Bernstein, Basil 118–20
Beveridge Report (1942) 233, 234, 248, 261, 375
Buddhism 31, 300
Bills, parliamentary
  interest groups and 216, 217
  readings of 198
Birmingham (W. Midlands) Council 200
birth control
  see contraception, family, family planning
birth rate 135, 151, 152, 167–9, 240
  crude 385
  demographers and 147, 150
  stability, reasons for 152
birth, registration of 147
Blondel, Jean 204, 206, 213
Booth, Charles 228, 233
Booth, General William 228, 246
borstals 323, 324

bourgeoisie 385, 401, 405
Boy Scouts Association 141
Britain (UK)
  abortion 168
  advertising expenditure 190
  birth rate 151, 152, 240
  census in 147-9
  death rate 152, 153, 226
  emigration from 156-9, 168
  family in 47-102
  government 195-222
  immigration 156-9, 168
  life expectation in 147, 150-6, 167-9, 226,
    240, 241
  population 147-62, 164-7, 167-9
  religion 302-12
British Broadcasting Corporation (BBC)
  182-6
broadcasting 182-9
Brougham, Lord 107
Bullock Committee (1975) 132, 281
bureaucracy 385, 394
Burnham, Dr James 44, 274
Burt, Sir Cyril 109
Butler Act (1944) 108

Cabinet, function of 198
Calvinists 27
Cambridge University 84, 115, 127-9, 137
Campaign for Nuclear Disarmament (CND)
  217, 248
Canada
  emigration to 158
  immigration from 158
  industrial relations 281
cannabis 340-2
capital (wealth) 28, 257, 386
capitalist economy 257, 386
Caribbean immigrants 157
case-study method 386
caste (Indian) 30, 31, 387
Catholics, as voters 209
  see also Roman Catholic Church
census 146, 147
  in ancient Rome 147
  confidential nature of 146, 147
  controversy over 147
  data from 13, 146
  enumerators 146
  form for 148, 149
Central Redundancy Fund 265
Chadwick, Edwin 227
Charity Commissioners 247
children

employment of 73, 74, 258
  separation from family 55, 56
  television, impact of 186-9
  see also education, schools
Children and Young Persons' Act (1969) 323
Children's Act (1948) 234
China, People's Republic of 55, 56, 270
church
  attendance 301-12
  class and 308
  power and status 27
Church of England 97, 302, 304-6, 309-12
cinema 177
Citizens' Advice Bureaux 236, 320
civil employment 258
class 387, 405
  and speech patterns 52, 117-20
  and status 42
  classification of 36, 37
  constitution of 28-30
  definition, criteria 35
  differences 40-2
  economic factor of occupation 40
  life-style and 40-2
  self-assigned 34-38
class-consciousness 35
classless society 35, 40
cohort 102, 387, 398
collectivist 36
colleges of education 85, 251
coloured population in UK
  see Commonwealth immigrants
conjugal family role 59, 61, 62
commerce, development of 27
commercial television 183-6
Common Law 295
Common Market
  see European Economic Community
Commonwealth immigrants 156-9, 358-63
  in central London 167
  skills of 158, 159
  see also New Commonwealth
Commonwealth Immigrants Acts (1962, 1968)
  360, 362, 363
communal living 102
communes 55, 270
communication
  advantages and disadvantages 177
  industry 176, 177
  means of 176, 177
Communism 388
communities as groups 2
community 388
  close-knit 2, 60, 63

loose-knit 65
community homes for young people 323
community service for offenders 323
community spirit 380
commuters (London) 167
comprehensive education 112–17, 124
  advantages of 114
  disadvantages of 115
  expansion of 113, 114
Comte, Auguste 1, 9
Conservative Party 196, 202–4, 210, 211
  aims 211
  and comprehensive education 113
  and industrial relations 281
  financial support for 213
constituency members, influence of 213
contest mobility 34, 388
contraception 101, 239, 250, 311, 394
  and family size 71, 167
  and living standards 152
  objections to 171
  contraceptive pill 85, 90
  see also family planning
conurbations 164, 389
Cooley, Charles Horton 176
coroners 357
correlation 16, 389
council housing 242–6
County Councils, responsibilities of 200
Courts Act (1971) 318, 319
courts of law 318–20
crime 331–45, 371
Criminal Justice Acts (1967, 1972) 322, 323,
  325, 327, 328, 349
criminal statistics 334, 335
cross sectional study 389
Crown courts 319
cultural class systems 178
cultural democracy 178
culture 51, 53, 60, 105, 295, 296, 298, 389
  differences in 367, 368
  of society 251
cumulative discipline 9
curriculum 105, 117
custodial function 323
customs 298
Czech immigrants in UK 156

data, accumulation 8, 11, 22
Davies, W. H. 231
death penalty 313, 325
death rate 152–6, 226
  crude 152, 153, 390
  decline, reasons for 153

death, registration of, data from 147
declining industry 261
deferential voter 390
deferred gratification 120
delinquency 12, 81, 100, 390
demand, effective 257
democracy 195, 221
Democratic Labour Party 214
demography 4, 145, 147
demonstrations, function of 217
Dennis, Henriques and Slaughter 285
Department of Education & Science 113
Department of Employment 259
Department of Health & Social Security 238
depopulation 165
deprived children and nursery education 121
descent 390
detention centres 323
detoxification centres 349
deviancy 331–57, 390
Devolution Act (1978) 222
Diamond Commission (1976) 267
direct grant grammar schools 114, 125
  see also education
discrimination 390
distribution of labour 261
distribution of opportunity, and social
  mobility 33
District councils, responsibilities of 200
division of labour 391
divorce 75, 86, 87, 90–100, 250, 311, 313
  age at 98
  rates 93, 94, 302
  undefended proceedings (1977) 95
Divorce Reform Act (1969) 87, 95, 313
Domesday Book 145
Donovan Report 260, 280
Doré, Gustave 226
downward mobility 32
drugs 338–45
  addiction to 339
  and mass media 344
  cigarette smoking 340
  dependency 339
  habituation 339
  illegal possession and selling of 345
  nicknames for 341
  see also alcohol, alcoholism
Durkheim, Émile 1, 272, 274, 300, 354
dysfunction 11

East enders and occupations 37
Easter Day communicants 306
ecology, problem of 379

economic change, effect of 40
economic function of education 105
economic growth and class 33
economic systems and unemployment 230,
 261–5
economy and employment 254–88
education 105–41, 391–2
 ability and attainment 123–34
 adult 139
 and social class 117–34
 and social mobility 33
 arguments in 130–4
 basic 115
 colleges 135
 comprehensive 112–15, 124
 development of 107–17
 direct grant schools 114, 125
 effect on status 37
 eleven-plus examination 110, 111, 114
 expenditure 105
 formal methods 105, 131–3
 functions of 105, 106
 further 126, 127, 134–9, 251, 263
 grammar 108–12, 124–6, 220
 home background and 118
 nursery 120–2, 236
 political function of 106
 polytechnics 135, 136
 pre-school, and playgroups 89, 372, 373
 primary 110, 132, 133
 private schools 110, 124–6
 public education 107
 public schools 110, 133, 134, 220
 pupil-teacher ratio 114
 secondary 78, 84, 85, 109–17
 secondary modern 108–12, 220
 selective function 106
 sixth form colleges 113
 socio-cultural factor in 118
 stabilising function of 105
 standards and employment 130, 255
 streaming 113, 122, 130, 131, 338
 system, growth of 107–9
 technical schools 108–10, 220
 three-tier system 108
 universities 65, 84, 85, 127, 128, 133, 137–9,
 220
 vocational training 135
 see also schools; teachers; Government White
 Papers
Education Acts (from 1870) 84
Education Act (1870) 74
Education Act (1944) 84, 109–12, 122
Education (Provision of Meals) Act (1926)
 233

Einstein, A. 380
elderly, welfare for 240
election by majority 203
electorate 201–9
Eliot, T. S. 377
elites, elitism 44, 195, 219, 392
embourgeoisement, process of 39, 40, 392
emigration 156–8, 168, 392
empirical discipline 9, 392
empirical method of investigation 11, 12
employer and employed, relationship between
 277–81
employment
 classification of 258, 259
 full, effect of 261, 262
 of women 78–80, 81, 82, 83, 87–9, 259, 260
 over-full 261
 see also unemployment
Engels, F. 28, 275
entrepreneur 257
enumerators (census) 146
Equal Opportunities Commission 88, 89
Equal Pay Act (1970) 82, 87, 89, 259
Erikson, E. H. 51
Establishment, the 219–21
 composition of 219, 220
Estate systems 26, 31, 392
 status in 26, 27
Estates General 27
ethnic group 358, 393
Eton public school 134
Europe
 infant mortality in 155
 see also Western Europe
European Economic Community (EEC) 158,
 214, 222, 281, 374
 effect on immigration 158
 holidays in 374
European immigrants in UK 158
executive (government) 196–9
expectation of life 393
ex-prisoner 333
Eysenck, H. J. 124, 215, 216

factors of production 257
Factory Acts (1833, 1847) 68, 73
factory system, development of 68, 153, 154
family 47–102, 393
 bilinial 50, 51
 and birth control 72
 as a group 49
 and questionnaire 21
 and social mobility 372
 environment and class 40

extended (consanguine) 49, 50, 53, 59, 60, 65, 68, 81, 368, 379
  home-centred 184
  in industrialised societies 58–60
  impact of technology on 75
  matriarchal 51
  matrilineal 50, 390
  of origin 48, 49
  of procreation 49, 65
  one-parent 350
  patriarchal 50
  patrilineal 50, 53, 390
  planning 74, 90, 250
    see also contraception
  roles
    conjugal (nuclear) 48, 49, 62–4, 66, 88, 89, 368
      see also nuclear family
    joint conjugal 64, 66
    segregated conjugal 62, 64
    sex and 52
    woman's 70, 75–88, 89
  social function of 51–55, 60
  size 71, 77, 151–4, 167–9
  social status 69
  structure 49, 65, 69
  symmetrical 88, 101
  traditional 60–2, 184
  types of 48–51
  Welfare State and 250–2
Family Allowance 235
Family Allowance Act (1945) 234
family planning 168, 239, 250, 311
Family Planning Association 168
  see also contraception
Farming 30
fecundity 394
fertility 394
Firmin, Thomas 225
Fisher Act (1918) 108
Fletcher, Ronald 288
floating voters 204, 206
folkways 297, 298, 394
Ford, Henry 271, 274
formal language (elaborated code) 119
formal social control 294, 295
French Revolution 26, 27, 221, 377
Freud, Sigmund 51
Friendly Societies 225
functionalist theories 9
further education 126, 127, 134–9, 251, 263
  see also education

Gamblers Anonymous 246

General elections
  floating voter 204, 206
  marginal seats 204
  voting at 202, 203
General Strike (1926) 230
geometric rate, population 147
Ghana 53
Girl Guides Association 141
government 195–222, 395
  Ancient Greeks and 195
  Establishment 219–21
  executive 197–9
  formation of 196, 197
  function 197
  local 199–201
  meaning of 195
  powers of 197–9
  working-class participation 28, 29
Government Social Survey (1968) 115
Government Training Centres 250, 265
Government White Papers
  education 113, 121
  immigration 362
  prisoners 325
  social insurance 234
grammar schools 108–12, 124–6, 220
  see also education
grants
  education 107
  student 125
Great Depression (1920–33) 230
Greater London
  decrease in population 167
  government 200
Greater Manchester Council 200
groups 2, 396, 406
  behaviour patterns in 2, 3, 7
  characteristics of 1, 2
  primary and secondary 176
  stratification 26–32

Hadow Report (1926) 108
Hall-Jones scale 30, 37
Halsey Education Priority Report (1972) 121
Hanoverian succession, opposed by Tories 210
Harrow public school 134
health authorities 238
Herbert, A. P. 313
hereditary titles in House of Lords 197
heredity 396
heroin 341, 342, 344
Heyerdahl, Thor 379
hierarchy 396

Himmelweit, Dr Hilde 188, 189
Hinduism 31, 300
historical theories 9
holidays 284, 374
Home Office 321, 328, 363
Home Secretary 316, 328
hospitals and specialist services 238
House of Commons 196-8
House of Lords 196, 197, 310, 320
Houses of Parliament 196
house purchase 42
Housing Acts (1890, 1972, 1974) 242, 243, 244
housing associations 244
housing, privately rented 243
Hulton Readership Survey 347
hypothesis 396

illegitimacy 349, 350
immigrants
  Commonwealth 358-63, 366, 367
  medical staff 361
  police and 316
immigration 156-9, 168, 396
  and legislation 157, 158, 360-3
  restriction of 157
  see also Government White Papers, migration
Immigration Act (1962) 157
income, distribution of 265-9
Independent Broadcasting Authority (IBA) 184-6
Independent Television Authority (ITA) 179, 183
India
  and caste system 26
  immigrants from 156-9
  independence, effect of 156
  infant mortality rate 155, 156
individual, the
  class and education of 372, 373
  inherited characteristics 371, 372
  society and 294, 371-80
  work and welfare 373-5
individualist perspective 36
industrial action, see strikes
industrial relations 280, 281
Industrial Relations Acts (1971, 1974) 281
Industrial Revolution 153
industrial societies 26
industrialisation 29, 32
Industrial Training Boards 265
infant mortality 71, 155, 156
  comparisons 155, 156
  in UK 155

informal social control 295-8
informative advertising 190
informative journalism 180
in-service training 135
Institute of Race Relations 157, 365
intelligence quotients (IQ) 124, 372
  see also education
interest groups 216-19, 396-7
intergenerational mobility 34
internal migration 165-7
internalisation 397
international statistics of density 165
inter-pupil relationships 118
interview 397
interviews, formal and informal 20
intra-household consultation 21
investigation
  principles of 11
  questionnaires 18-21, 402
  samples in 12-16
  social surveys 17, 18
  see also questionnaires
Ireland (Eire)
  advertising expenditure 190
  migration from 156, 358
Israel 55, 56, 270, 296

Jackson, Brian (and Marsden, D.) 124, 273
James Report (1972) 135
Jehovah's Witnesses 308
Jenkins, Roy 214
Jews
  migration of 156, 358
  orthodox 307, 358
Joint Council for the Welfare of Immigrants 363
Joint Industry Committee for National Readership Surveys (JICNRS) 180, 181
Jones, D. Caradog (and Hall, John) 30, 37
Judges of Appeal 197
judicial system 317-23
judiciary 197-9
juvenile courts 319
juvenile delinquency 334-8

karma, doctrine of 31
Kenya 53, 156
Keynes, Lord 261
kibbutzim 55, 56, 270, 296, 397
Kohlberg, L. 51

labour
  division of 270-2
  free mobility of 157-9

Labour Government
  and comprehensive education 113
  and welfare 233, 234
Labour Party 196, 202–4, 211, 212
  aims of 212
  constitution of 212
  contributions to 213
land ownership and status 27
Lane Committee 351
Law, the 312–29
Law Lords 197
Leeds, conditions in 227
Leeds (West Yorks) Council 200
Leeds University 127, 128, 192
legal aid 97, 320, 321
Legal Aid and Advice Act (1969) 320
Legal Aid and Assistance Act (1972) (1974)
  320
legislation 197–9
legislature (Parliament) 197–9
leisure 140–1, 282–8, 374
  five ages of 286–8
Liberal Party 196, 202–4, 212
life-cycle, family 49, 80, 81
life expectation 85, 152–6, 159–64, 167–9,
  226, 240, 241
  effects of increased 155, 167–9
life peers 197
Life Peerages Act (1958) 197
life-style and class 35, 120
Liverpool (Merseyside) Council 200
lobbies 216–19
local authorities
  and social services 200, 233
  housing 242, 243
  welfare services 233, 234
Local Education Authority 107
local government 199–201
  expenditure 200
  functions 199, 200
  income of 200
  survey on management of 200
  two-tier system 200
  voting for 200
Local Government Act (1972) 200
London
  and Commonwealth immigrants 167
  conditions in 228
  population increase 166
London University 84
longitudinal study 22
Lords Spiritual 197
Lords Temporal 197

magistrates' courts 318–20
Malthus, Thomas 147, 150, 151
managerial revolution 274
Manchester University 84
manifesto, election 219
manual worker, self-assigned class of 34–8
Mao, Tse-Tung 44
marginal seats 204
marriage 56, 57, 60, 61, 90–100, 250, 398
  age 92
  in Victorian society 69, 70, 73, 75, 90
  rates 90, 91
  registration of 147
married women, employment of 69, 259, 260
  see also family
Married Women's Property Act (1870, 1882)
  75, 86
Marsden, Dennis (and Jackson, B.) 124, 274
Martin, D. A. 302, 304–8
Marx, Karl 1, 9, 28, 29, 32, 34, 43, 272, 275,
  374
Masai family 53, 54, 56–8
  marriage 54
mass communication 176
mass media 176–92, 398
  and drugs 344
  and suicide 355
  role of 215
mass-production 270–2
maternity allowance 235, 250
Matrimonial Causes Acts (1857, 1937) 87, 95
Mayhew, Henry 18
Mead, G. H. 51
means test 230
media
  advertising expenditure 190
  and character assassination 191
Medical Council on Alcoholism 348
medical practitioners 238, 239
Members of Parliament 196, 197, 374
  affiliation and pressures on 216, 217
  education of 214, 220
  influence on 213
  occupations of 218
mentally disordered, benefits for 240
metaplets 56
meteorology 8
Methodists 246, 304, 306
metropolitan county councils 200
middle class 28–30
  achievement 118–20
  affluence of 230
  and political power 44
  and the police 316

and the Welfare State 41, 42
culture of 105, 125
extended family 66, 67
family 65–7, 90
  ambitions 66, 67
  education 65
  father in 73
  size 71, 72, 83
  upbringing 73
  woman's role in 66
grammar schools and 124–6, 131
growth of new 32
Labour vote of 209
law breakers 335
new 32
perspective 35, 36
prosperity 41
school-leavers 373
Midlands, migrant population of 165
mid-point sample survey 146
migration 398
  to UK 156–9
  within UK 164–6
  see also immigration
Mill, J. S. 75
Mills, C. Wright 44
ministers (government) responsibility of 197
minority groups and interests 357–69
Misuse of Drugs Act (1972) 345
mixed economy 277, 278
mobility, contest and sponsored 373
modelling
  personal, positional and immitative 52, 403
morality and the law 312, 313
mores see social mores
Mosca, Gaetano 44
Moslem Society 57, 332
mothers and young children, benefits for 235, 239, 240
motivation and social mobility 33
Motor Manufacturers Association 216
Mundella's Act (1880) 107

National Assistance Act (1948) 234
National Association of Boys' Clubs 141
National Children's Bureaux 121, 129
National Conference of Labour Women (1969) 259
National Council for Social Service (NCSS) 248
National Council for the Unmarried Mother and her child 350, 352
National Health Service 59, 85, 101, 159, 235–9, 269, 351

family planning on 85
and immigration 159
National Health Service Act (1946) 234
National Industrial Relations Court, action of 281
National Insurance Acts (1906, 1911, 1946) 233, 234
National Insurance (Industrial Injuries) Act (1946) 234
National Insurance Scheme 236
National Society for the Prevention of Cruelty to Children (NSPCC) 217, 248
National Union of Mineworkers (NUM) 218
Nazi Germany 296, 376
Newcastle Commission (1861) 130
Newcastle (Tyneside) Council 200
New Commonwealth 167
Newspapers 178–81
Newspaper Press Directory 179
New Towns Act (1946) 234
non-ethical discipline 9
non-patrials 363
non-workers 258
norms 295–7
North Atlantic Treaty Organisation (NATO) 378
North of England, migration from 165
Norwood Report (1943) 108, 109
nuclear (conjugal) family 48, 49, 58, 59, 62, 65, 68, 368
  see also conjugal family
nuclear weapons 378
nursery education 120–2, 236, 372
nursery school, benefits of 120–2

obsolescence, planned 263
occupational structure
  and social mobility 30, 33
  five-point scale 29, 400
occupations
  class and status of 29, 30
  classification of 282
  index of 34
  of parents, selection by 128, 129
  sons' relative to fathers' 34
offences 317–23
  civil 318
  criminal 318–20
  indictable 317, 318, 334
  non-indictable 317, 318, 334
Office of Health Economics 347
Office of Population Censuses and Surveys 169, 350
Old Age Pensions 233

old age pensioners, lack of representation 218

old age, and poverty 232

services for the aged 240–2

old people 54

social contact 62–3

old people's home 251

oligarchy 195

Open University 139

opinion poll 12, 202, 400

sampling 12

Organisation for Economic Cooperation and Development (OECD) 79

Orphans' and Widows' Pensions 233

Orwell, George 189

Owen, Robert 225

owner-occupied houses 242, 244

Oxford University 84, 115, 129, 130, 137

Pakistan Act (1973) 363

Pakistan

immigrants from 363

Pareto, Vilfredo 44

Parker, S. R. 285

Parliament 196–9

see also legislature

Paris, municipal election 200

parole 328

Parole Board 328

participant observation 22, 400

pedestrians, lack of influence of 217–18

peer group 51, 118, 400

penal systems 323–9

People's Republic of China 55, 56, 270

perfect mobility 34

permissive society 350

physically handicapped, benefits for 240

Piaget, J. 51

Plaid Cymru (Welsh Nationalists) 222

playgroups 121

Plowden Report (1967) 121, 122, 132

Plymouth Brethren 308

police 252, 295, 314–16, 321

Police Act (1976) 316

Police Complaints Board 316

Polish immigrants in UK 156

political attitudes 214–16

political functions of education 106

political levy 213

political parties

influence on MPs 213

membership of 213, 214

motivation 214–16

political sociology 196

politics

meaning of 195, 196

interest groups 216–19

pollution 379

polygyny 56

polytechnics 251

Poor Law Acts (1601, 1834) 225, 226

Poor Law Relief (Public Assistance) 234

population

arithmetic rate of growth 147

birth rate 135, 151, 152, 167–9, 240, 385

census 146, 147

data on 168

death rate 152–6, 226, 390

density 164–7

distribution 159–7

emigration and immigration 156–9, 168, 392, 396

food supplies and 147, 150, 151

growth of 147–9, 400

infant mortality and 155, 156

internal migration and 165–7

of Elizabethan London 166

size or 147–9

world trends 169–71

poverty 225–32, 401

line 232

reasons for 231, 232

trap 233

Powell, Enoch 159, 214

power 43, 44

and class 43, 44

and force 44

in estate systems 26

through ownership 27

Pregnancy Advisory Service 351

pregnancy, pre-marital 98

prejudice 364, 365

press, the 178–82

influence of 190–2

Press Council 192

pressure groups 216–19, 396–7, 401

pre-test survey 17

primary workers 259

Prime Minister 197, 198

primitive society 254, 270

see also Masai, Sisala

printing as communication 176

prisons 322–9

Private Member's bills 198

and interest groups 217

privatised working class 63–5, 75, 101, 401

probation service 252, 321

professional associations as interest groups 217

proletariat 32, 385, 401, 405
promotional interest groups 217
PROP 248, 328
protective groups 217
Protestants, and industrialisation 27
psephology 202
psychology 6
public health measures and population 154
public language (restricted code) 119
public and private schools 110, 133, 134, 220
 see also education
Public Health Acts (1848, 1875) 227
Public Schools Commission 133
punishment, theories of 317
pupil-teacher
 ratio 114
 relationships 117, 118

qualitative approach 22
quantitative approach 11, 22
Queen of England, function in government
 197-9
questionnaires 18-21, 402
 interviewer 20, 402
 mail 20, 21, 402
 pre-coded 19, 402
 see also investigations

race 402, 403
race relations 363-9
Race Relations Acts (1962, 1965) 368
racial prejudice and discrimination 365-7
radio 182-3
 as communication 176
 pirate radio 177, 178, 182
Radio Caroline 182
Radio London 182
raising of the school leaving age (RoSLA) 116
recidivism 327
redundancy 265
Reform Acts (1832, 1867) 202, 210
regional differences and employment of
 school-leavers 33
Registrar General 29, 30
 and census 146
 and occupation 282
 five-point scale of occupational structure 29
Rehabilitation of Offenders Act (1974) 327,
 328
Reith, Lord 182
religion 298-312
 prophetic function 301
 statistics on 304
religion and social control 298-312

religious beliefs 90, 251, 298-300
religious knowledge, decline in importance 312
religious rites 301, 302
Rent Act (1965) 243
respondents 18, 19, 402
response rate 18
retirement pensions 250
retraining 265
rites 301, 302
rites de passage 309
Robbins Report (1963) 130
role 403
Roman Catholic Church 27, 306, 355
 and contraception 171
Roosevelt, F. D. 12
Rowntree, B. Seebohm 18
royal assent 199
Royal Automobile Club (RAC) as interest
 group 216
Royal Commission on Trade Unions and
 Employers' Associations 280
Royal Military Academy 134
Royal Society for the Prevention of Accidents
 216
Royal Society for the Prevention of Cruelty to
 Animals (RSPCA) 217
Ruskin College 130
Russell Report (1973) 139
Russia, see Union of Soviet Socialist Republics

Salvation Army 228, 246, 304, 309
 see also suicide
Samaritans 357
sample frame 14, 404
samples, in investigations 13, 404
sampling 16
 random 13, 404
 systematic 14
 cluster 15
 stratified 15
 quota 15
 judgement 15
Sandon's Act (1876) 107
Sanitary Commission (1869) 227
school
 boards 107
 function of 105, 106
 leaving age 115-17
 leavers 33
 neighbourhood of 126
 training in job skills at 105
 transfer, age of 122
 uniform for 105
 see also education; teachers

School Intention Survey (DES, 1975) 85
Schools Council 117
Scotland, migration from 158
Scott, C. P. 191
Scottish National Party (SNP) 222
secondary modern schools 108–12, 220
secondary workers 259
secularisation 302–12, 405
Secretary of State, responsibility of 197
sects 308
segregated conjugal family 62, 64
sentencing offenders 321–3
Sex Discrimination Act (1975) 82, 88, 259
Sex Disqualification Act (1919) 87
Shadow Cabinet 197
Shaftesbury, Lord 228
Sheffield (S. Yorks) Council 200
Shelter 248
sibling 49, 405
Silkin, S. C. 313
Sisala 53, 55–7
sixthformer, new 114
slums 244
Smiles, Samuel 225
social behaviour-pattern 39, 294
social change 145
social class 28–30
  newspapers and 180, 181
  of individual 372, 373
  stratification 28–30, 43
  voting and 209
  see also class
social control 292–328, 406
  formal 294–5
  informal 295–8
social differences 26, 28
social factors and suicide 355
social group 292–4, 406
social institution 406
social insurance, White Paper on 234
social interaction 294
social mobility 32–4, 406
social mores 296, 297
social order 27, 292–4
social perspectives 35, 36
social problems 331–69
social relationship 3, 4, 38, 75, 274
social science 4–7, 8
Social Science Research Council 231, 365
social selection 129
social services 235–52
social status 26, 34, 52, 288, 409
social stratification 407
social structure 3, 4, 38–40, 68, 101, 145, 407

social surveys 17, 407
social system 3, 407
socialisation 51–3, 80, 82, 83, 105, 408
  anticipatory 53, 403
  primary 51, 397
society
  and the individual 371–80
  approaches to study of 1–23
  culture of 51, 53, 60, 105, 295, 296, 298, 389
  deviant in 331–7
  disagreement in 292, 293
  dynamism of 39
  family in 51–5
  future of 377–80
  religion in 301–12
  rules of 294–8
  shaping 375–7
  strata 26–32
  see also welfare society
socio-linguistics and learning 52, 117–20
sociologists 2, 3, 47, 51, 55, 58, 130, 141, 145, 162, 293, 354
  and hypothesis 11
  approach of 11, 23
  function of 8, 11, 12, 380
sociology 1, 2
  as a science 7
  banned USSR 1
  characteristics of 8–11
  political 196
  recognition of 380
Socrates 140, 141
South of England, migrant population 165
Sovereign, function of 197–9
Soviet Union, see USSR
Speaker of the House of Commons 221
special needs group 231
Speenhamland system (1795) 226
Spens Report (1938) 108, 109
sponsored mobility 34, 408
statistics 8, 16
  in sampling 15
status 41, 42, 408–9
  achieved 54, 408
  ambiguity 141
  ascribed 54, 408
  class and 43
stereotype 120, 409
stratification 26, 408
stratified diffusion, principal of 72, 101
strikes 280, 281, 374
Strutt, Jedediah 270
suburbanisation 166
suicide 353–7

anomic 355
altruistic 355
attempted 353
egoistic 354
see also Samaritans
Suicide Act (1961) 353
summary jurisdiction 318
Sunday school 307, 308
supplementary benefit 232
survey, pre-test, pilot 17, 18
surveys, social see investigation
suspended sentence 322

taboos 31
Tanzania 53
Tasaday people 254
Taverne, Dick 214
Tawney, R. H. 27
taxation and income-levelling 269
teachers, social class of 120
technical schools 108–10, 220
technological society 85
technology, advance of 33, 274–7
technostructure 275
teenage spending 140
television 183–9, 213
  and violence 186–9
Television Act (1964) 183
tertiary workers 259
Third Estate, rise of 27
Titmuss, Professor R. M. 269
Tomalin, N. 340
Tories 210
totalitarian regimes, registration in 147
Townsend, P. 2, 14
Trade Unions 29, 88, 90
  and family life 69
  and strike action 280, 281
  as interest group 216
  function 278, 280
  influence and power 218
  types of 280
  women in 79, 80
Trades Union Congress (TUC) 281
trading 27
traditional family 60–2, 184
traffic offences 334
transport and leisure 286
tripartite system 108–12, 124
truancy 81
Tunstall, Jeremy 284

Uganda 176
Ugandan Asian immigrants 360

underdeveloped countries and population
  increase 169–71
unemployment 230, 261–5
  long-term 265
  reasons for 264
Union of Soviet Socialist Republics (USSR)
  1, 378
Unions, general and craft 280
United Kingdom (UK) see Britain
United Kingdom Immigrants' Advice Service
  363
United States of America (USA)
  advertising expenditure 190
  codified law and constitution of 295
  doctors from Britain 159
  drug-taking in 344
  economic gain through immigrants 159, 237
  emigrants to 158, 159
  persons per square km 165
  population 170
  residents in UK 158
  voting in 202
universities 65, 84, 85, 127, 128, 133, 137–9,
  192, 251
  'new' 137
  'redbrick' ('city') 127, 137
unmarried mothers 349, 350
upper class 30, 36, 69, 73, 86, 98
upward social mobility 32, 40, 65, 152
urban dispersal 166
urbanisation 409
  and family life 67–70

vaccines and infant mortality 155
vagrants and census 146
values 298
variable 409
Veblen, Thorstein 288
villeins 26
voluntary organisations 246–50
voluntary workers 248
voters 201–9
  deferential and pragmatic 209
voting
  by age 207
  by class 209
  by region 208, 209
  by religion 208, 209
  by sex 206

Wales, migrants from 165
wealth
  distribution of 265–9
  ownership and power 27–8

Weber, Max 9, 27, 28, 29, 43, 300
welfare services, abuse of 235
welfare society 225–52
Welfare State 41, 42, 59, 67, 69, 90, 154,
     233–46, 250–2, 375
  and parents 152
  and voluntary organisations 246–50
  development of 232–5
Western Europe
  advertising expenditure 190
  emigrants to 158
  see also Europe
West Indian immigrants 157, 358–60
white-collar workers 30, 277, 410
White Papers, see Government White Papers
Williams, Shirley 187
Willinck Commission on Police (1962) 316
Wilson, Harold, government of 203
Winchester public school 134
Wing village campaign 217
women
  education of 84, 85
  employment of 77–80, 81, 82, 83, 87–9
  extension of rights to 87, 88
  family role 75–89, 298
  labour force 76–80
  legal rights 86–8
Women's liberation movement 89
work
  and leisure 282–8
  and the economy 254–69

Worker's Educational Association (WEA) 139
working class 68
  affluence of 140
  and trade unions 29
  background and educational success 111,
     112, 114, 125–30
  children 73, 74, 118–20, 251
  education and 85, 124–6
  family size 72
  in government 28
  law breaker 335–8
  marriage 90, 91
  politics 209, 214–16
  self-assigned class 36
  youth and youth service 141, 337
working population 259
  and dependent population 258
World Health Expert Committee on
     addiction-producing drugs 346
World Wars
  effect of 160
  World War I 160, 230, 380
  World War II 231

youth clubs 140, 236
youth culture 139–41, 262–3, 286, 410
youth employment service 236
youth movements 141

Zũni Indians 51